Schriftenreihe
Kommunikation in Politik und Wirtschaft

edited by
Prof. Dr. Andrea Römmele
Prof. Dr. Sabine Einwiller

Volume 5

Andrea Römmele | Henrik Schober [Eds.]

The Governance of Large-Scale Projects

Linking Citizens and the State

Nomos

Die Deutsche Nationalbibliothek lists this publication in the Deutsche Nationalbibliografie; detailed bibliographic data is available in the Internet at http://dnb.d-nb.de.

ISBN 978-3-8329-7879-2

1. Edition 2013

Preface

Andrea Römmele, Henrik Schober

Kathmandu, the capital city of Nepal, is chronically short of drinking water. In order to improve this situation, plans were made to divert water from three rivers and lead it to the city. The so called Melamchi Water Supply Project would affect 17 villages inhabited by indigenous people, the Hyolmo, forcing them to relocate. Moreover, a number of sacred sites alongside these rivers might be destroyed. A truly large-scale infrastructure project of about half a billion US Dollars, the planning process took more than four decades. In all these years, however, the government of Nepal did not care to discuss impacts of the project with the Hyolmo people who constantly raised concerns, especially since 2004.

Things began to change in 2007, when the government of Nepal ratified the International Labor Organization's convention 169 which states that indigenous people "shall participate in the formulation, implementation and evaluation of plans and programmes for national and regional development which may affect them directly". At this point, the Hyolmo people started a campaign to make the government live up to the standards of the ILO convention. By summer 2009, agreements were made between the government of Nepal and representatives of the indigenous people, but the Hyolmo claimed that the government was falling short in terms of implementation. They still were not part of the process and no government official consulted with them. Because of that, they turned to the Asian Development Bank (ADB) which is the main donor of the project along with the government of Nepal. The Hyolmo wrote a letter and asked for help. Two months later, they decided to make a film about their situation and – just like the letter – they addressed it to the ADB. This film was put up on the internet, and it soon went viral.

Since then, millions of viewers around the world watched the half hour clip "Dear Asian Development Bank" (see http://vimeo.com/8050625). The basic message of this film is not fundamental opposition but a demand for participation. It gives insights to the story of the Hyolmo and their struggle for recognition and is, thus, a blueprint for popular demands all over the world. Many people are willing to contribute to huge endeavors like the water supply project at stake. The Hyolmo are well aware that people in Kathmandu need drinking water. They just do not accept sacrifices without even being asked first.

In this respect, the story of the Hyolmo people is both, a warning sign and an encouragement to politicians, managers, planners and citizens around the world. It shifts the discourse as it brings in new perspectives on government and governance. It points out that huge infrastructure projects can and will face similar challenges everywhere in the world – no matter if the country is big or small, rich or poor, developing or developed. It claims that there are many stakeholders involved – some of which you probably do not even notice when you get started –, and that all of them must be recognized and treated fairly. It calls for participation and for adequate measures to ensure it. All these messages are universal, and they show why we need to think about the governance of large-scale projects.

This being said, the governance of large-scale projects of course is a topic too big to be discussed in one book. However, many issues raised in the case of the Hyolmo people struggeling for recognition are relevant for all sorts of large-scale projects. Thus, they can be applied to the concepts and cases presented in this book although most of them are situated in the OECD world. Basically, just like the case of the Hyolmo campaign, the present volume is not about definite answers but about new perspectives on the issue. It brings together scholars and practicioners of various fields and disciplines who each have a unique view on the topic and offer fascinating insights into the theory and practice of the governance of large-scale projects.

In the first section entitled "Framing participatory governance", the editors offer a concept of participation and inclusion of citizens within the planning and implementation of large-scale projects. They argue that modern democratic systems might have difficulties to implement new binding procedures, but they are open to public consultation which, in turn, will develop certain dynamics decision-makers cannot ignore. Christopher Gohl goes on to describe a pragmatistic theory of democracy which recognizes informal political participation as a valuable resource and seeks to overcome certain dilemmas of traditional modes of participation. Gunnar Folke Schuppert reminds us that communication is crucial to any kind of governance and calls for a new way of local democracy that includes communicative provisions by which citizens may shape and contribute to decision-making at an early stage. Paul Webb argues that participatory procedures have an effect on people's attitudes towards the state and, thus, may help to tackle the issue of democratic disenchantment. Key messages of this section are:

1. Public participation aiming to deliver policy advice is a joint endeavor of politicians, administrative staff, interest groups, and citizens. Thus, there must be transparency, cooperation and equal rights among all participants.
2. Process design is crucial to the success of participatory arrangements. Their functionality and fairness must be a priority all those involved agree on. Facilitators such as moderators need to pay close attention so as to make sure that communication within such arrangements meets the these criteria.
3. Citizens ask for both, participation and representation. Accordingly, political parties and institutions should take participatory processes as an additional, valuable source of advice rather than regarding them as threats.

The book then goes on to describe "Modes of inclusion and deliberation". Claudia Ritzi opens this section with a discussion on deliberative forums as a deliberative extension of the representative democratic process, and presents the case of a German city network. Wolfgang König and Mathias König also focus on city and local policy when introducing the concept of deliberative governance arenas which bring together an entire system of decision-making in one room. Sarah Bastgen and Katrin Winkler compare online-based liquid democracy to other modes of direct participation and sketch out the potential of internet democracy. Henning Banthien, Andrea Versteyl and Martina Richwien suggest how a current legal framework of formal participation could be interlinked with informal dialogue processes. Johannes Staemmler explores ways to include civil society in local decision-making and argues that city governments may enable new ways of cooperation by framing policy issues accordingly. Among others, this section offers the following takeaways:

4. Large-scale projects require modes of governance that reflect their inherent challenges and characteristics. In addition to focusing on fair and just decision-making, procedural legitimacy must be established and maintained throughout the process.
5. The voices of the citizens are crucial for participatory arrangements and need to be heard. In order to be able to successfully participate, however, citizens also need to be well informed about the opportunities and limits of modes of participation.
6. Participation is not necessarily a matter of institutional arrangements. Along with formalized procedures, informal modes of participation may offer valuable insights and advice.

The third section presents a variety of "Cases of participation in large-scale projects". Thamy Pogrebinschi and Fabiano Santos report from the homeland of participatory democracy and show how national public policy conferences can drive legislative activity in the Brazilian Congress. Carmen Sirianni discusses how an agency of the federal administrative state, the US Environmental Protection Agency (EPA), can enable collaborative civic action. Emanuela Saporito and Daniela Ciaffi look into the dynamics that may unfold in the course of a cross-border infrastructure project, a section of the Pan-European Corridor V railway connecting Turin and Lyon. Kjetil Holgeid and Mark Thompson focus on the IT dimension and explain why some large-scale projects succeed while others fail. Arne Spieker and Marko Bachl discuss the German infrastructure project Stuttgart 21 and analyze public arbitration discussions as a new measure for alternative dispute resolution. A variety of recommendations derives from the cases presented in this section:

7. Public broadcasts on participation may leave most recipients focusing on arguments which support their opinion, but they also raise a project's legitimacy by fostering mutual understanding for competing positions.

8. There is not one recipe for successful participation since specific political and institutional environments frame the conditions of success. This notwithstanding, every public agency or institution has the opportunity to open up to new modes of public dialogue.
9. Clashes of cultures regarding modes of participation – e.g. in cases where two or more political or administrative systems are involved – are difficult to handle. At the same time, they offer great chances of mutual learning and democratic improvement.

Finally, the last section offers food for thought and ways to get involved. Stefan Schaible describes the democratic challenges ahead, and Andreas Hoffelder gives examples of participation in large-scale projects from around the world. One key message of this section is this:

10. Politics and public administration need to improve their provisions for strategic, holistic planning. This includes modes of mediation and arbitration as well as a general openness towards public dialogue.

The editors of this volume are indebted to a variety of people and institutions without whom this book would not exist. First of all, we would like to thank the authors who are a great inspiration and wonderful colleagues. We are also very grateful to the Volkswagen Foundation for funding a symposium on the governance of large-scale projects held at the Hertie School of Governance in Fall 2011. The people at Nomos Publishers were most helpful in the process of designing and producing the book. Samantha Ferrell and Kate Fanale did a tremendous job proof reading the chapters. Andreas Hoffelder and Johannes Staemmler were a great support in both, the organization of the symposium and the preparation of the book. All of these people – and many more – contributed to this book in an invaluable way. The responsibility for any errors or flaws, of course, remains with us.

We hope you enjoy reading this book, and would be more than happy to see more works tackling the vague but fascinating topic of "The Governance of Large-Scale Projects".

Table of Contents

III Cases of participation in large-scale projects

IV What's next?

I

Framing participatory governance

How To Link Citizens And The State: Reasons for – and First Steps Towards – a Participatory Mode of Governance

Andrea Römmele and Henrik Schober

Participation in governance is a new trend term. The following essay examines different versions of the concept and outlines their corresponding opportunities and limits. On this basis, it will be shown that society is a knowledgeable resource as well as a valuable advisor. Including citizens' perspectives may increase both the quality and legitimacy of political decision-making. Because of that, continuous participation can and should be secured within political systems in order to improve the basis of information upon which political decisions are made. These considerations lead to a concept of policy-oriented participatory societal consultation which is suggested as a supplement to more traditional ways of policy advice.

1 Introduction

Modern democracies are based on parliamentary representation which is guaranteed by the electoral provisions of equal participation and contestation. Recently, governments are increasingly challenged by citizens who feel that they are not adequately represented. Citizen movements call for modes of continuous and issue-oriented participation which exceed casting a ballot every four or five years. However, provisions for direct democracy are difficult to implement in certain political and constitutional environments since executive and legislative decision makers are hesitant. As a consequence, the debate increasingly focuses on rather soft modes of participation which allow citizens to interact with politicians while institutional provisions of political decision making remain unaffected. These participatory arrangements offer opportunities for citizens to consult with policy makers.

This is especially true for large-scale infrastructure projects. The demonstrations and citizens' movements against a new airport in London or the railway construction project "Stuttgart 21" show the huge level of citizens' involvement with such projects and the need for modes of participatory policy making which transform protest into feasible policy input. The governance of large-scale infrastructure projects deserves special attention since it comprises a variety of stakeholders including politics, administration, corporations, and interest groups as well as non-governmental organizations and citizens' movements. Furthermore, the issues to be discussed are linked to a broad range of academic disciplines, e.g. economics, public policy, sociology, law, public administration, business administration, or information technology. Then, again, recent events show that no matter *who* makes decisions in *what* field, the inclusion of citizens is key for the success of any project which is – or could be – subject to public attention.

2 A weak link?

The ideal that citizens actively participate in political happenings, thereby contributing advice, is anything but new. The reality in representative democracies is, however, different: instead of directly and comprehensively taking part in political decision-making, one merely votes, leaving everything else to the chosen representative. That this system has been proven is beyond question. Its limits and weaknesses are certainly well known; such as for example that minority opinions are often not taken into account or are repressed (cf. Tocquevile 1959). Current rates of voter turnout are declining in nearly all established democracies, which is further evidence that fewer citizens view the act of voting as sufficiently appropriate for political participation.

This leads to reason that the strong and continual participation of citizens can strengthen the democratic quality of a political system. Accordingly, corresponding ideas and theories of deliberative democratic participation have been intensively discussed for quite some time (cf. including the groundwork by Habermas 1981; as well as Barber 1984; and recently Sen 2009). Participation processes have also increasingly been derived from this work (cf. Fishkin 2009), but such processes have mainly been critically assessed, needing to be justified and defended in detail.

One reason for this is the uncertainty in politics and society about what exactly a political system with forms of participation other than the act of voting might look like. In order to shed some light on the matter, we would like to suggest and expound upon the concept of policy-oriented, deliberative societal consultation: the inclusion of citizens in political questions that are discussed and to a certain degree answered through the provision of advice or recommendations. The first comprehensive discussion on participatory societal consultation concerns the new role of citizens, the media, and experts in the realm of public discourse and consultation (Leggewie 2007). It is argued that experts in the "argumentative turn" (cf. Fischer/Forester 1993) no longer consider themselves to be strongly objective, but rather bring their own positions into the political process. Through an exchange with citizens, scholars can thus develop suggestions for policy that stem from the center of society. Other forms of policy advice that normally take place among the political elite can thereby be complemented and in some cases partially replaced.

We argue that "participatory societal consultation" could add substantial value to the ways in which large-scale projects are governed. The concept must certainly be more clearly defined – the more so, as it does not exclusively apply to large projects of the kind that is discussed in various chapters in this book. Moreover, there are many different goals associated with the concept. E.g., one could argue that processes involving citizen participation should lead to binding decisions on precisely defined policy issues. However, political decision-makers tend to be somewhat hesitant towards such formats. Because of that, we will focus on participatory societal consultation which is not binding but rather consultative. This, again, makes them easier to apply and implement since political costs are lower. This notwithstanding, civic input still is substantial and there are informal institutions in place which are able to generate lot of public pressure that could be called "soft power" (Nye, 2004).

Against this background, participatory societal consultation could be seen as an alternative source of policy advice (cf. Schober/Römmele, 2011). It roots on the one hand in public exchange and on the other hand in public access to consultative processes. Classic policy advice has already succeeded in clarifying its self-image, but participatory societal consultation in comparison need further systematization. Only in this way can one succeed in using its potential for improving and sustaining the incorporation of citizens into the political process, thereby improving the quality of democracy.

Examples of policy-oriented participatory societal consultation already exist in the form of civic forums, conferences, planning committees, or participatory budgeting. In order to be accepted and sustainably entrenched in the collective consciousness of citizens, the essence of participatory modes of governance and its potential to be used in policy advice must be clearly defined and clarified.

3 The Challenges of Deliberation

The point of reference for participatory societal consultation is the concept of deliberative democracy. According to Jürgen Habermas, this form of communication is based on discourse ethics (cf. Habermas 1992). The result is thus not determined by the structure of the advising process, because the communication explicitly takes places "eye to eye" and must be "communicatively connected." This means that each discourse participant must be willing to understand the other side and formulate answers that are equally understandable. At the same time, it means that all participants must be prepared to tolerate other standpoints and to move away from his or her own opinion, should another argument be more convincing. Such a deliberate approach is affiliated with five challenges (for details, see Cohen 1989 and the overview by Schaal/Heidenreich 2006):

- *Popular sovereignty:* Joshua Cohen describes popular sovereignty as a paradox: The people should be autonomous and at the same time be capable of being governed. Deliberative democracy can solve this seeming contradiction, in that civilians are explicitly assigned parallel roles: that of regents, that of the executive body, and those that are affected by decisions. For participatory societal consultation it means that broad segments of the population must be targeted for inclusion, in other words, that it can't be a mere discourse of the "democratic elite" (cf. for example Dahrendorf 1965).
- *Institutions and Values:* According to Cohen, the second challenge is that while the political system should be built on common institutions, the citizens should contribute individual values (cf. Cohen 1989). This connection of the micro and macro levels is classically ensured by the logic of aggregation (cf. Coleman 1990), which plays an important function in the policy cycle. Participatory societal consultation is thereby challenged to find mechanisms by which the aggregation of interests can be improved.
- *Preferences:* Supplementary to the above-mentioned process of arriving at a compromise, a further goal of deliberative discourse is to increase the compatibility of the preferences of citizens: Via the process, the differing positions should converge with one another, allowing the most precise compromise possible to be reached. Participatory societal consultation thus must organize dialogues within which participants can exchange ideas and develop an understanding of other perspectives.
- *Cost of Implementation:* A deliberative exchange preceding a decision not only leads to more applicable compromises, but also can reduce the costs of implementation of the decision. When a decision already in the process of being formed is based on general agreement, unintended outcomes that were not or could not have been the subject of discourse might still be fundamentally accepted. Participatory societal consultation thus must also bear in mind that participants are actually able to participate and thereby indentify with what is undertaken.
- *Legitimacy:* The fifth and also most fundamental challenge of deliberative democracy, according to Cohen, is the increase of the democratic legitimacy of the political system. In the major categories of input, output, and process legitimacy (cf. Luhmann 1969 and Scharpf 1999), input legitimacy is especially addressed, touching upon the process of political decision-making. The central argument is that the participation of citizens represents an important complement to the too often nontransparent as well as non-disclosed work of the political and administrative elite. Here, deliberative democracy is confronted with two problems, however. On the one hand, the extent to which the preferences of those persons participating in the discourse are representative of the majority is questionable, given that the (relatively small) group of already politically interested citizens may be over-represented in the discourse (cf. Leggewie/Bieber 2008). On the other hand,

the image of the active, critical, and political citizen – as prominently portrayed by Benjamin Barber in the concept of a "strong democracy" (cf. Barber 1984) – also represents demands that might overwhelm many citizens. Even if some have a certain interest in politics and society, it shouldn't be assumed that the feeling is equally strong among all citizens and on all topics (cf. Waltzer 1983).

4 Weak Points of Classic Policy Advice

The demand of the research community surrounding Claus Leggewie was the new positioning of policy advice with the help of deliberative societal consultation. Even in its "classic" manifestations, policy advice has always sought a connection to society. Civil society organizations and the general population were nevertheless seldom – and then only selectively – seen as actors with their own preferences and dispositions that should be considered in a strategic consultation process. Rather, these social groups were the target groups of political initiatives.

In the following, the weak points of classic policy advice will be outlined. These points haven't quite been remedied by policy-oriented, deliberative societal consultation, but can nevertheless complement the "old form of policy advice."

- *Legitimacy:* There is no form of classic policy advice that can claim legitimization through the people. It's also not necessary in every case: For example, consultation during an election campaign doesn't need to involve the general population. It would, however, be desirable if citizens could be heard in the decision-making process in precisely those areas where public institutions are advised and the advice is followed.
- *Agenda Setting:* Classic policy advice, despite its increasingly more discursive characteristics, still reacts to the wishes as well as the commissions of politics and executes the corresponding advisory services. The possibility that citizens themselves define the subject under discussion is, however, rare. Here, one depends upon the central role of the media in political agenda setting.
- *Public Sphere:* Policy advice is thus only public when politicians wish it to be. Although university studies or the expert opinions of institutes are often published, currently, consulting on sensitive topics is mostly held behind closed doors. While this may correspond to the logic of politics, the logic of society is based on information and discussion.
- *Participation:* Factors such as low transparency, information, and discussion could once again be reasons why political participation is declining at the moment – not only in the form of voter participation, but, for example, the development of rates of party membership also speaks loud and clear. That social capital which, without

a doubt, is still present in the population is instead used differently (for example, in the vast landscape of clubs and associations).

5 Society in the Consultation Process

The presented weaknesses of "classic" policy advice form the starting point for deliberations that make the case for opening the concept and even more so for a fundamental change in the structure of advising. Renate Mayntz already thought in 1994 that the "dual policy advising model," which is based on the transfer of expertise from scholars to politicians, is no longer suitable in many aspects and a shift to addressing citizens must take place (cf. Mayntz 1994). In the continuous debate that has since sprung up, it has furthermore become clear that the people cannot only play an important role as recipients, but also as senders of advice. A prominent example is the thesis of James Surowiecki on "The Wisdom of Crowds" (cf. Surowiecki 2004). He argues that groups of people can come to "better" decisions than individuals, as long as they use the potential of the "wisdom of crowds" correctly.

While this argument emphasizes the improvement of the input, the positive consequences for political output are also to be considered. By including the largest group of people possible in the decision-making process, and thereby the most opinions and positions, the chances grow that the political result exhibits a higher degree of inclusion and enjoys the trust of the people. In this way, participatory societal consultation can support political actors in finding suitable and "better" answers to current and future socio-political issues, as well as efficiently and effectively implementing these decisions.

Structurally speaking, the dual model of policy advice is expanded both on the side of the sender as well as the receiver. From this point, three new societal consultation constellations can be derived: On the one hand, society is classified as recipients of expertise sent by scholars (Type 1). On the other hand, society can also act as senders of expertise to politicians (Type 2) as well as directly address society itself (Type 3).

5.1 Characteristics of Participatory Societal Consultation

It is to be assumed that the actors and functions are not fully identical within the three listed advising constellations. They vary regarding the respective advising formats, actors, and results.

- *Formats:* Policy advice formats that take into account the inclusion of society, or are even based on such an inclusion, are not new *per se*. Civil society organizations thus traditionally request scientific expert opinion and can often trace their roots back to scientific initiatives (examples include Oxfam or Attac). Nevertheless, such advising formats do not meet the criteria of deliberative democracy, as they are not inherently discursive. Renate Martinsen, however, identifies four basic types of deliberative policy advice (cf. Martinsen 2006): mediation, the process of discourse, planning committees, and consensus conferences. These types are similar in that they are based on the assumption that advisors and advisees participate in an exchange on a previously defined, concrete topic. That such an exchange can also be organized in a decentralized manner, such as through social networks, further expands the spectrum of imaginable (and existing) forms of participatory societal consultation and especially opens possibilities of the third type, in which society advises itself.

- *Actors:* A considerable piece of uncertainty regarding the concept of participatory societal consultation goes back to the question of who exactly participates in the advising process and who organizes it. "Society" can fundamentally either be defined as "the people" and refer to the individual citizens, or be understood as "civil society" (cf. Anheier 2004) and focus on organized citizens. Civil society organizations, as well as politicians or scholars, can play a role in organizing formats for consultation. The media can also function as an actor (cf. Marschall 2007). It not only offers an arena for exchange, but also takes on an active role in the form of steering agenda setting, agenda surfing, and agenda cutting on the daily public agenda (cf. Brettscheinder 2004).
- *Results:* When discussing the results of consulting one has first to differentiate between outputs and outcomes. Along with the basic notion that policy advice and participatory societal consultation both express recommendations, with respect to outputs contextual knowledge for orientation and recommendations for action are also to be named. Since participatory societal consultation is also characterized by its discursivity, dissemination also takes place in continual feedback between politics and society, following the development of expertise. These recommendations are therefore valid as agreed-upon snapshots of opinions – in comparison to the singular, interest-oriented advice of traditional policy advice. In addition to the trust generated through the process as a main outcome of deliberative societal consultation, there is also the improved level of information of the participating citizens and the balancing of different, independent interests, leading ideally to new inputs capable of communicatively connecting. These desirable aspects, from the view of democratic theory, nevertheless must acknowledge that participatory societal consultation comes with pragmatic political difficulties. For example, a consultation held in public can lead to politicians holding back and only voicing statements that are in accordance with the official positions of their parties, whereas in a non-public, exclusive discussion they could deviate from the party line. Regarding the outcome, this could mean that no big political change results from

the procedure of deliberative societal consultation, as it must be prepared in a different context.

On the basis of previous deliberations, the three types of participatory societal consultation can be more precisely outlined (see Image X). The presentation of participatory societal consultation as an expansion of policy advice by means of the inclusion of citizen expertise correlates to the type of policy-oriented, deliberative societal consultation, which will be further considered in the following.

Image 1: Three ideal types of deliberative societal consultation

		Receiver	
		Politics	Society
Sender	Experts	**Classic Advising Forms** – Formats: "Dual" policy advice – Actors: Scholars, politicians – Results: Expert opinions, recommendations	**Public Consultation** – Formats: Not exclusively deliberative, target-group specific – Actors: Scholars, civil society (including the people) – Results: Information, awareness, mobilization
	Society	**Policy-Oriented, Participatory Societal Consultation** – Formats: Deliberative, oriented towards the entire population or a section thereof – Actors: The people (including civil society) in cooperation with scholars, politicians – Results: Balanced opinions, trust, legitimacy, knowledge transfer	**Citizen-Oriented, Participatory Societal Consultation** – Formats: Deliberative, oriented at target-groups as well as the general population – Actors: Civil society, the people – Results: Information, connected discourses

5.2 Policy-Oriented, Participatory Societal Consultation

Policy-oriented, participatory societal consultation is equally directed towards the political process and political institutions and is in this orientation comparable to classic, scholarly policy advice. Ideally, it is said that the expertise of citizens will replace that of academic and scientific experts. It has already been pointed out by Claus Leggewie (cf. Leggewie 2007), however, that a full replacement of policy advice by participatory societal consultation is not looming in the future. This advising model thus distinguishes itself much more through the combination of expert-based and citizen elements. For example, scholars can supply information on specific factual issues in citizen forums, which are professionally moderated by communications and participation experts. Citizens can then consider this information during the deliberation process. This model of participatory societal consultation thereby offers a way to integrate the idea of citizen participation into the logic of policy advice. Policy-oriented, participatory societal consultation thereby features its own specific characteristics:

- Advising actors are experts and citizens who together advise policy and find themselves in a cooperative relationship.
- Following the principles of deliberative democratic theory, they interact (at least approximately) in a coercion-free space.
- This space is nevertheless also professionally organized in order to enable a goal-oriented consulting process; participating coordinators and moderators distinguish their role by restraining themselves as much as possible when it comes to factual questions and showing high sensitivity when it comes to procedural questions.
- The initiative for such a consultation, as with the specific setting of the agenda, can be made on the side of politicians as well as by society.
- The goal of policy-oriented, participatory societal consultation is not to make binding decisions in politics. The focus is on advising politics by articulating and defining problems as well as searching for possible solutions and the formulating of appropriate measures.
- The authority for decision-making remains in politics, but an obligation to the citizens regarding the utilization of the outcome should nevertheless be built into the process.

Our suggested definition thus reads: Policy-oriented, participatory societal consultation constitutes an organized form of equal cooperation between citizens and scholars, in which suggestions for policy are not binding, but nevertheless are included in the decision process.

6 *Outlook*

The concept of policy-oriented participatory societal consultation corresponds to the five requirements of democratic theory, which have been formulated in the context of the discourse on deliberation and participation: It is not a purely elite discourse because the general population is given the opportunity to voice a sovereign opinion; minority opinions are appropriately accounted for because the advising process results in an agreed-upon compromise and does not strive for a majority decision; the continual exchange between scholars and citizens on the one hand, and between these two groups and politicians on the other allows for mutual learning and harmonization of preferences; the resulting compromise can be considered to be widely accepted among the people because they actively took part in the preparation; and the legitimacy of political outputs can be raised through the inclusion of a – ideally representative – portion of the population.

What is clear in all this, however, is that these theoretical possibilities also require implementation in the political process. The evidence that policy-oriented, participatory societal consultation can be helpful in remedying the weaknesses of "classic" policy advice regarding legitimacy, agenda-setting, and public participation can only be rendered through real projects and advising processes. This will be essential in coming years in order to come closer to the goal of raising the quality of democracy step by step and also thereby the legitimacy of the political system. Only when projects are implemented and also evaluated, can conclusions be drawn, which can be further used to help to improve the quality of procedures.

There remains a string of open questions, however: How does one anticipate and prevent overburdening citizens from whom the participatory societal consultation format demands a great deal of resources? How can a communicatively connected, participatory societal consultation be organized in a way that is actually recognized by politicians and administration and thus included in the political decision-making process? How can one prevent the problem of paying more attention to the stances of people who are ready and have the capacity to be engaged, compared to the positions of those who can't or don't want to actively participate? And last but not least: Is there an arena which should be "protected" from participatory societal consultation – for example the negotiation of political questions that should not include citizens? This and many more questions suggest a need for continual engagement with the topic of deliberative societal consultation. Policy makers are especially asked to be willing to test the innovative procedure of citizen participation, although it is not without risk for individual politicians or parties whose positions may not overlap with those of the people. For the political system as a whole, however, a wide, diverse application of new citizen participation procedures would offer enormous opportunities.

Bibliography

Anheier, Helmut K. (2004). Civil society: measurement, evaluation, policy. London: Earthscan.

Barber, Benjamin (1984). Strong Democracy: Participatory Politics for A New Age. Berkeley: University of California Press.

Brettschneider, Frank (2004). Agenda-Setting, Agenda-Cutting, Agenda-Surfing. Themenmanagement bei der Bundestagswahl 2002. In: Heinrich Oberreuter (Hrsg.), Der versäumte Wechsel. Eine Bilanz des Wahljahres 2002. München: Olzog, P. 9-34.

Cohen, Joshua (1989). Deliberation and Democratic Legitimacy. In: Alan Hamlin/Philip Pettit (Hrsg.), The Good Politiy. Normative Analysis of the State. Oxford: Oxford University Press, P. 17-34.

Coleman, James S. (1990). Foundations of Social Theory. Cambridge, MA: Harvard University Press.

Dahrendorf, Ralf (1965). Gesellschaft und Demokratie in Deutschland. München: Piper.

Fischer, Frank/Forester, John (Hrsg.) (1993). The Argumentative Turn in Policy Analysis and Planning. Durham: Duke University Press.

Fishkin, James (2009). When the People Speak. Deliberative Democracy & Public Consultation. New York: Oxford University Press.

Habermas, Jürgen (1981). Theorie des kommunikativen Handelns. Frankfurt am Main: Suhrkamp.

Habermas, Jürgen (1992). Faktizität und Geltung. Frankfurt am Main: Suhrkamp.

Leggewie, Claus (Hrsg.) (2007). Von der Politik- zur Gesellschaftsberatung. Neue Wege öffentlicher Konsultation. Frankfurt a.M.: Campus.

Leggewie, Claus/Bieber, Christoph (2008). Webforum. In: Norbert Kersting (Ed.), Politische Beteiligung. Einführung in dialogorientierte Instrumente politischer und gesellschaftlicher Partizipation. Wiesbaden: VS Verlag, 92-103.

Luhmann, Niklas (1969). Legitimität durch Verfahren. Neuwied: Luchterhand.

Marschall, Stefan (2007). Politik- und Gesellschaftsberatung in der „Mediendemokratie". In: Claus Leggewie (Ed.), Von der Politik- zur Gesellschaftsberatung. Neue Wege öffentlicher Konsultation. Frankfurt a.M.: Campus, P. 153-170.

Martinsen, Renate (2006). Demokratie und Diskurs. Organisierte Kommunikationsprozesse in der Wissensgesellschaft. Baden-Baden: Nomos.

Mayntz, Renate (1994). Politikberatung und politische Entscheidungsstrukturen: Zu den Voraussetzungen des Politikberatungsmodells. In: Axel Murswieck (Ed.), Regieren und Politikberatung. Opladen: Leske + Budrich, P. 17-29

Nye, Joseph S. (2004). Soft Power: The Means to Success in World Politics. New York: PublicAffairs.

Schaal, Gary S./Heidenreich, Felix (2006). Einführung in die Politischen Theorien der Moderne. Oplanden/Farmington Hills: Verlag Barbara Budrich.

Scharpf, Fritz W. (1999). Regieren in Europa. Effektiv und demokratisch? Frankfurt a.M.: Campus.

Schober, Henrik/Römmele, Andrea (2011) Grundverständnis und Potenziale politikbezogener Gesellschaftsberatung. In: Bertelsmann Stiftung (Ed.), Wie Politik von Bürgern lernen kann. Potenziale politikbezogener Gesellschaftsberatung.

Sen, Amartya (2009). The Idea of Justice. London: Allen Lane.

Surowiecki, James (2004). The Wisdom of the Crowds. Why the Many Are Smarter Than the Few and How Collective Wisdom Shapes Business, Economies, Societies and Nations. New York: Random House.

Tocqueville, Alexis de (1959) [1835/1840]. Über die Demokratie in Amerika. Stuttgart: Reclam.

Waltzer, Michael (1983). Spheres of Justice: a defense of pluralism and equality. New York: Basic Books.

Beyond Deliberation: Towards a Pragmatistic Theory of Collaborative Democracy

Christopher Gohl

The contribution of informal political participation to democratic governance is often misunderstood. Though popular among scientists and practitioners, both deliberative democratic theory and complex democratic theory fail to understand the contributions and challenges of many informal participatory procedures. This paper argues that these procedures are more adequately understood within a framework of collaborative problem resolution. Pragmatistic theory in the tradition of John Dewey provides a comprehensive frame of reference for understanding political participation, reframing theoretical problems such as the legitimacy/effectiveness dilemma between the input and output side of democracy, and raising more relevant practical issues such as the art of government and democratic governability. Pragmatistic democratic theory is a good foundation for the emerging conception of collaborative democracy.

1 The Problem: Understanding Participation in Governance

In the famous words of Abraham Lincoln, democracy is a "government of the people, by the people, for the people." People participate in their own self-government. "Whoever says democracy, means participation" (van Deth, 2009, p. 141), or, as Keim wrote: "The simplest definition of democracy, rule by the people, implies participation. To rule carries the unstated uncondition: to take part; yet the role of participation in democracy has never been agreed upon" (Keim, 1975, p. 1; see Hager, 2005, p. 16). The central problem any democratic theory needs to address is thus: to what end, and how, do or should people participate in government?

That question about both the purpose and procedures of participation is central to both practitioners and theorists of political participation. Different democratic theories give different answers to that question. These answers are highly contested. After all, these answers by implication address other questions of power and authority, legitimacy and acceptance, efficiency and effectiveness, and subject and object of democratic politics. They also describe, and (again by implication) often prescribe, different roles, capacities, and competences of the governing and the governed, different sets of institutions and procedures, and different understandings of polity, politics, and sometimes policy. That's a big list of possible disagreements, with direct consequences for the evaluation of practice. The issues in question are thus central issues not only for democratic theories, but for any political science. And they are the continuous subject of more practical debates and power struggles in democratic publics and polities.

In effect, democratic theories are a discourse that defines what can or can't be done in a democracy. For example, they define what politicians, administration officials, and corporate executives in charge of infrastructure projects should and shouldn't do when they provide leadership, govern, or plan and execute projects. In the larger scheme of things, the shape of democracies all over the world is shifting. While some see the advent of post-democracy (Crouch, 2004), others believe we now enter the global age of democracy (Zakaria, 2003). In any case, changes in the hardware and software of democracy – changes in its institutions and practices, as well as changes in the understanding of democracy – are changes in the operating system of countries, or even of continents, in the case of the European Union. A sound and practical understanding of different concepts of participation is especially relevant to understanding and shaping such change.

Yet, this article will advance the argument that so far, popular and dominant democratic theories simply fail to understand participatory procedures and their complex contributions and challenges in regard to democratic governance. While they may be neat and consistent in the realm of democratic theory, they fail to make a practical difference for a better democracy. Misleading categories breed irrelevant theoretical knowledge and practical frustration. Both deliberative democratic theory and complex democratic theory don't get to the fact that political participation procedures are most adequately understood when they are understood as (parts of overall) procedures of collaborative problem resolution. In contrast, "collaborative democracy" is best understood through pragmatistic theory.

In order to understand the merit of different democratic theories, the object, elements, and challenges of democratic theory will be discussed.

2 *Object, Elements, and Challenges of Democratic Theory*

In order to fully understand and appreciate any specific democratic theory, one needs to understand the object of their theory. Only then is it possible to compare and judge who wins the contest of best explanations. Of course, the object of democratic theory itself is already subject to interpretation, and moreover, subject to historical change. In fact, one of the reasons older democratic theories can come out of fashion is that they fail to grasp new developments. Hence, any theory that wants to offer enduring explanations of democratic practice needs to be able to move along with its target. To this effect, it needs to be sufficiently complex and dynamic.

This part of the argument will discuss democracy as a contested concept – a discussion that provides clues as to the achievements expected from democratic theory

(2.1). It will then highlight the changing nature of participation as a challenge to democratic theories (2.2), and prepare the discussion of three different types of democratic theory in the following parts of the argument (2.3).

2.1 Democracy as Contested Concept

Democracy is taken to be an "essentially contested concept" (Gallie, 1956). In reference to Gallie, Lakoff defines four main features of *contested concepts*: "First, a contested concept has an uncontested core. (...) Second, the concept must be evaluative, that is, it must be used to make value judgments. Third, it must have a complex structure – it must be complicated enough to allow for variations. And fourth, it has to have parts that are subject to variation; these are often underspecified, vague enough to allow details to be elaborated in more than one way" (Lakoff, 2006, p. 23f.).

In regard to democracy and participation, that means that (1) some form of participation of the governed in government is part of the uncontested core of democracy. (2) Democracy and participation are normative concepts, used to make evaluative judgments. The main principles of a specific concept express a specific purpose and perspective on democracy. (3) Any concept of democracy and participation must be sufficiently complex to allow for variations. (4) There have to be elements that can be specified and varied. These elements concern the inventory of the *how* of any democracy – specified roles and procedures, ranging from party and parliament to direct democracy, informal participation, democratic discourse, and forms of a democratic public sphere.

Any comprehensive democratic theory that does justice to these four features necessarily combines norms with empirical sensitivity. It also needs to be able to accommodate a great variety of forms of democratic practice. Moreover, if the object of explanation is changing, it needs to be able to explain the changes.

Any given concept (or discourse) of participation defines its own universe of expectations, judgments, and possible actions. In consequence, democratic theory gains critical importance for political science, consultancy, and action – its contests are repeated, in other form and other degrees of subtleness, in the square of public opinion.

2.2 The Changing Object of Democratic Theory: New Participatory Procedures

In democracy, new developments are plenty these days. A decade ago Kleger has argued that there are three kinds of historical democratic transformations (Kleger, 1999a, p. 170): the transnationalization of democracy, a trend towards more direct democracy, and a trend towards more negotiation democracy. He describes these processes as comprehensive, self-reflective democratization processes of trial and error. And comprehensive these processes seem to be – any Google search demonstrates that abundant arguments can be found for the transformation of practically all elements of democracies: the transformation of elections, of political communication, of the public sphere, of citizenship, of democratic governance, of political parties, of parliaments, and of political leadership. It may be part of the uncontested consensus of democratic theorists that democracies today are in the process of transformation – though whether it is a transformation in degree or kind, and whether welcome or not, is contested.

Since democracy in its broadest sense means participation in self-government, this article assumes that any transformation of democracies can be understood in terms of the changes of the forms of participation in self-governance. Hence, these procedures of participation become the focal point of theoretical reflection. Generally, formal and informal procedures may be distinguished. The formal ones are methods written into law, such as elections, citizen consultations, direct votes, or rules of procedures in parliament. Informal procedures are procedures of participation for citizens (both the unconcerned and aggrieved), advocates, observers, experts, decision makers, or any stakeholders of a given problem.

Such informal participatory procedures are a current source of bewilderment for democratic theorists. In the past two decades, they sprung up like mushrooms after the rain, and in all shapes and forms (Gohl, 2011, p. 86-94 for an overview). They are called action planning, appreciative inquiry, area forums, backward mapping, blind walk, brainstorming, card technique, C.E.A.T., citizen advisory groups, citizens' jury, citizens' panels, citizens' summits, community advisory panels, community development, community organizing, conversation cafes, coproduction, deliberative mapping, deliberative polling, deliberative workshops, delphi survey, democs, design charrettes, dialogue, dynamic facilitation, empowerment circle, E-petitions, focus groups, forum theatre, or future search – to name but a few different methods and practices in alphabetical order.[1]

Arbitration, mediation, planning cells, or open space are among the better-known methods. Processes of arbitration and mediation have recently caught the public imagination in Germany, when the decade-long protest against a four billion Euro infrastructure project (by conservative estimates) in the heart of the city of Stuttgart built up to confrontations between grannies and police forces. A respected political figure, Heiner Geissler, was finally called in, and his arbitration was televised – a first in Germany – though not the first attempt to mediate between an angry public, government officials, and investors (Susskind & Field, 1996; Geis, 2005). Earlier participatory processes that were of some larger prominence were Agenda 21 processes – local, regional, and national multi-stakeholder processes of sustainable development

1 See www.peopleandparticipation.net, and www.iaf-methods.org for hundreds of participatory methods.

(Hemmati, 2002; Jonuschat et. al, 2007). These participatory methods, processes, and practices are all social constructs, shaped by local and historical context. Some of them are methods of group facilitation, their duration measured in hours. Others are processes that take years. Some of them are very well defined methods, with written rules of procedures. Others show a greater degree of improvisation, and are sometimes called "hybrid procedures" for their mix of methods.

2.3 Answers to the Challenge of New Participatory Procedures

Different theories, ranging from democratic theories to theories of group psychology, and urban planning to governance theories, see different elements of such participatory procedures (Gohl, 2011, p. 84-85). However, surprisingly little systematic research and empirical analysis have been conducted. Earlier assessments such as "[t]here is little systematic research on the nature and consequences of deliberation in real settings ... " (Mendelberg, 2002, p. 152), or "[u]nfortunately, empirical research on deliberative democracy has lagged significantly behind theory" (Delli Carpini, Cook & Jacobs, 2004, p. 316) still ring true today. The main reason may be that no unified model of participatory procedures has been agreed upon. "A widely recognized gap in the field of deliberative democracy is the lack of a synthesis of the purposes and design of various methods for deliberation that are employed around the world, and the policy environments in which they occur" (Levine & Hasselblad Torres, 2007, p. 14). "In the public participation domain, unfortunately, the key concepts are not generally well defined, even after several decades (or, some might argue, centuries or even longer) of sporadic research interest" (Rowe & Frewer, 2005, p. 252). Different exercises in the typology of participatory procedures (Rowe & Frewer, 2005; Fuhrmann & Stock, 2006; Renn, 2008; Geißel, 2008; Fuhrmann, 2009) have demonstrated problems, rather than providing convincing solutions (Levine & Hasselblad Torres, 2007, p. 40; Gohl, 2011, p. 109-119). Taking a clue from innovation theory, Helmut Klages concludes that participatory procedures are in a pioneering phase, characterized by a "plurality without system" (Klages, 2007, p. 58).

To be sure, there are theories that seem to rise to the occasion of explaining the contribution of informal participatory procedures to democratic governance. One type of theory that has long gained a certain prominence in that regard is the family of theories and models of deliberative democracy. There are many reasons why this may be so. First of all, it is a theory with enough breadth to explain the empirical occurrence, and normative necessity, of "government by discussion" (Feindt, 2001). Secondly, it is deep enough to encompass the design of democratic societies on a macro-level, and the design of participatory procedures for groups of people on a micro-level. Thirdly, it is also practical enough to inform the new design of such procedures. Indeed, a few early theorists, such as Fishkin (1991), themselves invented procedures based on the theory, such as the "Deliberative Opinion Poll" or "Deliberation Day" (Saretzki, 2010, p. 126-132). Moreover, theorists and practitioners also formed the Deliberative Democracy Consortium (DDC) in 2003, shaping an increasingly differentiated discourse (Gastil & Levine, 2005). And finally, the discourse on deliberative democracy was blessed with rich intellectual foundations on both sides of the Atlantic, laid out by Seyla Benhabin, Amy Gutman, and Jürgen Habermas, among others.

As German government and administration officials begin to gradually turn their interest towards the contributions and challenges of political participation, another theory seems to be rising in prominence – complex democratic theory, once conceived in the early seventies of the last century by Frieder Naschold and Fritz Scharpf, represented mainly by the work of the latter after the death of the former. Both were early theorists of administration and the organization of government, and Scharpf is one the pioneers of the governance discourse in Germany. A normatively sober theory, government officials and governance schools alike appreciate complex democratic theory for the pragmatic clues it provides in regard to a general understanding of the challenges of participatory procedures.

However, these theories have serious shortcomings. In fact, they confuse more than they enlighten in regard to the contributions and challenges of participatory procedures to democratic governance (3 and 4). It is time to turn attention to another kind of democratic theory – to pragmatistic democratic theory (5), which is much better suited to explain a comprehensive collaborative democracy.

3 Deliberative Democratic Theory

3.1 Government by Discussion

The family of deliberative democratic theory is characterized by a consensus that the process of deliberation is the source of democratic legitimacy (Strecker & Schaal, 2001, p. 120). "Government by discussion" (Feindt, 2001) means that rules are established when the forming of the political will in the decision-making process includes reciprocal understanding and rational argumentation. That is more than just preference aggregation and bargaining over interests. The democratic process of decision making realizes itself in intertwined arenas of discourse, which are open to all sorts of reasons (Strecker & Schaal, 2001, p. 100). Central criteria of the deliberative-democratic system are the inclusion of all citizens in the forming of the political will, the respective opportunities to participate, and the chance for an enlightened understanding of the issues (Gastil, 2008, p. 5-8). Forums and forms of democratic communication and deliberation are found in institutions of civil society, in real and digital publics, in parliaments, administrations, as well as the courts (ibid, p. 284).

Not all political communication is deliberation in the precise sense. "When people deliberate, they carefully examine a problem and arrive at a well-reasoned solution after a period of inclusive, respectful consideration of diverse points of view" (ibid, p. 8). Deliberation in concrete cases is sometimes referred to as a specific discourse that takes place in "fora of communication," in which "arguments are exchanged and are tested in regard to their validity and in accordance to definite rules. Neither the prestige of participants nor their status plays a role in this" (Knaus & Renn, 1998, p. 444). According to Renn (2008), the purpose of a deliberation procedure is to debate criteria of truth, establishing normative validations in regard to the veracity of an argument. In that view, the rationality of a deliberation calls for an integration of all relevant arguments in order to reach consensus through argumentation. As an example, Renn points to citizen forums and deliberative juries. In a broader and more pragmatic definition by Kastenholz, discourse should "contribute, amongst other things, to establish a shared basis of knowledge, make an argument transparent and comprehensible, integrate societal preferences and normative concepts, enhance the acceptance and basis of legitimacy of decision, and thereby also prevent conflicts and arbitrate in existing conflicts" (Kastenholz, 2002, p. 2).

A typical foundation of all specified rules of discourse is the discourse ethic of the "Theory of Communicative Action" of Habermas (Habermas, 1981). Habermas replaces a substantial notion of rationality with a procedural concept of rationality, concentrating on language as the foremost medium of the construction of reality (Keller, 1997, p. 318). Habermas defines discourse as the form of communication characterized by argumentation, in which problematic validity claims are discussed and analyzed in regard to their justification. To lead a discourse, it thus becomes necessary to step out of the context of action and experience. No information is exchanged, but rather arguments, which serve the justification or rejection of problematic claims to validity (Habermas, 1984, p. 130f.).

In that view, discourse is a reflexive process of understanding to test claims of validity, based on language, and unburdened of the constraints of action, experience, and decision. In the course of discourse, the reciprocal exchange of arguments in the form of acts of speech are tested without regard to the prestige and status of persons, but according to defined rules of validity claims (Habermas, 1981; Kreß, 2000). In a discourse, participants explicitly test the validity of their norms and arguments. Habermas' discourse ethic commands respect, fairness, reciprocity, and intersubjective comprehensibility. It calls for a dismissal of any strategic, instrumental communication on the part of the participants. Habermas thus defines an ideal speech situation – preconditions of communication that make the better argument the decisive factor of rational validity claims. "Discourse has become an ideal, discoursivity a criteria of quality to test the dignity and capacity for legitimacy of processes of forming the political will. (...) The claim of discoursivity becomes the theoretical model of a successful practice" (Nennen, 2000, p. X).

3.2 A Critique of Deliberative Democracy

Theories of deliberative democracy view democracy, at heart, as one large conversation that takes place in many different arenas, not just parliaments. Its usual output is a piece of well-reasoned advice in the form of a report or a recommendation to decision makers. Whether and under what circumstances the promise of a better political outcome is ever realized, is subject to the criteria of "better outcome." But experience and empirical research shows that it is plausible to expect that deliberation, under specified circumstances, delivers more consensus, less partisanship, a stronger acceptance of results, and rational, evidence-based, if not morally sound results (Elster, 1998). Indeed, "experts are often surprised and impressed by the quality of the public's deliberations, judgments, and actions" (Levine, Fung & Gastil, 2005, p. 2).

It is easy to criticize deliberative democracy from a theoretical point of view when one prefers another theory that addresses issues that are obviously neglected – the competitive nature of voting, for example. The first main critique from the point of view of participatory procedures is that most of them simply don't function according to deliberative standards. For example, neither a group exercise such as brainstorming, nor politically relevant public mediation processes are unburdened by the constraints of action, experience, or decision. For both, creativity and new information are vital – indeed, almost all participation procedures are generative in function. Negotiation, including strategic bargaining, is an integral part of any mediation. For many participation procedures, the goal is to overcome rational discourse, and earn the fruits of emotion and experience. There is no conceivable reason why participative procedures should adhere to deliberative standards beyond the rules of a civil discussion.

Secondly, deliberative democracy focuses only on the input side of government, and in a wholly conservative manner. Ideally, decision makers ask citizens to participate and dispense a piece of well-reasoned advice. If deliberation lacks such an official mandate, it is of no relevance – and even if it has a mandate, the logic of the recommendation seldom fits into the schedule, rationality, and competence of the decision maker all at once. That is a potential hotbed of frustration, since participants – in practice, and against the standards of deliberation – develop some passion for their recommendations. They want to generate change.

The third critique is a strategic critique, and it includes the two previous critiques. Theorists of deliberation usually share the normative urge of a more inclusive, deeper democracy. Yet, their idea of participation is blind to the logic of politics as it is. As

Michael Walzer reminds deliberation enthusiasts: "a democratic political process (...) is (...) pervasively nondeliberative" (Walzer, 2007, p. 134). Indeed, it is often competitive to a fault. To transform the existing logic, it is simply not enough to frame citizens as people who need to be asked to advise decision makers in a rational way. To generate change, participation procedures must also address issues of power, competence, and implementation. Democratic theory needs to go beyond mere deliberation.

4 Complex Democratic Theory

4.1 Democratic Government as Arrangement of the Power by the People, for the People

The presuppositions of democracy as a "contested concept" (II.1) are also presuppositions that have determined the design of the so-called "Complex Democratic Theory," as advanced by Frieder Naschold (1968; 1969; 1971), and, more prominently, Fritz Scharpf (1970; 1975; 1985; 1988). His concept has shaped the scientific discourse on democracy in Germany. In the wake of "Stuttgart 21," a major infrastructure project in the southern part of Germany that was met with years of protest and resulted in a last minute effort of public arbitration, Scharpf's theory is beginning to shape practical debates about a (supposed) conflict between the desire of citizens to participate more, and the necessity of government to plan and execute projects effectively.

Dating back to the seventies of the last century, complex democratic theory was designed to bridge the gap between normative claims – at the time advanced by proponents of participatory democracy – and empirical feasibility. In that respect, it was consciously crafted as an ambitious project of the social sciences – as a "Theory of Democracy Between Utopia and Adaptation" (Scharpf, 1970). It was an answer to the shortcomings both of the (empirical, affirmative, and rather elitist) theory of pluralism, and the (normative, emancipatory, and rather popular) theory of participative democracy, both of which shaped the democratic discourse in the United States (Herzberg, 2001, p. 9f., Hager, 2005, p. 25).

The aim of complex democratic theory was to construct a theory, which sensibly conciliated normative goals of democracy with empirically existing institutions and procedures. According to Schmidt, the central question of the whole endeavor was "How can government be maximally effective and democratic at the same time, so that a maximum of collective welfare is reached and the emergence of totalitarian rule is avoided?" (Schmidt, 2003 169, quoted in Holtkamp, Bogumil & Kißler, 2006, p. 82). The central problem, as complex democratic theory sees it, is thus what appears to be an obvious antagonism between calls for more participation, and the productive efficiency of the political system (Hager, 2005, p. 9).

The central theoretical strategy is to frame that problem in terms of complexity, and to design a theory that is able to process such complexity. The theory is designed to function as a calculator of many different variables, able to calculate the combination of both practical and theoretical, normative and empirical variables. The complexity of complex democratic theory comes from two sources – first, the complexity of the object, the interrelations of democracy; and secondly, from the scrupulous architecture of a modern theory of the social sciences which tries to systematically facilitate normative and theoretical reflection with empirical observations of functions. So before any vote is actually cast and observed, this is already a complex theory (compare Schmidt, 2000, p. 299; and Hager, 2005, p. 19-24 on options in the design of social science theories).

The classical, even canonical distinction between the input and output of democratic processes stems from the central theoretical strategy to design a theory dealing with complexity. Scharpf presupposed that there is a large plurality of principally irreducible democratic goals of different democratic actors, which could and should not be reduced by a theoretical decision. "Scharpf's innovation lies in the axiomatic concentration of this plurality into two opposing command variables, 'input' and 'output'. This is the very source of the legitimacy/effectiveness dilemma that is now part of the standard repertoire of democratic theory (compare Dahl, 1994, Schmidt, 1997)" (Hager, 2005, p. 25f.). Normative demands of more inclusive participation are disciplined by the orientation of the theory towards output and empirical observations (Schmidt, 2000, p. 296). The plurality of normative goals are bundled into two main command variables which describe possible accomplishments of democracy: (1) legitimacy of the input side through democratic inclusion in decision making, which is government by the people; and (2) legitimacy of the output side, which derives from the ability to effectively and appropriately execute democratic decisions, and is government for the people.

Scharpf's first step was to analyze empirical variables of both the input and output side. By combining these variables with normative goals on both sides, Scharpf hoped to identify a practical potential for democratization. Scharpf expected to enable a certain dosage of more participation, and an improvement of intelligent regulation on the government side (Schmidt, 2000, p. 294f.). While potentially conflicting, both input and output legitimacy were to complement each other. "Authentic expression and unaltered implementation of the will of the people" and "the collective problems and interest of real existing members of the polity" were to be balanced by institutional mechanisms, refining the will of the people in terms of facts, law, and an orientation towards the common good (Scharpf, 1997: section 2.2).

If that were an easy task, the legitimacy/effectiveness dilemma would have been but a temporal thesis of democratic theory. In his work, Scharpf went on to place the emphasis on the output side of government. "Sorting out all of Scharpf's proposal, one gets the impression that all in all, the postulate for participation is evacuated from the realm of political decision making. (...) The extension of the theory shows an emphasis of the 'planning democracy' on successful planning despite, and not through participation" (Hager, 2005, p. 28f.). Scharpf went on to become a prominent analyst of the loss of steering capacity of the national state, and a leading thinker in the governance debate, which is often more descriptive than interested in normative goals (Walk, 2007, p. 34).

4.2 A Critique of Complex Democratic Theory

Complex democratic theory succeeds in providing a comprehensive structure of normative and analytical categories with which democratic government can be explained and understood. The meticulous architecture of the theory allows for an integrated and complex synopsis of democratic systems. It also highlights the interrelatedness of factors in a democratic system. And the dilemma it posits between participation and government is a successful focal point because it popularizes certain divisions inherent in democratic thought between norm and claim on one hand and fact and performance on the other. Democratic theories often pit people against politicians, represented against represented, governed against governing, deliberation against decision, and decentralized articulation and self-determination against central and binding decision making. On the input side are the theoretical sovereign, amorphous electorate, the critical public, and the plurality of actors of civil society; on the output side practical authorities, concrete actors, defined roles, and professional government. Here the normative will, there the empirical way.

In that tradition, analytical empiricists demand empirical proof that the wish for new and more forms of participation really do lead to better results. Even theorists of democratic deliberation rush to make that argument. In Germany, proponents of more participation gladly point to the challenge of chancellor Willy Brandt from 1969, "to dare more democracy" (Beck & Ziekow). In that view, more democracy is a risk that needs daring. Since it is common knowledge that too many cooks spoil the broth, that frame of view is immensely popular. Complex democratic theory makes it debatable.

From the viewpoint of participatory procedures, any critique must begin with the focus of the theory on the macro-systematic side of democracy. It is impossible to deduct anything practical or enlightening that would explain aspects of participatory procedures, which are phenomena on a micro, and at best, meso-level. Though his categories "legitimacy" and "effectiveness" inspire the research of participatory procedures, these categories are not really relevant to participants and facilitators: "Our exploration of facilitators' observations suggest that two concepts familiar to small group researchers – participant satisfaction and group productivity – provide overarching standards by which participants and facilitators alike judge deliberative processes" (Mansbridge et al., 2006, p. 1).

The second critique is that, like deliberative theory, complex democratic theory sees participation wholly on the input-side. Moreover, Scharpf focuses on traditional forms of an authentic expression of the popular will, and his main interest here is the justification of majority rule (Scharpf, 1999, p. 17). So he never focuses on new kinds of participation procedures and their specific contributions to government. His view of participation stays below complexity level. It is in that view that the legitimacy/effectiveness dilemma must be understood. It has its reason in theoretical design choices that turn a blind eye to participation procedures on a micro or meso-level. In one bold stroke of theoretical assumption, the division between legitimacy through participation and legitimacy through effective government is thus dramatized and turned into a dilemma.

One mark of the good quality of a theory is the potential for reflexive self-correction. Complex democratic theory may have the categories for self-correction in regard to participatory procedures. Not the least of it is a conception of the political process as a process of "problem treatment" ("*Politik als Problemverarbeitung*": Scharpf, 1973; see Jann and Wegrich, 2003). It is an integral, but not popular part of complex democratic theory. A kindred conception of politics as problem resolution is central to pragmatistic theory, and turns a sharp eye on the blind spot of complex democratic theory – elements of political input, throughput, and output which are relevant to participatory procedures.

5 Pragmatistic Democratic Theory

5.1 Democracy as Problem Solving

The pragmatistic tradition of political theory is more comprehensive than pragmatistic democratic theory. Pragmatism, basically, is a school of thought that rejects the difference between theory and practice that Greek philosophy has written deep into Western thinking. It fills up the divide by positing that what is true is what effects a difference in reality. Any word, any conception, any idea is seen as an instrument with which reality can be handled in a meaningful way. Consequently, truth is found through experiment, so the truth in a problematic situation affects its resolution. In his famous pragmatistic maxim, Peirce proposes to "[c]onsider what effects, that might conceivably have practical bearings, we conceive the object of our conception to have. Then, our conception of these effects is the whole of our conception of the object" (Peirce, 1998 [1902], CP 5.2). In that sense, pragmatism is a method: "Pragmatism is that method of reflection which is guided by constantly holding in view its purpose and the purpose of the ideas it analyzes, whether these ends be of the nature and uses of action or of thought." (ibid: CP 5.13 note 1).

It is in the context of his complementary work on epistemology, the philosophy of science, educational theory, and experimental action that the work of John Dewey on democracy must be understood. Dewey describes the process of politics as cooperative problem resolution (Jörke, 2003, p. 233). In his empirical contribution to pragmatistic democratic theory, de Souza Briggs (2008) speaks of "Democracy as Problem Solving." Dewey's basic thesis is that democracy is a communal practice of cooperative and experimental problem resolution, producing intelligent solutions for an interdependent world. His central question is how collective problem resolution procedures should be shaped, or in other words: how democracy should be organized. Since democracy is basically understood to be a collective epistemological enterprise of experimentation, pragmatists like to quote Alexis de Tocqueville who wrote: "In democratic countries, knowledge of how to combine is the mother of all other forms of knowledge; on its progress depends that of all the others" (Tocqueville, 1995, p. 517; cf. de Souza Briggs, 2008, p. 8).

One important context of Dewey's conception of politics as a process of collective problem resolution is his critique of the "Great Society," the societal reality of the American mass democracy in the first decades of the 20th century (Jörke, 2003, p. 203). According to Dewey, where the interdependency of economic development is increasing, the place of relevant political decisions and democratic shaping grows ever more distant to the people. More and more people feel disconnected and don't see their interests represented by politicians, while they also have no starting point for resistance – so apathy grows (Jörke, 2003, p. 128). Against that diagnosis, Dewey sets his idea of a "Great Community." It is a space where individuals develop and grow as individuals, self-determined and self-organized. "A democracy is more than a form of government: it is primarily a mode of associated living, a conjoint communicated experience" (Dewey, 1964, p. 121, quoted in Jörke, 2003, p. 205). According to Dewey, the Great Society is transformed into the Great Community, where democracy as mode, mechanism, and method of collective, experimental problem resolution is implemented. In a democracy as a problem resolving community, all politics begins where the consequences of an individual's action affect other individuals involuntary, thus prompting a need for regulation. Where interdependent problems cannot be resolved alone, a public and cooperative political action comes into being (Dewey, 1991, p. 12ff.).

Dewey's classical model of a collective problem resolution process is a process of *social inquiry* (Krüger, 2000; Rost, 2003). It is a prototypical participatory process where participants go through a whole cycle of problem resolution. They do so in a cooperative, experimental manner. It starts with a concrete problem, or more specific: with a problematic situation, usually characterized by complexity. That situation will have to be transformed into an unproblematic situation. That calls for creative action – indeed, Hans Joas calls pragmatism a "theory of situated creativity" (Joas, 1996, p. 197). Creative action effects the transformation through reorganizing the problematic situation until it is unproblematic. The reorganization is a process where reflection and action on probation gear into each other (Jörke, 2003, p. 213). The key element of this process is the conceptions held by participants. To the given facts, they inscribe a certain meaning that is relevant in regard to the aspired changes (Dewey, 2003, p. 100f.). Not all of the given facts are relevant to the resolution of the problem, and hence, not all facts need to be assigned certain conceptions. It is up to experiment (informed, of course, by prior experience) to find those conceptions that really effect changes. The true meaning of a conception lies in the modification of reality that follows the application of this conception (Dewey, 2003, p. 18).

The experimental and reflective problem resolution includes all steps from analysis to implementation. In his work "Logic: The Theory of Inquiry," Dewey describes the different phases of that inquiry: the qualification of a situation as a problematic, the experimental and rational test of a hypothesis, the reflexive establishment of a relationship between conception and reality, and the construction of judgment (Dewey, 2002; Krüger, 2000, p. 212-227; Rost, 2003). Where this process of inquiry takes place in public, democracy as process of inquiry fulfills itself. Rost argues that the practice of such public inquiries would result in a "continuously planning society" (Rost, 2003, p. 12). Such a society could be understood as a learning society, continuously reconstructing the consequences of problematic situations and searching for solutions. Its political process is not about making collectively binding decisions, but about resolving collectively shared problems (Fuhrmann, 2001; Gohl, 2001, p. 7).

5.2 Participatory Procedures as Problem Resolution Procedures

In his book *Democracy as Problem Solving*, Xavier de Souza Briggs (2008) describes examples of successful problem resolution in cities all over the world. In his review of the book, Archon Fung subsumes Briggs' book into a tradition of democratic thought where "a democratic society is one that has the power to achieve the common aims of its citizens" (Fung, 2010, p. 132). He outlines three insights. "First, these cases of successful problem solving result neither from pure public deliberation in which good reasons trump self-interest, nor from bare-knuckled brawls in which interest backed by superior power carries the day. (...) actors and groups with diverse interests share enough in common (the problem they face) to engage in a kind of joint planning and action that involves some elements of deliberation leavened with heavy doses of negotiation" (ibid, p. 132). Moreover, the participating parties "manage to engage in an intellectual process in which they actually learn – they uncover empirical features of the situation that they are in, they learn about each other, and they invent better (more effective, mutually beneficial) solutions to the problems they face" (ibid, p. 133).

As second insight, Fung describes success as a function of linking the politics and policy, decision-making processes with implementation and public action "in a pragmatically reciprocal way." The boundaries between input and output, between articulating the will of participants and taking action for implementation break down. Politics as problem resolution is a collaborative effort that calls into question the old view that the formation of political will is a bottom-up process, and the implementation of decision is top-down. That is the third insight: "In Briggs' account, initiative can come from either the top or the bottom of the local social structure. (...) Though these cases differ in their origins, they are similar in that they all achieve broad-based inclusion in the medium term. This inclusion, of local elites as well as broader constituencies and private, civic, and governmental actors, is an essential ingredient in solving (...) decentralized problems" (ibid, p. 133). Fung concludes that for Briggs, democratic inclusion is not just right, but also good in terms of results.

The cases of Briggs provide a contemporary commentary of Dewey's public inquiry and problem resolution processes. Pragmatistic democratic theory provides a frame of reference that includes deliberation, and addresses questions of input, throughput, and output of democratic governance. It will be argued in the final conclusion that participatory procedures are multi-faceted political procedures, which are more adequately understood in terms of such collective resolution processes.

6 *Conclusion: Reframing the Debate About Collaborative Democracy and Collective Problem Resolution*

Participatory procedures are multi-faceted procedures that cannot be reduced to deliberation or the authentic expression of popular will on the input side of democratic governance. Instead, they are more adequately understood when they are understood as (condensed parts of) collective problem resolution processes, which Kleger has called "organized dialogues" (Kleger, 1999a, p. 193; 1999b, p. 317; 2004, p. 185). Organized dialogues are multi-faceted participative procedures with the potential purpose of generating comprehensive collaborative transformation. They include less ambitious procedures such as group facilitation that leads to a better understanding of participants and problems, procedures of deliberation aimed at dispensing advice to decision makers, and procedures of public engagement, action, and implementation commonly believed to be part of the output dimension of democratic governance (Gohl, 2011, p. 119-127).

Participatory methods can be tagged and categorized according to their specific contributions to collective problem resolution. As processes, they should be shaped according to strategic purposes best described as effects or outcome (Gohl, 2010). In structuring participation, considerations of input, throughput, and output remain relevant: "Democracy is a recipe for structuring the participation of stakeholders in solving problems that confront them collectively in a way that (1) makes significant decisions as accessible and inclusive as possible and (2) avoids patterns of domination, subject to the aim of (3) producing outcomes that are recognized as promoting legitimate interests and values" (Briggs, 2008, p. 312). That is another way to express the emergent concept of collaborative democracy, which has been called "government with the people" (Noveck, 2009). It really is government of the people, by the people, and for the people – a process of inclusive, problem resolution as organized by concerned actors.

Taken seriously, democracy as problem resolution changes the logic of politics, which is not to make collectively binding decisions, but to solve collectively shared problems. It reframes the problem of complex democratic theory, the legitimacy/effectiveness dilemma, as the challenge of the capability of democracies to solve problems. Briggs calls it "civic capacity" (Briggs, 2008), Fung suggests it better be called a "craft" (Fung, 2010, p. 133), and Kleger "democratic governability" (Kleger, 1999a, p. 179; Kleger, Karolewski & Munke, 2004, p. 526; similar Gohl, 2010, p. 132-168). Alongside considerations of systemic capacity, the competence of democratic actors, neglected since the demise of conceptions of statesmanship and the art of government, becomes an issue of scientific interest again. Pragmatic democratic theory is an action theory of governance.

For patching up the deficencies of the other theories, for its ability to accord these theories a proper place in the comprehensive scheme of things, and for its potential to move the practice of democracy beyond theoretical problems and desirable standards of discourse to better (and then more) democracy, the guiding frame of reference for the understanding of participatory procedures should be a pragmatistic conception of collaborative democracy as collective problem resolution. For increasingly complex, globalized, and learning society, this is an adequate understanding of the operating system of politics.

Bibliography

Beck, K., & Ziekow, J. (eds.) (2011). Mehr Bürgerbeteiligung wagen. Wege zur Vitalisierung der Demokratie. Wiesbaden: VS Verlag.

Briggs, X. (2008). Democracy as Problem Solving. Cambridge, MA: MIT Press.

Crouch, C. (2004). Post-Democracy. London: Polity Press

Dahl, R. A. (1994). A Democratic Dilemma: System Effectiveness Versus Citizen Participation. Political Science Quarterly, 109(1), 23-34.

Delli Carpini, M. X., Cook, F. L., Jacobs, L. R. (2004). Public Deliberations, Discursive Participation and Citizen Engagement. A Review of the Empirical Literature. Annual Review of Political Science, 7, 315–344.

Dewey, J. (1964). Demokratie und Erziehung. Braunschweig: Georg Westermann Verlag.

Dewey, J. (1991). The public and its problems. Athens: Swallow Press.

Dewey, J. (2002). Logik. Die Theorie der Forschung. 1. Aufl. Frankfurt am Main: Suhrkamp.

Dewey, J. (2003). Philosophie und Zivilisation. 1. Aufl. Frankfurt am Main: Suhrkamp.

Elster, J. (ed.) (1998). Deliberative Democracy. Cambridge: Cambridge Univ. Press.

Feindt, P. H. (ed.) (2001). Regierung durch Diskussion? Diskurs- und Verhandlungsverfahren im Kontext von Demokratietheorie und Steuerungsdiskussion. Frankfurt am Main: Lang.

Fishkin, J. S. (1991). Democracy and deliberation: New Directions for democratic reform. New Haven: Yale University Press.

Fuhrmann, R. D. (2009). Prozedurale Politik. Auf dem Weg zu einer politischen Verfahrenstheorie. Dissertation an der Privaten Universität Witten/Herdecke gGmbH, Fachbereich Wirtschaftswissenschaft.

Fuhrmann, R. D. (2001). New Politics. Politische Techniken für das 21. Jahrhundert. Veranstaltung vom 24. Januar 2001. Stuttgart.

Fuhrmann, R. D., & Stock, A. (2006). Partizipative Verfahren optimal auswählen und anpassen. Die Meta-Matching-Method (MMM): Ein Grundwerkzeug für kommunale Planer und Entscheider. Neues Verwaltungsmanagement, 39(2), 1–39.

Fung, A. (2010). Review of Xavier Briggs' Democracy as Problem Solving: Civic Capacity in Communities Across the Globe. City and Community (February 2010), 132-134.

Gallie, W. B. (1956). Essentially Contested Concepts. Proceedings of the Aristotelian Society, 56, 167-198.

Gastil, J. (2008). Political Communication and Deliberation. Thousand Oaks, CA: Sage.

Gastil, J., & Levine, P. (2005). The Deliberative Democracy Handbook. Strategies for Effective Civic Engagement In The Twenty-First Century. 1. ed. San Francisco, Calif.: Jossey-Bass.

Geis, A. (2005). Regieren mit Mediation. Das Beteiligungsverfahren zur zukünftigen Entwicklung des Frankfurter Flughafens. 1. Aufl. Wiesbaden: VS Verl. für Sozialwiss.

Geißel, B. (2008). Wozu Demokratisierung der Demokratie? Kriterien zur Bewertung partizipativer Arrangements. In A. Vetter (ed.), Erfolgsbedingungen lokaler Bürgerbeteiligung (29–48). 1. Aufl. Wiesbaden: VS Verlag.

Gohl, C. (2001). Bürgergesellschaft als politische Zielperspektive. Aus Politik und Zeitgeschichte, 2001(6–7): 5–11.

Gohl, Christopher (2010). Organisierte Dialoge als Strategie. Ed. by the Bertelsmann Stiftung (Schriftenreihe Zukunft Regieren. Beiträge für eine zukunftsfähige Politik, 9/2010). Gütersloh: Bertelsmann. Online at http://www.bertelsmann-stiftung.de/cps/rde/xbcr/SID-A3554A-D1-9EA009C2/bst/xcms_bst_dms_32218__2.pdf, zuletzt geprüft am 31. Dezember 2011.

Gohl, C. (2011). Prozedurale Politik am Beispiel organisierter Dialoge. Wie politische Beteiligung professionell gestaltet werden kann – eine Grundlegung. Münster: Lit Verlag.

Habermas, J. (1981). Theorie des kommunikativen Handelns. Frankfurt am Main: Suhrkamp.

Habermas, J. (1984). Vorstudien und Ergänzungen zur Theorie des kommunikativen Handelns. Frankfurt am Main: Suhrkamp.

Hager, L. (2005). Wie demokratisch ist direkte Demokratie? Eine Wachstumstheorie der Demokratie - Volksinitiativen in Kalifornien. Wiesbaden: VS Verlag.

Hemmati, M. (2002). Multi-stakeholder processes for governance and sustainability. Beyond deadlock and conflict. London: Earthscan.

Herzberg, C. (2001). Wie partizipative Demokratie zu politisch-administrativen Verbesserungen führen kann - der Bürgerhaushalt von Porto Alegre. Münster: Lit.

Holtkamp, L., Bogumil, J., & Kißler, L. (2006). Kooperative Demokratie. Das demokratische Potenzial von Bürgerengagement. Frankfurt am Main: Campus.

Jann, W., & Wegrich, K. (2003). Phasenmodelle und Politikprozesse. Der Policy Cycle. In K. Schubert (ed.), Lehrbuch der Politikfeldanalyse (71–105). München: Oldenbourg.

Joas, H. (1996). Die Kreativität des Handelns. 1. Aufl., [1. Dr.]. Frankfurt am Main: Suhrkamp.

Jonuschat, H. (ed.) (2007). Partizipation und Nachhaltigkeit. Vom Leitbild zur Umsetzung. München: Oekom.

Jörke, D. (2003). Demokratie als Erfahrung. John Dewey und die politische Philosophie der Gegenwart. Wiesbaden: Westdeutscher Verlag.

Keim, D. W. (1975). Participation in Contemporary Democratic Theories. In J. R. Pennock & J. W. Chapman (eds), Nomos XVI: Participation in politics. The Yearbook of the American Society for Political and Legal Philosophy. New York: Lieber.

Keller, R. (1997). Diskursanalyse. In R. Hitzler & A. Honer (eds): Sozialwissenschaftliche Hermeneutik. Eine Einführung (309-333). Opladen: Leske + Budrich.

Klages, H. (2007). Beteiligungsverfahren und Beteiligungserfahrungen. Bonn: Friedrich-Ebert-Stiftung.

Kleger, H. (1999a). Was heißt: "Die Idee der Demokratie ist reflexiv geworden?". In: Angehrn, Emil; Baertschi, Bernard (eds): Demokratie und Globalisierung. Democratie et mondialisation. Studia Philosophica, Sonderheft: 167–195.

Kleger, Heinz (1999b). Stadtregion und Transregion. Herausforderungen politischer Theorie heute. In: Greven, Michael; Schmalz-Bruns, Rainer (eds): Politische Theorie heute. Ansätze und Perspektiven. 1. Aufl. Baden-Baden: Nomos-Verl.-Ges.: 385–414.

Kleger, Heinz (2004). Der Konvent als Labor. Texte und Dokumente zum europäischen Verfassungsprozess. Münster: Lit (Region - Nation - Europa, 25).

Kleger, Heinz; Karolewski, Ireneusz Pawel; Munke, Matthias (2004). Europäische Verfassung. Zum Stand der europäischen Demokratie im Zuge der Osterweiterung. 3., aktualisierte und erweitete Aufl. Münster: Lit Verlag (Region – Nation – Europa).

Kreß, Angelika (2000). Repräsentation – Partizipation – Diskurs. Zur demokratietheoretischen Begründung verfahrensgesteuerter Diskurse. In: Nennen, Heinz-Ulrich (ed.) (2000): Diskurs. Begriff und Realisierung. Würzburg: Königshausen & Neumann: 197-238.

Krüger, Hans-Peter (2000). Prozesse der öffentlichen Untersuchung. Zum Potential einer zweiten Modernisierung in John Deweys „Logic: The Theory of Inquiry“. In: Hans Joas (ed.): Philosophie der Demokratie. Beiträge zum Werk von John Dewey, Frankfurt/ M. (Suhrkamp) 2000: 194-234.

Lakoff, George (2006). Moral politics. How liberals and conservatives think. 2. ed. [Nachdr.]. Chicago, Ill.: Univ. of Chicago Press.

Levine, Peter; Fung Archon; Gastil, John (2005). Future Directions for Public Deliberation. In: Journal of Public Deliberation, Volume 1, Issue 1, 2005, Article 3.

Levine, Peter; Hasselblad Torres, Lars (2007). Where is Democracy Headed? Four Years of DDC Research and Practice. ed. by Deliberative Democracy Consortium (DDC). Online verfügbar unter http://www.thataway.org/main/wp-content/uploads/2008/10/where_is_democracy_headed_report.pdf, zuletzt geprüft am 30. März 2009.

Mansbridge, Jane; Hartz-Karp, Janette F.; Amengual, Matthew; Gastil, John (2006): Norms of Deliberation. An Inductive Study. Edited by The Berkeley Electronic Press. Berkeley.

Mendelberg, Tali (2002). The deliberative citizen. Theory and Evidence. In: Delli Carpini, Michael X (eds.): Political decision-making, deliberation and participation. Amsterdam: Jai (Research in micropolitics, 6): 151–193.

Naschold, Frieder (1968). Demokratie und Komplexität. Thesen und Illustrationen in der Politikwissenschaft, Politische Vierteljahresschrift 9: 494-518.

Naschold, Frieder (1969). Organisation und Demokratie. Untersuchung zum Demokratisierungspotential in komplexen Organisationen. Kohlhammer, Stuttgart.

Naschold, Frieder (zusammen mit Wolf Dieter Narr) (1971) Systemsteuerung, Bd. II. Band zwei des dreibändigen Werkes: Einführung in die moderne politische Theorie. Kohlhammer Verlag, Stuttgart 1971. 3. Aufl.

Nennen, Heinz-Ulrich (ed.) (2000). Diskurs. Begriff und Realisierung. Würzburg: Königshausen & Neumann.

Noveck, Beth Simone (2009). Wiki Government. How Technology can make government better, democracy stronger, and citizens more powerful. Washington D.C.: Brookings Institution Press.

Peirce, Charles Sanders (1998). Collected papers of Charles Sanders Peirce. Edited by Charles Hartshorne, Paul Weiss, Arthur W. Burks. Bristol: Thoemmes.

Renn, Ortwin (2008). Risk governance. Coping with uncertainty in a complex world. London: Earthscan (Earthscan risk in society series).

Rost, Sophia (2003). John Deweys Logik der Untersuchung für die Entdeckung des Politischen in modernen Gesellschaften. Münster: Lit (Region - Nation - Europa, 19).

Rowe, Gene; Frewer, Lynn J. (2005). A Typology of Public Engagement Mechanisms. In: Science, Technology & Human Values, Jg. 30, H. 2: 251–290.

Saretzki, Thomas (2010). Strategie als Herausforderung für deliberative Demokratietheorie. In: Raschke, Joachim; Tils, Ralf (eds) (2010): Strategie in der Politikwissenschaft. Konturen eines neuen Forschungsfelds. 1. Aufl. Wiesbaden: VS Verl. für Sozialwiss.: 121-150.

Scharpf, Fritz W. (1970). Demokratietheorie zwischen Utopie und Anpassung. Konstanzer Universitätsreden 25. Constance: Universitätsverlag.

Scharpf, Fritz W. (1975). Policy-Making in the German Federal Bureaucracy (with Renate Mayntz). Amsterdam: Elsevier.

Scharpf, Fritz W. (1973). Planung als politischer Prozeß. Aufsätze zur Theorie der planenden Demokratie. 1. Aufl. Frankfurt am Main: Suhrkamp (Theorie).

Scharpf, Fritz W. (1985). Die Politikverflechtungs-Falle: Europäische Integration und deutscher Föderalismus im Vergleich, in: Politische Vierteljahresschrift, 26. Jg., Nr. 4: 323–356.

Scharpf, Fritz W. (1988). The Joint-Decision Trap. Lessons from German Federalism and European Integration. In: Public Administration 66: 239-287.

Scharpf, Fritz W. (1997). Demokratische Politik in der internationalisierten Ökonomie, MPIfG Working Paper 97/9, November 1997.

Scharpf, Fritz W. (1999). Governing in Europe. Effective and Democratic? Oxford/ New York: Oxford University Press.

Schmidt, Manfred G. (1997). Demokratietheorien (2. Auflage). Opladen: Leske + Budrich.

Schmidt, Manfred G. (2000). Demokratietheorien. Eine Einführung. 3. überarb. und erw. Aufl., Opladen: Leske + Budrich.

Schmidt, Manfred G. (2003). Die ‚komplexe Demokratietheorie' nach drei Jahrzehnten. In: Mayntz, Renate; Streek, Wolfgang (eds): Die Reformierbarkeit der Demokratie – Innovationen und Blockaden. Festschrift für Fritz Scharpf, Frankfurt a.M.: 151-172.

Strecker, David & Schaal, Gary S. (2001). Die politische Theorie der Deliberation: Jürgen Habermas. In: Brodocz, André / Schaal, Gary S. (eds): Politische Theorien der Gegenwart, Band II. Opladen: UTB: 89-128.

Susskind, Lawrence; Field, Patrick (1996). Dealing with an Angry Public: The Mutual Gains Approch to Resolving Disputes. New York: The Free Press.

Tocqueville, Alexis de; Mayer, J. P.; Lawrence, George (1995). Democracy in America. 1. Perennial Library ed., [Nachdr.]. New York, NY: HarperPerennial.

Van Deth, Jan (2009). Politische Partizipation, in: Kaina, Viktoria; Römmele, Andrea (eds): Politische Soziologie. Ein Studienbuch. Wiesbaden: VS Verlag für Sozialwissenschaften: 141–161.

Walk, Heike (2007). Partizipation in der sozial-ökologischen Forschung. Ergebnisse der Querschnittsarbeitsgruppe Partizipation. In: Jonuschat, Helga (ed.): Partizipation und Nachhaltigkeit. Vom Leitbild zur Umsetzung. Ergebnisse des Workshops „Partizipation und Nachhaltigkeit – Der Teufel steckt im Detail" am 23. September 2005 in Berlin. München: Oekom (Ergebnisse sozial-ökologischer Forschung, 7), 13–27.

Walzer, Michael (2007). Thinking Politically: Essays in Political Theory. Selected, edited, and with an introduction by David Miller. Binghamton, N.Y.: Vail Ballou Press.

Zakaria, Fareed (2003). The Future of Freedom: Illiberal. Democracy at Home and Abroad. New York, N.Y.: W.W. Norton and Co.

Zum Leitbild einer kommunikativen lokalen Demokratie

[Envisioning a Communicative Local Democracy]

Gunnar Folke Schuppert

This contribution argues that there is a bias to contemporary debates on civic inclusion into government decision-making. It sets out to overcome the previous focus on the concept of civic participation and suggests a theoretical perspective which combines communication and governance. With "governance" understood as "governance as and by communication" it sketches out a new method of allowing citizens to actively participate in public policy-making.

While traditional participation models are structured to fulfill certain purposes and produce distinct outputs (both of which are usually defined by administrative authorities), communicative governance should be introduced at an earlier stage of the policy process. Citizens should not only get involved after the scope and aim of the process has been defined, but ought to play an active role from early on; they should contribute to agenda-setting and to the shaping of the processes. To accomplish this, a new style of democratic policy-making on the local level has to be based on continuous communication among those being involved and affected.

This concept of a communicative democratic procedure is based on five pillars: democratic theory, constitutional theory, governance theory, decision-making theory and conflict theory. Those five elements fuel every democratic process. In this article, each one of them is assessed regarding its potential and impact for public policy-making, and it aims at combining them into a procedural structure that allows citizens to develop ways to handle political issues through communication. This seems to be an adequate supplement to administrative behavior since the latter's acceptance is eroding and the information asymmetry between decision-makers and decision-takers is vast and more and more subject to criticism.

This paper proposes a concertedly produced equity roadmap ensuring procedural fairness. Its layout is crucial. The designer of the process becomes a key figure within the whole concept of communicative local democracy. S/he is in charge of the functionality and fairness of the communication process. Expectations of the designer are therefore high regarding her/his professionalism, impartiality and authority. In the end, all of this is needed to enable the development of modern communicative processes to satisfy demands of citizens, politics and administrations alike.

1 Die Ausgangslage

1.1 Zur erodierenden Akzeptanz infrastruktureller Planungsentscheidungen

Zum Beleg für diesen im Ergebnis wohl unstreitigen Befund möchten wir einige Sätze aus einem Beitrag von Wolfgang van den Daele und Friedhelm Neidhardt zitieren, der von Versuchen handelt „mit Argumenten Politik zu machen“, und die wie folgt lauten:

> „Probleme der Akzeptanz sind die zweite wichtige Erklärung für den Trend zu mehr Verhandlung, Dialog und Partizipation. In wichtigen Problemfeldern ist die Abnahme beschlossener Politiken offenbar nicht mehr gewährleistet. Größere Planungs- und Standortentscheidungen lösen häufig Bürgerproteste und rechtlichen Dauerstreit aus, der alles blockiert. Die Ursachen für die gestiegene Konfliktintensität dürften in der Sensibilisierung für die Umweltprobleme und für die Ambivalenzen von Modernisierungsdynamik bei der Bevölkerung im Allgemeinen liegen sowie in der Mobilisierung von lokalem Widerstand durch die Umweltbewegung oder ihre Organisationen.“ (van den Daele/Neidhardt 1996, S. 9ff.)

Diese Sätze sind nicht etwa als Kommentar zu „Stuttgart 21“ geschrieben worden, sondern stammen aus dem Jahre 1996 und finden sich in dem 96er-Jahrbuch des Wissenschaftszentrums Berlin mit dem heute noch genauso aktuellen Titel „Kommunikation und Entscheidung“. Von diesem Zusammenhang von Kommunikation und Entscheidung soll auch in diesem Beitrag die Rede sein.

1.2 Zum Ruf nach intensiver Bürgerbeteiligung bei Großprojekten

Dieser Ruf ist so unüberhörbar und so vielstimmig erschallt, dass es auch hier genügt, eine Stimme als repräsentativ auszuwählen. Unsere Wahl ist dabei nicht etwa auf Vertreter von Umweltverbänden oder Bürgerinitiativen gefallen, vielmehr soll jemand zu Wort kommen, der im Ministerium für Verkehr, Bau und Landesentwicklung des Landes Mecklenburg-Vorpommern das Referat „Verkehrskonzepte, Bürgerbeteiligung“ leitet, also dem häufig gescholtenen Bereich der planenden Verwaltung angehört. In seinem „post Stuttgart 21“ geschriebenen Beitrag attestiert Reinhard Wulfhorst im August 2011 den Auseinandersetzungen um den Bahnhofsneubau geradezu „schockartige Wirkungen“, die weit über dieses Einzelvorhaben hinausreichen. Er meint eine Art Grundkonsens für mehr Bürgerbeteiligung feststellen zu können, ein Konsens, der die Chance bietet, eine Bürgerbeteiligung auf den Weg zu bringen, die diesen Namen wirklich verdient (Wulfhorst 2011, S. 581):

> „Auch aus der Wirtschaft sind ungewohnte Töne zu hören. Der Deutsche Industrie- und Handelskammertag hat sich beispielweise im Zusammenhang mit dem geplanten Planungsvereinheitlichungsgesetz für ‚eine frühzeitige, breite und kontinuierliche Beteiligung der Öffentlichkeit‘, Mediationsverfahren und die Beibehaltung des zwingenden Erörterungstermins ausgesprochen. Solche Einlassungen einer Wirtschaftsorganisation, die fast wörtlich mit Forderungen der Umweltverbände übereinstimmen, wären noch vor Jahresfrist kaum denkbar gewesen. Damit scheint sich ein breiter gesellschaftlicher Kon-

> sens herausgebildet zu haben, der die Chance bietet, eine Bürgerbeteiligung insbesondere bei Großprojekten auf den Weg zu bringen, die diesen Namen wirklich verdient."

Wenn dies richtig ist, sind wir alle aufgefordert, aus dieser Chance etwas zu machen. Aber wie?

1.3 Von der Partizipationsperspektive zur Notwendigkeit eines „communicative turn"

Wenn man darüber nachdenkt, welche Folgerungen aus den Befunden einer erodierenden Akzeptanz von hoheitlichen Planungsentscheidungen sowie dem Ruf nach intensiverer Bürgerbeteiligung zu ziehen sind, so scheinen uns drei sich zwar überschneidende, vom Ansatz aber doch sehr verschiedene Antworten in Betracht zu kommen.

Die erste Antwort könnte darin bestehen, die ja durchaus vorhandenen Beteiligungsverfahren anreichernd zu verbessern oder auch mit reformerischem und innovativem Elan neue Beteiligungsmodelle zu entwerfen. Was die erste Strategie angeht, so wäre dafür etwa der Beitrag des Verwaltungsrechtlers Thomas Groß repräsentativ, der unter dem Titel „Stuttgart 21: Folgerungen für Demokratie und Verwaltungsverfahren" auf Verbesserungen der Partizipation in Planungsverfahren zielt (Groß 2011). Diesen Weg wollen wir nicht beschreiten. Aber auch als Designer eines neuen Beteiligungsmodells wollen wir uns nicht versuchen. Wenn man nämlich einen Blick auf den 2010 von der Bertelsmann-Stiftung veröffentlichten Überblick über die „Charakteristika neuer Beteiligungsmodelle" wirft – von der ehrwürdigen Planungszelle bis zum World Café – so stellen sich ganz von alleine Zweifel daran ein, ob es Sinn macht, diesen sechzehn (!) vorgestellten Beteiligungsverfahren noch ein siebzehntes hinzuzufügen. Auch diesen Weg wollen wir daher nicht gehen.

Eine zweite Antwort könnte darin bestehen, das Denken in Kategorien des Verwaltungsverfahrens und die facettenreiche Welt von Beteiligungsmodellen zu transzendieren und eine eher kulturwissenschaftliche Perspektive zu wählen. Als repräsentativ dafür haben wir einen soeben erschienenen Beitrag von Ulrich Sarcinelli (2011) wahrgenommen, in dem er eine „neue Kommunikations- und Beteiligungskultur" einfordert. Im Originalton heißt es dazu bei Sarcinelli wie folgt (ebenda, S. 324):

> „Dies alles spricht für eine andere, stärker bürgergesellschaftlich durchwirkte Kommunikationskultur. Gemeint ist damit gerade nicht ein medienzentrierter Verlautbarungsstil mit politischen Sprechern, Öffentlichkeitsarbeitern, Beratern und Spindoctors; einer Art von Kommunikation, die sich als hochspezialisierte Sozialtechnologie versteht, eine zur Politik hinzutretende Vermittlungstechnik und von der Politik separierte Sphäre von Kommunikationsprofis zur Generierung von Aufmerksamkeit und Legitimationsbeschaffung. Notwendig ist vielmehr eine Kommunikation, die in eine ‚horizontal und vertikal differenzierte(n) Regelungsstruktur' (Mayntz 2009, S. 11) passt; eine Kommunikation für ein ‚komplexes Arrangement verbundener Arenen' (Benz 1998, S. 201f.) mit Schritten hin zu einer neuen Beteiligungskultur. Dies will gelernt sein, muss eingeübt und gepflegt werden, um wechselseitiges Vertrauen zu schaffen. Die Stadt muss sich als modernes, kommunizierendes und verhandelndes Ge-

> meinwesen nicht zuletzt dadurch bewähren, dass die Bürger ernst genommen und ihnen neue Diskursräume und Beteiligungsplattformen geboten werden. Die neue Kommunikations- und Beteiligungskultur ist anstrengend. Sie verursacht hohe Transaktionskosten und sie ist kein Pazifizierungsgarant."

Auch diesen Weg wollen wir nicht beschreiten; und zwar nicht deshalb, weil er – wie Sarcinelli warnt – vielleicht zu anstrengend wäre, sondern weil wir den – wie man ihn nennen könnte – kommunikationskulturellen Ansatz radikalisieren und mit Impulsen aus der Governance-Forschung verbinden möchten.

Wir möchten in diesem Beitrag die bisherige Partizipationszentriertheit der Debatte über bürgerschaftliche Beteiligung an staatlichen Entscheidungsprozessen überwinden und eine kombinierte kommunikations- und governancetheoretische Perspektive ins Spiel bringen, die Verwaltungsräume als Kommunikationsräume begreift und „Governance" vor allem als „governance as and by communication" versteht (vgl. zu „governance as communication" Schuppert 2006; 2007). Es geht also darum, das, was gemeinhin unter der Überschrift der bürgerschaftlichen Beteiligung diskutiert wird, als Kommunikationsprozesse auszugestalten und zu organisieren (vgl. erste Überlegungen dazu bei Schuppert 2011), und zwar von Anfang an – also schon in der Phase des „agenda-settings" – und nicht etwa nur als Kommunikation innerhalb feststehender Verfahrensstrukturen. Vielmehr ginge es darum – und hierin liegt das Neue und Weiterführende – auch die Verfahrensstrukturen selbst kommunikativ zu entwickeln, sie also als Produkt eines Kommunikationsprozesses, nicht als festgeschriebenen Rahmen für Kommunikation zu begreifen. Bevor wir dazu einige, diese kommunikationswissenschaftliche Perspektive konkretisierende Überlegungen vortragen, wollen wir das uns vor Augen stehende Leitbild einer kommunikativen lokalen Demokratie theoretisch möglichst umfassend fundieren und dazu verschiedene Theoriestränge zusammenzuführen versuchen.

2 *Zur theoretischen Fundierung des Leitbildes einer kommunikativen lokalen Demokratie*

Das theoretische Fundament, auf dem unser Leitbild einer kommunikativen lokalen Demokratie aufruht, besteht aus fünf Pfeilern im Sinne von fünf sich überlappenden, aber analytisch zu trennenden Argumentationssträngen. Diese fünf Argumente sind

- das demokratietheoretische Argument
- das verfassungstheoretische Argument
- das governancetheoretische Argument
- das entscheidungstheoretische Argument und
- das konflikttheoretische Argument.

Im Folgenden wollen wir alle fünf Pfeiler einer kurzen Inspektion unterziehen, um uns im Anschluss daran an einer ersten Zwischenbilanz zu versuchen.

2.1 Das demokratietheoretische Argument

Zweifellos ist das an erster Stelle zu nennende Argument für eine kommunikative lokale Demokratie das demokratietheoretische Argument, und zwar genauer die Vorstellung und der Anspruch der sog. deliberativen Demokratietheorie (zu ihr Feindt 2001; Strecker/Schaal 2001), dass es möglich sei, „durch Argumente Politik zu machen" (van den Daele/Neidhardt 1996). Der deliberativen Demokratietheorie ist dazu die kommunikationstheoretische Perspektive sozusagen von vornherein eingeschrieben, ein Zusammenhang, wie er schöner als in der Regierungserklärung Willy Brandts vom 28. Oktober 1969 kaum zum Ausdruck gebracht werden kann. Die in ihr formulierte Botschaft hieß „Mehr Demokratie wagen", ein damals politischer Schlüsselbegriff, der in dieser Regierungserklärung wie folgt transportiert wurde (hier zitiert nach Anna-Bettina Kaiser 2009, S. 139):

> „Wir wollen mehr Demokratie wagen. Wir werden unsere Arbeitsweise öffnen und dem kritischen Bedürfnis nach Information Genüge tun. Wir werden darauf hinwirken, daß durch Anhörungen im Bundestag, durch ständige Fühlungnahme mit den repräsentativen Gruppen unseres Volkes und durch eine umfassende Unterrichtung über die Regierungspolitik jeder Bürger die Möglichkeit erhält, an der Reform von Staat und Gesellschaft mitzuwirken. [...] Mitbestimmung, Mitverantwortung in den verschiedenen Bereichen unserer Gesellschaft werden eine bewegende Kraft der kommenden Jahre sein. Wir können nicht die perfekte Demokratie schaffen. Wir wollen eine Gesellschaft, die mehr Freiheit bietet und mehr Mitverantwortung fordert. Diese Regierung sucht das Gespräch [...];wir brauchen Menschen, die kritisch mitdenken, mitentscheiden und mitverantworten."

Aber gerade wegen dieses so verlockenden Versprechens der deliberativen Demokratietheorie politische Lösungen dadurch finden zu können, dass man sich kommunikativ und argumentativ auf eine gemeinsame für vernünftig gehaltene Lösung konsensual verständigt, ist Vorsicht hinsichtlich der mit ihr möglicherweise verbundenen „Kollateralschäden" geboten. in ihrem Beitrag von 1996 haben Wolfgang van den Daele und Friedhelm Neidhardt auf die zentrale Stellschraube hingewiesen, wer, in welcher Rolle und mit welcher deliberativen Kompetenz an solchen Deliberationsprozessen teilnimmt (ebenda, S. 13):

> „Bei Deliberationen in den Entscheidungsarenen ist das Netzwerk der beteiligten Akteure sehr viel enger [als bei Diskussionen über Leitideen, G.F.S.]: Politiker, die sich des Issue annehmen, Fachbeamte aus den einschlägigen Bürokratien, Spezialisten aus den Parteien, Sprecher der involvierten Interessenverbände und über Gutachten oder sonstige Beratungskontexte eingebundene Experten. In der ‚policy community', die direkt Einfluß auf die Formulierung konkreter Politiken nimmt, bleibt politische Deliberation das Prärogativ eines Elitenzirkels; der Normalbürger oder die Öffentlichkeit spielen dabei keine unmittelbare Rolle".

Auf diese Achillesferse des deliberativen Politikmodells, die sich mit der Formel „je mehr Deliberation, je mehr Exklusion“ auf eine griffige Formel bringen lässt (vgl. dazu Klatt/Walter 2011), wird notwendigerweise noch zurückzukommen sein.

2.2 Das verfassungstheoretische Argument

Das uns genauso wichtige verfassungstheoretische Argument für das Leitbild einer kommunikativen lokalen Demokratie bezieht sich auf die Stellung des Bürgers im demokratischen Verfassungsstaat: diese Stellung des Bürgers ist weder die des Untertanen des längst überwundenen Obrigkeitsstaates, noch die des Konsumenten oder Kunden eines ökonomisierten Staatsverständnisses, sondern die des Mitgestalters des Gemeinwesens, dessen mitverantwortlicher Bürger er ist (zu den verschiedenen Bürgerbildern und ihrem rechtlichen Niederschlag siehe Susanne Baer 2006). Zwei Schlüsselbegriffe sind an dieser Stelle aufzurufen, die für das Leitbild einer kommunikativen Verwaltung (weiterführend dazu Anna-Bettina Kaiser 2009) von zentraler Bedeutung sind.

2.2.1 Grundrechtsschutz durch Verfahren

Der erste Schlüsselbegriff heißt „Grundrechtsschutz durch Verfahren“, womit die „Entdeckung“ der Verfahrensdimension für die Effektuierung des Grundrechtsschutzes in der Rechtssprechung des Bundesverfassungsgerichts gemeint ist. Zu dieser Rolle des Bundesverfassungsgerichts als Motor der Kommunikationsbeziehungen zwischen Verwaltung und Bürgern heißt es bei Anna-Bettina Kaiser zusammenfassend wie folgt (ebenda, S. 160f.):

> „Der Durchbruch für die Idee des Grundrechtsschutzes durch Verfahren – und damit ist regelmäßig gemeint: Grundrechtsschutz über Kommunikationsmuster in Verwaltungsverfahren – wurde […] in der Mühlheim-Kärlich-Entscheidung (BVerfGE 53, 30) erreicht. Hier fand eine Entwicklung ihren Höhepunkt, die sich durch einen allmählichen Bedeutungszuwachs des Verfahrens für die Grundrechtsentwicklung auszeichnet […].
> Ein entscheidender Grund, abseits von gesellschaftlichen Partizipationsforderungen […] zu einer Aufwertung des behördlichen Verfahrens (und damit automatisch der Kommunikationsmuster) zu gelangen und folglich die Partizipationsdebatte zu verstärken, war die sich auch in der Rechtsprechung einstellende Einsicht, dass mit der Zunahme von Planungsverwaltung und Ermessensvorschriften verstärkt Rechtsschutzlücken entstehen würden, die nur durch eine Aufwertung des Verwaltungsverfahrens kompensiert werden könnten (Kompensationsfunktion des Verfahrens und der Kommunikation).“

2.2.2 Der „status activus processualis“

Der zweite Schlüsselbegriff heißt „status activus processualis“, eine Begriffsschöpfung, die wir Peter Häberle (1972) verdanken, der damit die klassische, auf Georg Jellinek (1905) zurückgehende Unterscheidung von status passivus und status activus des Bürgers um eine prozessuale Dimension erweitert hat. Dieser dem Bürger im demokratischen Verfassungsstaat zukommende „status activus processualis“ lässt sich gleich zweifach begründen:

Steht im freiheitlichen, pluralistisch verfassten Verfassungsstaat das Gemeinwohl nicht von vornherein fest und kann es auch nicht ex cathedra von wem auch immer verkündet werden, sondern ist es erst im Prozess der demokratischen Willensbildung, also „ex processu“ hervorzubringen (näher dazu mit weiteren Nachweisen Schuppert 2002), so steht dem Bürger – dies ist der erste Argumentationsstrang – in diesem Prozess der Gemeinwohlhervorbringung eine aktive, mitgestaltende Rolle zu, eben ein „status activus processualis“

Die zweite Begründung ist grundrechtstheoretischer Natur und wurde von Peter Häberle geliefert. Die Schubkraft seiner Argumentation wird uns von Anna-Bettina Kaiser wie folgt eindringlich nähergebracht (ebenda, S. 148f.):

> „Der zweite, sehr wirkmächtige Weg, sich der Partizipationsidee zu nähern, wurde von P. Häberle […] 1971 – auf der Staatsrechtslehrertagung zu dem Thema ‚Grundrechte im Leistungsstaat‘ eingeschlagen. Anders als […] (vorher) wurden vermehrte Partizipationschancen des Bürgers nicht mehr über ein Verfassungsprinzip, sondern über die Grundrechte zu konstruieren versucht, wofür der Berichterstatter freilich nichts weniger als eine grundlegende Reform der Statuslehre G. Jellineks, mithin der bis dahin herrschenden Grundrechtsdogmatik vorschlug.
> Nicht minder revolutionär als dieser antizipierte Umbau der Dogmatik war freilich bereits die wirklichkeitswissenschaftliche Bestandsaufnahme, die Häberle Anlaß für die Suche nach neuen Grundrechtsdimensionen bot und in der er die Partizipation des Bürgers und eine Kommunikation zwischen Verwaltung und Bürger ausdrücklich verknüpfte. Das Verhältnis zwischen Bürger und Staat sei durch das Leistungsrecht ein grundlegend anderes geworden: ‚Das dem Leistungsrecht eigene aktiv sozialgestaltende Moment läßt Kooperations-, Kommunikations-, Partizipations-, Verfahrens- und Organisationsformen in den Vordergrund rücken.‘ (Häberle 1972, S. 47). Zwar würden Elemente von Befehl und Zwang nach wie vor existieren, jedoch habe der ‚status (passivus) subiectionis‘ seine grundlegende Position zugunsten des ‚status activus‘ eingebüßt.“

2.3 Das governancetheoretische Argument

Wenn wir jetzt neben den normativen Argumenten der Demokratie- und Verfassungstheorie die Governancetheorie die Bühne betreten lassen, so deshalb, weil auch aus der Governanceperspektive deutliche Signale in Richtung einer immer wichtiger werdenden „governance as and by communication“ empfangen werden können. Als „Signalgasten“ – so heißen bei der Marine diejenigen Crewmitglieder, die Signale senden – wollen wir insoweit Klaus Offe und Stein Ringen heranziehen.

2.3.1 Signals and Information as a resource of public policy

In einem noch unveröffentlichten Beitrag hat sich Claus Offe unlängst mit dem Thema „Signals and Information as a Resource of Public Policy“ (Offe 2010) beschäftigt und hier dargelegt, dass der Staat – was weitgehend unstreitig sein dürfte – nicht nur durch Gebote und Verbote das Verhalten seiner Bürger zu steuern versucht – der sogenannte Command und Control-Ansatz – oder durch negative und positive Anreize, sondern auch durch das Aussenden von Signalen und die Verbreitung von Informationen, eine Steuerungstechnik, die man als Steuerung durch Überzeugungsprogramme bezeichnet hat (König/Dose 1993). Offe nennt dies – und diesen Begriff greifen wir gerne auf – „ruling through signals“.

Aber nicht dieser Befund ist es, der uns eigentlich daran interessiert, sondern die weitergehenden demokratietheoretischen Folgerungen, die Offe an diesen Befund knüpft. Wenn nämlich Signale und Informationen Ressourcen staatlicher Steuerung darstellen, dann müsse dem auf der Seite der Steuerungsadressaten das Recht entsprechen, die Offenlegung der relevanten Informationen verlangen zu können, da nur auf diese Weise ein Raum öffentlichen bekannten Wissens hergestellt werden könne: „For by making disclosure of critical information mandatory and easily available for actors on the demand side, clients and customers would no longer have to rely on contingent pieces of information and individual propensities to complain. Instead, they would be transformed into a ‚public‘ with a reflexively shared knowledge (‚all of us know that everyone else knows‘) of significant information and its implications for action – and hence for public policies aiming at the alteration of action.“ (Offe, S. 6)

Auf diese Weise werde – und hier nun kommen wir zu der demokratietheoretischen Pointe – so etwas wie Partizipation durch geteiltes Wissen ermöglicht, eine Partizipationsform, die er als „cognitive participation“ bezeichnet und die er den eher traditionellen Partizipationsformen wie dem Wahlrecht, der Vereinigungsfreiheit und dem Stiften und Zuwenden wie folgt zur Seite stellt: „To the extent such access to knowledge would be institutionalized, an additional fourth and largely underdeveloped channel of democratic participation would be opened in addition to the three more conventional participatory modes (of voting, joining, and donating): the channel of cognitive participation.“ (Offe, S. 7)

Auch hinsichtlich dieser so plausibel entwickelten „cognitive participation“ steht allerdings wie ein schwer zu verscheuchendes Gespenst das Problem von Inklusion und Exklusion, und damit die Frage, ob wir es hier erneut mit einer Variante einer Elitenkommunikation zu tun haben.

2.3.2 The Powerlessness of Powerful Government

In einem unveröffentlichten „discussion paper“ von 2005 hat der norwegische, aber in Oxford lehrende Politikwissenschaftler Stein Ringen die Frage diskutiert, wie Regierungen es bewirken, dass das auch umgesetzt wird, was sie politisch wollen : „To rule is to make things happen in society.“ Die dafür zu Gebote stehenden Instrumente reichen von hoheitlicher Anordnung über die Methode regulierter Selbstregulierung bis zu rechtlich unverbindlichen Überzeugungsprogrammen. Vor allem aber müssen Regierungen ständig kommunizieren, um Unterstützung für ihre Politik einzuwerben, ihre auf Vertrauen beruhende Autorität zu festigen und um „leadership“ auszuüben. Zu dieser Seite der Kommunikation aus der Perspektive einer auf die Steuerungsressource Kommunikation angewiesenen Regierung, also nicht aus der demokratietheoretisch basierten Perspektive der Bürgerbeteiligung heißt es bei Ringen in einer – wie wir finden – zitierenswerten Passage wie folgt (Ringen 2005, S. 11f.):

> „Governments rule by taxing, spending and regulating, but that is not enough. They in addition depend on speaking. They need to inform, to explain, to ‚sell‘ their policies, to make themselves trusted or at least believed, to encourage, to persuade – and to manipulate when that is called for. A Government needs to be seen and heard and to make itself the centre of attention, to out-manoeuvre those trying to out-manoeuvre it. It needs to control the issues that become salient in the press and public awareness and to not let others take hold of the agenda. It needs to lead and to display leadership. […]
> Governments ‚spin‘, and so they must. This is an ancient art. Winston Churchill stands as perhaps the greatest European political leader in modern times. His genius as Prime Minister during World War II was more in communication than in administration, in his speeches and his display of confidence, determination and energy. This was pure signal politics and contributed decisively to effort, morale and co-operation. Governments today live in a harsher environment in which leadership is less accepted and trust thin (O'Neill 2002). Political gamesmanship has shifted away from the traditional arena of parliamentary politics and into arenas dominated by media, organised interests, single-issue pressure groups, and corporations with huge public relations departments. Politics itself revolves strongly around agenda issues: battles over which issues political battle is to be fought over. This is a war of words as much as of action. The moment the government is driven on to the defensive it is on the run. It simply must speak, more and more and ever more loudly, so as to subdue those others who threaten to bring it out of balance and off course. It has to force others into the position of responding to it, or be their victim. It has to conceal what it is unable to get done, make murky compromise look like decisive action and magnify its achievements. It will overdo it, that cannot be avoided – but the risk of looking foolish is for nothing compared to the risk of letting others take ownership of the agenda. Spin is not something a government has the luxury of choosing to indulge in or not. It is the face of a government that rules.“

2.4 Das entscheidungstheoretische Argument

Bereits in unserer Verwaltungswissenschaft aus dem Jahre 2000 hatten wir Gelegenheit, uns mit dem Zusammenhang von Entscheidungsprozessen und Kommunikation zu beschäftigen und hatten dazu unter der Überschrift „Entscheidungsprozesse als

Kommunikationsprozesse“ Folgendes notiert (2000, S. 740): „Entscheidungsprozesse sind Kommunikationsprozesse. Damit werden automatisch die Qualität der Kommunikationsbeziehungen und die Kommunikationsfähigkeit der handelnden Akteure zu wichtigen Voraussetzungen [...] der Entscheidungsqualität“. In gleichsinniger Weise hat sich auch Wolfgang Hoffmann-Riem (1994) geäußert, der dazu Folgendes zu Protokoll gegeben hat (a.a.O., S. 22):

> „Verwaltungshandeln als Entscheidungshandeln ist auf die Verfügbarkeit von Informationen und die Sicherung einer angemessenen Informationsaufnahme und -verarbeitung angewiesen. Informationen über Tatsachen und Werte (Interessen), über potentielle Folgen sowie angemessene Lösungswege lassen sich nur begrenzt auf einseitige Anforderung hin ‚abrufen‘; sie werden vielmehr häufig erst in einem Interaktionsprozeß ‚generiert‘. Damit werden Kommunikationsfähigkeit, Kommunikationsnetzwerke und Interaktionsstile zur Ressource ‚richtiger‘ Entscheidungen.“

Wenn sich dies aber so verhält, dann kommt natürlich der Frage, ob die Chancen der Kommunikationsteilhabe fair verteilt sind, eine zentrale Bedeutung zu; zu diesem unter der Überschrift „Stärkung der kommunikativen lokalen Demokratie“ immer wichtiger werdenden Gesichtspunkt hatten wir 2000 Folgendes niedergeschrieben (ebenda, S. 745f.):

> „Wenn Entscheidungsprozesse vor allem Informationsverarbeitungsprozesse sind, dann ist es entscheidend für die Qualität von Entscheidungen und für die Chance ihrer Richtigkeit – Entscheidungsrichtigkeit –, daß die für die jeweilige Entscheidung benötigten Informationen möglichst umfassend, rasch und zuverlässig zur Verfügung stehen. Sowohl die rechtliche Ausgestaltung des Verwaltungsverfahrens als auch die Kommunikationspraxis der Verwaltung sind daher stets in zweierlei Hinsicht in den Blick zu nehmen: sie sind einmal – dies ist gewissermaßen die instrumentell-technische Seite – daraufhin zu überprüfen, ob sie eine ausreichende Informationsversorgung der Verwaltung gewährleisten; sie sind zum anderen aber auch danach zu befragen, ob die in jeder Ausgestaltung von Kommunikationsbeziehungen liegende Zuteilung von Diskurs – und damit Einflußchancen sachgerecht ist oder sich eher zu einer strukturellen Asymmetrie der Kommunikationsteilhabe verfestigt.“

Auf diesen Gesichtspunkt einer Asymmetrie der Kommunikationsteilhabe wird gleich noch einmal zurückzukommen sein.

2.5 Das konflikttheoretische Argument

Die politische Kultur einer Gesellschaft wird nicht nur durch ihre Institutionenkultur und ihre Kommunikationskultur, sondern ganz entscheidend auch durch ihre Konfliktkultur bestimmt, also durch die Art und Weise, wie mit Konflikten umgegangen wird (ausführlich dazu Schuppert 2008). Es ist das Verdienst insbesondere von Ralf Dahrendorf, die Konfliktkultur in Deutschland gewissermaßen „hoffähig“ gemacht zu haben, indem er das Vorhandensein von Konflikten zur universellen sozialen Tatsache erklärte und daraus die Notwendigkeit ableitete, mit ihnen konfliktregulierend umzugehen (Dahrendorf 1961, S. 228): „Konflikte verschwinden durch ihre Regelung nicht; sie werden nicht einmal notwendig weniger intensiv: in dem Maße aber, in dem es gelingt, sie zu regeln, werden sie kontrollierbar und wird ihre schöpferische Kraft in den Dienst einer allmählichen Entwicklung sozialer Strukturen gestellt."

Eine der vielversprechendsten und zuletzt wieder im Zusammenhang mit „Stuttgart 21" praktizierten Methoden der Konfliktverarbeitung besteht in der „Konfliktbewältigung durch Verhandlungen" (Hoffmann-Riem/Schmidt-Aßmann 1990), eine Strategie, die insbesondere im Bereich der Umweltpolitik vielfach praktiziert (Fietkau/Weidner 1998) und in Deutschland vor allem unter dem Oberbegriff der Mediation diskutiert wird (weiterführend von Schlieffen 2007).

Darüber ist viel geschrieben worden. Hier sind lediglich zwei Punkte festzuhalten. Einmal, dass Mediationsverfahren extrem kommunikationsintensive Verfahren sind, in denen es häufig zunächst einmal darauf ankommt, eine gemeinsame Sprache zu finden, ein Befund, der für die Rolle des Mediators bedeutet, vielfach als Kommunikationshilfe und Übersetzer tätig zu sein. Heiner Geißler hat die zentrale Bedeutung dieser Aufgabe – was immer man sonst von dem Mediationsverfahren „Stuttgart 21" halten mag – überzeugend vorgeführt. Zum anderen ist festzuhalten, dass die Möglichkeiten selbst des professionellen Mediationsverfahrens ideologisch aufgeladene Konflikte einer konsensualen Lösung zuzuführen, eher gering sind. Bei Helmut Weidner heißt es dazu in einem Rückblick auf die Forschung des WZB zu diskursiven Konfliktlösungen mit einem deutlich skeptischen Unterton wie folgt (Weidner 2011, S. 21f.):

> „Welchen Diskussionsstand die Verfahrensbeteiligten unter diesen Bedingungen auch immer erreicht haben mögen: Die Letztentscheidung obliegt den zuständigen politisch-administrativen Institutionen, die sich nun mit den Mediationsergebnissen förmlich arrangieren müssen. Und alles steht im Schatten des Rechtswegs, den jeder Berechtigte beschreiten kann, egal wie hoch der Konsens in der Mediation war. Die externe Determination von Verfahren zu Großkonflikten ist demzufolge so stark, dass rundum erfolgreiche Verfahren eher unwahrscheinlich sind. Sie sind im Übrigen auch nicht billig zu haben. Denn zu den monetären Kosten kommen noch die Belastungen durch Zeitaufwand, schwierige Überzeugungsarbeit sowie mögliche Imageverluste. Das betrifft vor allem NGOs, deren Unterstützer häufig eine harte, eher kompromisslose Haltung erwarten."

2.6 Versuch einer Zwischenbilanz

Alle fünf vorgestellten Theorieansätze belegen aus jeweils unterschiedlicher Perspektive die Notwendigkeit einer kommunikativen Verwaltung, die nicht nur die Bürger von Fall zu Fall und häufig in einem zu späten Stadium des Entscheidungsprozesses an Verwaltungsplanungen partizipieren lässt, sondern die umfassend und von Anfang an den Bürger als Dialogpartner begreift. Anna-Bettina Kaiser hat dafür die folgende gefällige Zusammenfassung gefunden (Kaiser 2009, S. 27f.):

> „Nicht zuletzt ist in dem Konzept des mündigen Bürgers, auf dem die bundesrepublikanische Demokratie beruht, der Kommunikationsaspekt bereits enthalten. Denn mündig zu sein heißt, so steht es schon im Wörterbuch der Gebrüder Grimm, einen Mund zu haben, sprechen zu können."

Andererseits ist an mehreren Stellen klargeworden, dass das schöne Bild einer kommunikativen Verwaltung in einer deliberativen Demokratie zwei hässliche Flecken aufweist, die nicht nur den Genuss des Betrachters stören, sondern die das Bild insgesamt entwerten könnten; dies ist zum einen das Inklusions-/Exklusionsproblem, zum anderen das Problem einer asymmetrischen Verteilung der Diskurschancen.

Was das hinreichend bekannte Exklusionsproblem angeht, so mag es an dieser Stelle genügen, wenn wir Wolfgang Merkel kurz das Wort geben, der dazu mit der gebotenen Klarheit für die gemeinhin als Musterland der Demokratie geltende Schweiz Folgendes angemerkt hat (Merkel 2011, S. 12):

> „Selbstexklusion der Unkundigen: Eine jüngere Studie von mehr als 150 Volksabstimmungen in der Schweiz hat gezeigt, dass die Bürger, die an den Abstimmungen teilnehmen, weit kompetenter in politischen Fragen sind als die Gesamtheit der Stimmberechtigten. Es kommt zu einer ‚Selbst-Selektion der Inkompetentesten' wie der Schweizer Autor Hans-Peter Kriesi schreibt: Die ‚Inkompetentesten nehmen typischerweise nicht an den Abstimmungen teil'. Es sind die besser gebildeten Bürger, die das ‚Volk' in Referenden vertreten. Vertreter einer elitären Demokratie könnten argumentieren, dass dies durchaus wünschenswert sei, da dadurch auf gleichsam ‚natürliche' Weise unvernünftige Entscheidungen ‚unvernünftiger' Bevölkerungsschichten unwahrscheinlich würden. Dass dies ein elitär-konservatives Argument ist, scheint den Referendumsbefürwortern verborgen geblieben zu sein."

Hinzu kommt für den Fall der gemeinsamen Deliberation „aller Stände", dass die Kommunikations- und damit Einflusschancen entsprechend dem Bildungsniveau der Beteiligten in der Regel asymmetrisch verteilt sind. Da die kommunikative Kompetenz – wie vielfach belegt worden ist (vgl. mit weiteren Nachweisen van den Daele 2005) – schichten- und milieuspezifisch unterschiedlich ausgeprägt ist, sind die „gebildeten Stände" dadurch strukturell eindeutig begünstigt, die weniger Ausdrucksstarken hingegen haben das Nachsehen, was wiederum ihre Tendenz zur Selbstexklusion verstärkt.

Da diese beiden schwer zu verscheuchenden Gespenster strukturelle Ursachen haben, steht nicht zu erwarten, dass die geschilderten Asymmetrien von alleine verschwinden. Es bedarf also gezielter Eingriffe, die die Architektur und die Regelungsstrukturen des intendierten Kommunikationsprozesses an wichtigen Stellschrauben verändern. Drei solcher Stellschrauben sind in ihrer weichenstellenden Funktion leicht erkennbar und bieten sich als Ansatzpunkte für gezielte Veränderungen geradezu an.

Die erste Stellschraube bezieht sich auf das Inklusionsproblem oder – anders gewendet – das Problem der Gewährleistung von Repräsentativität. Wie immer die Kommunikationsprozesse im Einzelnen organisiert sein mögen – als Anhörungstermin, als Diskussionsforum oder als Bürgerparlament –, man wird nicht umhinkönnen, Instrumente einzusetzen, die den Repräsentationsdraht „künstlich" erhöhen. Ein solches Instrument ist die Zusammensetzung der Kommunikationsarena nach dem Zufallsprinzip, eine Methode, wie sie insbesondere von Hans J. Lietzmann engagiert propagiert wird (Lietzmann 2011, S. 240):

„Deswegen plädiere ich deutlich dafür, die Teilnehmer am Dialogverfahren im Zufallsprinzip über die Einwohnermeldeämter auszuwählen und anzusprechen. Sie sollen persönlich und individuell aufgefordert werden, sich zu beteiligen. Solche Zufallsverfahren sind inzwischen breit ausgetestet und auch vielfach angewandt und erprobt. Die Praxis solcher alleatorischen Verfahren, solcher Zufallsauswahl, wird international zunehmend angewandt, und zwar gerade dort, wo die plurale Differenzierung und die soziale Fragmentierung die Repräsentativität der politischen Entscheidungsträger in Frage zu stellen droht – auch und besonders dort, wo immer wieder der Vorwurf einer zu selektiven und zu partiellen Planungskommunikation erhoben wird.“

Eine zweite Stellschraube besteht – und dies wird insbesondere im Politikfeld der integrierten Stadtentwicklungsplanung diskutiert (Bundesverband für Wohnen und Stadtentwicklung e.V. 2011a) – in der Nutzung der sog. Milieuforschung, wie sie etwa von der Forschungsgruppe Sinus Socio Vision (siehe dazu Bundesverband für Wohnen und Stadtentwicklung e.V. 2011b) betrieben wird, die – wie das nachstehende Schaubild zeigt – verschiedene Milieus unterscheidet, die jeweils eine eigene Sichtweise auf die Probleme der Stadtentwicklung und Stadtplanung haben.

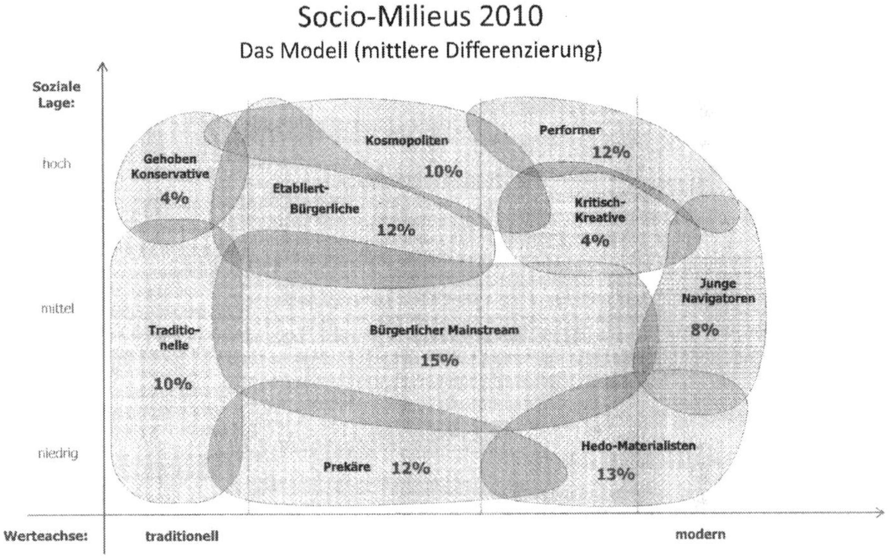

Gelänge es – so die ebenso einfache wie überzeugende Grundidee – mit den Milieus ins Gespräch zu kommen, würde dadurch die Chance auf eine verbesserte Inklusion deutlich erhöht. Bei Sebastian Beck heißt es dazu unter der Überschrift „Milieuorientierte Demokratie“ in bedenkenswerter Weise wie folgt (Beck 2011, S. 61):

„Die Milieus sind ein Brennglas auf die Bürgergesellschaft. Sie bieten einen strategischen Zugang, um Stadt und lokale Demokratie vom Bürger her zu entwickeln. Allen Befürchtungen zum Trotz ist die Stadtgesellschaft weder individualistisch fragmentiert noch partizipationsverdrossen. Vielmehr verfügen alle Milieus über spezifische Zugangsformen zu politischem Engagement. Die Art und Weise, wie Partizipation und Politik in der Praxis verlaufen, ist einfach per se mittelschichtslastig: intellek-

> tuelle Diskussionsveranstaltungen, die Art und Weise der Debatte in den großen politischen TV-Talkshows, das ist eine kulturelle Welt, die bestimmten Bildungsmilieus sehr nah ist. Diese Welt ist damit aber auch zutiefst selektiv. Das Panorama lebensweltlicher Partizipationszugänge ist deutlich breiter. Eine milieuorientierte Demokratie – etwa im Bereich der Stadtentwicklung – könnte durchaus inklusiver sein und Erosionstendenzen des demokratischen und solidarischen Miteinanders in der Stadtgesellschaft entgegenwirken."

Milieuspezifische Kommunikationsangebote zu machen, erscheint aber nicht nur deswegen sinnvoll, weil damit die spezifischen Perspektiven der verschiedenen Milieus in die jeweiligen Kommunikationsprozesse eingespeist werden können, sondern auch deshalb, weil das Potential für ein lokales Engagement milieuspezifisch sehr unterschiedlich ausgeprägt ist und deswegen eine gezielte Ansprache erforderlich erscheint.

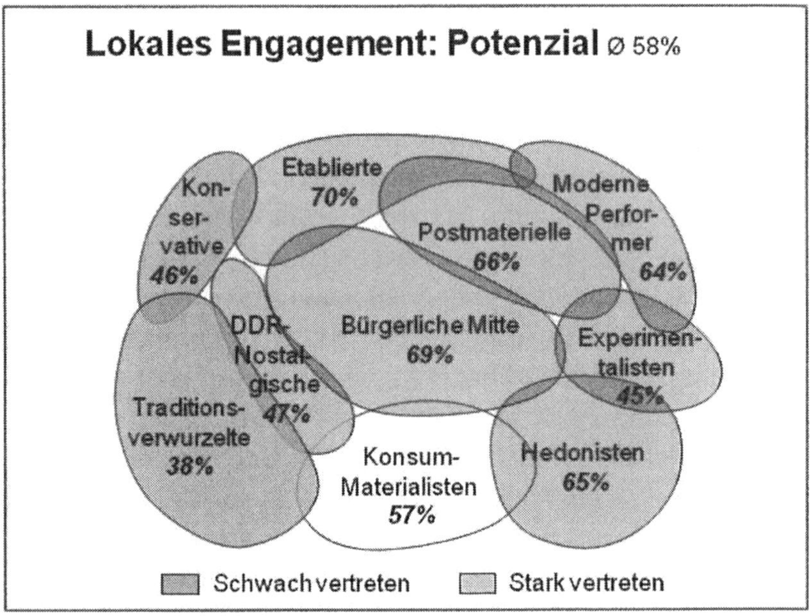

Quelle: Schaubild bei Beck 2011, S. 64.

Die dritte Stellschraube bezieht sich auf die schon besprochene Notwendigkeit, bei den jeweiligen Kommunikationsprozessen eine diskursive Chancengleichheit zu gewährleisten. Unseres Erachtens ist diese Aufgabe nur lösbar, wenn der jeweilige Kommunikationsprozess durch eine von allen Beteiligten akzeptierte, neutrale Person moderiert wird, für die wir im Anschluss an Christopher Gohl (2010) die Bezeichnung „Verfahrensgestalter" vorschlagen. Dieser Begriff scheint uns besser als der des Mediators zum Ausdruck zu bringen, dass es bei der Umsetzung des Leitbildes einer kommunikativen lokalen Demokratie nicht primär um Konfliktmittlung durch Verhandlungen geht – das auch –, sondern um die Organisation von Dialogen. Es geht also um Organisation von Kommunikation.

Es kann daher nicht überraschen, dass auch in der Mediationsforschung stets die kommunikative Aufgabe des Mediators hervorgehoben wird (vgl. etwa Madigan et al. 1990); wir selbst haben in einem zusammenfassenden Diskussionsbeitrag zu einer Tagung über „Konfliktbewältigung durch Verhandlungen" vorgeschlagen, die folgenden zwei Typen von Mediation zu unterscheiden (Schuppert 1990, S. 331):

- „Mediation as negotiation, eventuell verbunden mit compensation. Dieser Typ von Mediation wird insbesondere verwendet bei der Klärung von Standortfragen, sei es für Chemiebetriebe, für Mülldeponien, sei es für spezielle Aids-Kliniken.
- Mediation als Kommunikationshilfe bei Gesprächen mit Experten. Bei diesem interessanten Typ von Mediation moderiert der Mediator das Gespräch der Experten untereinander und das Gespräch der Experten mit den Betroffenen und den politischen Entscheidungsträgern, sei es, um die Ursachen für abweichende Wertungen aufzudecken, sei es, um die Unterschiede in der Folgenprognostik (worst-case-analysis versus more-likely-case analysis) herauszuarbeiten."

3 Zur schwierigen Aufgabe der kommunikativen Organisation von Kommunikation

Den klassischen Partizipationsmodellen ist häufig vorgehalten worden, dass der Bürger an etwas beteiligt wird, was als Produkt – meistens in Gestalt eines von der Verwaltung in langwierigen Abstimmungsprozessen mit den sogenannten „Trägern öffentlicher Belange" erarbeiteten Planentwurfs – bereits feste Konturen hat und das nunmehr vom Bürger kritisiert oder abgelehnt werden kann. Claus Offe hat in diesem Zusammenhang stets anschaulich von der undankbaren Rolle des Bürgers gesprochen, schon Beschlossenes ex post skandalisieren zu müssen. Dies ist in der Tat unbefriedigend. In vielen Diskussionsrunden, an denen wir in letzter Zeit teilgenommen haben, war daher uni sono davon die Rede, dass die Bürgerbeteiligung möglichst früh einzusetzen habe, gewissermaßen schon im Stadium der nur erahnbaren Konturen eines Infrastrukturprojekts. Mit dieser Forderung nähern wir uns dem eigentlichen Problem, das noch weit komplexer ist und für dessen Lösung Vorbilder rar gesät sind.

3.1 Kommunikative Herstellung von Kommunikationsstrukturen

Was mit dieser Überschrift gemeint ist, ist leicht zu erklären: Die Kommunikation mit den Bürgern und den – je nach Fall und Problem – unterschiedlichen „stakeholdern" hat nicht erst einzusetzen, wenn der Plan oder das Projektdesign schon „fertig" ist, um dann – etwa als Planfeststellungsverfahren – geordnet durchgeführt zu werden. Vielmehr muss schon die Frage, worüber genau und mit welcher Erörterungstiefe ein Kommunikationsprozess in Gang gesetzt werden soll, kommunikativ entschieden werden, wozu insbesondere auch die Frage gehört, wie der ins Auge gefasste Kommunikationsprozess eigentlich ablaufen, d.h. strukturiert werden soll.

Gleichsinnige Überlegungen haben wir in der Literatur eigentlich nur bei Reinhard Wulfhorst (2011) gefunden, der deswegen auch etwas ausführlicher zu Wort kommen soll; Wulfhorst schlägt ein von ihm so genanntes „Kommunikations- und Beteiligungsscoping“[1] vor, dessen Funktion er wie folgt erläutert (ebenda, S. 589):

> „Es sollte deutlich geworden sein, dass eine Kommunikations- und Beteiligungsstrategie nur dann erfolgreich sein kann, wenn sie den jeweiligen Umständen des Einzelfalls angepasst wird. Jede Bürgerbeteiligung ist so gesehen ein ‚Unikat‘. Entscheidender Garant für das Gelingen ist deshalb eine verfahrensmäßige Begleitung und Einhegung, die diesen Prozess organisiert und ihm Struktur verleiht. Als Auftakt und zugleich entscheidenden Weichensteller möchte ich ein ‚Kommunikations- und Beteiligungs-Scoping‘ vorschlagen. Es wird zum frühestmöglichen Zeitpunkt, also in der Anfangsphase der Planung, durchgeführt. Ähnlich dem Scoping der Umwelt(verträglichkeits)prüfung, das den Rahmen für die zu untersuchenden Umweltauswirkungen festlegt (vgl. §§ 5 und 14 f UVPG), wird hier ein Fahrplan für die Kommunikation mit den Bürgern und deren Beteiligung aufgestellt. Dieser Termin sollte allerdings dem hier vertretenen Ansatz entsprechend freiwillig sein, sodass von einer gesetzlichen Regelung abzuraten ist.“

Was hiermit vorgeschlagen wird, ist nichts anderes als eine kommunikativ hergestellte Beteiligungs-Roadmap, wobei eine Roadmap – nach Auskunft von Wikipedia – dazu dient, „langfristige Projekte in einzelne, leichter zu bewältigende Schritte zu strukturieren, wobei Unsicherheiten und mögliche Szenarien zur Zielerreichung betrachtet werden“. Da wir eine solche Beteiligungs-Roadmap nicht nur für eine weiterführende Idee halten, sondern hierin die einzige Möglichkeit sehen, der klassischen Partizipationsfalle – fertiger Plan, zu späte Bürgerbeteiligung – zu entgehen, soll Wulfhorst

1 Das „Scoping“ ist Teil der gesetzlich geregelten sog. Umweltverträglichkeitsprüfung (UVP-Gesetz vom 01.08.1990). Zu dieser heißt es im „Grundkurs Umweltrecht“ von W. Kahl und A. Voßkuhle (1998) wie folgt:
„Ziel der UVP ist es, möglichst frühzeitig unter Beteiligung der Öffentlichkeit und derjenigen Behörden, deren Aufgabenbereich berührt ist, die Auswirkungen eines Vorhabens auf die Umwelt zu ermitteln, zu beschreiben und zu bewerten [...]. Die umfassend angelegte Prüfung [...] soll [...] Umweltschutzgesichtspunkten bei der Entscheidungsfindung mehr Gewicht verleihen [...].
Der Ablauf der UVP, die regelmäßig von der Behörde durchzuführen ist, die auch über die Zulässigkeit des Vorhabens entscheidet, lässt sich wie folgt skizzieren:
Unterrichtung der zuständigen Behörde über das geplante Vorhaben, die den voraussichtlichen Untersuchungsrahmen (d.h. Gegenstand, Umfang und Methode der UVP) zusammen mit dem Vorhabenträger erörtert und abstimmt, wobei andere Behörden, Sachverständige (Gutachter) und Dritte (Gemeinden, Umweltverbände, Bürgerinitiativen) herangezogen werden können (sog. Scoping-Verfahren).
Einreichung der erforderlichen Unterlagen durch den Vorhabenträger
Einholung von Stellungnahmen anderer Behörden
Anhörung der Öffentlichkeit
– (8) [...].“.

Gelegenheit gegeben werden, konkretisierend noch Folgendes vorzutragen (ebenda, S. 589):

> „Die Ausgestaltung des Kommunikations- und Beteiligungs-Scopings erfolgt einzelfallbezogen. Bei vielen unproblematischen Genehmigungsverfahren wird es sich in einer kurzen Verständigung zwischen dem Vorhabenträger, dem Bürgermeister der betroffenen Gemeinde, Vertretern des Gemeinderats und der späteren Zulassungsbehörde darüber erschöpfen, zu welchem Zeitpunkt und auf welche Weise die Bürger erstmals informiert werden. Am anderen Ende der Skala denkbarer Fallgestaltungen stehen raumbedeutsame und vorhersehbar hoch umstrittene Infrastruktur(groß)vorhaben. Hier wird ein eigener Scoping-Termin angesetzt, an dem insbesondere verschiedene Repräsentanten der Bürgergesellschaft sowie von Vereinen und Verbänden, der Vorhabenträger, Vertreter der betroffenen politischen Ebene und der Medien sowie die für die Zulassung des Vorhabens zuständigen Behörden teilnehmen. Die Leitung übernimmt ein unabhängiger Moderator, auf den sich die Teilnehmer verständigt haben. Sämtliche Fragen der Kommunikation und Beteiligung, insbesondere die soeben aufgezeigten Eckpunkte, gehören auf die Tagesordnung. Ein wichtiges Thema ist die Frage, ob die bestehenden formellen Beteiligungsmöglichkeiten ausreichen oder durch konsultative Verfahren angereichert werden sollen."

Damit sind wir schon beim nächsten und letzten Stichwort angelangt.

3.2 Zur zentralen Rolle des Verfahrensgestalters

Eine Schlüsselfigur innerhalb des ganzen Konzepts einer kommunikativen lokalen Demokratie ist die Person des Verfahrensgestalters (ausführlich dazu Gohl 2010, S. 83ff.), der die Aufgabe hat, den Dialog mit den Bürgern zu organisieren und dabei die Einhaltung der vereinbarten Spielregeln zu gewährleisten. Der Verfahrensgestalter ist aber nicht nur für die Funktionsfähigkeit des jeweiligen Kommunikationsprozesses von zentraler Bedeutung, sondern auch für die Gewährleistung eines fairen Verfahrens, und zwar aus den folgenden Erwägungen.

Beobachtbar war in letzter Zeit eine Erosion der Akzeptanz von Verwaltungsentscheidungen, und zwar auch von solchen, die sowohl den politischen wie den administrativen Entscheidungsprozess ordnungsgemäß und ohne erkennbaren Rechtsverstoß durchlaufen haben. Dieser Befund einer schwindenden Akzeptanz erscheint in gewissen Grenzen plausibel, wenn die Beteiligten das Gefühl haben können, dass die Karten in dem Entscheidungsspiel unfair verteilt sind, z.B. deshalb, weil die Diskurs- und Einflussmöglichkeiten der Beteiligten eine deutliche Asymmetrie aufweisen. Ein Kommunikationsprozess mit asymmetrischen Diskurschancen kann der zentralen Aufgabe der Gewährleistung einer prozeduralen Fairness schlicht nicht gerecht werden und verfehlt daher seine Funktion. Hier ist eine kompensatorische Funktion des Verfahrensgestalters als Kommunikationshelfer unverzichtbar. Aus diesem Befund ergeben sich hohe Anforderungen an die Professionalität, die Unparteilichkeit und die Autorität des Verfahrensgestalters, die nicht einfach zu erfüllen sind (siehe dazu Gohl 2010, S. 89ff.). Versucht werden muss dies trotzdem.

Baer, Susanne (2006), Der Bürger im Verwaltungsrecht. Subjektkonstruktion durch Leitbilder vom Staat, Tübingen.

Beck, Sebastian (2011), Warum milieuorientierte Demokratie?, in: Bundesverband Wohnen und Stadtentwicklung e.V. (Hrsg.), Dialog, Zur Stärkung Lokaler Demokratie, Bonn, S. 61ff.

Benz, Arthur (1998), Postparlamentarische Demokratie? Demokratische Legitimation im kooperativen Staat, in: Michael Greven (Hrsg.), Demokratie – eine Kultur des Westens?, Opladen, S. 201ff.

Bertelsmann-Stiftung (Hrsg.) (2010), Politik beleben, Bürger beteiligen. Charakteristika neuer Beteiligungsmodelle, Gütersloh.

Bundesverband Wohnen und Stadtentwicklung e.V. (Hrsg.) (2011b), Milieumodelle 2011 für Mehrheitsgesellschaft und Migranten, www.vhw.de (Stand: Juli 2011).

Dahrendorf, Ralf (1961), Gesellschaft und Freiheit. Zur soziologischen Analyse der Gegenwart, München.

Feindt, Peter Henning (2001), Regierung durch Diskussion? Diskurs- und Verhandlungsverfahren im Kontext von Demokratietheorie und Steuerungsdiskussion, Frankfurt am Main.

Fietkau, Hans-Joachim/Weidner, Helmut (1998), Umweltverhandeln. Konzepte, Praxis und Analysen alternativer Konfliktregelungsverfahren, Berlin.

Gohl, Christopher (2010), Organisierte Dialoge als Strategie, veröffentlicht als Beitrag 9/2010 der Reihe „Zukunft regieren. Beiträge für eine zukunftsfähige Politik“ der Bertelsmann-Stiftung, Gütersloh, 208 Seiten.

Groß, Thomas (2011), Stuttgart 21: Folgerungen für Demokratie und Verwaltungsverfahren, in: Die Öffentliche Verwaltung (DÖV), 64. Jahrgang, S. 510ff.

Häberle, Peter (1972), Grundrechte im Leistungsstaat, in: Veröffentlichungen der Vereinigung Deutscher Staatsrechtslehrer (VVDStRL) 30, S. 43ff.

Hoffmann-Riem, Wolfgang/Schmidt-Aßmann, Eberhardt (Hrsg.) (1990), Konflikbewältigung durch Verhandlungen, Bd. I/II, Baden-Baden.

Hoffmann-Riem, Wolfgang (1994), Ermöglichung von Flexibilität und Innovationsoffenheit im Verwaltungsrecht, in: derselbe/Eberhard Schmidt-Aßmann (Hrsg.), Innovation und Flexibilität des Verwaltungshandelns, Baden-Baden, S. 10ff.

Jellinek, Georg (1905), System der subjektiven öffentlichen Rechte, 2. Aufl. Tübingen.

Kahl, Wolfgang/Voßkuhle, Andreas (Hrsg.) (1998), Grundkurs Umweltrecht. Einführung für Naturwissenschaftler und Ökonomen, 2. Auflage, Heidelberg/Berlin.

Kaiser, Anna-Bettina (2009), Die Kommunikation der Verwaltung. Diskurse zu den Kommunikationsbeziehungen zwischen staatlicher Verwaltung und privaten in der Verwaltungsrechtswissenschaft der Bundesrepublik Deutschland, Baden-Baden.

Klatt, Johanna/Walter, Frank (2011), Entbehrliche der Bürgergesellschaft? Sozial Benachteiligte und Engagement, Bielefeld.

König, Klaus/Dose, Nikolai (Hrsg.) (1993), Instrumente und Formen staatlichen Handelns, Köln/Berlin/Bonn/München.

Magidan, Denise/Susskind, Lawrence/Weinstein, Alan (1990), Vorüberlegungen für eine verbesserte Konfliktbewältigung im Umweltbereich, in: W. Hoffmann-Riem/E. Schmidt-Aßmann (Hrsg.), Konflikbewältigung durch Verhandlungen, Bd. I, Baden-Baden; S. 151ff.

Mayntz, Renate (2009), Governance-Theorie: Erkenntnisinteressen und offene Fragen, in: Edgar Grande/Stefan May (Hrsg.), Perspektiven der Governance-Forschung, Baden-Baden, S. 9ff.

Merkel, Wolfgang (2011), Entmachten Volksentscheide das Volk? Anmerkungen zu einem demokratischen Paradoxon, in: WZB-Mitteilungen 131, März 2011, S. 10ff.

Offe, Claus (2010), Signals and Information as a Resource of Public Policy, unveröffentlichtes Manuskript.

O'Neill, Onora (2002), A Question of Trust, Cambridge: Cambridge University Press.

Ringen, Stein (2005), The Powerlessness of Powerful Government, unveröffentlichtes discussion paper, 25 Seiten.

Sarcinelli, Ulrich (2011), Politische Kommunikation in der Bürgergesellschaft, in: Forum Wohnen und Stadtentwicklung 6/2011, S. 321ff.

Schlieffen, Katharina, Gräfin von (2007), Der Mediationsstaat, in: Dieter Gosewinkel/G.F. Schuppert (Hrsg.), Politische Kultur im Wandel von Staatlichkeit, WZB-Jahrbuch 2007, Berlin, S. 181ff.

Schuppert, Gunnar Folke (2000), Verwaltungswissenschaft. Verwaltung, Verwaltungsrecht, Verwaltungslehre, Baden-Baden.

Schuppert, Gunnar Folke (2002), Gemeinwohl, das. Oder: Über die Schwierigkeiten, dem Gemeinwohlbegriff Konturen zu verleihen, in: Gunnar Folke Schuppert/Friedhelm Neidhardt (Hrsg.), Gemeinwohl – Auf der Suche nach Substanz, WZB-Jahrbuch 2002, Berlin, S. 19ff.

Schuppert, Gunnar Folke (2005), Governance im Spiegel der Wissenschaftsdisziplinen, in: Schuppert (Hrsg.), Governance-Forschung. Vergewisserung über Stand und Entwicklungslinien, Baden-Baden, S. 371ff.

Schuppert, Gunnar Folke (2008), Politische Kultur, Baden-Baden.

Schuppert, Gunnar Folke (1990), Resümee und Ausblick, in: Wolfgang Hoffmann-Riem/Eberhard Schmidt-Aßmann (Hrsg.), Konfliktbewältigung durch Verhandlungen. Informelle und mittlerunterstützte Verhandlungen im Verwaltungsverfahren, Nomos 1990, S. 327ff.

Schuppert, Gunnar Folke (2007), Governance as Communication. Das Beispiel von European Governance, in: Otfried Jarren et al. (Hrsg.), Entgrenzte Demokratie? Herausforderungen für die politische Interessenvermittlung, Baden-Baden, S. 287ff.

Schuppert, Gunnar Folke (2011), Bürgerdialog, lokale Demokratie und Urban Governance aus kommunikationstheoretischer Perspektive, in: Bundesverband für Wohnen und Stadtentwicklung e.V. (Hrsg.), Dialog: Zur Stärkung lokaler Demokratie, Bonn, S. 43ff.

Strecker, David/Schaal, Gary S. (2001), Die politische Theorie der Deliberation: Jürgen Habermas, in: André Brodocz/Gary S. Schaal (Hrsg.), Politische Theorien der Gegenwart, Bd. I, Opladen: UTB, S. 89ff.

Van den Daele, Wolfgang/Neidhardt, Friedhelm (1996), „Regieren durch Diskussion" – über Versuche, mit Argumenten Politik zu machen, dieselben (Hrsg.), Kommunikation und Entscheidung. Politische Funktionen öffentlicher Meinungsbildung und diskursiver Verfahren, WZB-Jahrbuch 1996, Berlin, S. 9ff.

Van den Daele, Wolfgang (Hrsg.) (2005), Diskurs und Governance. Abschlussbericht der Forschungsabteilung „Zivilgesellschaft und transnationale Netzwerke", WZB-Diskussion-Paper SP IV 2005-103, Berlin.

Weidner, Helmut (2011), Im Südwesten nichts Neues. Ein Rückblick auf WZB-Forschung über diskursive Konfliktlösung, in: WZB-Mitteilungen 131 (März 2011), S. 21ff.

Wulfhorst, Reinhard (2011), Konsequenzen aus „Stuttgart 21“: Vorschläge zur Verbesserung der Bürgerbeteiligung, in: Die Öffentliche Verwaltung (DÖV). 64. Jahrgang, S. 581ff.

The Changing Nature of Citizen's Attitudes Towards the State: Causes and Solutions

Paul Webb

In this paper, I reflect on what has changed in people's attitudes towards the state, its major institutions and political actors, and consider the reasons for these changes. I shall also consider some of the solutions that have been proposed to the problems constituted by attitudinal change, and in particular, to the contention that the answer lies in the development of innovative modes of citizen participation in political decision-making.

1 Introduction

There is an extensive literature on the changing nature of citizen attitudes to the state in the established democracies, and many observers accept that there is now a considerable body of evidence attesting to widespread popular dissatisfaction with the political process and its major institutions and actors. Typical of the evidence is that relating to political parties, a key target for the malcontents. Although they are of course almost universally regarded as essential components of democratic regimes and key to the process of securing effective political representation, mobilizing voters, organizing government and shaping public policy across the world's democracies today, both new and old, parties (and politicians) are often perceived in very negative terms: among other things, they are said to be self-interested, untrustworthy, corrupt, and challenged by other actors in respect of what the political functions they perform. The relevant evidence takes in a range of both individual-level and aggregate-level indicators, including: an increase in electoral volatility since 1960, and a concomitant rise in the fragmentation of party systems, reflecting in part the emergence of new anti-establishment and populist organizations; a widespread fall in electoral turnout since 1990, and an even more widespread decrease in the proportion of voters claiming strong partisan affinities, or joining political parties across the established democracies. At the same time, however, there has been a burgeoning of citizen membership and activity through interest groups and social movements, which gives the lie to the any possibility that we are witnessing a generalized turning away from political engagement by citizens. Even so, there is widespread evidence of public disaffection with representative democracy's central institutions and actors. For instance, the wave of World Values Survey data gathered since 1999 across more than 70 countries reveals that on average only 19 percent of citizens living in democratic nations express 'quite a lot' or 'a great deal' of confidence in political parties; and there is very little variation in this basic pattern across areas as diverse as Latin America (16.8%), post-communist Eastern Europe (18.8%) and the established democracies (21.9%) (Webb & White 2007: 353). Trust in parties, governments, legislatures and parliaments is general low across America and the EU, while falling proportions of citizens trust politicians to act in the common good or simply even to care about what ordinary citizens think (Pharr & Putnam, 2000: ch.1; Stoker 2006: ch.2; Hay 2007: ch.1).

This disillusionment does not appear to be associated with a corresponding erosion of belief in the value of democracy per se: it is not that disappointment with the way the established democracies work leads to a widespread conviction that democracy has been tried and found wanting (Hay 2007: 32), and should therefore be replaced by a more authoritarian form of politics. Rather, the overwhelming proportion of citizens are 'dissatisfied democrats' who see the cure for democracy as 'more (and better) democracy', to paraphrase James Madison (Dalton 2004).

Others, however, are not so sure that there is a really a problem stemming from the frustrations of 'dissatisfied democrats', or anything else for that matter, for they would take issue with the basic premise that generalized political disillusionment has really grown at all in a clear, cross-national trend over time. Pippa Norris stands out as good example of this in her recent book *Democratic Deficits* (2011), in which she reviews the empirical evidence and concludes that, by and large, there is no clear cross-national trend, but only a rather muddled picture of trendless fluctuation when everything is seen as a whole.

It's not easy to make sense of this sharp discrepancy of outlook: how can researchers as influential as Russell Dalton (2004) and Pippa Norris take such divergent views of the same material? Close inspection suggests that differences of methodological approach might go some way towards explaining the apparent discrepancy: for one thing, they do not use exactly the same empirical evidence, although there is overlap. For istance, with respect to Europe, Norris relies largely on a few indicators drawn from the Eurobarometer survey, and focuses on the period from 1998-2008 (see especially the tables and figures in Chapter 4 of *Democratic Deficits*), while Dalton draws mainly on national election survey data going back to the 1960s and 1970s. Moreover, where the latter tends to looks at net change from the beginning to the end of the period, the former produces time-series graphs showing the whole pattern of fluctuation at the points in between. Norris's time-series are bound to give a stronger impression of fluctuation than Dalton's, therefore. So, some of the divergence of view is methodological in nature, though it is also perhaps due in part to the individual researcher's personal inclination to see the glass half-full or half-empty. I would argue that, even if it is not always easy to discern clear trends over time in some countries, there can be no disputing the fact that many established democracies do suffer from significant to high levels of negative public orientations towards the state and political elites, and that in some cases, these things certainly have grown (Dalton 2004: ch.2).

So, while we should not be duped into imagining that there was ever a Golden Age of public respect and admiration for our leaders and institutions, I think there is at the very least a case to answer on the charge-sheet against many of the world's longest established democratic polities. There is less deference towards the institutions and elites of representative politics, more cynicism, and more disappointment than might be regarded as entirely healthy. So, why are these attitudes as widespread as they are, and maybe growing?

2 *Explaining the political disenchantment*

There are a number of possible explanations which we can discern in the literature. Dalton (2004) points to a combination of two major factors, principal among which is the rising expectations of government that citizens have. This is particularly true of the young, the better educated, the more affluent, and the post-materialist. While these are the very groups that have most directly benefited from the spread of affluence, their expectations have increased the most, as has their tendency to criticise political elites, institutions and processes. Yet they do not represent a threat to democracy per se; on the contrary, these 'dissatisfied democrats' are driven by a passion for the democratic creed that fosters disillusionment with the way current political processes operate. They often have a high sense of political efficacy and they expect to be able to play a direct role in influencing and shaping decisions – occasional and marginal participation through the orthodox channels of representative democracy is not enough for them.

A second general source of decreasing political support, for Dalton, is the growing complexity of contemporary political agendas. This is spawned by the proliferation of new issue dimensions and a commensurate mobilization of political interest groups and social movements across advanced industrial democracies. The expansion of the political agenda to accommodate new debates over environmental quality, social norms, lifestyle choices, multiculturalism, and other social and cultural issues can be seen as a kind of triumph of interest articulation over interest aggregation. In such fluid, multidimensional policy space it can be very difficult for governments to satisfy most of the people most of the time. Citizen mobilization against major infrastructural projects which impact heavily on local environments provides a good example of this. In effect, then, this is an argument that 'poor performance' – or at least, the perception of poor performance by governments - lies at the root of the problem.

A third factor which should not be overlooked is the common complaint that modern parties and politicians fail to offer voters a meaningful choice, as they converge around a limited range of ideological or programmatic options. Typically, this line of criticism today contends that there has been a narrowing of political space in Western democracies around a neo-liberal consensus (Hay 2007: 159). This has been exacerbated by the narrowing of electoral competition which has been driven by the adoption of political marketing techniques by parties. The net effect of this has been to restrict the domain within which politicians may act, or articulate a convincing case for political action. This in turn simply serves to undermine the point of politics in the eyes of many citizens.

Fourthly, we should not overlook the role of the mass media, the central mechanisms through which most citizens gain most of their information about politics. There have been a number of vocal critics of the role of the media in respect of the portrayal of politics in recent years, notably John Lloyd (2004) and Meg Russell (2005). Gerry Stoker points to four main lines of criticism against the media: that the media 'dumbs down' politics by focusing on the 'immediate, the scandalous and the negative'; that it increasingly fuses reporting and opinion in a provocative way; that is actively spreads a 'culture of contempt', as exemplified by the type of encounter in which the interviewer's underlying if unstated question to the politician appears to be 'why is this bastard lying to me?'; and that the media place themselves above politics and democracy as self-appointed arbiter and judge (Stoker 2006: 128-9). These criticisms are broad in scope, but they are not irrelevant to the widespread perception that parties cannot make a difference. Dumbing-down, trivialization, and generalized contempt all feed the sense that party politics cannot really achieve positive outcomes, and that consequently it matters little which of the major alternatives is in power.

A final line of explanation, which has probably been heard rather less often, but which seems nevertheless to be stated with increasing frequency these days, is that public disaffection with politics and the state stems as much from the shortcomings of the citizens themselves. In the UK, for instance, a number of writers including Meg Russell (2005), Gerry Stoker (2006), and Matt Flinders (2010) have argued in various ways that at least part of the problem reflects the fact that many citizens simply do not understand that in politics 'you don't always get what you want' (Bale et al 2008), that it is often 'messy, inefficient and conflict-ridden' (Hibbing & Theiss-Morse 2002), that it entails compromise, incremental policy changes, and sub-optimal outcomes. Meg Russell, for instance, argues that one of the sources of citizen misunderstanding about politics is the pernicious effect of a culture of consumerism in our societies:

> 'It is difficult to find anything more antithetical to the culture of politics than the contemporary culture of consumerism. While politics is about balancing diverse needs to benefit the public interest, consumerism is about meeting the immediate desires of the individual. While politics requires us to compromise and collaborate as citizens, consumerism emphasises unrestrained individual freedom of choice. While politics recognises that there are always resource constraints, modern consumerism increasingly encourages us to believe that we can have it all now.' (Russell 2005: 10)

Alternatively, Matt Flinders (2010: 3) contends that:

> 'The public have become politically decadent in their expectations of what politics should deliver...people 'hate' politics because they simply do not understand it, and they are generally not helped to understand it by the media (or university professors of politics for that matter).'

3 Solving the problem of political disenchantment

Needless to say, one's view of the cause of the problem tends to shape the response that one would regard as appropriate. Broadly speaking, if you think that the key to the problem lies mainly in the frustrations of dissatisfied democrats who find that the established systems of representative democracy – chiefly parties, elections and parliaments – do not fulfil their expectations, then you will probably conclude that the answer lies in institutional innovations that provide enhanced opportunities for direct participatory involvement – citizen initiatives and referendums, deliberative polls, citizen assemblies, voter juries, small scale online interactions between representatives and constituents, and so on. Indeed, there is widespread interest in participatory democracy in general, and in various forms of deliberative or 'dialogic' democracy in particular (see, eg, Pateman, 1970; Bessette 1980; Cohen 1989; Fishkin 1991; Nino 1996; Ackerman & Fishkin 2004). These are often favoured as solutions to the problem of political alienation, and enthusiasm extends beyond political theorists: In the UK, The Power Inquiry (2006) advocated more participation, among other things, and commissioned the American academic James Fishkin to run its own deliberative exercise in January 2010. The British government's own Green Paper, *The Governance of Britain* (CM7170 2007), proposed use of citizen juries in local politics and the White Paper *Communities in Control* (CM7247 2008) advocated the spread of participatory budgeting in local government. While these policy ideas were instigated by the Labour government that left office in 2010, its Conservative-Liberal Democrat successor has not rejected these proposals, and indeed, has embraced innovations such as online petitions which must generate parliamentary debates if signed by 100,000 citizens, introducing a 'public reading stage' of parliamentary bills to give people the chance to comment online, and giving people the right of initiative to call local referendums. Other countries, of course, already have longstanding traditions of direct democracy, anyway (USA, Germany, Italy, Switzerland), while at European level there is significant official interest in the potential of participation through e-democracy (Council of Europe 2009). Looked at one way, provision for greater recourse to participatory democracy – or at least, to direct democracy - may be a way of meeting the demands of legions of cognitively mobilized 'dissatisfied democrats', but it may also in part be about parties attempting to reduce the domain in which they are directly accountable for policy decisions – a voluntary relinquishing of power and a deflection of responsibility for some problems that are intrinsically difficult to solve. This, of course, takes us back to the views of writers like Colin Hay, who see in such 'de-politicization' a primary cause of political disenchantment rather than its cure.

Indeed, not all observers are convinced that greater participatory democracy holds the solution to the problem. For one thing, those who doubt that there really has been a significant erosion of public confidence in the processes and institutions of representative democracy, are unlikely to regard these are likely to prove very worthwhile steps; if you don't feel that there is a problem in the first place, then why would you need a solution? But even some of those who do accept that there is a problem, do not necessarily agree that greater participation will supply the required cure. Thus, those who feel that citizen disaffection has more to do with the failure of many citizens to understand the nature and possibilities of politics are unlikely to see the extension of participatory rights and opportunities as being likely to solve the problem; they are more inclined to argue that better civic education, and/or steps to regulate the media – albeit a politically a very sensitive idea – would be more worthwhile (Russell 2005). Relatedly, there are researchers who see the extension of participatory rights as beside the point because such measures ignore the fact that most citizens are not very interested in politics and simply do *not* want to be further involved. The most striking example of this line of argument in recent years has been contributed by John Hibbing and Elizabeth Theiss-Morse in their research on American voters. They offer a stark challenge to the participatory visionaries:

> The last thing people want is to be more involved in political decision-making: They do not want to make political decisions themselves; they do not want to provide much input to those who are assigned to make these decisions; and they would rather not know the details of the decision-making process… This does not mean that people think no mechanism for government accountability is necessary; they just do not want the mechanism to come into play except in unusual circumstances (Hibbing & Theiss-Morse 2002: 1-2).

As Clive James (2009) might put it, democracy is '...that political system that leaves me free not to care about it.' Hibbing and Theiss-Morse summarise the orientations of American citizens as a preference for some kind of 'stealth' arrangement, whereby citizens know that democracy exists, but expect it to be barely visible on a routine basis – an attitude that they describe as naïve and unfeasible. The upshot of their Stealth Democracy study is that the authors criticise both the naïveté of popular attitudes towards politics, and the insistence of some observers that participatory democracy provides the solution to its current discontents. The alleged benefits of participatory - especially deliberative - democracy are portrayed by Hibbing and Theiss-Morse as 'wishful thinking', and they point out that research tends to reveal that it only works under very limited conditions. 'Deliberation will not work in the real world of politics where people are different and where tough, zero-sum decisions must be made…real deliberation is quite likely to make them hopping mad or encourage them to suffer silently because of a reluctance to voice their own opinions in the discussion' (2002:

207). They cite a variety of research evidence to debunk three of the major claims of the participationists: that deliberative and participatory democracy produces better decision-making (actually, the most powerful personalities often dominate, whether or not they are the best-informed or most rational); that it enhances the legitimacy of the political system (in fact, face-to-face conflict just exacerbates people's anger and resentment (Morrell 1999); and that it leads to personal development (again, it just exacerbates the sense of powerlessness, inadequacy and marginalization of the weakest participants). Indeed, Diana Mutz (2006) has gone so far as to argue that high-intensity deliberation around political differences can actually reduce the inclination of many people to participate in politics, because of the desire to avoid conflict. So, borrowing from the terminology of principal-agent analysis, we might say that the conclusion of writers like Hibbing and Theiss-Morse is that citizens (the principals) prefer to guard against their agents' (politicians and parties) presumed tendency to shirk, not through 'police-patrol' oversight – direct, continuous and proactive – but through 'fire-alarm' oversight – mediated, episodic and reactive (McCubbins and Schwartz, 1984). Like Schudson's 'monitorial' citizens, they are watchful and engaged in surveying the political scene rather than gathering information intensely, 'poised for action if action is required' (Schudson 1999: 8), but eschewing direct involvement as much as possible.

That said, recent research from the USA now suggests that the pessimism of writers like Hibbing, Theiss-Morse and Mutz may be exaggerated. Using a blend of experimental and survey designs, Neblo et al (2009) have investigated American voters' hypothetical willingness to deliberate and their actual behaviour in response to a real invitation to deliberate with their member of Congress, and found that willingness to deliberate in the US is much more widespread than sceptics like Hibbing would suggest, and that it is precisely the demographic groups that are least likely to participate in traditional partisan politics – and therefore those whom we would expect to express the stealth democracy perspective - who are actually most interested in deliberative participation. However, these findings depend crucially on the particular form of deliberation between citizens and elected representatives that is implemented. Similarly, Bengtsson and Mattila (2009) have found that in Finland people with less education, with less political knowledge and those who feel that the political system does not respond to their needs – again, those we might expect to have 'stealth democratic' attitudes – are actually most likely to want greater use of direct democracy in their political system. Of course, it can be argued that direct or referendum democracy is not at all the same thing as deliberative democracy or high-intensity participation. Still, it clearly requires a greater degree of political engagement on the part of ordinary citizens than a purely partified form of representative democracy does.

4 *Conclusions: Dissatisfied Democrats or Stealth Democrats?*

In this article, I have briefly reviewed the debate about how far there has been a significant growth of popular disenchantment with the major institutions and processes of the democratic state, about the causes of such developments (among those who do accept that attitudinal shift has taken place), and about the potential for participatory democracy to supply an effective solution to the problem. It seems to me that the literature points to at least two rather different type of disenchanted citizen: drawing on existing terminology from the literature, we can distinguish 'dissatisfied democrats', who are likely to be middle class, educated, active and articulate devotees a highly engaged body politic, from 'stealth democrats', who are likely to be of lower socio-economic status, less well-educated, less interested or engaged in politics, who are absorbed largely by private concerns, and who only consent to participate in order to keep untrustworthy elites in check. The implications of this distinction should not be underestimated for, following Mutz, it would seem to follow that more intensive forms of deliberative participation would at best only be effective in respect of the dissatisfied democrats, but would be counter-productive with respect to the stealth democrats. While the former may chafe at the participatory limitations of traditional forms of representative democracy, and might thrive in a more participative environment, the latter could actually be more vulnerable to political marginalization, for they are less likely to take to direct and active engagement. They have traditionally depended on parties as key interlocutors and tribunes of their social group interests, but their parties (typically social democratic or labour in orientation) have often lost this role through strategic adaptation. Without representative parties that express their social identities and serve as communities of political learning, as was once the case, these citizens retreat into a disaffected and alienated take on politics. These feelings will only be exacerbated by evidence of 'feather-bedding' by self-interested politicians and parties (Hibbing & Theiss-Morse: 121-124).

Research that directly engages with this issue remains at an early stage (Webb et al 2010), but it could carry important implications for the reforms that the political elites who attempt to respond to the problem of democratic disconnect devise. New forms of radical participatory democracy may not be the answer that some envisage them to be; reforming existing systems of representative democracy may be of far greater import, since few citizens are likely to care for more demanding levels of political involvement. For the time being, however, this issue remains open to much more empirical research.

Ackerman, Bruce & James S. Fishkin (2004) *Deliberation Day* (New Haven: Yale University Press).

Bale, Tim, Paul Taggart and Paul Webb (2006) 'You can't always get what you want: Populism and the Power Inquiry', *Political Quarterly* 77: 195-216, April-June.

Bengtsson, Asa and Miko Mattila (2009) 'Direct democracy and its critics: Support for direct democracy and stealth democracy in Finland' *West European Politics*, 32/5: 1031-1048.

Bessette, Joseph (1980) 'Deliberative Democracy: The Majority Principle in Republican Government', in *How Democractic is the Constitution?* (Washington, D.C.: AEI Press), pp. 102-116.

Cohen, Joshua (1989) 'Deliberative Democracy and Democratic Legitimacy', from A.

Hamlin and P. Pettit (eds), *The Good Polity*. (Oxford: Blackwell), pp. 17-34.

CM7170 (2007) *The Governance of Britain* (London: The Stationery Office).

CM7247 (2008) *Communities in Control: Real People, Real Power* (London: The Stationery Office).

Council of Europe (2009) *Electronic democracy: Recommendation CM/Rec(2009)1 and explanatory memorandum (2009)* (Strasbourg: Council of Europe Publishing).

Dalton, Russell J. (2004) *Democratic Challenges, Democratic Choices: The Erosion of Political Support in Advanced Industrial Democracies* (Oxford: Oxford University Press).

Fishkin, James S. (1991) *Democracy and Deliberation* (New Haven: Yale University Press).

Flinders, Matthew (2010) 'In defence of politics', *Political Quarterly*, 81: 309-326.

Hibbing, John and Elizabeth Theiss-Morse (2002) *Stealth Democracy: Americans' Beliefs About How Government Should Work* (Cambridge: Cambridge University Press).

James, Clive (2009) *A Point of View*, BBC Radio 4, broadcast 4.12.09 (available at http://www.bbc.co.uk/programmes/b006qng8)

Lazer, David, Michael Neblo, Kevin Esterling and Kathy Goldschmidt (2009) *Online Townhall Meetings: Exploring Deomocracy in the 21st Century* (Washington DC: Congressional Management Faoundation), available at http://nposoapbox.s3.amazonaws.com/cmfweb/Online-Town-Hall-Meetings-Report.pdf.

Lloyd, John (2004) *What the Media are Doing to our Politics* (London: Constable and Robinson).

McCubbins, Matthew and Schwartz, Thomas (1984) 'Congressional Oversight Overlooked: Police Patrols versus Fire Alarm', *American Journal of Political Science*, 28:1, 165-179.

Morrell, Michael E. (1999) 'Citizens' Evaluations of Participatory Democratic Procedures: Normative Theory Meets Empirical Science' *Political Research Quarterly*, 52/2, pp. 293-322

Mutz, Diana C. (2006) Hearing the Other Side: Deliberative versus Participatory Democracy (Cambridge: Cambridge University Press).

Neblo, Michael, Kevin M. Esterling, Ryan P. Kennedy, David Lazer, Anand E. Sokhey (2009) *Who Wants to Deliberate – and Why?* (Cambridge Mass: Harvard Working Paper RWP09-027, September).

Nino, C.S. (1996) *The Constitution of Deliberative Democracy*. (New Haven: Yale University Press).

Norris, Pippa (2011) *Democratic Deficits: Critical Citizens Revisited* (Cambridge: Cambridge University Press).

Pateman, Carole (1970) *Participation and Democratic Theory* (Cambridge: Cambridge University Press).

Pharr, Susan J., and Robert Putnam (2000) *Disaffected Democracies: What's Troubling the Trilateral Countries?* (Princeton, NJ: Princeton University Press).

Power Inquiry (2006) *Power to the People: The Report of Power, an Independent Inquiry into Britain's Democracy* (London: Power Inquiry; available at http://www.powerinquiry.org/report/index.php).

Russell, Meg (2005) *Must Politics Disappoint?* (London: Fabian Society, 2005).

Schudson, M. (1999). *The Good Citizen: A History of American Civic Life.* (Cambridge, Mass: Harvard University Press).

Stoker, Gerry (2006), *Why Politics Matters: Making Democracy Work* (Basingstoke: Palgrave Macmillan).

Webb, Paul, Tim Bale and Paul Taggart (2010) *Deliberative versus parliamentaryt democracy in the UK: An Experimental Study,* (Sussex: Sussex European Institute Working Paper 118.)

Webb, Paul & Stephen White (2007) *Party Politics in New Democracies* (Oxford: Oxford University Press).

II

Modes of inclusion and deliberation

A Second Stage: The Revitalization of Democratic Legitimacy with the Help of Deliberative Forums

Claudia Ritzi

This article discusses procedural reforms that might help to relieve the crisis of legitimacy in contemporary societies. It argues, on the basis of theoretical reflections and the results of empirical research, that a deliberative extension of the representative democratic process is more recommendable than the further strengthening of direct democratic forms of decision-making, because deliberative processes offer the opportunity to decide e.g. on large-scale projects in a comprehensive and future-oriented way and promise to strengthen the decisions' procedural legitimacy. At the end of the paper, the "vhw-Städtenetzwerk" is described, a network of 15 German cities that plan to implement deliberative forums in 2012/2013 to strengthen their citizens' inclusion in the democratic process and their support of important political decisions.

1 Introduction

Few social scientists these days doubt that our system of parliamentary representation is in a crisis of legitimacy. We are faced with rising levels of political disenchantment not only in Germany, but also in other western democracies, and more and more people have the impression that their interests and beliefs are no longer adequately represented in the parliamentary system – no matter which party or coalition holds the power. Also conventional forms of political participation are used by a decreasing number of people, while more and more citizens take part in political protests (see e.g. Hay 2007; Dalton 2004; Embacher 2009).

That this crisis of legitimacy limits the political systems' capacity to govern these days seems to be obvious with regard to decision-making processes on large-scale projects: the conflict about the building of a new train station in Stuttgart (known as "Stuttgart 21") is just one example of the increasing number of projects in Germany and elsewhere in Europe that today are challenged not only by tight budgets but also by the resistance of large parts of the citizenry. In the long run, such a situation is not only dangerous in that it promotes the development of political structures that Colin Crouch and other authors described as "post-democratic" (Crouch 2004; Ritzi & Schaal 2010) but also because it threatens future-oriented development, especially of metropolitan areas.

But what to do in a democracy when general elections fail to generate the necessary amount of legitimacy that the political system needs in order to act successfully? This article argues that a deliberative extension of the representative democratic process in such a situation is a highly recommendable measure, because it offers not only the opportunity to decide on large-scale projects in a comprehensive and future-oriented way, but it also promises to strengthen the decision's expected legitimacy.

To substantiate this thesis, in a first step we will refer to Niklas Luhmann's concept of "procedural legitimacy" (Luhmann 1975) and identify reasons and indicators for today's crisis of representative democratic decision-making with focus on large-scale projects. We will argue that decisions of special relevance and/or decisions that are bound to high costs compared to other policies are typically confronted with a more specific demand structure and also offer certain other characteristics that challenge the acceptability of the representative political decision-making process. Therefore their sensitivity to the consequences of political disenchantment and other indicators of the legitimacy crisis is especially high.

In a second step, different ways of increasing the acceptance of decisions on large-scale projects are discussed. In most of the literature, two types of procedural reforms have been described as promising: the introduction of direct democratic forms of decision-making and the implementation of procedures based on Jürgen Habermas' theory of deliberative democracy (Habermas 1997). Both strands will be discussed and compared in section 2. This comparison leads to the conclusion that regarding large-scale projects, the implementation of deliberative groups from the perspective of legitimacy seems to be more promising than the increased use of direct democratic referendums, because deliberative modes of consultation are able to build a "second stage" of legitimacy that supplements the legitimacy of representative processes in an adequate way by enhancing its "epistemic procedural legitimacy."

In addition to these reflections, in the third and last section the practical relevance of deliberative modes of decision-making processes will be emphasized: here the *Städtenetzwerk* (city-network) will be described, a cooperation of (at the moment) 15 German cities[1] that have committed to each implement at least one deliberative forum in 2012/2013 to take part in the so far most expansive test of the effects of such forums on legitimacy in Germany. This project aims at strengthening the legitimacy of local political decision-making not only by introducing deliberative forms of citizen communication, but also by using a recruiting strategy that is more inclusive than the self-recruiting mechanisms that dominate other forms of participation.

1 The exact number can change, because cities which are interested to join the network can do so at any time.

In his influential study "*Legitimation durch Verfahren*" (procedural legitimacy), Niklas Luhmann (1975) explains why the acceptance of democratic procedures by citizens is the most important source of legitimacy in modern societies, which are marked by plurality and complexity. He argues that whenever decision-making processes are confronted with contradicting opinions and cannot refer to a shared belief in the existence of substantial truths, the quality of a policy can only be perceived by citizens as a consequence of the quality of the democratic process, because substantially anything can become "true" in a parliamentary deliberation and vote. So "truth is no longer just a value but becomes a social mechanism that fulfills an assignable function" (Luhmann 1975, p. 23) and legitimacy describes the capacity of a political system "to engender and maintain the belief that the existing political institutions are the most appropriate ones for the society" (Lipset 1960, p. 64).

From this viewpoint, legitimacy is less a normative than an empirical concept, it primarily results from the citizen's belief in political processes, and its evidence is based on the acceptance of a policy by the citizens (see Weber 1992). Democratic citizens may accept a political decision even though it contradicts their personal opinion because either they believe in the authority of their political leaders and/or because they believe in the rationality of the political process. As Luhmann argues, belief in the rationality of a political process gains importance in plural societies and modern democracies because leaders' authority declines.

Referring to this concept of political legitimacy, we can interpret the increasing frequency of critique and protest against political decisions and democratic authorities as clear indicators of a legitimacy crisis in a democracy (Menzel 1980, p. 36; Barnes et al. 1979). For Germany, data from the "ALLBUS" (German General Social Survey) has proven such a trend since the 1980's. Especially younger cohorts here show increasing activity regarding unconventional forms of political participation, which mostly are forms of political protest (Lengfeld et al. 2000; Hadjar & Becker 2009; Dalton 2004).

Even better indicators than the participation in political protests might be the number of referendums and the number of petitions for a referendum in a given country (*Bürgerbegehren/Bürgerentscheide*). But unfortunately, for Germany it is not possible to offer a reliable interpretation of such data, because the institutional regulations and settings of such forms of participation and decision-making have been changed continuously. While in the early years, after the founding of the Federal Republic, direct democratic forms of decision-making played a marginal role, today all federal states offer their citizens opportunities for petitions and referendums on the local and state level, even though the relevant regulations (especially the quorums) still differentiate substantially (Schiller 2005; Decker 2010).[2]

For the same reasons as it is difficult to offer a quantitative long-term evaluation of the general perception of the legitimacy of the decision-making process in Germany, it is also difficult to analyze Germans' attitudes towards large-scale projects, whereby the term "large-scale" is meant to mark projects which are of special influence to the economic, social, or cultural future development of a city or region, which go along with noticeable changes for the citizens (at least during the construction process), and/or which are bound to high expenditures. Also, large-scale projects are often characterized by incongruent cost-benefit structures of different social groups: while, for example, the building of an airport runway leads to noise exposure of a relatively small part of the region's inhabitants, it also enables a large number of people to benefit from the improved infrastructure. As we will see later, this characteristic challenges the democratic practice of majority decision and it limits the sanctioning potential of voting in the eyes of the citizens. At this point it has to be mentioned, because it also complicates the measurement of the people's general perception of large-scale projects, that such data has not only to be analyzed regarding the numbers of supporters and critics, but also has to be interpreted carefully regarding the respondents' personal affectedness by certain projects – but very often this information is not available.

Despite these methodological problems, almost all political scientists these days believe that citizens' average evaluation concerning large-scale projects would be even more clearly marked by increasing criticism than other kinds of policies (Renn 2011). So there is not only a general crisis of legitimacy in Germany that manifests in an increasing number of political protests and other forms of unconventional political participation, its effects also become most visible in cases of large-scale decision-making. What theoretical insights might help to explain this development?

Using Easton's terminology (Easton 1975), we can assert that decisions on large-scale projects often suffer from a lack of support compared to the amount of conflicting demands they are confronted with. Regarding large-scale projects, people offer a comparatively precise and stable set of wants and demands that determine the level of specific support the political system will gain by deciding for one or another option. Being faced with this rather fixed set of individual preferences, the level of diffuse support becomes even more important for the legitimacy of political decision-making on large-scale projects than it is for other policies. But this level seems to be declining. As Fuchs et al. (2002) have argued, trust in political institutions and in democratic procedures can be seen as one indicator of diffuse support. But while the general sup-

2 On the level of the Federal Republic, German citizens have no right to initiate direct democratic decision making. A referendum on this level would only be possible for decisions on a new constitutional document (article 146 GG) or on a restructuring of the German territory (article 29 GG) (for an overview on direct democracy in Germany see Weixner (2006)).

port for democracy in Germany is still high, the development of trust in single democratic institutions shows a negative trend over time (von Beyme 2010; Klingemann 2000; Klingemann et al. 2006).[3] The decreasing levels of trust, especially in professional politicians and parliamentary institutions, but also in other experts that may appear as consultants in the political process, is one reason for the people's increasing rejection of large-scale projects: they do not trust in the politicians' and political institutions' potential to make the right decisions and they are afraid of the results of the political process, especially when it comes to important topics and projects.

But not only did trust in politicians and political institutions decrease at the end of the 20th century, citizens in many established democracies also give poor marks to how their political system functions. Referring to the growing gap between many people's strong adherence to democratic values on the one hand and their rather negative evaluation of the existing structure and performance of representative democratic government on the other hand, Norris et al. (1999) describe the emergence of "critical citizens" at the end of the last millennium. Those "dissatisfied democrats," as Norris also calls them, are often politically interested and engaged, but not satisfied with their political system's performance. So they appear very likely to be supporting the protestors against large-scale projects to express their dissatisfaction with the functioning of the political system and to try to improve its results from their perspective, because they believe that democratic structures are something worth fighting for (Geißel 2011).

The growing number of "critical citizens" also led to a demand for more participation, a demand that is closely connected to the increase of direct democratic forms of influence and decision-making. From this perspective, protests against large-scale projects are often not only oriented against the projects themselves, but are also meant as protests against the decision-making processes. Here we can witness, "that the decision-making process is at least as important as the decision itself" (Renn 2011). Especially those with a strong socio-economic background have uttered this wish for more direct influence on politics in recent years in Germany, especially when a political decision affects them personally.

But if more and more people act politically according to "NIMBY (not in my backyard) logic," their wish might be problematic: to act according to such an egoistic or infantile logic means that the citizens – as stated in parts of the literature more commonly today than it was in the past (Kraft & Clary 1991; Barber 2007) – prioritize their self-interested preferences and are not willing to accept personal disadvantages, even when they might lead to an increase in public welfare. As it was already mentioned, urban planning often is characterized by an unequal allocation of costs and benefits: while typically a large but anonymous group of people profits at rather low individual rates, a comparatively small group of people bear the costs or risks (that

3 For international data see e.g. Norris (1999, p. 6).

often are individually high). Also, while the costs appear to the citizens the moment a political decision is made, the profits and benefits often are long-term effects of a project, and additionally often those who are affected by the decisions are not (only) those who can influence it by their voting behavior. The less integrated and connected a society is, the lower the willingness of a negatively affected member to accept the project or measure will be, and the more distinct his/her orientation towards its present instead of its future effects will be (Putnam 2000; Renn 2004).

So for democratic systems, societal disintegration that leads to a loss of common sense and an increase of self-interested political participation within the community is in at least two respects problematic: structural majorities will dominate the results of elections so that the opponents of large-scale projects, especially those who are gravely affected by a project, won't perceive voting as a fair instrument for being heard, but will rather feel the need to start protests. Also, their protests challenge the democratic system because they make it more difficult for politicians to gain acceptance for measures that are intended to serve the public good – especially when only those citizens who are directly concerned by a decision become politically active.

To sum this up we can state that decisions on large-scale projects offer characteristics that make their acceptance and legitimacy even more vulnerable than those of other policies today. They are confronted with an unusually precise demand structure and often lack the resources to generate the corresponding amount of support. In addition to this, politicians and political institutions are confronted with sinking levels of trust, with a more and more critical perception of the political system's performance and functioning, as well as with some citizen's demands for more options to influence the political decision-making process. These aspects have led to a high number of political protests against large-scale problems in past years, which may hinder urban development and thus in the long run threaten the common welfare.

Even though the legitimacy crisis seems to be a consequence of societal changes and the people's perceptions of and attitudes towards politics and the political system rather than a direct consequence of procedural reforms or a worsening of democratic performance, mainly procedural reforms have been discussed in the literature in the past few years to slow down or even stop this trend. Especially politicians have criticized this approach as not being oriented towards the causes, but faced with the irreversibility of societal changes, procedural reforms seem to be the only option to react to challenges that result from the problems of legitimacy, especially of political decision-making on large-scale projects.[4] Therefore in the following section two kinds of

4 For an overview on possible solutions see e.g. Stoker (2006, p. 190ff). Another alternative might be the introduction of presidential regimes on the federal state level. Such a model has been discussed in Germany since the 1950s, but faced with sinking levels of trust in politicians and the citizen's claim for more participatory options, it lost influence within the last few years (see Decker 2004).

procedural reforms will be presented and their effects are discussed in the light of the identified reasons for the legitimacy crisis of large-scale projects.

3 Participatory reforms as solutions to the legitimacy crisis

To figure out how to strengthen the legitimacy of large-scale projects, we first have to identify variables that can be influenced politically and are of relevance to the citizen's acceptance of political decisions. The inclusiveness and transparency of the political process and a decision's perceived quality constitute such variables and will therefore be discussed in the following, referring to theoretical and empirical research. At the end of the section we will compare in how far direct democratic and deliberative forms of consulting or decision-making seem to be adequate means to positively impact these criteria. Do they seem to be able to strengthen the citizen's trust in political decision-making and can they help to overcome the problems that result from weakened social ties in today's society?

3.1 Three characteristics of legitimate democratic decision-making

Whatever kind of decision-making process is given, there will always be supporters and opponents whenever a large-scale project is planned and decided on politically. But from normative theory and empirical research we can derive at least three characteristics that strengthen a democratic process' entitlement to support as well as its actual acceptability: first, the more *inclusive* a political process is, the more likely its result is to be a legitimate one in the eyes of the citizens. Second, the more *transparent* a democratic decision-making process is, the more acceptable its results are. And third, the higher the *perceived quality* of political planning and decision-making is, the more legitimate they become.

Inclusion is an important criteria for democratic legitimacy, because it stresses the democratic notion that Dahl (1991, p. 31) formulated in the "strong principle of equality": "All members of the association are adequately qualified to participate on an equal footing with the others in the process of governing the association." Because it not only refers to the legal equality that *theoretically* empowers all people in the same way, but also to the de facto equality that describes the patterns of *actual* participation, it points to an important weakness of today's representative democracy: the fact that some social groups participate with significantly higher likelihood and frequency than other groups, which are not legally but de facto excluded from the democratic process. For example, Armin Schäfer proved in a recent study that this exclusion influences the legitimacy of political decisions, because people who do not participate conventionally in the political process – i.e. legally by free choice, but also because of social mechanisms that are hard to overcome – are especially critical towards the acceptability of political decision (Schäfer 2011, p. 10ff.; see also Merkel/Petring 2012) Such inequalities conflict with the democratic notions of inclusion and equal citizenry and therefore also challenge democratic legitimacy.

Second, we can state that the more *transparent* a democratic process is, the more acceptable its results are and the more citizens will trust in its quality and legitimacy. Transparency in this context means that citizens should be able to receive sufficient information on the project (costs, result, etc.) but also on alternative options and the party's and politicians' positions in the decision-making process. To theoretically justify the importance of transparency for democratic quality and acceptability, we can again refer to Dahl (1991), who emphasizes the relevance of transparency by showing that it gravely affects a democracy's quality. Policy-making "behind closed doors" may improve the quality of the politician's deliberation (Chambers 2004), but is still perceived critically by citizens.

Manfred G. Schmidt identifies the lack of transparency as a crucial reason for people's dissatisfaction with democracy in Germany (Schmidt 2006, p. 521). At least on the local level, this lack of transparency is mostly not the result of secretiveness of the local political or administrative actors, but rather a consequence of changes in the media structure and media reception, and also it reflects the people's general distrust in their representatives. Nevertheless, citizens' impression that they are not well informed regarding large-scale projects, as the example of Stuttgart 21 illustrates, is a problem for the legitimacy of democratic decisions.

As a last relevant attribute for the evaluation of procedural reforms that seek to strengthen legitimacy, we have to mention the *perceived quality* of political planning and decision-making. While the analysis of democratic quality is a wide and complex field of research (e.g. Munck & Verkuilen 2002), the perceived quality of democratic decision-making is a simpler construct. It asks whether the citizens, independent from their personal interests and preferences, believe that a certain decision-making process is suited to lead to high-quality results. This indicator, among others, aims at the evaluation of the role that professionals and experts play in today's political process, especially when it comes to decisions on large-scale projects. While many people on the one hand appreciate decision-making through professionals because they believe them to be competent and knowledgeable, on the other hand they tend not to trust politicians and experts because they assume that they might act in favor of their personal rather than the public interest (e.g. Peters 1999).

So the perceived quality of a decision-making process is based on two notions that are often discussed as contradicting in the literature: the trust in professional expertise and the distrust in professional deciders. An ideal democratic decision-making process would be able to integrate them by convincing the public of the trueness of the actor's motives as well as of their competence – and of course it would be inclusive and transparent.

In the following we will use *inclusiveness*, *transparency*, and *perceived quality* as indicators to evaluate the legitimizing potential of direct democratic and deliberative forms of political decision-making on large-scale projects. These two institutional designs have been discussed intensely in the literature as solutions to the legitimacy problems of modern policy making, especially with regard to large-scale projects, but so far they have rarely been compared.

3.2 Direct democracy as a solution to the legitimacy crisis?

In Germany, direct democracy is most often considered when it comes to a discussion on how to fight the legitimacy crisis. This is not only the due to the latest enhancements of institutionalized opportunities for direct democratic decision-making in this country, but also with regard to the Swiss example. Germany's small neighbor state offers an institutional setting that is oriented towards consensus and participation, mainly by direct democratic referendums. And even though some of the Swiss's decisions are highly controversial internationally (e.g. the 2009 national ban on the construction of minarets), Swiss people assign their political system comparatively better grades in a variety of support measures and therefore should be seen as less disenchanted with their system than other industrialized countries might be (e.g. Dalton 2004, p. 57ff.). Also, the Swiss example seems to falsify some scientists' anxiety that direct democracy leads to status quo oriented policies (Germann 1993, p. 230f.).

Obviously, direct democracy offers the closest link between political decision-making and the citizen's opinions and interests and also its *theoretical inclusiveness* is all encompassing – what indeed makes it appear as a promising instrument to achieve legitimate decision-making (Decker 2010, p. 574f.). But from the standpoint of *actual inclusiveness*, direct democracy appears more problematic: not even half of the Swiss population participates in most referendums in Switzerland (*Bundesamt für Statistik* 2011). In Germany, the situation seems to be similar, even though of course the number of referendums is much smaller here. The voter turnout rates of direct democratic forms of decision-making are generally lower than those of elections. Additionally, such forms of decision-making offer an even stronger social bias than other forms of participation (Schäfer 2011). So its high theoretical inclusiveness and its possible legitimizing power is confronted with a low actual inclusiveness, which is marked by a far-reaching exclusion of certain social groups. Because there are not any signs visible that hint at a mitigation of this effect, we have to note mixed results regarding the potential of direct democracy in strengthening today's democracy's inclusiveness.

A more optimistic perspective offers our second criteria: *transparency*. As we know from direct democratic procedures in Germany and Switzerland, such forms of decision-making stimulate intense media coverage on the concerned topic, as well as the increased attention of citizens towards this coverage. From the perspective of the media, direct democratic forms of decision-making have high news values because they are politically influential, they represent conflictive and clear-cut-issues, and they offer a limited timeframe (Kampwirth 1999; Marcinkowski 2004, 2007). Also direct democratic decision-making supports the intensity of interpersonal communication on the referendum's topic, which additionally enhances the citizen's feeling of transparency and enlightenment (Rehmet et al. 1999, p. 162f.; Benz & Stutzer 2007).

Regarding the *perceived quality* of direct democratic decision-making, there is considerable speculation, but unfortunately a lack of substantial information. In this article we cannot quote a single study that analyzes the effects of direct democracy on a decision's perceived quality, so we must refer to studies based on different but related research questions. As Fishkin (2009) does in his studies on deliberative polling, one might interpret changes in opinions and voting intentions as signs for a successful process. Successful communication processes and opinion change lead quasi-automatically – so at least is the assumption of theorists – to an improvement of the (perceived) quality of a political decision. In analogy to these assumptions, one might interpret the effects of political campaigning on citizen's attitudes: as Longchamp (2003) shows, a significant number of citizens change opinions and voting intentions as a reaction to the campaigns for a direct democratic decision-making process. But to claim that this change automatically leads to a higher perception of the quality of the referendum's result seems to be highly speculative.

Therefore, two other empirical studies appear to be more adequate in giving us at least hints as to the effect of direct democracy on the (perceived) quality of direct democratic decision-making. Lutz and Hug (2006) show for a number of states that the possibility of doing a referendum leads to a closer connection between the citizens' opinions and the actual political decisions, which should also lead to a higher perceived quality of political decision in the eyes of the citizens. Blume et al. (2009) try to measure the financial effects of direct democratic decision-making. They come to the result that initiatives by citizens lead to increasing expenditures, while referendums that are initiated by politicians reduce the community's or state's expenditures. Again, this interpretation is a bit speculative, but assuming that citizens' perception of the quality is highly influenced by its costs (as usually is the case with large-scale projects), their direct democratic power over the expenditures should enhance their satisfaction with the results.

On the basis of this tentative interpretation of empirical results and without further research, we cannot be sure of the effects of direct democratic decision-making on the perceived quality of these political decisions. There are indicators for positive effects, but we don't know enough about other effects that might result e.g. from the weaker influence of experts on these decisions. We have better knowledge regarding the other two factors, inclusiveness and transparency. Direct democracy here seems to be able to strengthen the legitimacy of large-scale projects, because it integrates the citizens more closely into the political process and improves their knowledge and interests for such decision-making processes at a moment when the decision is not yet made but can still be influenced by them.

But still there is one main problem for the legitimacy of large-scale projects that cannot be solved by this mode of decision-making: it cannot help effectively close the widening gap between groups of citizens that do participate in the political process and other groups that exclude themselves or that are more and more excluded from it. It might help to improve a decision's legitimacy in the eyes of Norris' "critical citizens," but it will probably not be able to reach those people who are already more or less completely truncated from politics and the political process. In the following we will argue how and why deliberative processes might be better suited to integrating this growing group of citizens.

3.3 Deliberative consultation as a solution to the legitimacy crisis?

Within a few years, deliberative democratic theory has turned from a "theoretical statement" into a "working theory" (Chambers 2003) that is applied in a large number of research areas. In the first years after this "deliberative turn" (Dryzek 2000) in political science, research focused on testing central theoretical principles by analyzing deliberative processes that either already existed in practice (e.g. by analyzing jury or parliamentary debates) or that were "constructed" for research purposes but that had no or hardly any influence on "real" politics (like e.g. James Fishkin did in his deliberative polls).[5]

On the basis of the knowledge we gained from these studies, today we are able to design deliberative settings that aim not only at a further development of the deliberative theory, but that are also meant to influence political practice and to react to some of the problems that democratic decision-making is confronted with. The German "city network" (*Städtenetzwerk*) that will be presented in the next section is one example that proves the current relevance of this work. But before we will explicate this project in detail, we first should shortly describe what "deliberative forums" are and take a closer look at existing results of empirical deliberative research to argue why we believe that the implementation of such forums is a promising measure to strengthen the

5 For an overview on studies that differentiate between real-world deliberations and deliberative processes in a laboratory setting, see Schaal & Ritzi (2009).

legitimacy of decision-making processes on large-scale projects. Again we will therefore refer to our three criteria of inclusion, transparency, and perceived quality.

According to the theory of deliberative democracy, legitimacy in modern societies results not only from equal participation opportunities but also from the justifiability of norms on the basis of rational argumentation. Therefore, deliberation describes communication processes in which arguments are exchanged in a way that the "unforced force" of the better argument prevails (see Habermas 1997, p. 147, p. 225ff.), or in the words of Joseph Bessette (1994, p. 46): "Deliberation is a reasoning process in which the participants seriously consider substantive information and arguments and seek to decide individually and to persuade each other as to what constitutes good public policy." Even though classic deliberative theory is normative and includes counterfactual ideals and assumptions, it is possible to set up communicative settings in practice that aim at establishing a kind of discourse that comes close to the theoretical ideal. Such settings are what we refer to when talking about "deliberative forums."

In such forums, a certain number of citizens meet to discuss a political problem or conflict. To identify the "best argument" in the course of the deliberation – which, according to deliberative theory should lead to the "best" decisions and to a high degree of consensus under the participants of the deliberation – it is necessary that the communicative process fulfills certain minimum requirements: first, it has to be marked by *non-coerciveness*, which means that all participants are free to make their arguments and have the same rights and chances to be heard in the deliberative process. The second requirement we call *reciprocity and equal respect*. It means that the participants should listen to each other and regard each other as equals; they should respect the opinions and positions of the others and take them into account while presenting their own arguments so that power differentials between participants are excluded from the deliberation. The third requirement is the *justifiability* of all relevant statements in a deliberation: this requirement excludes (ideally) all statements from the deliberative process that are not based on rational arguments. The deliberative model in this way aims to overcome NIMBY-type arguments "by getting citizens to cooperatively solve policy dilemmas rather than simply vote on policy options" (Chambers 2003, p. 317).

If a political institution wants to set up a discursive setting that fulfills these criteria, the size of a deliberating group has to be limited, which leads to an exclusion of large parts of the citizenry and therefore stands in opposition to a core ideal of democratic theory and representative democracy: equality.[6] Therefore, and for legal reasons as well, we do not suggest laying any decision-making power in the hands of a deliberative group, but rather regard such groups mainly as influential consulting agencies, whose

6 To illustrate this necessity, Fishkin describes the "trilemma" of the participatory ideals: equality, quality of the deliberation, and number of included people. Because not more than two of these ideals could be reached in one process, we have to choose two of the three ideals. Fishkin comes to the conclusion that deliberative quality is generally of higher importance than a high number of participants (Fishkin 2009, p. 46f.).

recommendations are not legally binding but have to be taken into account in all relevant (representative) decision-making arenas. The deliberating group also should be a representative sample of the relevant political community, which can be reached with the help of a random selection of participants, so that all relevant standpoints, attitudes, and views are included in the deliberation. Only then does a deliberative process fulfill the theory's dictum, whereas all addressees must have come to the same decision if they had been its authors.[7]

To make sure that reciprocity and equality is given, a facilitator should accompany the deliberative talks. His/her task is to encourage all participants of the deliberative group (especially those who are less educated and self-confident than other group members) to speak and to ensure that all positions are heard and that all arguments are taken into account by the others.

Last but not least, comprehensive media coverage is important for the success of deliberative processes. In complex modern societies, only mass media are able to generate the necessary public attention, transparency, and a sufficient level of information to enable citizens to gain trust in a political process and to perceive it as legitimate. So only when there is media coverage the consultation of political representatives by deliberative groups can be successful in the eyes of the general public.

If all these requirements are given, the introduction of a deliberative consultation process can set up a "second stage" of legitimacy in the context of representative democracy that supplements the existing sources of political legitimacy by adding a second dimension of political support that is based on the work of the deliberative forums and that might be called "epistemic procedural legitimacy" (see figure 1). While in the representative model legitimacy is mainly a result of processes of informational exchange between the public and the politicians and of course of conventional participation processes, in our model it can additionally result from the citizen's trust in the deliberative method and from its decision's epistemic quality.

7 Here we refer to Habermas' "discourse principle", which says that only such norms and values should prevail that would be accepted by all persons affected if they had taken part in the deliberation (Habermas 1997, p. 228).

Figure 1: Deliberative forums and the second stage of legitimacy in representative democracies.

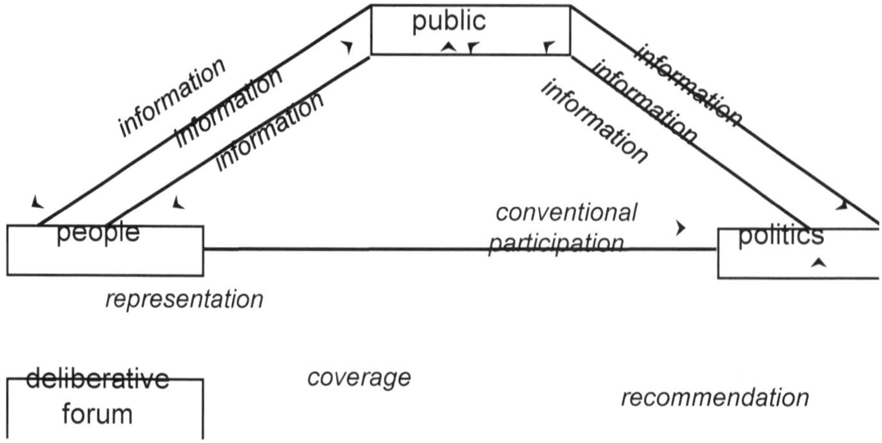

Even though the deliberative model can be used to involve citizens at every stage of policy formation (Chambers 2003, p. 317), when it comes to large-scale projects it is recommended to involve them before binding decisions have to be made by politicians (Ritzi & Schaal 2011). The example of "Stuttgart 21" proves that a deliberative process can be helpful in a crisis situation, but the continuing protests after the deliberative arbitration between opponents and supporters of the new train station also shows that its pacifying effects have been of limited scope. As we believe a stronger legitimizing effect could have been expected if a deliberative setting had been implemented at an earlier stage of the planning. This expectation can be substantiated with regard to the effects of deliberative processes on inclusiveness, transparency, and the perceived quality of a deliberatively found decision.

As already mentioned, the *inclusiveness* of deliberative groups is on the one hand limited: compared to direct democratic forms of decision-making, only a few people here get the chance to participate, which might disappoint those citizens that wish to be included more intensely in the democratic process.[8] But on the other hand, exactly because it is not based on self-recruiting, the deliberative group method offers the chance to generate a more representative group of participants than other forms of citizen involvement do. James Fishkin et al. therefore by lot generated a representative sample of citizens that are invited to participate in the deliberative polls, which are one

8 To prevent this and to offer all citizens the chance to participate in deliberative processes, Bruce Ackerman and James Fishkin (2004) proposed a second kind of deliberative process: the introduction of annual "Deliberation Days".

kind of deliberative group process.[9] They proved that the invitation to participate in a deliberative group in most cases leads to a more representative group of participating citizens than self-recruiting-methods do (Fishkin 2009, p. 43ff.). It is also possible not only to generate a representative sample of citizens who are invited to participate in the deliberation, but to ensure, with the help of quotas or by lot, that the actual deliberative group mirrors a community's socio-economic and/or lifestyle profile.

So while theoretical inclusiveness is better in direct democratic forms of decision-making, deliberative group consultations offer a higher potential of actually integrating a larger number of social groups in the political process. In light of the causes of the legitimacy crisis that have been described in the first section, to us the latter seems to be the more important task. So we believe that deliberative methods are superior to direct democratic methods regarding their potential to strengthen democratic legitimacy on the basis of improved inclusiveness – at least when there is a facilitator that makes sure that all participants not only are physically present but actively involved in the deliberation (Mendelberg 2002).

Because deliberative groups have not been implemented very often in practice, we don not yet have significant empirical data that analyzes their influence on our second factor: *transparency*. But again, we can refer to Fishkin's deliberative polling studies that mostly took place in successful cooperation with certain media channels, which covered the polling and deliberation process. Even though the deliberative method is so far widely unknown in the general public, the journalists' and the people's interest in the deliberative polling weekends was substantial, so that we might expect public attention on the results of the deliberative consultation processes to be as high as the public's interest in the coverage on direct democratic decision-making. Results from a case study on deliberative talks in a Bangladesh election campaign also support this expectation (Raman & Bhanot 2008).

The *perceived quality* of democratic decision-making can be supposed to improve with the help of deliberative groups. As deliberative theorists argue and empirical studies have proven, compared to ordinary polling or decision-making via referendum, deliberative methods lead to a higher degree of knowledge on the relevant issues. Also, many participants change their opinions, while the talks following the deliberations are more strongly orientated towards the common good than before, and most of the groups reach increasing rates of consensus through the deliberative process.[10] So there

9 James Fishkin developed the method of deliberative polling to use public opinion research for decision making processes without being confronted with the problem of uninformed and unreflected political preferences. Citizens are invited to gather at a single place for a weekend in order to discuss a given issue. Their opinions regarding the issue are measured before and after the weekend, so that it is possible to compare the deliberatively "laundered" with the pre-deliberative opinions (Fishkin 2009).

10 For an encompassing overview see Mansbridge (2010, p. 56ff.).

are good reasons for the presumption that the results of deliberative consultation processes are of a higher degree of rationality compared to direct democratic procedures.

More difficult is the comparison to the results of decision-making processes in traditional representative institutions like parliaments or municipal councils, where a high level of expertise is pre-given and an above average level of orientation towards the common good can be expected as well.[11] But being faced with the citizen's rising distrust in professional politicians, expert-driven decision-making in the political process and important representative institutions, the inclusion of a group of randomly selected citizens in the representative process offers legitimizing potential independent from the representative's knowledge and orientations. As Jane Mansbridge points out, it probably will take a while for the public to give methods like deliberative polling "the credibility and respect that they deserve. When they earn that respect, as I hope and believe they will, this new institution will be a boon to democracy, in underscoring the intelligence and capacity of the citizenry, in giving the citizens involved the experience of responsibility of others, and in guiding the polity toward better outcomes" (Mansbridge 2010, p. 60).

So regarding decisions on large-scale projects, we can conclude that instead of further strengthening direct democratic action, as it has been done in Germany within the last 20 years, it seems preferable to implement newer forms of participation that are based on deliberative democratic theory and that can generate epistemic procedural legitimacy. If a randomly selected group of citizens takes part in a deliberative consultation process, we can expect the decision to be characterized by a higher degree of legitimacy than a decision that was made with the help of a referendum. Deliberative methods can be expected to have the same positive effects on a process' transparency as direct democratic forms of action and they achieve even better results regarding the decisions' perceived quality and the representative inclusion of citizens.

4 Democratic deliberation in practice: The German city-network

After years in which large parts of the political elite seem to have held hope that their decisions and institutions will regain legitimacy just by themselves, today many politicians have realized that they need to react to the crisis they are faced with. Especially the huge protests against "Stuttgart 21" have demonstrated the need for action, but even before that, some representatives in Germany started to look out for new forms of decision-making processes that might be able to generate support for large-scale

11 It is hard to prove that deliberatively found decisions are of higher quality than the representative's decision. But as Cass Sunstein proves, deliberative methods can compensate for knowledge differences: At the end of deliberations, in most cases the non-professional group members come to qualified results as political experts (Sunstein 2006).

projects and to strengthen such projects' legitimacy. The *Verband für Wohnen und Stadtentwicklung* (vhw, a national association of towns and cities) recognized this development and in 2010 founded the German *Städtenetzwerk* (city network), in which up to 15 German cities now take part. All these cities, which differ largely in size and socio-economic and demographic structures (part of the network includes e.g. Berlin, Bergisch Gladbach, and Stuttgart), are planning to set up deliberative consultation processes in 2012/2013 to invite their citizens to participate in communal decision-making processes on topics like education, integration, and urban development.

This network is not only notable because it is the first time in Germany that such a large number of cities introduced a comparable setting of deliberative citizen participation, but also because the vhw plans to send out invitations to participate in a deliberative group only to a certain number of citizens that have been selected by lot. This form of "recruitment" will help to integrate not only politically interested citizens in the process, but also to integrate citizens that have a social background in which politics have low priority (so called *politikferne Milieus*). As in the studies of James Fishkin, a random sample of citizens will be invited to take part in the deliberative forums. But different from the deliberative polls, the sampling will be weighted according to certain milieus' affinity to politics. Citizens from lifestyle-milieus where most people do not participate in the political process will be overrepresented, so that the deliberative group has a better chance to mirror the relevant population.

The vhw-approach is based on the perception that lifestyles are better indicators for political behavior than socio-economic factors alone are (Sinus 2009; Jost 2007), which results from the notion that today any political process that wants to be perceived as fair and legitimate should make special efforts to guarantee not only formal equality but also *de facto* equality, which means that there are no systematic biases within the group of participating citizens.

The recruiting of the sample according to lifestyle indicators follows three aims: first it helps to reintegrate disaffected citizens in the decision-making process. Second, it leads to an inclusion of citizens who have never or hardly ever participated in the democratic process before (a group that includes, not least, people with an immigration background). And third, it contributes to the formation of policies and political decisions that are better adapted to the needs, wishes, and preferences of those citizens that will be affected by the decisions. Also the vhw plans to set up partnerships with local media, so that the deliberative forums will be accompanied by close media coverage, which is supposed to lead to legitimizing effects not only on the side of the deliberation's participants, but also on the side of the other citizens.

The city-network wants participants of the deliberative forums not only to reflect on a pre-given topic (e.g. the question of how and where to build a community center), but also to develop recommendations for this decision. These recommendations will be forwarded to the municipal or district council (depending on where the representative decision on the topic is made) and to the administration. Even though the deliberative forum's resolutions are not of binding power, they can be expected to have decisive influence over the representative's decision, because in advance of the deliberative procedures, all municipal councils involved in the city-network have declared that they will take the recommendations seriously.

So from the perspective of the cities and the vhw, the setting up of a deliberative "second stage" promises to establish new forms of cooperation between citizens, their political representatives, and the administration. The innovative process is supposed to also be used in the future, especially when decisions on large-scale projects or other unusually contentious decisions have to be made (Rohland & Kuder 2011, p. 6f.). If the city-network proves to be a successful project, this could be a first step to turning the mainly protest-driven German trend towards referendums (*Bürgerbegehren/Bürgerentscheide*) into a trend of new cooperation between the citizens and the state. From a scientific perspective, the *Städtenetzwerk* is also a project of special interest: the 15 deliberative forums, which will take place in 2012/2013 and will be evaluated by political scientists from the Helmut Schmidt University (directed by Prof. Dr. Gary S. Schaal), offer a unique opportunity to evaluate the effects of deliberative forms of citizen participation on political legitimacy as well as to gain knowledge on questions like "which topics seem to be especially appropriate for discussion in deliberative forums?", "do different community-sizes affect the deliberation's success?", or "do deliberative methods offer chances to integrate citizens who usually do not participate in the political process?".

Thus political practice as well as university research set high hope in the city-network. Even though we today cannot know whether and to what extent these hopes will be fulfilled by the deliberative forums, as we have tried to argue in this article, they can at least be perceived as well-reasoned.

Bibliography

Ackerman, B., & Fishkin, J. (2004). *Deliberation Day.* New Haven/London: Yale University Press.

Bundesamt für Statistik. (2011). http://www.bfs.admin.ch/bfs/portal/de/index/themen/17/22/lexi.topic.1.html [02.11.2011]

Benz, M., & Stutzer, A. (2007). *Direct Democracy and Citizen's Information about Politics.* In: Z.T. Pállinger, B. Kaufmann, W. Marxer, & T. Schiller (Ed.) *Direct Democracy in Europe. Developments and Prospects* (pp. 125-142). Wiesbaden: VS Verlag für Sozialwissenschaften.

Bessette, J. M. (1994). *The Mild Voice of Reason. Deliberative Democracy and American National Government.* Chicago: University of Chicago Press.

Chambers, S. (2003). Deliberative Democratic Theory. *Annual Review of Political Science 6*, 307-326.

Chambers, S. (2004). Behind Closed Doors: Publicity, Secrecy, and the Quality of Deliberation. *The Journal of Political Philosophy*, 12(4), p. 389-410.

Dahl, R. A. (1971). *Polyarchy: Participation and Opposition*. New Haven: Yale University Press.

Dahl, R. A. (1991). *Democracy and Its Critics*. 2. Edition. New Haven: Yale University Press.

Dalton, R. J. (2004). *Democratic Challenges, Democratic Choices. The Erosion of Political Support in Advanced Industrial Democracies*. Oxford: Oxford University Press.

DBB (Datenbank Bürgerbegehren und Bürgerentscheide in Deutschland). (2011). http://www.datenbank-buergerbegehren.de/beteiligung.php [2.11.2011]

Decker, F. (2010). Zwischen Placebo und Erfolgsmodell: Direkte Demokratie auf der Landesebene. In: *Zeitschrift für Parlamentsfragen 41*, 564-579.

Decker, F. (2004). Die Regierungssysteme in den Ländern. In: *ders. (Ed.): Föderalismus an der Wegscheide?* Wiesbaden: VS Verlag für Sozialwissenschaften, 169-201.

Dryzek, J. S. (2000). *Deliberative Democracy and Beyond: Liberals, Critics, Contestation*. Oxford (UK): Oxford University Press.

Easton, D. (1975). A Re-Assessment of the Concept of Political Support. In: *British Journal of Political Science 5(4)*, 435-457.

Fishkin, J. S. (2009). *When the People Speak. Deliberative Democracy and Public Consultation*. Oxford: Oxford University Press.

Fishkin, J., & Luskin, R. C. (2005). Experimenting with a Democratic Ideal: Deliberative Polling and Public Opinion. In: *Acta Politica 40 (3)*, 284-299.

Fishkin, J., Luskin, R. C., Panaretos, J., Siu, A., & Xekalaki, E. (2008). Returning Deliberative Democracy to Athens: Deliberative Polling for Candidate Selection. *Paper presented at the meetings of the American Political Science Association,* Boston, MA, 28-31 August. http://cdd.stanford.edu/

Fishkin, J. S., Camarano, E., Luskin, R. C., & Siu, A. (2010). *Deliberative Participatory Consultation: The First Deliberative Poll in Porto Alegre*. http://cdd.stanford.edu/research/papers/2010/fishkin-porto-alegre.pdf [07.11.2011]

Gabriel, O. W., & Völkl, K. (2004). Politische und soziale Partizipation. In: O.W. Gabriel, E. Holtmann (Ed.): *Handbuch Politisches System der Bundesrepublik Deutschland* (pp. 523-573). München/Wien: Oldenbourg.

Geißel, B. (2004). Responsivität und Responsivitätswahrnehmung – Thesen zu einem undurchsichtigen Verhältnis. In: *Zeitschrift für Politikwissenschaft 14. (4)*, 1239-1259.

Geißel, B. (2011). *Kritische Bürger. Gefahr oder Ressource für die Demokratie?* Frankfurt am Main: Campus.

Germann, R. E. (2003). Aufnahme plebiszitärer Elemente ins deutsche Grundgesetz: Was lehren die Schweizer Erfahrungen. In: W. Link, E. Schütt-Wetschky, & G.Schwan (Ed.) *Jahrbuch für Politik* (pp. 219-258). Baden-Baden: Nomos.

Habermas, J. (1997). *Between Facts and Norms*. Cambridge: Polity Press.

Hadjar, A., & Becker, R. (2009). Bildungsexpansion und politisches Engagement – Unkonventionelle politische Partizipation im Zeitverlauf. In: I. Node, A. Evers, & A. Klein (Ed.): *Bürgergesellschaft als Projekt* (pp. 101-124). Wiesbaden: VS Verlag für Sozialwissenschaft.

Jost, F. (2007). Mein Haus – mein Quartier – meine Stadt. Sinus-Milieus und bürgerschaftliches Engagement. In: *Reihe „Bürgergesellschaft" der Konrad-Adenauer-Stiftung Nr. 4*. Bonn: KAS.

Kampwirth, R. (1999). Volksentscheid und Öffentlichkeit. Anstöße zu einer kommunikativen Theorie der direkten Demokratie. In: T. Schiller (Ed.): *Direkte Demokratie in Theorie in kommunaler Praxis* (pp. 17-68). Frankfurt a. M.: Campus.

Karpowitz, C. F., & Mendelberg, T. (2007). Groups and Deliberation. In: *Swiss Political Science Review 13 (4)*, 645-662.

Kraft, M. E., & Clary, B. B. (1991). Citizen Participation and the Nimby Syndrome: Public Response to Radioactive Waste Disposal. In: *The Western Political Quarterly, Vol. 44, No. 2 (Jun., 1991)*, 299-328.

Lengfeld, H., Liebig, S., & Märker, A. (2000). Politisches Engagement, Protest und die Bedeutung sozialer Ungerechtigkeit. In: *Aus Politik und Zeitgeschichte B 7-8/00*, 22-31.

Lipset, S. M. (1960): *Political Man. The Social Bases of Politics*. Garden City: Doubleday & Company.

List, C., McLean, I., Fishkin, J., & Luskin, R. C. (2000). Deliberation, Preference Structuration, and Cycles: Evidence from Deliberative Polls. *Paper presented at the University of Texas School of Law Conference on "Deliberating About Deliberative Democracy"*. www.nuff.ox.ac.uk/users/list/structuration081001.pdf [07.11.2011]

Mansbridge, J. (2010). Deliberative Polling as the Gold Standard. In: *The Good Society 19 (1)*, 55-62.

Marcinkowski, F. (2004). Deliberation, Medienöffentlichkeit und direktdemokratischer Verfassungsentscheid – Der Fall Liechtenstein. In: *Beiträge Liechtenstein-Institut Nr. 21*.

Marcinkowski, F. (2007). Beyond Information and Opinion. The importance of public communcation in the referendum process. In: Z. T. Pállinger, B. Kaufmann, W. Marxer, & T. Schiller (Ed.): *Direct Democracy in Europe* (pp. 94-107). Developments and Prospects. Wiesbaden: VS Verlag für Sozialwissenschaften.

Mendelberg, T. (2002). The Deliberative Citizen: Theory and Evidence. In: M. C. Delli Carpini, L. Huddy, & R. O. Shapiro (Ed.*): Research in Micropolitics, Vol. 6: Political Decision-Making, Deliberation and Participation* (pp. 151-193). Greenwich: JAI.

Menzel, J. (1980). *Legitimation staatlicher Herrschaft durch Partizipation Privater*. Berlin: Duncker & Humblodt.

Merkel, W., & Petring, A. (2012). Politische Partizipation und demokratische Inklusion. In: T. Mörschel, & C. Krell (Ed.): *Demokratie in Deutschland* (pp. 93-119). Wiesbaden: Springer VS.

Munck, G. I., & Verkuilen, J. (2002). Conceptualizing and Measuring Democracy. In: *Comparative Political Studies, Vol. 35, No. 1*, p. 5-34.

Peters, H.-P. (1999). Das Bedürfnis nach Kontrolle der Gentechnik und das Vertrauen in wissenschaftliche Experten. In: J. Hampel, & O. Renn (Ed.): *Gentechnik in der Öffentlichkeit. Wahrnehmung und Bewertung einer umstrittenen Technologie* (pp. 225-245). Frankfurt a. M.: Campus.

Putnam, R. D. (2000). *Bowling Alone: The Collapse and Revival of American Community*. New York: Simon & Schuster.

Raman, V. V., & Bhanot, A. (2008). *Political crisis, Mediated Deliberation and Citizen Engagement: A case study of Bangladesh and Nirbachoni Sanglap.* http://downloads.bbc.co.uk/worldservice/pdf/wstrust/Bangladesh_Sanglap_Governance.pdf [07.11.2011]

Rhemet, F., Weber, T., & Pavlovic, D. (1999). Bürgerbegehren und Bürgerentscheide in Bayern, Hessen und Schleswig-Holstein. In: T. Schiller (Ed.): *Direkte Demokratie in Theorie und kommunaler Praxis* (pp. 117-164). Frankfurt a. M.: Campus.

Renn, Ortwin (2004). The Challenge of Integrating Deliberation and Expertise: Participation and Discourse in Risk Management. In: T. McDaniels , & M. J. Small (Ed.): *Risk Analysis and Society: An Interdisciplinary Characterization of the Field* (pp.289-366). Cambridge: Cambridge University Press.

Ritzi, C., & Schaal, G. S. (2010). Politische Führung in der Postdemokratie. In: *Aus Politik und Zeitgeschichte 2-3/2010*, 9-15.

Ritzi, C., & Schaal, G. S. (2011). Wie Bürgerbeteiligung besser gelingt. Bürger-Juries und die vier Versprechen der deliberativen Demokratietheorie. In: *vhw Schriftenreihe, Band 3: Dialog* (pp. 38-42). Berlin: Verband für Wohnen und Stadtentwicklung.

Rohland, P., & Kuder, T. (2011). Dialog: Zur Stärkung lokaler Demokratie. In: *vhw Schriftenreihe, Band 3: Dialog* (pp. 3-7). Berlin: Verband für Wohnen und Stadtentwicklung.

Schaal, G. S., & Ritzi, C. (2009): *Empirische Deliberationsforschung. MPIfG Working Paper.* http://www.mpifg.de/pu/workpap/wp09-9.pdf

Schäfer, A. (2011). Affluence, Inequality and Satisfaction with Democracy. In: O. Gabriel, & S. Keil (Ed.): *Democracy and Society in Europe.*

Schmidt, M. G. (2006). *Demokratietheorien: Eine Einführung. 3rd Edition.* Wiesbaden: VS Verlag für Sozialwissenschaften.

Sinus Sociovision (2009). *Informationen zu den Sinus-Milieus 2009.* Heidelberg: Sinus Sociovision.

Sunstein, C. R. (2006). *Infotopia: How Many Minds Produce Knowledge.* New York: Oxford University Press.

Weber, M. (1992). Die drei Typen der legitimen Herrschaft. In: *ders.: Soziologie, weltgeschlichtliche Analysen* (pp. 151-166). Politik, Stuttgart.

Weixner, B. M. (2006). Direktdemokratische Beteiligung in Ländern und Kommunen. In: B. Hoecker (Ed.): *Politische Partizipation zwischen Konvention und Protest* (pp. 100-132). Opladen: Verlag Barbara Budrich.

Deliberative Governance Arenas as a Model for the Governance of Communal and Administrative Reforms

Wolfgang König, Mathias König

This paper deals with the research questions of how communication between stakeholders (e.g. politics, business, and citizens) could be improved, and what a possible mode of civic participation and deliberation might be. The paper argues that "Deliberative Governance Arenas" (DGA) might be one possible model that allows the institutional space for the deliberation process. Through deliberative governance arenas, policy makers get the whole system into one room, which could result in creative solutions for a particular issue that are quantitatively different from solutions found by a small group. The use of such processes could activate citizens and strengthen their faith in democratic processes. These deliberative governance arenas allow the inclusion of different components of knowledge.

1 Rationale

At least since the occurrence of the civil protests against the infrastructure project "Stuttgart 21," it has become obvious that modern citizens demand that politics and administration allow them to become intensively involved in project development and decision making. This applies even more to projects with conflict potential. Thus, recent decreased voter participation does not indicate that citizens have become less interested in politics. All current representative surveys of the population have rather shown that direct participation is precisely what citizens expect from "true" democracy. At least since the 1990s, all western democracies have suffered from symptoms of crisis that are aimed at the core of representative democracy in particular: confidence in the representative elites. The loss of confidence on the part of the citizens towards their elites is mainly based on disappointed expectations (Kaina 2002), i.e. the non-validation of constructs of reality (Schmidt 1992). The aim of this paper is to show how participatory governance can be successful in complex procedures, using the Deliberative Governance Arenas (DGA) approach of public involvement in the frame of the large-scale project of communal and administrative reform (*Kommunal- und Verwaltungsreform*) in the German federal state of Rhineland-Palatinate as a concrete example. After all, communal and administrative reforms are considered "elite projects" of regional planning which should be valid for several decades. During implementation, they face massive resistance mostly on the part of the citizens because their concepts of reform are different. In addition, such reforms change the local governance system. This paper starts by introducing the DGA approach, then analyzes the example of Rhineland-Palatinate, and finally discusses the consequences of the findings for the DGA approach.

2 *Deliberative Governance Arenas*

Modern societies are increasingly facing more and more complexity, which they must learn to deal with. It is thus assumed that complexity grows within a political system, and that this increase may therefore be mastered by applying a higher degree of democracy (Hellmann & Fischer 2003). Here, "democracy" "only" refers to a structural, constitutionally established arrangement of the political system (Czerwick 2008) and remains unclear as a term of analysis with regard to the actual multi-layered regulation processes. The qualitative change in human experience in transformation processes requires a "democratic experimentalism," since the solutions found in traditional structures do not provide any satisfactory answers (Keupp 2003). The DGA approach was developed in order to overcome the issues of analysis.

2.1 Basic assumptions

Knowing the varieties and various conceptions of democracy, political elites must not "forget" that the current rules of representation reduce the complexity of democracy only in the short term, as this may become counterproductive in an increasingly complex society. Politicians are more than representatives for the people. They also stand for the existing "constitutional construct of democratic reality." Accordingly, they are the target of the frustration of citizens, whose construct of democratic reality is not limited to formally established criteria. Eventually, citizens become disappointed by the *kind* of democratic reality, which does not correspond to their "constructs of reality." As a consequence, it is not "the" reality that is at issue, but the basic assumption of the psychological approach of the German "social constructivism." Here, it is assumed that the personal constructs of reality of individuals are mainly created within the social discourse, while the individuals may also redefine their reality (König & König 2011b). This puts the "grammar of politics" (Fach 1997), i.e. the way of solving social problems, into analytical focus. The governance theory or perspective allows a "totality in perspective" (Kooiman 2003) and thus the carrying out of analyses aimed at identifying social regulation processes beyond the constitutional reality. In addition to the coordination of collective acting, the governance perspective describes mechanisms and processes of cause and effect that should result in coordination (Benz, Lütz & Schimank 2007). The starting point is the emphasis on system rules and system properties, which generate sociopolitical interaction by means of new procedures, aiming at increasing legitimacy and effectiveness (Kooiman 2006). If the assumptions of the governance theory are reflected back on the basic assumptions of constructivism, it becomes clear that the theory addresses the described "reality checks." This is essential for political elites, as a strategy for acting can be derived from this understanding of constructivism and governance.

2.2 DGA approach

Deliberative Governance Arenas are "spaces enabling regulation processes" of deliberative communication, which are generated in the frame of governance processes and are aimed at involving and integrating specific target groups, respectively. The objective is to integrate the citizens in a regulation chain, while actively communicating the necessity and the purpose as well as the transparent use of results. A context defined by institutional rules where individuals are interacting represents an arena. Thus, arenas are regulation zones for negotiations between diverging particular interests. Here, the focus is not on the decision mode of (political) decisions but on the conditions that are required to be able to regulate highly complex issues. A DGA may be formed in various ways, be it by the communicative effects of direct democracy or by various methods of participation (König & König 2011a). The scope and the focus of analysis, respectively, with regard to regulation structures and their sphere of action in a DGA may range from punctual involvement in a concrete matter (politics) over continuous institutionalization of participation (politics and policy), up to the meta-level and the philosophy of governance itself (through an overall concept) (König & König 2011a):

Figure 1: Perspectives of “Deliberative Governance Arenas”

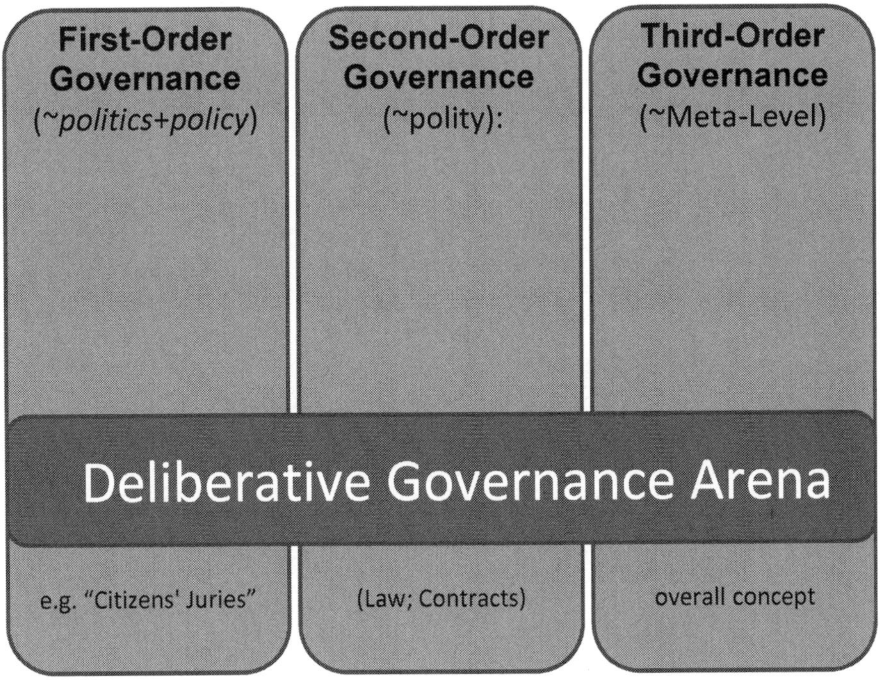

(König & König 2011a, p. 66)

3 "Deliberative Governance Arenas" in Rhineland-Palatinate

3.1 Communal and administrative reform as a governance process

The last communal and administrative reform in Rhineland-Palatinate took place 30 years ago. It was an elite project of the political parties CDU and SPD and led to massive resistance on the part of the citizens. The then-controversial issue was the newly founded associations of municipalities, i.e. a local administrative reform as an element of regional planning. Those associations were formed to ensure the self-governance of very small municipalities in Rhineland-Palatinate. Several small municipalities each were combined to form associations of municipalities under professional administration. This provoked considerable resistance on the part of the citizens, as sometimes municipalities were combined which, for historical and cultural reasons, were not able or willing to cooperate. The current key issue of the reform is again the local administrative reform as an instrument of regional planning, in terms of whether and how the associations of municipalities can be maintained even with a declining number of inhabitants, or whether they might have to merge. In case of mergers, the new communal area and the associated resources, the political majorities, and the distance to the point of administration may change. Theoretically, the reform can affect all associations of municipalities in Rhineland-Palatinate, but partly also counties, and towns with county status. Due to the fragmented character of Rhineland-Palatinate, the majority of citizens are affected by the reform. There have been numerous communal and administrative reforms in Germany, and experience has shown that communal and administrative reforms are complex procedures that are difficult to communicate in general. During the problem identification and planning phase, possible consequences and contents are rarely elaborated upon in the media, as the informational value of the reforms is at that point low. The informational value is especially high only after the reforms have been resolved and are to be implemented, despite the ensuing resistance of people affected. In order to solve this paradox, the political public must be constantly informed during the process (Sarcinelli, König & König 2008).

Figure 2: The paradox of participation

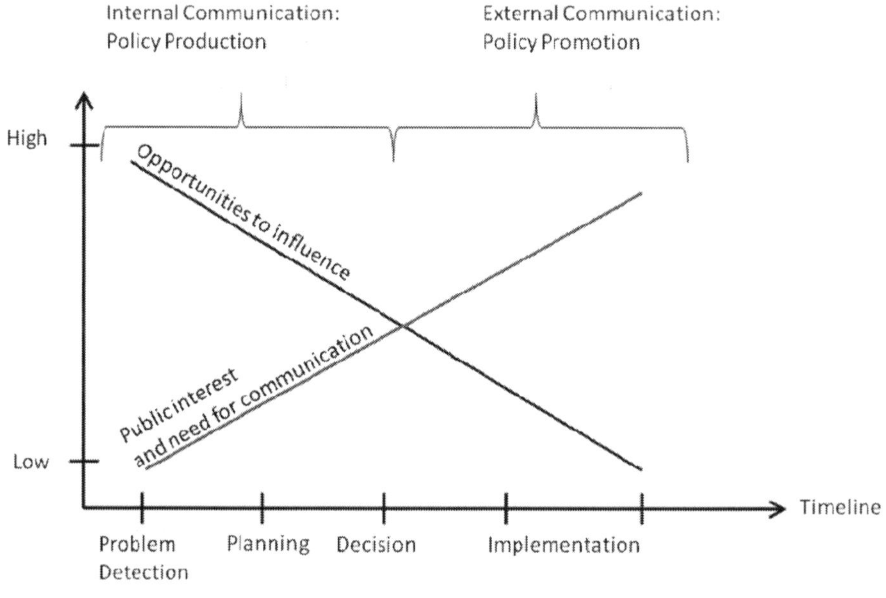

(König & König 2010, p. 131)

The paradox of participation thus refers to the process-design component of the DGA. The purpose component, however, has to be established by creating and applying an extended constructivism. Here, the question is how to apply the DGA.

3.2 DGA design and effect(s)

Public involvement began at the beginning of the reform planning process, not only at the end as a measure of subsequent legitimation. This was a political requirement prescribed by the Minister-President of the federal state of Rhineland-Palatinate who based his actions on the governmental concept of a "civil society." For the state government, civil society means that the citizens should be more closely involved in political processes in general, and that they should play their role as citizens and not as customers. With the participation of citizens in the course of the communal and administrative reform, Rhineland-Palatinate shows that civil society is not just an idea, but a viable way of living politics, as the Minister-President formulated. The objective is not to abolish representative democracy, but to complement it in a useful way in order to improve the output of political decisions. Thus, participation in the form of a DGA can be regarded as an element of political communication, because participation allows the communication of information and knowledge both on the part of politics towards the citizens and on the part of the citizens towards politics. Participation can also become an instrument of political consulting, as citizens subject political projects to a rationality test or reality check. In this way, "blind spots" in the planning can be detected. Participation leads to a discursive examination of an issue because any relevant arguments are heard and evaluated. This proceeding is successful because communication takes place with the people affected, who can then evaluate the arguments of politics and introduce their own arguments, if required. Thus the people affected act as consultants (König & König 2010). In the sense of constructivism, the number of individuals that create similar constructs of reality is important (Hejl 1992). Below, the DGA design will be laid out and effects will be described using the Citizens' Jury as an example:

Nine Regional Conferences (October-November 2007): Regional Conferences took place in Worms, Mainz, Ludwigshafen, Speyer, Koblenz, Neuwied, Pirmasens, Trier, and Kaiserslautern. In total, over 2,500 persons participated in the Regional Conferences. The communal and administrative reform was brought to public awareness. The target group mainly comprised of municipal officers and functionaries (veto players, experts) who discussed the reform with the Minister of the Interior (about 2-3 hours per conference).

Five Citizens' Congresses: So-called Citizens' Congresses (moderation method of the Future Conference) took place in Bingen, Ludwigshafen, Kaiserslautern, Trier, and Lahnstein in the spring of 2008. Those congresses were promoted with the slogan "*Meine Meinung zählt*!" (My opinion counts!), and all citizens were invited to participate. In a widespread media campaign, citizens were invited by mail and via radio advertisements and public posters. About 1.2 million flyers were distributed to citizens' mailboxes in the state. The state government also advertised participation in the congresses through radio spots and on posters. At each congress, between 150 and 250 citizens (mostly people with honorary political posts), in groups of eight people per group, discussed possible improvements to the administration and the criteria of a regional reform.

Figure 3: Changes in ratings of statements concerning reforms in the course of the planning procedure (Citizens' Jury) (N=140)

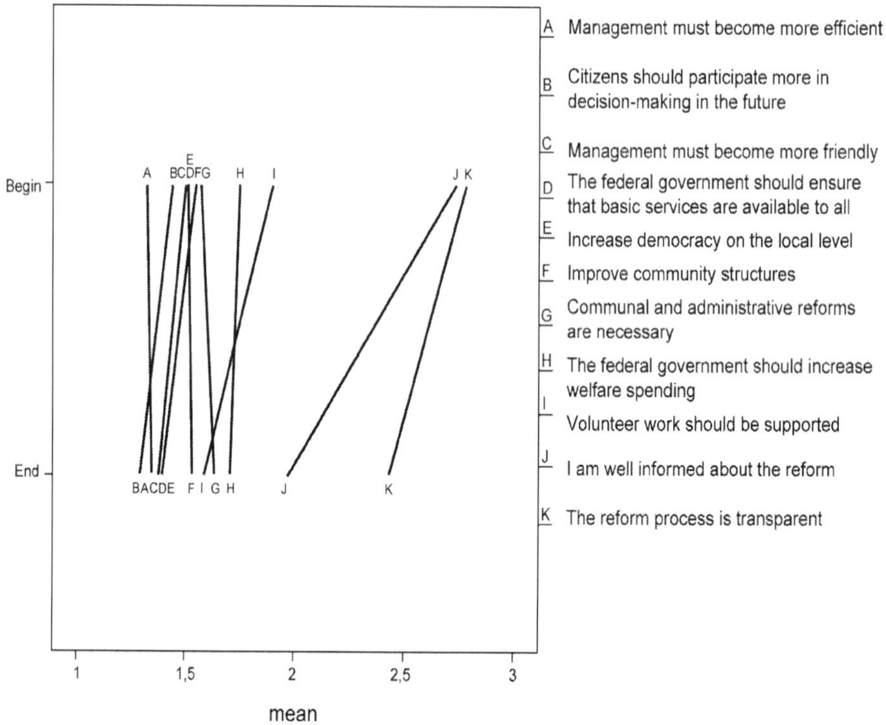

(König &König 2012, p. 52)

Six Citizens' Juries (June 2008): After the Citizens' Congresses, six so-called Citizens' Juries were established in Vallendar, Pirmasens, and Prüm in June 2008. As representatives of "city" regions, the city of Pirmasens, which also has county status, was selected together with the *Verbandsgemeinde* (association of municipalities) Pirmasens-Land. As representatives for the "urban" regions, *Verbandsgemeinde* Vallendar was selected together with the city of Bendorf, and for the "rural" regions, *Verbandsgemeinde* Prüm was selected together with *Verbandsgemeinde* Arzfeld. The "Citizens' Jury" had been developed by Peter C. Dienel in the 1970s, and has become well known internationally in the meantime. In each Citizen's Jury, 25-30 randomly selected persons worked together for four days. This method allowed the reduction of statistical distortions with regard to the composition of participants in the Citizens' Congresses. The objective was to collect detailed ideas and proposed solutions from participants living in various regions and structurally different areas of the state.

At the beginning and at the end of the meeting, the participants in the Citizens' Juries were interviewed in writing. Figure 2 summarizes the results from six Citizens' Juries.

> "It becomes clear that citizens' beliefs change through the procedure. They demand in particular the support of voluntary work by citizens and gain trust in the political process of the reform transparency and knowledge" (König &König 2012, p. 52).

The results of the Citizens' Congresses and Citizens' Juries were summarized by the Ministry of the Interior. On this basis, the opinions of the citizens were collected via 10,000 telephone interviews of adult inhabitants in a statewide representative population survey between March 23 and June 5, 2009. The results of the representative survey have shown that the involvement of citizens had a positive effect with regard to awareness, as the majority of the population of Rhineland-Palatinate (60 percent) knew in the spring of 2009 that the state government was working on a communal and administrative reform. Half of the persons interviewed who had learned about the reform felt sufficiently informed, the other half would have liked to obtain more information. More than 80 percent appreciated that citizens were so closely involved in the reform planning process. In the fall of 2010, the state government started the "stage of voluntariness" where the municipalities were given the opportunity to "look for" partners for a merger themselves. This way, the demands of the citizens for more involvement in the reform process were fulfilled, while handing down a considerable part of the conflict-bearing complexity to the municipalities. There, the regulation arenas to be created will be of particular importance. For this reason, 14 associations of municipalities with various problems, and which were especially affected by the reform, were selected for an elite survey. The survey is representative with regard to the local representation of the political parties CDU and SPD, voter groups, and the FDP, respectively. Just *Bündnis90/Die Grünen* (The Green Party) are underrepresented, while the group of "independent local municipal officers" is overrepresented as compared to their representation in the state. In total, 155 elected municipal officers were interviewed. A clear majority of the respondents (84 percent) spoke in favor of the stage of voluntariness for their municipalities. A vast majority of the respondents (78 percent) consider the participation of citizens as an instrument of efficient governing, and spoke in favor of involvement of the citizens in the reform planning process (89 percent). A majority of the respondents (60 percent) also wish to involve the local citizens in the stage of voluntariness. A vast majority of the respondents deem financial support, the provision of know-how, and support in participation processes to be factors for success of the stage of voluntariness; support in participation processes is most often requested by the respondents (90 percent) (Sarcinelli, König & König 2011). In the qualitative parts of the survey, the elites interviewed partly mentioned being "overstrained," as complex involvement of citizens beyond the existing legal provisions had not been part of the scope of work and daily administrative life of the respondents so far (Sarcinelli, König & König 2010).

4 Conclusion and discussion

In the frame of the accompanying scientific research, it became obvious that the satisfaction of the citizens with regard to the created DGA grew with the intensity of the participation method. The citizens' willingness to participate was high, and the citizens were interested in further involvement in the reform process (Sarcinelli, König & König 2009). The procedural design of the DGA and the resulting structured regulation arenas may be regarded as successful operationalization of an "extended constructivism," as the citizens were successfully won over to the complex topic of regional planning. The dilemma of regional planning is that, apart from experts, the purpose-component is usually not institutionally validated by the citizens. In addition to the punctual arenas for problem resolution, the current modification of the municipal codes reduced the quorum for citizens' referendums and decisions and established an "experimental clause," which more easily allows for the involvement of citizens on a new legal basis. This participation requirement is "marketed" under the government motto of a "civil society." In summary, the empiric results indicate that both the citizens and the political elites validate the DGAs and their results positively. In the course of the reform, the further design of DGAs seems to become the key challenge on the local level within the municipalities. A successful operationalization in the frame of the large-scale project of a "communal and administrative reform" in the German federal state of Rhineland-Palatinate, however, will depend on the degree of support for the local political elites in this new management of complexity, as this form of governance is highly experimental (König & König 2011b). The consequences resulting from the findings for the DGA approach described are synoptically summarized in Figure 3:

Figure 4: Consequences for governance management

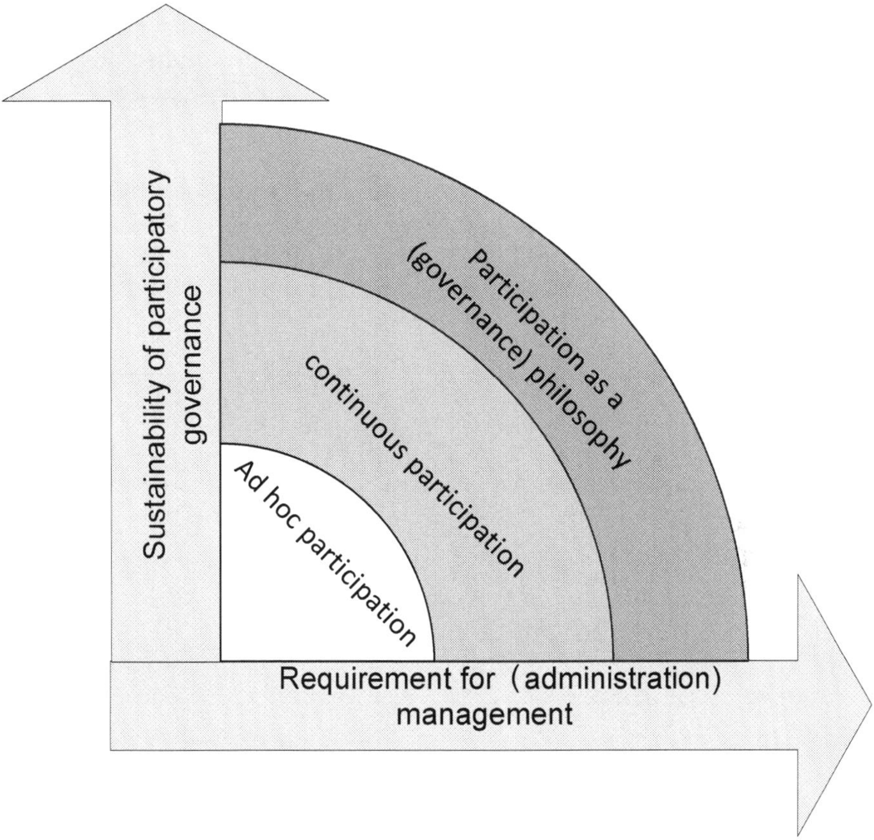

The following items from this representation may be discussed: From the point of view of the decision makers, the question of whether the participation of citizens makes sense generally only arises after an "acceptance problem" has occurred. The arbitration procedure in the case of "Stuttgart 21" is one such example. The problem is that such "emergency involvement" – with uncertain outcome – does not represent any sustainable management of participation, as punctual emergency involvement tends to reduce the trust in politics and administration. These are "only" measures for subsequent legitimation and no actual sustainable relationships of cooperation.

Continuing participation in a range of topics makes more sense in terms of strategy, as cooperation – and thus participation – is necessary for achieving cooperative performance. As a rule, such participation arrangements are made in the so-called "third sector," i.e. particularly on the level of clubs and societies. The "simple" citizens mostly do not know those arrangements and remain uninvolved, as, in the opinion of the decision makers, they are not needed at the round table for a successful fulfillment of the tasks.

But the trend of clubs and societies having problems gaining new members – "active" members in particular – continues, as the population is less willing to bind itself to institutions and associations. For this reason, it will be decisive to open up the regulation and participation arenas. Here, politics and administration often object, because this would result in "new confusion."

This will happen if no philosophy of participation has been worked out which might serve as orientation for management processes. Therefore, for a successful modern administration, clarification is needed as to what the overall concept and the management philosophy should look like from a strategic point of view.

Bibliography

Baecker, J., Borg-Laufs, M., Duda, L. & Matthies, E. (1992). Sozialer Konstruktivismus - eine neue Perspektive in der Psychologie. In S. J. Schmidt (Ed.), *Kognition und Gesellschaft. Der Diskurs des radikalen Konstruktivismus 2* (pp. 116-145). Frankfurt am Main: Suhrkamp.

Benz, A., Lütz, S., Schimank, U. & Simonis, G. (2007). Einleitung. In A. Benz, S. Lütz, U. Schimank & G. Simonis (Eds.), *Handbuch Governance. Theoretische Grundlagen und empirische Anwendungsfelder* (pp. 9-25). Wiesbaden: VS, Verl. für Sozialwiss.

Beck, K. (2011). *Politik geerdet. Ein Essay*. Berlin: Vorwärts-Buch.

Berger, P. L. & Luckmann, T. (1984). *Die gesellschaftliche Konstruktion der Wirklichkeit. Eine Theorie der Wissenssoziologie*. Frankfurt am Main: Fischer Taschenbuch Verl.

Czerwick, E. (2008). *Systemtheorie der Demokratie. Begriffe und Strukturen im Werk Luhmanns* (1st ed.). Wiesbaden: VS, Verl. für Sozialwiss.

Decker, F. (2005). Die Systemverträglichkeit der direkten Demokratie. Dargestellt an der Diskussion um die Einführung von plebiszitären Elementen in das Grundgesetz. *Zeitschrift für Politikwissenschaft, 4*, 1103-1147.

Fach, W. (1997). Die letzte Reform. Über den neuen „öffentlichen" Dienst. In E. Grande & B. Eberlein (Eds.), *Modernisierung des Staates?* (pp. 163-176). Baden-Baden: Nomos-Verl.-Ges.

Glasersfeld, E. (1996). *Radikaler Konstruktivismus. Ideen, Ergebnisse, Probleme*. Frankfurt am Main: Suhrkamp.

Hejl, P. M. (1992). Die zwei Seiten der Eigengesetzlichkeit. Zur Konstruktion natürlicher Sozialsysteme und zum Problem ihrer Regelung. In S. J. Schmidt (Ed.), *Kognition und Gesellschaft. Der Diskurs des radikalen Konstruktivismus 2* (pp. 167-213). Frankfurt am Main: Suhrkamp.

Hellmann, K.-U. & Fischer, K. (2003). Niklas Luhmanns politische Theorie in der politikwissenschaftlichen Diskussion. In K.-U. Hellmann, K. Fischer & H. Bluhm (Eds.), *Das System der Politik: Niklas Luhmanns politische Theorie* (pp. 9-16). Wiesbaden: Westdt. Verl.

Janisch, P. (1992). Die methodische Ordnung von Konstruktionen. Der Radikale Konstruktivismus aus Sicht des Erlanger Konstruktivismus. In S. J. Schmidt (Ed.), *Kognition und Gesellschaft. Der Diskurs des radikalen Konstruktivismus 2* (pp. 24 - 41). Frankfurt am Main: Suhrkamp.

Kaina, V. (2002). *Elitenvertrauen und Demokratie. Zur Akzeptanz gesellschaftlicher Führungskräfte im vereinten Deutschland.* Wiesbaden: Westdt. Verl.

Keupp, H. (2003). Lokale einrichtungen zur Förderung bürgerschaftlichen Engagements: Freiwilligenagenturen, Selbsthilfekontaktstellen, Senorenbüros u.Ä. - Chancen und Restriktionen. In Deutschland. Enquete-Kommission Zukunft des Bürgerschaftlichen Engagements (Ed.), *Bürgerschaftliches Engagement in den Kommunen* (pp. 13-51). Opladen: Leske + Budrich.

König, M. & König, W. (2010). Politische Kommunikation durch regierungsinitiierte Bürgerpartizipation? Die politisch Kommunikation im Kontext der Bürgerbeteiligung im Rahmen der Kommunal- und Verwaltungsreform in Rheinland-Pfalz. In K. Mok & M. Stahl (Eds.), *Düsseldorfer Forum Politische Kommunikation. Beiträge des 5. Düsseldorfer Forums Politische Kommunikation* (pp. 129-148). Berlin: Frank & Timme.

König, M. & König, W. (2011a). Deliberative Governancearenen. Die Überwindung kooperativer Problemlösungen in der deutschen Parteiendemokratie. *Journal für Generationengerechtigkeit*, 2, 65-69.

König, M. & König, W. (2011b). Deliberative Governance Arenen als Operationalisierungsvariante politischer Partizipation und Kognition. Politische Psychologie, 1, 98-110.

König, M. & König, W. (2012). Government public opinion research and consultation Experiences in deliberative marketing. In J. Lees-Marshment (Ed.), *The Routledge Handbook of Political Marketing.* (pp.48 -60). London/New York: Routledge.

Kooiman, J. (2003). *Governing as governance.* London [u.a.]: SAGE.

Kooiman, J. (2006). Governing as Governance. In G. F. Schuppert (Ed.), *Governance-Forschung. Vergewisserung über Stand und Entwicklungslinien* (pp. 149-172). Baden-Baden: Nomos Verl.-Ges.

Patzelt, W. J. (1998). Ein latenter Verfassungskonflikt? Die Deutschen und ihr parlamentarisches Regierungssystem. *Politische Vierteljahreszeitschrift, 4*, 725-757.

polis+sinus (2009). *Repräsentativbefragung im Rahmen der Bürgerbeteiligung zur Kommunal- und Verwaltungsreform. Ergebnisdokumentation.*

ProDialog (2009). *Nichtwähler in Deutschland. Panelbefragung zur Bundestagswahl 2009.* Berlin.

Sarcinelli, U. & König, M. (2010). Die Chancen von Politikberatung durch Bürgerbeteiligung – Das Beispiel der Kommunal- und Verwaltungsreform in Rheinland-Pfalz. *Newsletter Wegweiser Bürgergesellschaft ,6,* 1-6.

Sarcinelli, U., König, M. & König, W. (2008). Bürgerbeteiligung als Politikberatung? Ein "Werkstattsbericht" im Rahmen der Kommunal- und Verwaltungsreform in Rheinland-Pfalz. *Zeitschrift für Politikberatung ZPB, 3-4*, 586-594.

Sarcinelli, U., König, M. & König, W. (2009). *Bürgerbeteiligung im Rahmen der Kommunal- und Verwaltungsreform in Rheinland-Pfalz. Gutachten zur ersten und zweiten Stufe der Bürgerbeteiligung Oktober 2007 – September 2009.* Mainz/Landau: Staatskanzlei und Ministerium des Inneren und Für Sport Rheinland-Pfalz.

Sarcinelli, U., König, M. & König, W. (2010). Bürgerbeteiligung im Rahmen der Kommunal- und Verwaltungsreform in Rheinland-Pfalz. Gutachten zur Bürgerbeteiligung in der Freiwilligkeitsphase. Leitfaden für kommunale Gebietskörperschaften. Retrieved April 25, 2011, from http://www.ism.rlp.de/fileadmin/ism/downloads/moderne_verwaltung/kommunal-_und_verwaltungsreform/LeitfadenUniKoLaB%25C3%25BCrgerbeteiligung.pdf&ct=ga&cad=:s7:f2:v 0:d1:i1:ld:e1:p0:t1284913869:&cd=Xb-m1u5S-4Ys&usg=AFQjCNFZovWy8skoH1hN1CeujdAvrJEjiQ

Sarcinelli, U., König, M. & König, W. (2011). Bürgerbeteiligung in der Kommunal- und Verwaltungsreform. Aus Politik und Zeitgeschichte, 7-8/2011.

Schmidt, S. J. (1992). Medien, Kultur: Medienkultur. Ein konstruktivistisches Gesprächsangebot. In S. J. Schmidt (Ed.), *Kognition und Gesellschaft. Der Diskurs des radikalen Konstruktivismus 2* (pp. 425-450). Frankfurt am Main: Suhrkamp.

Liquid Democracy – Participation Model of the 21st century?

Sarah Bastgen, Katrin Winkler

In the following, the concept of liquid democracy is at first theoretically located and further clarified with regard to its mode of operation and precise fields of application. The article then goes on with the comparison of the concept with two other, current procedures of direct citizen participation as well as the analysis of a first implementation of the liquid democracy principle on the basis of the study commission entitled "Internet and Digital Society." By means of this comparison, both the potentials of liquid democracy as a method of citizen participation in the 21st century and the challenges, as wells as its limitations, are shown. The elaborations indicate the need for an extensive process of citizen education so as to fully exploit the existing opportunities for participation.

1 Introduction

The discussion on the reforming of the democratic system has been an element of various academic as well as media articles for quite some time. In particular, the progressing change of social environments places new demands on parliamentary democracy. At present, representation is constrained both by territorial and legislative terms. Personal environments, however, have changed with the effect that traditional social structures are breaking down and citizens' willingness to become involved in politics has changed as a result. Nowadays, political interest and participation is much more individualized, specialized, and also issue-specific. This development is caused by the decline of social cleavages and increasing pluralization, so that significant effects of the social structure are replaced by minor effects of specific socio-structural characteristics and the volatility of the electorate increases (Decker & Neu, 2007). In recent years, such a development has also been obvious in Germany. Thus, stagnating and falling voter turnouts, respectively, the growing political discontent, and the gradual loss of trust in political representatives manifests itself in increasing non-institutionalized, unconventional political participation:

"The fact that traditional forms of politics and political participation became less attractive to citizens as well as the fact that the magnitude of political integration within institutionalized politics has weakened – especially with regard to the young and the citizens of Eastern Germany –, should be considered warning signals." (Federal Bureau of Statistics, Wiesbaden, 2011, p. 376; translation by S.B. and K.W.)

Moreover, this also explains the circumstances that cause, in spite of the desire for more participation, most parties to still register a dramatic decrease in members (Niedermayer, 2011) and why election turnout stagnates or even declines. Projects and subjects like Stuttgart 21, non-smoker protection in Bavaria, or the school reform in Hamburg provide us with a perspective other than that of the passive citizen who is turned off by politics and clearly reveals a citizen's willingness to shape society. Those political issues demonstrate the need for procedures and methods that complement the traditional instruments of representative democracy. One of the concepts that seems to be exceedingly promising in this respect is that of liquid democracy.[1]

The concept, which is characterized by deliberative and discursive structures, has been discussed for some years, primarily on the internet. So far it has very rarely been a subject of scientific research. Liquid democracy is subjected to the assumption that all decisions in a democratic system should be genuinely based on the participation of each and every citizen. The term liquid democracy is to be understood as an allegory for the development of a new democratic concept, in which the existing personnel and institutional boundaries should be liquefied and, in doing such, democratic processes are supposed to become more dynamic. The actual term is an artificial name, which encompasses single political process ideas, such as delegated voting, as well as larger political participation concepts, up to the vision of a new political system. An analytically selective definition does not exist to date.

2 Liquid democracy - theoretical discourses

In the center of democracy as the only legitimate form of government are people as the sum of all individuals. In its political self-determination, the people constitute the state and thus become the sovereign (Frevel, 2004, p. 59). Since the exercising of authority is inevitably accompanied by the restriction of the civil rights and liberties as well as the self-determination of the individual, it has to be attributed – due to the democratic principle – to the will of the people in its function as sovereign (Kohler-Koch, Conzelmann & Knodt, 2004) and therefore must guarantee an effective political linkage mechanism. Authorization, accountability, and control are mechanisms that aim at linking decisions to the citizen's will. Consequently, norm setting and the exercise of sovereign authority are based on the continuous participation of the citizens *de jure* and *de facto*. Participation takes place in a direct form – through the negotiation of decisions within a discursive process, in which each citizen is allowed to participate, or by means of elected representatives. Control and effective political linkage, however, can only be realized if political processes are transparent and accountable. Another

1 The concept of liquid democracy is also defined as direct parliamentarianism or delegated voting (cf. Liquid.net).

normative standard is the socio-political principle of equality (Waschkuhn, 1998, p. 7). Ideally, in a democracy, the preferences of all citizens are considered according to a sophisticated criterion of equality (Hüller, 2006); at least equal political chances and open structures for those who are willing to participate must be guaranteed. Therefore politics are legitimized to the extent which they provide equal opportunities in consideration of citizen's interests and at the same time are suitable for accomplishing tasks and making decisions that are accepted by those affected and the citizenry. At the same time, those who exercise power have to be accountable to those they govern (Benz, 2005, pp. 267-268). Each democratic system – be it representative or direct – has to meet those standards.

In modern mass democracies like Germany, governmental institutions regulate community affairs; political parties and elected representatives are in charge of political will formation and interest aggregation. The central role of representatives is based on the reasoning that the inclusion of all citizens in any decision-making processes – an essential condition for the democratic ideal of the agora – is not feasible when considering the size of modern democracies. Besides, the citizens do not have the time, the political interest, or the necessary expertise to take part in every decision and vote in a reasonable manner (Riklin, 1980, p. 517) or to make informed decisions (Kriesi & Trechsel, 2008, pp. 61/63). The problems of the unequal participation of individual groups as well as the abstinence of lower social strata are also stated in this context (Linder, 1992, p. 128; Möckli, 1993, pp. 4/16). Therefore, institutions and procedures are required to receive the interests of the citizens and consider those so as to realize the democratic principle (Schmidt, 2000, p. 257). Representatives of direct and participatory democracy theories state, on the other hand, that according to this reasoning people's participation in the democratic process is not only mostly limited to going to the ballot box, but also that the will of the people is not put into effect due to the principle of majority rule. Furthermore, they refer to the risk that in the course of the development of political parties into cartel parties (Katz & Mair, 1995, 2009; Koole, 1996) and election campaign machineries, including the aim for voter maximization and the approach to the so-called median voter, the political profile of a party and therefore the creation of distinct collective identities could be lost (cf. convergence hypothesis, e.g. Saalfeld, 2007). Consequently there would no longer be a legitimate representation of the people, especially since party discipline – as unwritten law, the pre-forming of political decisions by experts and lobbyists hidden from the public gaze, and the fact that representatives are only subject to their own consciences (cf. second sentence of Article 38 par. 1 of the Basic Law for the Federal Republic of Germany) do not attest an independent exercise of power (Geser, 1996, p. 38). Accordingly, instruments with corrective and controlling functions need to be granted to citizens, to eliminate the democratic dilemma, to diminish the lack of input legitimacy, and to thus meet the democratic standards described above. This refers to an effective organization of the process of will formation and interest mediation, which assures the authentic participation of the citizens. Ideally, the citizen's interests should be directly transferred into the political process – as genuinely as possible and without any intermediary layers. A great importance is thus attached to active citizens' participation and effective exertion of influence on politics.

Those assumptions are also the basis of the concept of liquid democracy. Accordingly, liquid democracy is a form of democracy located in the sweet spot between representative and direct democracy. It is conceptualized as a sort of hybrid of existing concepts of democracy, which allows for elements of voting, representation, and participation as well. The citizens shall not only be represented, but also be allowed to become actively involved in politics – including simple as well as complex issues.

On the basis of concrete issues, each citizen is supposed to decide whether to delegate his/her vote – for instance due to a lack of expertise and/or limited capacities – to vote by him-/herself, or to abstain from voting – though, an obligation to participate is not intended. In principle, every interested citizen is allowed to participate in the discourse and ballot process – the exclusiveness of legitimacy caused by representative decision making is significantly reduced. The approach however, does not imply the abolition of political parties.

Liquid democracy's special characteristic is that the mode of participation can change (constantly). At the same time, this feature is the key instrument of control, which differentiates liquid democracy from traditional representative democracy. Each citizen is allowed to reclaim his/her vote and to delegate it to someone else. The other option would be to participate directly since s/he has already gained adequate expertise due to discussion, reading, or reflection.

Since individuals develop recommendations and decisions – without any intermediary layers – the legislative process is controlled and adjusted (if need be) directly by the citizens. The effective mechanism linking politics to the will of the people is guaranteed. At the same time, this approach leads to almost equal opportunities to participate and strengthens the pressure on politicians and parties to make decisions in line with the will of the community. Improved transparency, the comprehensive inclusion of all stakeholders in a deliberative will formation process and consequently an increased input and output legitimacy are inherent to the concept. Accordingly, liquid democracy implies a long-term integrating function regarding political and societal sections within processes of decision making and implementation (Linder, 2005, p. 256). It acts like a catalyst for broadening the political agenda and a political space that accepts opposing views (Foerster, 1953, p. 153). Moreover, a sociopolitical balance function is inherent in this new method of citizen participation since political competences are controlled not only *ex ante* but also *ex post*.

Referring to these elaborations, liquid democracy can be understood as a form of deliberative democracy. The procedural understanding of democracy, which underlies the model of deliberative democracy, is based on the quality and the institutional conditions of political communication as key criteria and sources of legitimacy. In particular, the discursive character of the political process has a legitimizing effect (Nanz & Steffek, 2005, p. 82). The focus is on participatory and open structures for the expression of collective will, in contrast to parliamentary interest aggregation (Scheuch, 2003, p. 54). The key principles of deliberation are (1) accountability towards those affected by decisions and (2) inclusiveness, which means consideration of all interests and arguments relevant stakeholders may have (Cohen & Sabel, 2003). Both principles can be realized by the participation of either the persons concerned or their representatives in the political will formation process and/or by linking will formation to a public sphere that is characterized by horizontal and vertical permeability.

3 The internet as a democratic instrument

Until now, the inclusion of all citizens has not been feasible. The new information and communication technologies – particularly the internet – however, allow for a rethinking and reforming of representative systems into more democratic ones which include the substantial and above all active involvement of the citizens in political will formation and decision-making processes. It allows not only a response to existing yet neglected needs to participate, but also the reestablishment of democratic functions that have been poorly implemented up to now: for instance the protection of minorities is strengthened through equal rights to express one's opinion independently of that opinion's influence. Furthermore, the access to politically relevant information and its availability is maximized; the responsiveness is enhanced by means of multiple touching points.

Ergo, the internet and the opportunities of participation associated with the medium allow for democratic discourse even in complex societies and make a large-scale dialogic process of will formation possible in the first place. The medium sets the stage for the principle of assembly implied in the concept of democracy through online debates, in which every citizen is allowed to participate. The results of the latest ARD/ ZDF online study (ZDF & Hessischer Rundfunk, 2011) show that the internet is now used by 73% of the German population (2010: 69.4%), including a considerably strong increase in those citizens 60 and above. Now 34.5% of this age group are online – a growth rate of 23% when compared to 2010. In addition to wide coverage, the internet almost eliminates temporal, spatial, and financial limitations in communication. Moreover, it allows not only for highly transparent political processes by means of persistent electronic storage and processing options, but ensures a high degree of inclusiveness (Cohen & Sabel 2003). According to Geser (1996, p. 37), the internet now for the first time provides the opportunity to make legislative proposals, consultation processes, and the individual behavior of the legislators fully accessible to all those interested and herewith create the cognitive requirements, which are essential for a rational exercise of political rights. The internet has become the agora of the 21st century, so to say.

4 *Liquid democracy as a liquefaction of democratic definitions*

Liquid democracy provides a solution for the practical implementation of democracy in the form of a digital agora. The fundamental notion of this theoretical framework is the "liquefaction" of certain democratic confines. Based on the application of adequate software (such as adhocracy, liquid feedback of the *Piratenpartei* (Pirate Party)), all interested persons are able to voice their concerns and preferences and to exercise their political rights in a digital discussion forum on the internet.

Although there is hitherto no unambiguous definition of the term, the analysis of liquid democracy as an addendum for the actual representational system proves productive with regard to new methods of civic participation.[2] With regard to Germany, this explicitly refers to an addendum of the respective state parliament by so-called policy-parliaments (cf. Liquid.net),[3] whereby every citizen will be provided with direct access to information on policies. In this respect, the liquefaction of democratic confines concerns both the participatory and the substantial dimension of the political system. The temporal dimension shows change in that the classical election (every 4 years) is used side by side with quorum elections, time limit elections, and permanent elections. A quorum election will make sense if in a very short time a certain issue enjoys public popularity along with a solution or recommendation within a policy-parliament. The quorum functions as a socio-political seismograph for issues relevant to a large portion of society. In contrast, a time limit election aims to reduce the risk of an overly long decision-making process in case of urgent problems. Though issues that admit no delay are subjected to the discursive process, they require prompt agreement for a decision. This modus operandi of elections can be understood in response to the critique that public dialogues are reform-resistant and retain the status quo (Waschkuhn, 1998, p. 510). Adventitiously a permanent election will occur since diverse issues are continuously discussed by intra-policy-parliaments, which ultimately resolve themselves in votes.

2 The following partially modified and added arguments are basing on the elaborations of the German registered association Liquid Democracy.

3 Liquid.net is a site of the registered association Liquid Democracy that presents basic approaches of the direct parliamentarianism and liquid democracy theory. Retrieved Feb. 10, 2012, from http://wiki.liqd.net/Direkter_Parlamentarismus/Einf%C3%BChrung.

Chart 1: Liquefaction of democratic dimensions

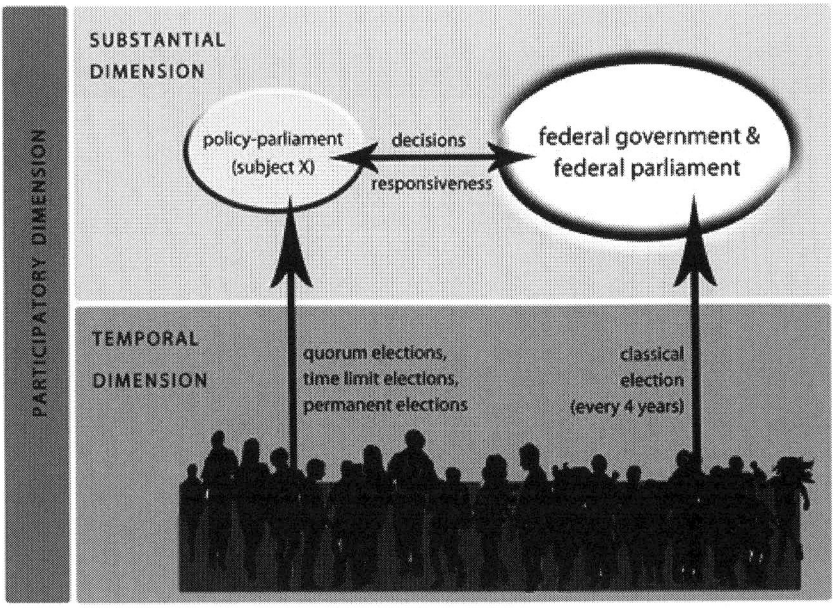

Source: Created by the authors

As an elementary substance of liquid democracy, the principle of delegated voting becomes first priority. According to this, the advantages of the representative and direct democracy will be integrated in a system that allows every citizen to participate directly or to delegate his/her vote to representatives, alliances, and/or parties. With regard to the political process, this means that there will be preceding policy-parliaments ahead of the legislative parliament, where concrete issues are discussed and developed.

Discussion forums, commentary runs, comparisons of texts and text annotation, co-text differentiations (according to the wiki principle), and also short opinion screenings, polls, and votes will be offered as tools of discourse. The crucial element is the transparency of the process. An easily comprehensible overview of what was discussed and what modified, what the actual state is, what the objectives are, which further steps exist, and what the next possibilities of participating are has to be ensured. Moreover, the cut-off points of participation have to be minimized in order to achieve proportionate "little" and "weaker" articles. Simultaneously, insignificant articles or abusive remarks have to be eliminated without censoring opinions (requirement of a netiquette).

Per se, every citizen holds one vote for every single decision on the respective issues in each policy-parliament. Within the policy-parliaments, every citizen has the opportunity to participate directly in the deliberative discussion and decision-making processes or to delegate the vote for an issue to another, active individual of the policy-parliament. Ergo one's own vote can be delegated to any other citizen who is entitled to vote or to a policy-specific alliance. Responsiveness as the indispensable condition of democracy is ensured since delegated votes are terminable at any moment: hence the participation modus operandi of each vote is liquid. The final responsibility for political acts permanently rests on the citizen, who can influence the decision him-/herself or, in case of delegating one's vote, implicitly back the decision.

Chart 2: Decision-making process with policy-parliaments

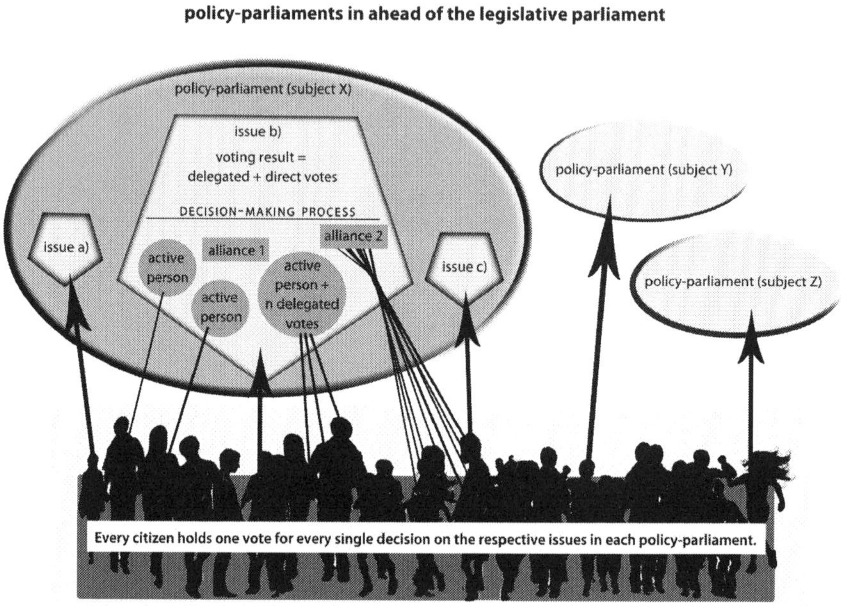

Source: Created by the authors

Alliances in policy-parliaments consist of active individual members, e.g. an association of opponents of nuclear power – irrespective of their party political affiliation or their memberships in NGOs – in the policy-parliament "environment" on the topic "renewable energy." These alliances are nonpartisan in the sense that individuals who have no party affiliation can be directly involved in the debate plus be associated with policy-parliament alliances. Nevertheless, it shall not be precluded that an alliance adopts a party's ideological character. If a topic of one policy-parliament concerns another issue of the same or another policy-parliament, the odds are that the alliance can be likewise engaged in an activity dealing with the additional issue – finally the individual holds one vote for every issue of each policy-parliament. The voting result for one topic of a policy-parliament includes both the delegated and direct votes.

By implication, the citizens can decide if some policy-parliaments have individual priority for themselves, so that by virtue of their personal stakes or corresponding expertise they contribute directly, delegate their votes, or even abstain from voting. The delegation of a vote to an individual or a member of an alliance has to be accepted by the delegates.

5 Current attempts at civic participation

In the recent past there have been diverse initiatives and efforts taking the political creative willingness at the German federal and the European level into account, such as the European Citizens' Initiative, which concedes European citizens direct participation in European politics: One million citizens are needed to request the European Commission to advance a legislative act for a specific issue.

In Germany there is volition to meet the increased demands on participation by means of continuous adjustments to the petition rights, especially online petitions, (modification of the legal framework for the work of the petitions committee of the German Bundestag) or online consultations (e.g. the "*Zukunftsdialog über Deutschland,*" initiated by Chancellor Angela Merkel 2011/12). The aspiration of these top-down proposals is to (re-)take the citizens' concerns seriously and, in this context, to enhance the responsiveness significantly. The immediate linkage of politics to society would be improved on the one hand to expedite the political legitimation of the representatives and on the other hand to consolidate the persistence of the democracy. But are these measures in a position to effectively meet the demands on participation and implicate a reduction of the democratic legitimacy deficit?

5.1 Online Petitions

In 2005, the German Bundestag integrated online petitions as a trial model. The online petition system was adopted permanently in October 2008 after the testing phase was completed successfully. The diversification of the petition right, as an everyman's right documented in Article 17 of the German Basic Law, now enables the addressing and co-signing of a petition online. In consequence, a simplification of individual participation rights proceeded. In the course of the reinforced utilization of online petitions, the petition committee modified the fundamental terms and conditions for requests and complaints in November 2011: The fixed term for co-signing as well as authoring articles on a discussion forum (substitute 3 with 4 weeks) was amended on January 1, 2012. Besides, there are plans for modification of the co-signing whereupon petition signing is completed using a standardized and pseudonymized form (Committee on Petitions of the German Bundestag, 2011a). Applicants for petitions and fellow signatories benefit from such a fundamental harmonization of standards.

However, on closer consideration of the petition procedure, the actual effect and hence the opportunities of influence become obvious: Petitions with a differential priority setting and urgency, respectively, could forward to the Federal Government by the Federal Parliament: the documents can be distinguished either as "material for one's work," as "suggestions," or as "considerations."[4] In 2012 a total of 16,849 petitions were counted, with a total number of 15,993 considered petitions (Committee on Petitions of the German Bundestag, 2011b, p. 11). 6,984 of the considered petitions underwent a parliamentary consultation. As few as 12 of those considered petitions were distinguished and referred by the Federal Parliament as "considerations" (0.08%) to the Federal Government. In addition, the German Bundestag referred 85 petitions as "suggestions" (0.53%), 123 petitions as "material for one's work" (0.77%), and 86 petitions as "plain assignments" (0.54%) to the Federal Government (ibid., p. 92). De facto only 306 (1.92%) of roughly 16,000 petitions which were considered in the German Bundestag were passed on to the Federal Government. In addition, not even half (43.68%) of the petitions were consulted in the German Bundestag and not more than 5.85% (936) of the petitions in the German Bundestag got abidance (Committee on Petitions of the German Bundestag, 2011b).

Against this background the extent to which the German Bundestag and the Federal Government, respectively, take the requests and the direct participation of the citizens seriously is questionable and the importance of citizens' suggestions in the following consultation and resolution process appears doubtful. The empirical explanation does not purport that the concerns of the citizens are received and implemented sufficiently. At least it is inexplicable to a citizen as to what extent his/her interests will be considered. But the democratic system is a long-term confidence system. In consequence, only if the concerns of the citizens are not observed alone but rather incorporated partially, at the very least by integrating them into policy guidelines and enforcing into effective action, will voters be mobilized and enabled for politics (Poguntke, 2000). However, the control mechanisms, which are indispensable for the protection of re-

4 "material for one's work": The contents are so important that they shall be integrated in actual or future reflections. "suggestions": The executive authority should reconsider its decision and it seems to be advisable to find a way out. "considerations": The consideration shows the government that the Federal Parliament demands an adaptation of decisions in the interest of the petitioners as quickly as possible.

sponsiveness, prove elusive in consequence of the deficient and hardly comprehensible petition proceeding.

5.2 "Zukunftsdialog über Deutschland"

The "*Zukunftsdialog*" by Angela Merkel was initiated in spring 2011. The project is divided in different sequences. At the center there are the three questions: *How do we want to live together?*, *What do we want to live from?*, and *How do we want to learn together?* In order to work out perspectives and political action proposals by means of an interdisciplinary cooperation, these three questions were discussed with 100 experts from scholarly fields and practice in the first instance. On February 1, 2012 the project transitioned into a new phase: the public dialogue, which aims at the discussion and the adaptation of citizen's requests and experiences for a future-oriented political practice. The discussion and the submission will be made by using a two-and-a-half-month online consultation, plus three additional discussion meetings in several German towns. Thereby the stimuli of the citizens shall influence the experts' discussion. Following this process, the suggestions shall be finalized, reviewed, evaluated, and also be published in a book, presumably in June 2012.

Initially the public dialogue as an internet-based consultation instrument is proving to be an adequate attempt to have regard for the citizens' willingness to shape society at the highest political level. Nevertheless here, too, arises the question of the actual charisma and stringent adaption of citizens' contributions. On the website of the online dialogue you can read:

"One objective of the public dialogue is to find out good ideas and practice examples [of the citizens]. That is why citizens could put their own suggestions for actions forward for discussion and they could report on their experiences." (www.dialog-ueber-deutschland.de)[5]

According to these explanations, it seems to be that the real cause is not the actual processing and implementation of the requests – i.e. true participation – but rather to foster a political expression of opinion and discussion. The way in which the contributions will ultimately find entrance into future political practices is not (yet) comprehensible to the citizens. The degree of responsiveness is low insofar as effective dialogue between citizens, the Federal Government, and the chancellor, respectively, does not occur.

5 www.dialog-ueber-deutschland.de is a site that presents the comprehensive work of the "Zukunftsdialog" published by the Press and Information Office of the Federal Government by order of the Office of the Federal Chancellor. Retrieved Feb. 20, 2012, from https://www.dialog-ueber-deutschland.de/DE/60-FAQ/faq_node.html;jsessionid=7936218994D01CE81F-C0D732E14A46A7.s6t2#a488004.

It is even a debatable point whether the capabilities of such an online consultation have been realized and whether or not the "products" of the citizens are taken seriously and given the respect due to them. One indication for this supposition is illustrated with the example of the statement of the initiator, Angela Merkel:

“Well, it is an approach for identifying oneself and being heard too. Democracy, if it comes to a decision, relies on representative results. That means we have to give everyone a chance to participate. Insofar I think it is more direct communication between politics and citizens, but not yet a new form of decision-making. […] But I think it is simply good that people just can contribute their ideas and above all things to network themselves, to evaluate their thoughts and thereby to learn of each other, to stimulate each other, without large barriers such as writing a letter and throwing it in a mailbox” (pol-di.net e.V.[6]/politik-digital.de).[7]

That was the answer of the chancellor to the question of whether or not online participation processes could be the gambit towards more direct democracy. This statement emphasizes that a vertical power relation still predominates in the linkage between politics and citizens (Ebert & Bazil, 2011). Especially the last sentence indicates and accentuates evidently that the exchange of ideas between politicians – themselves part of the citizenry – and citizens is not as important as the exchange of ideas within the society. According to these remarks, a realistic exertion of influence by the citizens is at least not envisaged. *Ad interim,* the *Zukunftsdialog* aroused public criticism inasmuch as it is still functioning as an election campaign activity of the current Federal Government and acting chancellor, respectively (Müller, 2012). Criticism to such an extent does not benefit the confidence of the citizens; it has counter-productive effects on general political participation and furthermore illustrates a non-transparent procedure.

With recourse to the previous examples, citizens’ effective political opportunities to influence politics are conspicuously deficient. Thus the high quorums, restrictive choice of topics, or the non-binding nature of petitions present a particular obstacle for direct participation. Likewise, it is problematic that in many cases the population is not satisfactorily informed before the implementation of a decision or even subsequent to decision-making processes – which are not sufficiently public and transparent.

6 pol-di.net e.V. / politik-digital.de: Live-Interview mit Angela Merkel. Steffen Wenzel im Interview mit der Bundeskanzlerin, Retrieved Feb. 11, 2012, from http://politik-digital.de/politik-digital-de-im-gespraech-mit-der-bundeskanzlerin/.

7 „Na ja, es ist ein Zugang, sich sozusagen kenntlich zu machen und auch gehört zu werden. Demokratie, wenn sie dann zur Entscheidung kommt, ist allerdings ja immer noch darauf angewiesen, dass wir repräsentative Resultate haben. Das heißt, wir müssen dann allen die Chance geben, bei etwas mitzumachen. Und insofern glaube ich, es ist mehr direkte Kommunikation zwischen Politik und Bürger, aber noch nicht eine neue Form der Entscheidungsfindung. […] Aber ich finde es einfach gut, dass Menschen ohne große Barrieren, Brief schreiben, in den Kasten werfen, einfach mal ihre Ideen mit eingeben können und sich vor allen Dingen auch vernetzen können, Gedanken bewerten können und damit ja auch vielmehr voneinander lernen, einander Anregungen geben entsteht [sic].“.

Against this background, de facto integration and civic participation are not optimal and occasionally, they contradict the main idea and ultimate ambition of democracy: sovereignty of the people. Only the sovereignty of the people can legitimize the exercise of representative sovereignty and authorize governmental institutions – now and then a forgotten aspect of democratic systems and political practice.

6 Implementation of liquid democracy: enquetebeteiligung.de and adhocracy

Against the legally binding character of petitions as an instrument of direct citizen participation, the participation offer of the study commission "Internet and Digital Society" installed by the German Bundestag follows the institution resolution:

"The study commission involves the public in its work to a special degree. The commission regularly informs on its activities as transparent as possible by providing and publishing information on the website of the German Bundestag. Furthermore the website offers options for participation which let public suggestions be known appropriately for the work of the commission" (German Bundestag, 2010, p. 4).

Hence, the platform enquetebeteiligung.de[8] and the modus operandi of the study commission, respectively, can be classified as a first attempt to realize the direct involvement of citizens in the discussion and decision-making process at a federal level. The commission is composed of 17 experts from the commission and the citizens as a collective actor – i.e. the "18th expert." Since the end of February 2011, citizens have had the possibility to comment on the working papers of the commission, to generate their own proposals, and to discuss them on the platform enquetebeteiligung.de. The platform thereby enables every citizen to ask questions on the subject. The platform is based on the concept of liquid democracy and thus it can be classified as a policy-parliament. The realization of the liquid democracy concept is ensued by the software adhocracy, which enables the practical implementation of a well-structured discourse and vote delegation:

"The parliament [German Bundestag] was the first in the world to use the internet to invite the interested public to cooperation on equal terms. [Also] a blog and a forum were set up to further improve the dialogue between the commission and the citizens" (Study commission "Internet and Digital Society" of the German Bundestag, 2011).[9]

Since the launch of the participation platform, 2,498 members, 241 proposals, 2,215 comments, and 13,073 votes have been recorded (date 20 February 2012). Within seven

8 Enquetebeteiligung.de is the participation platform that presents the work of the study commission "Internet and Digital Society" of the German Bundestag (https://enquetebeteiligung.de/).

9 „Als erstes Parlament weltweit nutzt [der Bundestag] das Internet, um die interessierte Öffentlichkeit zu einer Mitarbeit auf Augenhöhe einzuladen. [Außerdem] wurden ein Blog und ein Forum eingerichtet, um den Dialog zwischen der Kommission und den Bürgerinnen und Bürgern weiter zu verbessern.".

days (February 13 - 20, 2012) 64 new members joined the platform, the suggestions increased by 12, the comments showed an increase of 8 and the number of votes grew by 258 (Enquetebeteiligung.de).[10] The online forum also achieved success: 177 topics were discussed, 526 articles were prepared, and 11,521 users were registered by 20 February 2012 (Study commission "Internet and Digital Society" of the German Bundestag).[11] Against the background that the participation offers of the study commission are not communicated in the best possible way – for the purpose of a comprehensive information campaign – it becomes obvious that such participation opportunities are well frequented and of widely shared interest. The interim report also shows that the commission gives weight to the citizen suggestions for the following course of the discussion by including them in the reports of the respective project groups: "Two of twelve recommendations of action were adopted [for the interim report media competency of 21 October 2011] by the online participation platform enquetebeteiligung.de of the study commission" (Study commission "Internet and Digital Society" of the German Bundestag, 2012). On a positive note, the user-friendly surface allows greatly simplified access. Therefore the participation platform of the study commission can indeed be appreciated as an attempt to involve the citizens in processes of political will-formation by using methods of liquid democracy. Nevertheless, it should be noted that the study commission merely prepares decisions on complex and relevant issues. The reports therefore have the status of recommendations, but are not legally effective (cf. Rule 56, par. 1 & 4, Rules of Procedure of the German Bundestag, 2009, pp. 37-38).

One essential deficit is common to all of these examples: the supposed interest in the concerns of citizens on the part of the representatives (German Bundestag, 2012).[12] However, all examples show an engagement on the part of the political actors to include expressions of the citizens in the process of will formation. Measured against the petitions that underwent a parliamentary consultation, against the aim of the "*Zukunftsdialog*" and the statements of the chancellor, respectively, as well as the mere recommendatory character of the study commission by virtue of its function, the definitive influence should be evaluated as less than convincing.

Liquid democracy can thwart this loss of democracy due to the consequently transparent, discursive and deliberative process. Because of the broad participation of the citizens in every policy discussion, the politicians will be more or less forced to stringently aggregate the request of the people. Otherwise the representatives will risk their relationship of trust and thereby their re-election. As a result, the principle of liquid

10 As of 13 February 2012: 2,434 members · 409 suggestions · 2,207 comments · 12,815 votes; as of 20 February 2012: 2,498 members · 421 suggestions · 2,215 comments · 13,073 votes.

11 Study commission "Internet and Digital Society" of the German Bundestag is a site that presents the work of the study commission "Internet and Digital Society". (http://www.bundestag.de/internetenquete/.).

12 According to a user survey more than 70% of those who use the platform enquetebeteiligung.de believe that they cannot influence politics.

democracy promotes the departure of representatives, who are solely subjected to the characteristic style of their party and their individual conscience. Then, direct and long-term established participation will not be regarded as a problem of less expertise and qualitatively inferior decisions but rather it will be accepted as an optimal, individual, and collective exhaustion of human and social capital. Analogous to that, the vertical power relation between politics and state, respectively, and society will be reduced and decisions will achieve a higher degree of acceptance by the society. The democratic system will reach a new benchmark of confidence and thus stabilizes as well as ensures its own persistence.

7 Discussion: optimized, authentic democracy via liquid democracy?

> "[T]he participation of all citizens upon the debatably elucidative decision-making process" (Euchner 1969, as cited by Waschkuhn, 1998, p. 18)

Even if the concept of liquid democracy was discussed over the last few years as an instrument of reinforced citizen participation, its application is in the early stages of development and it is therefore applied in a restricted context: e.g. as a tentative method, similar to a test version of online consultation of the study commission "Internet and Digital Society" as well as an intra-party organization concept so as to implement grassroots democracy in the shape of liquid feedback as used by the *Piratenpartei* (Pirate Party) in Berlin. The existing experiments in liquid democracy implementation, e.g. the study commission, allow observation of such as well as how it is possible for people to work out (complex) topics of society in an objective and collaborative manner. There, citizens of the internet community can "meet" to discuss issues of the internet and its social impact and (consequently) work out productive common position papers. Due to the technical options, which are created by globalized communication networks now more than ever, daring more democracy appears to be (a goal) within reach. Nevertheless, as to the realization of liquid democracy as a new way of citizen participation, several important aspects shall be taken into account.

First of all, the risk of a digital divide should be considered – a social cleavage between people who have access to the internet and those who are excluded from access – be it because of a lack of know-how or of material reasons. In order to fulfill the democratic principle of equal opportunities and at least equal access to the political process respectively, it is necessary to ensure barrier-free internet access to every citizen. This could be realized in the form of free citizen participation cafes – e.g. in Administrative Offices for Citizens or similar public buildings. And even though the number of users is steadily increasing – above all among the older segment of the population – at least at this moment in time there is risk of an intergenerational conflict, especially because younger, well-educated (often male) actors are those who control modern information technologies, even today. This fact – in the context of a general over-aging of western industrial nations – can lead to certain sections of the population being critical of liquid democracy because they cannot handle these technologies well or they are unwilling to adapt. In order to use existing opportunities optimally and to establish liquid democracy as a new participation method as well as to increase the circle of users and the public range of the recommendations by policy-parliaments or study commissions, the democratic system needs the stringent integration of these participation options into political education schemes. Thus equal internet access and the development of citizens' skills for using liquid democracy instruments are mutually dependent. Ideally, everyone must have free access to education schemes and training opportunities in such a way that one can adequately and meaningfully contribute to the discourse.

The risk of dominance by an educated elite is an additional argument, which substantiates the centrality of more comprehensive education schemes as a requirement for realizing liquid democracy. Liquid democracy is grounded on written discursive processes, which benefit those with high cultural capital (Bourdieu, 1983) who can express themselves eloquently and persuasively. This may result in the development of an educated elite that occupies the opinion leadership and consequently the social prevalence. Against this background, actors who are less well educated or cannot express themselves appropriately in a written form are forced to content themselves with delegating their own votes. Therefore the participatory component would be mostly lost on these citizens. Only more comprehensive political education schemes can thwart the uncertainty of the elite development and allow for using immediate participation options in terms of the liquid democracy concept. Concomitant with this is the necessity of a comprehensive obligation on the part of politicians to inform. For instance the integration of all media as multipliers into policy-parliament decisions is easily conceivable. The interplay of providing public internet access points and education schemes as well as training opportunities together with a high amount of obligatory information antagonizes the potential risks of a digital divide, the manifestation of an educated elite, and the accumulation of information by few actors.

With regard to a broad establishment of the concept including an adequate political momentousness and impact, respectively, one must beg the question of inclusiveness. Liquid democracy has no circumscribed target audience. The concept is scalable in such way that it enables the implementation of discursive democratic processes at all levels and in all organization forms: i.e. in companies and in civil society organizations, in political parties and in initiatives, at the municipal level, or even at state, federation, or on a European level.

However the openness and the legal structure, respectively, of the process is a debatable point. Should every EU-citizen be allowed to participate in German policy-parliaments? There is no apparent reason against such dissolution of boundaries of the discourse – perhaps the process actually will be enriched by valuable (intercultural) expertise. First and foremost in the case of issues relevant to society as a whole, e.g. climate change or sustainability, there is no reason for limiting participation. Quite the opposite, the possibility of participation may contribute to the development of a European identity and as a result of this, to European integration. There might be further discussion on whether the right to vote should be restricted to particular groups, but not the participation in discussions itself.

Further, the question of safety and possibility of manipulation has to be clarified: Political processes are about the assertion of specific interests to others. Thus, a political prevalence automatically accrues. Hence all components of the political process have to be secured to manipulations to thwart the development of an oligarchy. Security applies to policy-parliaments and the same is true for democratic votes as the foundation of future legally binding decisions. During the discourse, it is crucial to consider all articles and that all articles of all citizens involved could be modified by the participants themselves – ideally with reference to the modification or history. An arrangement system – i.e. well-defined and universal rules for structuring articles must also exist so as to deal equally with every article. Above all, more extensive questions e.g. on the security of e-voting have to be discussed in public if liquid democracy software solutions will not only be used for structured discussions and preparations of opinions but rather for concrete and legally binding votes on topics which have subsequent and real consequences for the society. Furthermore these questions will have ultimate brisance in situations where decisions concern the whole society.

The risk that liquid democracy benefits an oligarchic sovereign reality is based on the option of delegating one's vote which is inherent in the concept of liquid democracy and which could result in the accumulation of votes by single actors or alliances. At this point, Robert Michels' "iron law of oligarchy" (1911) must be noted, which postulates a development appearing in all social systems: In the course of advanced bureaucratization, democratic social systems adopt oligarchic structures which ultimately corrupt the system (Giddens, 2009, p. 789). The key to abrogate the law lies in precisely preventing this bureaucratization. This is exactly where liquid democracy comes into play. So if institutional players succeed in clustering expert committees as temporary personal compositions, followed by their early rescission, there is an actual chance that the "iron law of oligarchy" cannot evolve.

The danger is that the participants of the policy-parliaments consequently choose to delegate their votes unto very few activists, thus the liquid democracy would degenerate into a representative democracy. However, it seems unlikely that pure direct or representative structures will be established. It is more probable that topics, which need a high degree of specific expertise and can only be contributed by certain social actors, will establish oligarchy structures. The solution is the implementation of extensive training measures that are able to establish an information equilibrium. In addition, an adequate statement based on the actual development status of liquid democracy cannot be made about the extent to which liquid democracy will increase citizen participation at the level of society as a whole. The concept allows every citizen to participate in the discourse of relevant topics and contribute personal ideas and proposals for solution. Liquid democracy also enables the creation of community structure independent of territorial regions. Thus, citizens are able to "assemble", e.g. at a federal level, and discuss problems relating to society as a whole. But the behavior of the people is not predictable: Will the general public actively participate or decide for oligarchically shaped structures? It is possible that the actors who are strongly involved in politics are also those who poll most of the votes. Hence, there is a chance that citizens will participate to a large extent, with the result that there will be no explicit opinion leadership and a very lengthy decision-making process.

8 Conclusion

As illustrated above, the concept of liquid democracy is a meaningful amendatory instrument in terms of the intensification of a discursive parliamentary process. Due to the fact that the citizens are the agenda setters (again), and beyond that, the *ex post* and *ex ante* controllers as well as revisers, the democratic and legitimacy deficit is mitigated. The democratic standards of accountability, transparency, and control, together with equal opportunities and open structures, respectively, for those who are willing to participate are met. This is because all methods of direct democracy implied by the concept of liquid democracy feature initiative, legitimacy, and approval functions as well as veto, revision, and balance functions. Moreover, an opposition function is attributed to the methods (Luthardt, 1994, p. 35).

These functions are particularly effective due to the fact that citizens' concerns can be constitutively involved in the political process. In case the concerns are voted on and approved in policy-parliaments, they have the direct and decisive effect of a suggestion or a consultation. Even if a concern is not approved, based on a public and transparent discourse, it results in an indirect effect: the informal adaption of this demand in the political agenda.

Hence, there is a need for comprehensive and partially profound education and development processes in terms of a new political culture so as to ensure the ideal of deliberative democracy inherent in the concept of liquid democracy und therewith as much civic participation as possible. Such processes require time and the willingness – in particular the willingness of political actors – to engage oneself in the new culture of civic participation. Simultaneously the social implementation of the altered culture of political participation is of major importance. However, this seems to be more likely the case, the more the citizens could perceive – through the political decisions – that politicians take their involvement seriously and that they actually influence politics.

As is generally known, electoral abstinence and the increase of unconventional participation are not necessarily associated with political apathy and disenchantment with politics: in contrast they are an indicator of the recovery of the people's own sovereignty qua the right to participate politically, which result in decisions broadly accepted by society. The empowerment of civil society in terms of decision making causes responsible and sustainable action. The inclusion of all stakeholders in political decisions and therewith decisions that concern society guarantees that the outcome reflects the preferences prevalent in the society and that governmental actions are linked to the will of the people. The paradox of participation can similarly be mitigated, since instead of including the citizens in the phase of decision-making and implementation, those affected by an issue are confronted with the consequences at the very beginning of the political process. Consequently, they are able to actively make use of their veto and control options.

In spite of the potential risks mentioned above and the fact that liquid democracy is a young concept, the implementation of which is not yet properly developed, it is worth working toward the realization of liquid democracy (German Bundestag, 2012), if for no other reason than to gain empirical results and to see how the concept proves itself.

Bibliography

Basic Law of the Federal Republic of Germany (as of July 21, 2010). Art. 38 Abs. 1 Satz 2 GG. Retrieved Feb. 20, 2012, from http://www.bundestag.de/dokumente/rechtsgrundlagen/grundgesetz/index.html.

Benz, A. (2005). Politikwissenschaftliche Diskurse über demokratisches Regieren im europäischen Mehrebenensystem. In: H. Bauer, P. M Huber & K. Sommermann (Eds.), Demokratie in Europa (pp. 253-280). Tübingen: Mohr Siebeck.

Bourdieu, P. (1983). Ökonomisches Kapital, kulturelles Kapital, soziales Kapital. In: R. Kreckel (Ed.), Soziale Ungleichheit (pp. 183-198). Göttingen: Schwartz.

Cohen, J. & Sabel C. (2003). Sovereignty and Solidarity in the EU. In: J. Zeitlin & D. Trubek (Eds.), Governing Work and Welfare in a New Economy: European and American Experiments (pp. 345-375). Oxford: Oxford University Press.

Committee on Petitions of the German Bundestag (2011a). Pressemitteilung vom 16.11.2011. Petitionsausschuss ändert Verfahrensgrundsätze. Retrieved Feb. 2, 2012, from http://www.bundestag.de/presse/pressemitteilungen/2011/pm_1111161.html.

Committee on Petitions of the German Bundestag (2011b). Der Jahresbericht des Petitionsausschusses. Ausgabe 2011. Retrieved Feb. 14, 2012, from https://www.btg-bestellservice.de/pdf/20460000.pdf.

Decker, F. & Neu, V. (Eds.). (2007). Handbuch der deutschen Parteien. Wiesbaden: VS Verlag.

Ebert, H., & Bazil, V. (2011). Das Bürgerbild in politischen Reden. Koblenz/Königswinter: University Koblenz-Landau & Verband der Redenschreiber deutscher Sprache. Retrieved Feb. 2, 2012, from http://www.aktive-buergerschaft.de/fp_files/Nachrichtendienst/Studie Buergerbild.pdf.

Federal Bureau of Statistics, Wiesbaden (2011). Datenreport 2011. Kapitel 14. Demokratie und politische Partizipation. Retrieved Feb. 12, 2012, from destatis database. https://www.destatis.de/DE/Publikationen/Datenreport/Downloads/Datenreport2011Kap14.pdf?__blob=publicationFile

Foerster, F. W. (1953). Schule und Charakter. Moralpädagogische Probleme des Schullebens. Recklinghausen: Paulus Verlag.

Frevel, B. (2004). Demokratie, (1st ed.). Wiesbaden: VS Verlag.

German Bundestag (2009). Rules of Procedure of the German Bundestag. Rule 56. Retrieved Feb. 14, 2012, from https://www.btg-bestellservice.de/pdf/80060000.pdf.

German Bundestag (2012). Experten: Internet hat nur eingeschränkte Wirkung auf politische Teilhabe. Enquete-Kommission „Internet und digitale Gesellschaft“ (Anhörung) - 19.03.2012, Retrieved Mar. 27, 2012, from http://www.bundestag.de/presse/hib/2012_03/2012_140/02.html.

Geser, H. (1996). Auf dem Wege zur "Cyberdemocracy"? Auswirkungen der Computernetze auf die politische Kommunikation. In H. Geser: Online Publikationen. Zürich: University Zürich. Retrieved Feb. 2, 2012, from http://www.geser.net/intcom/t_hgeser00.pdf.

Giddens, A. (2009). Sociology (6th ed.). Hoboken: John Wiley & Sons.

Hüller, T. (2006). Demokratisierung der EU durch bürgerschaftliche und zivilgesellschaftliche Partizipation. Retrieved Mar. 15, 2012, from https://www.dvpw.de/fileadmin/docs/2006x-Huller.pdf.

Katz, R. S., & Mair, P. (1995). Changing Models of Party Organization and Party Democracy: The Emergence of the Cartel Party. Party Politics 1 (1), 5–28.

Katz, R. S., & Mair, P. (2009). The Cartel Party Thesis: A Restatement. Perspectives on Politics 7 (4), 753-766.

Kohler-Koch, B.; Conzelmann, T. & Knodt, M. (2004). Europäische Integration - Europäisches Regieren. Wiesbaden: VS Verlag.

Koole, R. (1996). Cadre, Catch-All or Cartel? A Comment on the Notion of the Cartel Party. Party Politics 2 (4), 507-523.

Kriesi, H., & Trechsel, A. H. (2008). The politics of Switzerland: continuity and change in a consensus democracy. Cambridge/New York: Cambridge University Press.

Linder, W. (1992). Staatshandeln zwischen Akzeptanz und Blockade: Wie prägend ist das „Volk?“. In H. Abromeit & W. W. Pommerehne (Eds.), Staatstätigkeit in der Schweiz (pp. 121-143). Bern/Stuttgart/Wien: Haupt Verlag.

Linder, W. (2005). Schweizerische Demokratie. Institutionen, Prozesse, Perspektiven (2nd.). Bern/Stuttgart/Wien: Haupt Verlag.

Luthardt, W. (1994). Direkte Demokratie: ein Vergleich in Westeuropa (1st ed.). Baden-Baden: Nomos Verlagsgesellschaft.

Michels, R. (1911). Zur Soziologie des Parteiwesens in der modernen Demokratie: Untersuchungen über die oligarchischen Tendenzen des Gruppenlebens. Leipzig: Werner Klinkhardt.

Möckli, S. (1993). Stärken und Schwächen der direkten Demokratie in der Schweiz. Erweiterte Fassung eines Referates an der Delegiertenversammlung des Forums Helveticum. St. Gallen: University St. Gallen, Campus Koblenz. Retrieved Oct. 25, 2009, from http://www.ipw.unisg.ch/org/ipw/web.nsf/ SysWeb Ressources/202_1993/$FILE/202.pdf.

Müller, P. (2012). Kommunikation der Kanzlerin – Bürgerdialog empört die SPD. Retrieved Mar. 10, 2012, from http://www.spiegel.de/politik/deutschland/0,1518,818321,00.html.

Nanz, P. & Steffek, J. (2005). Legitimation durch Deliberation? Die Rolle der Zivilgesellschaft in der Supranationalen Politik. In: M. Knodt & B. Finke (Eds.), Europäische Zivilgesellschaft – Konzepte, Akteure, Strategien (pp. 79-102). Wiesbaden: VS Verlag.

Niedermayer, O. (2011). Parteimitglieder in Deutschland: Version 2011. Arbeitshefte a. d. Otto-Stammer-Zentrum, Nr. 18, Berlin: FU Berlin.

Poguntke, T. (2000). Parteiorganisation im Wandel. Gesellschaftliche Verankerung und organisatorische Anpassung im europäischen Vergleich. Wiesbaden: Westdeutscher Verlag.

Riklin, A. (1980). Stimmbeteiligung in der direkten Demokratie. In J. P. Müller (Ed.), Recht als Prozeß und Gefüge. Festschrift für Hans Huber zum 80. Geburtstag (pp. 513-528). Bern: Stämpfli Verlag.

Saalfeld, T. (2007). Parteien und Wahlen. Baden-Baden: Nomos Verlag.

Scheuch, M. (2003). Demokratie per Mausklick - Neue Informationstechnologien und ihre Auswirkungen auf Demokratietheorie. Stuttgart: ibidem- Verlag.

Schmidt, M. G. (2000). Demokratietheorien. Eine Einführung (3rd ed.). Wiesbaden: VS Verlag.

Study commission "Internet and Digital Society" of the German Bundestag (2011). Zwischenbericht der Enquete-Kommission „Internet und digitale Gesellschaft". Retrieved Feb. 20, 2012, from http://dipbt.bundestag.de/dip21/btd/17/056/1705625.pdf.

Study commission "Internet and Digital Society" of the German Bundestag (2012). Im Plenum: Zwischenberichte der Enquete vom 10. Januar 2012. Retrieved Feb. 20, 2012, from https://www.bundestag.de/internetenquete/Plenardebatte_2012-01-20/index.jsp.

Waschkuhn, A. (1998). Demokratietheorien. Politiktheoretische und ideengeschichtliche Grundzüge. München: R. Oldenbourg Verlag.

ZDF & Hessischer Rundfunk (2011). Pressemitteilung. ARD/ZDF-Onlinestudie 2011: 3 von 4 Deutschen sind online – starker Zuwachs bei den Über-60-Jährigen. Retrieved Feb. 20, 2012, from http://www.ard-zdf-onlinestudie.de/index.php?id=264.

Infrastructure and Participation: How Formal and Informal Participation Methods Can Be Interlinked

Henning Banthien, Andrea Versteyl, Martina Richwien

The aim of this paper is to outline an innovative approach by which to link formal and informal modes of participation. To this end the concepts of formal and informal participation will first be outlined and placed in relation to one another. Next, the current legal framework and practical implementation of formal participation will be presented, and the relevant legal amendment introduced and assessed. This will be expanded upon with an example of how a formal development procedure and an informal dialogue process can be interlinked and how the central points of overlap might be designed. The paper closes with a summary of the most important recommendations.

1. Introduction: Infrastructure Projects and Participation

When thousands of demonstrators collided with hundreds of police officers in Stuttgart's Schlosspark on September 30, 2010, people across Germany shook their heads in collective disbelief. No one had expected that a conflict surrounding the construction of a new train station could escalate in such a way. Since then, the debate surrounding on the infrastructure project "Stuttgart 21" has been regarded as a symbol of a country caught between renewal and paralysis: Everywhere, where large-scale projects are being planning, those responsible are now driven by "the fear of Stuttgart-style circumstances" – as the *Stuttgart Zeitung* newspaper's headline so memorably put it.

Infrastructure projects such as new roads, industrial facilities, power stations or airport runways have long stood for prosperity, job creation, and the further development of a region. From the point of view of investors, protests against such projects are difficult to comprehend. They are convinced: That which is economically desirable and which – through a process of planning permission – is recognised as being in the public interest, simply cannot be perceived as controversial by society. The perspective of affected residents or critical interest groups is, conversely, a very different one: They experience a far-reaching change in their environment and fear a decrease in their quality of life; they do not feel involved in the normal procedures and processes.

Infrastructure projects prototypically represent the challenges of modern networked societies: Individual interests and selective engagement broader determine societal debates. The internet and rapidly developing communications technologies hereby ensure that conflicts can develop at almost exponential rates. At the same time, it is indisputable that large-scale infrastructure projects will continue to be an integral and necessary part of our mobile, networked world: Economic, social, and cultural integration and globalisation increasingly demand infrastructural adaptations, such as in the transport system. And with the planned acceleration of the German transition to renewable energy and phasing out of nuclear power, the question of a "socially acceptable" design and implementation of such a transition – and its related infrastructure requirements – gains a new sense of urgency.

But what might contemporary and effective citizen participation in infrastructure projects look like? What are the roles of legal, formal methods of participation and of informal, flexible citizen participation? How can this interaction be organised and orchestrated so that the reliable and proven structures of formal methods can be complemented by the positive dynamics of informal forms of participation? Finally, what legally sound and empirical recommendations can be made with regard to the concrete design of future modes of participation in infrastructure projects?

In light of these questions, the aim of this paper is to outline an innovative approach by which to link formal and informal modes of participation. To this end the concepts of formal and informal participation will first be outlined and placed in relation to one another (Ch. 2). Next, the current legal framework and practical implementation of formal participation will be presented, and the relevant legal amendment introduced and assessed (Ch. 3). This will be expanded upon with an example of how a formal development procedure and an informal dialogue process can be interlinked and how the central points of overlap might be designed (Ch. 4). The paper closes with a summary of the most important recommendations (Ch. 5).

2. *Formal and Informal Participation and the Interlinking Thereof*

A fundamental understanding of formal and informal participation will be developed in this chapter. In addition it will show how to design successful linkages between different forms of participation, and which instruments of participation can be used for this purpose.

2.1. Formal Participation

2.1.1. Overview

Fundamentally, public participation as conceived of by legislators generally serves three functions:

- Expanding the knowledge-base of the administration
- Balancing conflicting interests / an appeasement function
- Anticipated legal protection

The methods differ with regard to those to be involved. While participation of the "public" is mentioned in the Bundes-Immissionsschutzgesetz (BImSchG, Federal Emissions Control Act), the Verwaltungsverfahrensgesetz (VwVfG, Administrative Procedures Act) as used for infrastructure projects (rail, streets, air transportation, etc.) foresees that…

…anyone whose interests are affected by this undertaking…

…may raise objection (§ 73, ¶ 4 of the VwVfG).

This, however, precedes the public inspection of application documents in every case. Due to the limitation of the right of objection, which applies to those whose interests are affected by the undertaking, the public hearing which follows is – according to the intention of the law – generally not open to the public. Rather, it is exclusive to those who have raised objections in a timely manner. In reality, a quasi-open public hearing – as determined by the approval authority – often takes place in such a process. The legislator has the legal protection of those affected rather than a societal dialogue with citizens about the project in mind – as is shown by the limitation (of the process) to those affected.

2.1.2. Perception

The design of the participation of the public and/or those affected takes place on multiple levels in infrastructure projects:

- Identification of needs under the Energiewirtschaftsgesetz (EnWG, Energy Economy Law)
- Regional planning procedures
- Planning approval procedures

A needs assessment only takes place in individual, legally regulated cases, such as, for example, in regional planning procedures. Such regional planning procedures are used to assess the spatial compatibility of various routes/alternative locations, while the approval procedures deal with the granting of approval for a specific project for which permission has been applied for.

From this it becomes clear: Planning is a process by which a project becomes more concrete, and which results in there being less leeway for alternatives with each progressive stage in the process. Leeway in the approval process for concrete projects is thus generally perceived as low because the decisions have actually already been predetermined in the preceding stages.

The preceding stages – the needs assessment and regional planning procedure – were, in the past and despite public participation, generally not perceived by the public as participatory. Some 5 to 10 years can pass between the respective planning and approval phases. In the case of Stuttgart 21, this was even the case for the legally binding planning approval process, which had been completed years earlier.

2.2. Informal Participation: Participation Culture and Process Knowledge

Informal participation is not a new phenomenon. It builds upon an already developed culture of participation and countless, already tested participation instruments. Hundreds of such processes have been implemented throughout Germany in recent decades – and many of them very successfully. None the less, businesses and administrations are often sceptical about accompanying complex planning and development processes, such as the implementation of infrastructure projects, with intensive and systematic informal forms of participation. They fear only encountering and engaging with the usual suspects, who show them up in public and want to discuss "every last nut and bolt" – only to then still remain opposed to everything.

Such fears are understandable yet unfounded – if participation is done correctly. It is important to remember that in such cases conflict escalates not due to disagreements on specific, substantive issues, but because those affected have the feeling that they are powerless to affect decisions that are made about their environment, community etc. This creates a relationship of mutual misunderstanding: The one side is labelled reckless profit maximisers, the other as the spoiled and notoriously "stonewalling" "angry citizen" (*Wut-Bürger*) or NIMBY.

Informal participation, when conceived of as supplementing formal processes and as a public discussion between applicants, leading administrative agencies, and participants, offers a space for the search for collaborative solutions. Long-sighted project developers can refer to a broad and successful body of practice in the effective participation of citizens and stakeholders.

When looking at successful participation processes in more detail it becomes clear that the selection of the appropriate procedure and the design of the process do more to determine success or failure than the choice of individual dialogue methods. Participation processes therefore largely revolve around the question of "How?" A substantial and substantive knowledge of processes design and architecture is necessary for the successful design and implementation of an informal participation process: Participation instruments continually need to be revised, readjusted, in order to find a flexible, resource-efficient, solution tailored to a particular infrastructure project and target group.

It's all about "how"

- ✓ How will the process be designed?
- ✓ What are the goals and rules?
- ✓ How will information be spread and to what target group?
- ✓ How will suggestions and feedback be collected?
- ✓ What is the result of the process and how will this be integrated into formal development procedures?

And last but not least:

- ✓ How does the leading agency understand its role in this process?

[Box] The various forms and instruments for public participation in planning processes can be generally divided according to their function in the process. The **information function** covers the full spectrum of public relations work and is either one-sided or dialogue-oriented. The **hearing** corresponds to the classic (formal) participation method. **Active participation** covers the active participation of stakeholders and/or relevant actors in the planning and decision-making processes of planning. It also comprises negotiation processes that are applied in the context of conflict resolution.

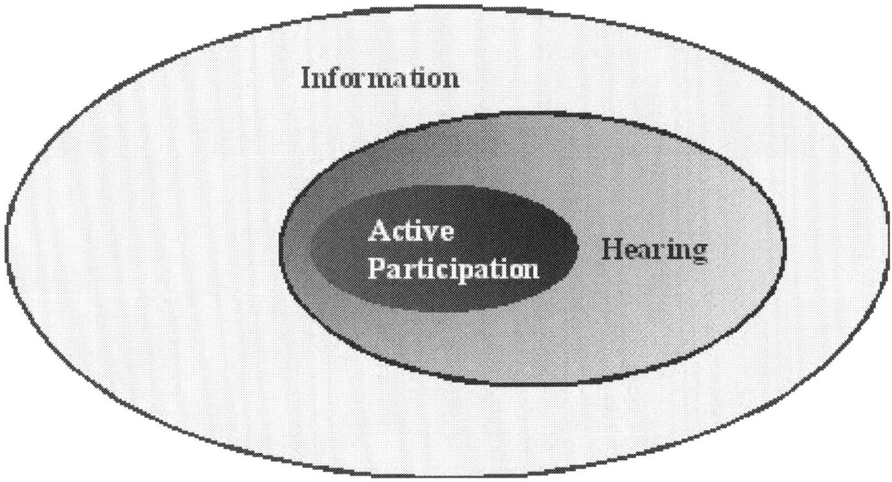

These specific participation functions typically address different audiences with differing levels of intensity. Three target groups can be differentiated:

- **Public sector bodies (*Träger öffentlicher Belange,* TöB)** are administrators of public issues whose hearing and involvement in a project is required by law.
- **Associations**, such as environmental groups, are involved in procedures under the umbrella of the Aarhus Convention. They are addressed in their function as affected groups (on environmental issues) as well as in "TöB-like" roles.
- The third group is **citizens** who are also to be involved in approval proceedings.

For successful approval proceedings, the central requirement is therefore to tailor the communication and the instruments of participation to the respective target group. While public sector bodies and associations are likely to be familiar with specialised laws, for example, a generic, understandable language and real opportunities for participation are essential for citizens.

The concrete design of informal methods of participation depends upon the framework conditions of the procedure. Dialogue processes can draw upon many tested instruments. The following diagram gives an overview of various instruments in relation to their influence on decisions – i.e. the opportunities for participation offered by a format – and the number of people reached with that format. When designing a process it is important to be aware of these options and to apply them strategically.

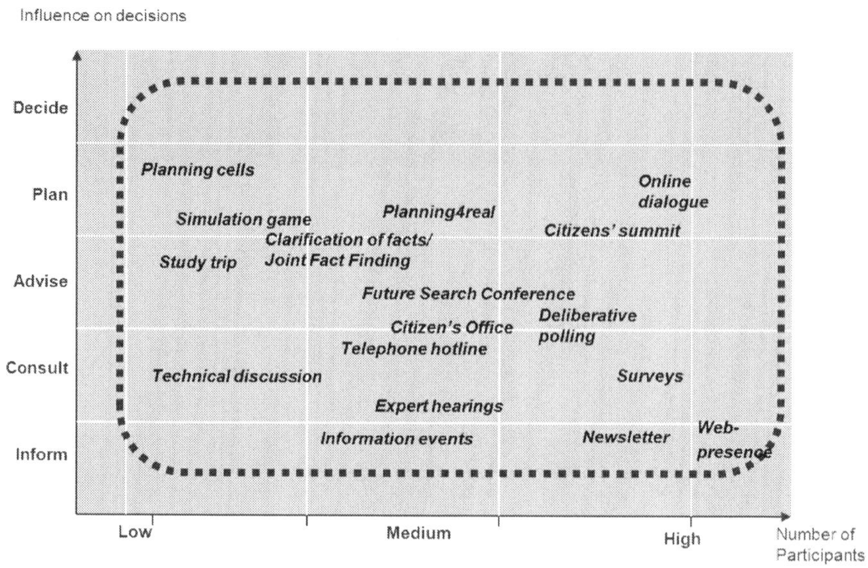

A multitude of differing instruments and tools are available for the design of participative processes. Alongside "classical" methods, known from relevant publications on facilitation methods, numerous methods can be found in practice that fit the individual conditions and goals of various processes. Here, different elements of the "classic" methods are combined with each other.

2.3. Connecting and Interlinking Development Procedures with Informal Processes

In order to create a tailored interplay of methods and processes, informal participation processes should not be tied too closely to development procedures in any formal way. It is important that informal processes retain the flexibility from which their added value is derived. Legal rules should, above all, stipulate at which point in the process broad public participation should occur and how the results will be integrated, but should not de facto formalise the informal process with statutory requirements. In combination, formal and informal procedures achieve qualitatively better participation, which brings with it a wider acceptance and often gives rise to new solutions and ideas for implementation.

The strength of informal participation lies in not being integrated into formal, legally curtailed processes. Within the context of informal participation it is possible to pose and address far-reaching, open questions. In doing so such they enable knowledge to be generated which goes beyond the formal procedure. Additionally, confidence in the participating persons and the institutions initiating the process is also strengthened through such informal procedures.

For this, informal participation needs a process which affords all parties involved the opportunity to meet "on equal footing", and which offers a space in which to search for common solutions. Informal participation can already be initiated in the run-up to the planning stage of a project, with the benefits soon clear: In doing so, all potentially affected stakeholders are brought to the table at an early stage. Timely, informal participation is in many cases already initiated at the regional planning stage, because it is at this level that the decision is made whether a project will be implemented at all, and the alternatives to implementing the project are reviewed. The legal duty to implement public participation in environmentally relevant projects offers appropriate options for linkages (such as strategic environmental reviews and impact assessments). Further, the discussion of strengthened, early public participation and its design can be conducted in the context of the Administrative Procedure Act (VwVfG) in order to reveal optional interfaces with informal participation.

The following figure depicts the core interfaces between formal/technical planning process and informal participation possibilities, using a levelling flowchart. Differences between preceding procedures and approval procedures as well as between various specific, relevant laws are not included.

Diagram: Hybrid Procedures: Linking technical development procedures and dialogue processes

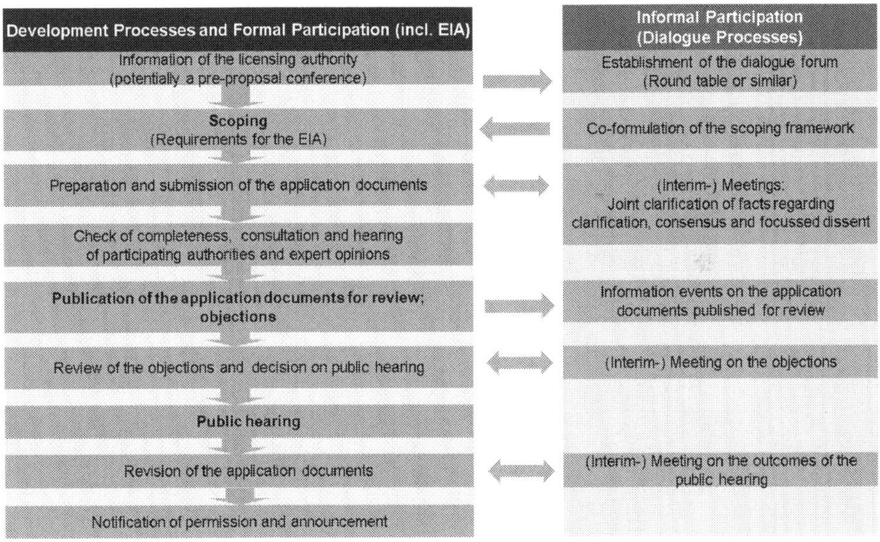

3. *Formal Participation: General Conditions for Public Participation in a Procedure and for Early Public Participation*

In this chapter, an overview of legal framework conditions will be drawn up and the options and potential for optimisation through early public participation will be analysed.

3.1. Public Participation at Various Stages of Approval for Infrastructure Projects

3.1.1. Preceding Procedures and the Testing of Alternatives

With procedures such as, for example, grid infrastructure planning, public participation takes place as part of the needs assessment under the Bundesbedarfsplangesetz (part of the EnWG). This is conducted under § 4, in combination with § 12a of the European Elections Act (EuWG), and takes place in the form of so-called consultations. On the basis of the needs assessment, route corridors are established as part of Federal Sectoral Planning under § 5 et seq. of the Netzausbaubeschleunigungsgesetz (NABEG, Law on the Acceleration of Grid Expansion). Finally, the planning approval for the individual routes under § 18 et seq. of the NABEG is drawn up and also includes public participation.

Public participation in the regional planning process for further infrastructure measures is regulated in § 15, ¶ 3, sentence 3 of the Raumordnungsgesetz (ROG, Regional Planning Act) in a non-mandatory fashion:

> "The public **may** be included in the implementation of a regional planning process."

The Federal States have made use of this in their state planning acts in different ways, with public participation provided for in some state planning acts. In addition, this public participation follows largely from the fact that an environmental impact assessment (EIA) or strategic environmental assessment (SEA) is mandatory within the procedures for infrastructure projects.

For all of these cases, § 9, ¶ 1, sentence 1 of the Gesetz über die Umweltverträglichkeitsprüfung (UVPG, Law governing Environmental Impact Assessments) stipulates that the concerned public "is to be heard on the basis of the documents laid out for public review." The public will be given the chance to comment (§ 9, ¶ 1, sentence 2 of the UVPG). Under § 9, ¶ 2 of the UVPG, the decision and its justification, should also be available for public review. If the plan is amended, the public is to be involved again (§ 9, ¶ 1, sentence 3 of the UVPG).

The timely submission of objections also paves the way for judicial protection regarding the approval decision: Precluded are of course those who have not raised objections in writing by the predetermined deadline (generally 1 month plus a fortnight). Further, the established case law – at least regarding the lawsuits of environmental associations – has also, meanwhile, significantly increased the material requirements for the particulars of objections being submitted.[1]

§ 9, ¶ 3 of the UVPG provides for corresponding public participation for the so-called upstream (regional planning) process. In doing so, however, legal claims (legal remedies) are not provided for in upstream processes.

3.1.2. Approval Procedures

Public participation has generally largely focused on approval procedures for concrete projects. § 9, ¶ 1, sentence 2 of the Law governing Environmental Impact Assessments (UVPG) stipulates that "the affected public" be granted the opportunity to comment on the respective project in a hearing. § 73, ¶ 4 of the Administrative Procedure Act (VwVfG) determines that "anyone, whose interests are affected by this project," can raise objections against the plan in writing within 2 weeks after the close of the period for raising objections. The relevant specific technical planning laws refer to each of the above provisions of the Administrative Procedure Act (VwVfG) regarding participation / the consultation of affected parties (for example, § 17 of the Federal Highways Act (FStrG), § 18 of the General Railway Act (AEG), § 9b, ¶ 5 of the Atomic Energy Act, § 10 of the Air Traffic Act, § 43a of the Energy Economy Law (EnWG), and § 38 of the Waste Management and Product Recycling Act (KrWG)).

3.1.3. The Steps of Public Participation

The design of public participation in the respective procedures generally includes the following steps:

- Application documents are made available for public review
- Objections can be raised
- Discussion of those objections that are submitted in a timely manner takes place

§ 73, ¶ 6 of the Administrative Procedure Act (VwVfG) contains no "rules of the game" for discussing objections that are submitted in a timely manner. For the emission control permit process, § 18 of the 9th Federal Emissions Protection Ordinance (BlmSchV) provides for the following:

1 See decision of the Federal Administrative Court (BVerwG) from 29 September 2011 (7 C 21.09 and from 9 August 2010 (9 B 10.10).

"The hearing is public...
The chief negotiator can determine that objections be bundled and discussed together. In this case, the order of discussion must be announced...
The chief negotiator moderates and can revoke the floor from those speakers who speak over the allotted time slot or make statements that do not concern the subject of the hearing or which are not linked in a factual context to the objection.
The chief negotiator concludes the discussion when its purpose has been fulfilled..."

With regard to the purpose of the discussion, § 14 elaborates as follows:

"The hearing is intended for discussing the objections submitted in a timely manner, insofar as this is significant for checking the permit conditions. It should give those who have raised objections the opportunity to expound upon their objections"

While it is regulated in emissions control laws that only objections relevant to the approval procedure must be addressed in the public hearing, the provisions of § 73, ¶ 6 of the Administrative Procedure Act (VwVfG) leave this open with regard to the planning approval process. In practice, both cases generally entail that objections not relevant to the permission procedure are also, at least partially, discussed. This is done with the pacifying function of the hearing in mind.

Objections not relevant to the approval procedure often pertain to the reasonableness and meaningfulness of the project, alternatives to the project, questions on financing, and – important to those affected – to the fear of a possible drop in real estate value.

Numerous appeals, applications and requests are generally put forward in the course of a public hearing. Insofar as the administration follows up or must follow up on these, significant delays in the proceedings and a possible redesign / re-planning cannot be avoided.

Often, such public hearings consist of hostile exchanges between professional technical advisors and lawyers. When this is the case it is clear that the heading has not met its statutory (pacifying) function (see Gaentzsch, 2010; Riese & Dieckmann, 2010; Versteyl, 2006; 2008; 2011).

When it comes to infrastructure projects, grid expansion and its role in Germany's transition to renewables and phasing out of nuclear power takes on particular importance. A new legal basis has been established for the development of national networks in the form of the Grid Expansion Acceleration Act (NABEG). The regulations are testimony to the legislator's view that an acceleration of grid expansion can only be conducted in dialogue with the citizens. The act therefore includes the further development of public participation in key contexts and steps of the process and can therefore act as a role model for other procedures.

3.2. Optimisation through Early Public Participation

3.2.1. Legal Basis

The draft of the so-called Planning Procedure Harmonisation Act has the aim of introducing and codifying so-called "early public participation." § 25 of the VwVfG-E ("Consultation, Advice") stipulates:

> *"The administration aims that the agency involved in the planning of the project with potentially non-negligible effects to the interests of a large number of third parties, inform the concerned public early on about the goals of the project, the means for implementation, and the assumed effects of the project (early public participation)."*

Decisive framework conditions are therefore that:

- it is a voluntary instrument of the project developer,
- which it is directed towards the "affected public",
- the project developer informs the administration of the outcomes.

The regulation applies to all approval procedures, i.e. to authorisation processes for industrial facilities, as well as planning approval procedures for infrastructure measures. The regulation does not include limitations on projects with EIA requirements.

In contrast to formal procedures, early public participation does not have any preclusive effects, i.e. non-participation has no effect on rights in the later approval process.

Through early public participation it is possible for the project developer to quickly recognise conflicts and optimise plans – and to do so at a point in time when there is a lesser risk of significant procedural delays. If the project developer does not already conducted such a voluntary public participation process as part of current legal requirements, there exists significant conflict potential at a later point in time, namely in the context of objections being submitted following the publication of plans for review and the hearing.

3.2.2. Possible Designs for Early Public Participation

§ 25, ¶ 3 of the VwVfG-E does not prescribe *how* early public participation should be conducted. As a result, leeway for various instruments exists:

Experienced project developers, who have conducted early public participation for a considerable period of time, have, up until now, regularly done this through public information provisions, events, etc., and have done so without linkages to the formal procedural steps.

In all projects in which an EIA is conducted, a so-called "scoping meeting" usually takes place in which the purpose and the scale of the EIA are determined. In accordance with § 5 of the Law governing Environmental Impact Assessments (UVPG), specialists and third parties can be consulted in this procedure (see Versteyl, 2011). As a result, the context of the scoping meeting could therefore lend itself as an opportunity for early public participation.

Such an interlinking with existing procedural steps can help prevent delays as this additional, early informal public participation makes supplementary, upstream procedural steps within formal processes unnecessary. This interlinking with participation opportunities in formal processes and procedures enables the inclusion of both recommendations on the content of the project and the procedures, as well as on the content of the EIA. The dialogue thus-begun with the public can be deepened in parallel to the further, formal procedural steps.

4. Recommendations for the Interlinking of Development and Dialogue Processes

So-far the legal frameworks of formal development procedures and the possibilities and instruments for informal participation processes have been presented. In a next step, the interfaces which have been identified (opportunities for interlinking) will be presented in order to delineate a functional, comprehensive format which is able to address current challenges. While specific interfaces have already been tested in practice (for example, at the Regional Dialogue Forum Frankfurt or City Train Mannheim), this paper aims to systematically describe the possible interfaces for linking formal and informal procedures. To this end, the following will present an illustrative example of an interlinking between a formal development process and a dialogue forum, with the latter the central building block of the informal procedure. In addition to detailing the constitution of the dialogue forum (goals, composition, and mode of operation) the example focuses on the most important interfaces between both types of procedure.

4.1. Goals, Composition, and Mode of Operation of Dialogue Fora

A dialogue forum seeks to create a space is which an open, trusting and transparent exchange between actors participating in a local or community project can take place. In order to mitigate the prevalent in-fighting, the entrenchment into established positions and the apportioning of, confidence-building measures and a new culture of exchange are initiated right from the outset of a dialogue forum (including established shared rules of the game). In order to ensure an effective and non-partisan process, the dialogue forum should be led by a neutral party which enjoys the strong confidence of all sides. Central goals and tasks of the dialogue forum are:

- *integrating* the various opinions and interests and achieving a trusting exchange,
- the *institutionalisation* of the exchange between the participating stakeholders and channelling this,
- *involving* concerned citizens and ensuring a comprehensive and *targeted flow of information*,
- creating *transparency* throughout the process (for example, through the publication of all relevant reports and minutes on the website of the dialogue forum),
- the early clarification of open *technical and substantive questions* (joint fact finding) by deciding together upon recognised third party experts and evaluators.

From a legal perspective it is to be recommended that the dialogue forum be given the status of a "body concerned with public matters" (Träger öffentlicher Belange, TöB) – i.e. be classed as an administrator of public issues. As a result, stakeholders that are not legally TöBs (such as citizen initiatives) can then participate in formal procedures.

Based on experience, a dialogue forum can best fulfil the goals and tasks detailed above when its mode of operation is based upon the following guidelines:

- *Composition*: The dialogue forum should be composed of the most important stakeholders. Opinions on the project should be balanced between the participants and this should be reflected in the forum's composition.
- *External Chairing*: An external actor must chair the forum to ensure the non-partisanship of the leadership and the transparency of the forum.
- *Consensus oriented*: The dialogue forum is an advisory body. It should, therefore, work in a consensus-driven manner and – as far as possible – abstain from majority votes. This also means that political "speeches" are to be avoided as much as possible from the outset.
- *Objectivity*: Jointly chosen experts are to be invited for the clarification of technical and substantive questions and integrated into the process of jointly clarifying facts. In addition, hearings or other expert events should be initiated on specific questions.
- *Transparency*: The meetings are public and minutes are posted online.
- *Information*: The events initiated by the forum serve to inform about the work of the forum (and the project). They equally have the task of bringing questions, regulations, and criticisms from citizens back into the dialogue forum. The flow of information is ensured through, among other things, public relations, a dedicated website, mobile information stands, information events, and a newsletter.

4.2. Central Interfaces

How a formal development procedure and an informal dialogue process can be effectively interlinked is presented in the following diagram. Thereafter the six most important interfaces are described in detail.

Diagram: Interlinking in the example of an informal dialogue process

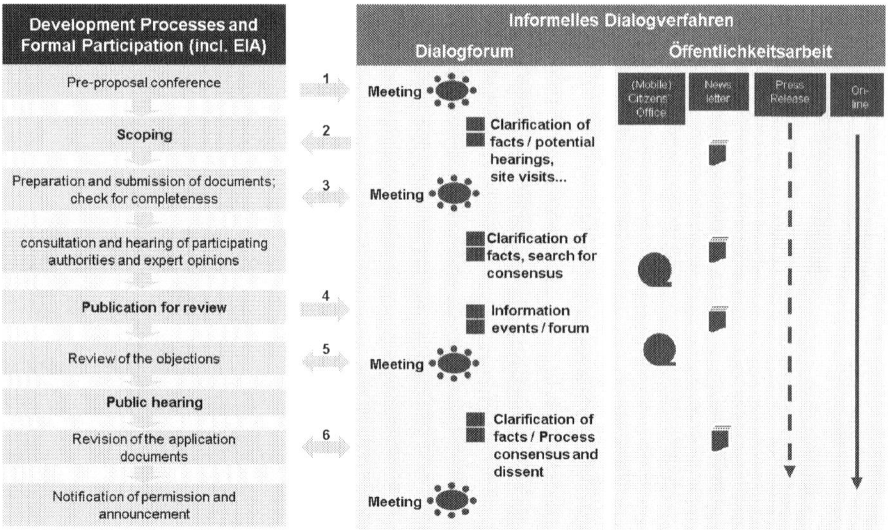

(1) Early Interlinking: Information and Establishment of a Dialogue Forum

To ensure an effective overall process, it is important that both the formal and the informal participation processes are designed together from the very beginning. Already at the stage when a project idea is formulated, the opportunities and limitations of citizen participation should be thought through. It is recommended that an analysis and mapping of actors be conducted. In this way it is possible to gear the scope and form of informal participation towards the planned infrastructure project (size, potential conflicts, and possible dynamics). Such a joint planning from the outset also enables to information flow of a formal development procedure and the dialogue process to be coupled from the beginning. This saves resources, mitigates misunderstandings, and ensures targeted communications.

Goal: The dialogue forum should be ready for operation shortly after the public announcement of the project. In this way arguments and interests can be channelled and made more matter-of-fact right from the beginning; personal hostilities and rising tension can be mitigated. The publication (the announcement of, or better, the widespread knowledge of) the project and the initiating of the dialogue process must go hand in hand in order to productively channel misgivings and objections from the beginning.

The first meeting of the dialogue forum can be run in the context of the pre-application meeting, which first advises on the mode, scope, and location of the project and collects relevant questions.

(2) Defining the Frame: Scoping Meeting and Formulation

It is at the scoping meeting that the topic as well as the scope and method of the EIA for the planning process are defined. In order to support the scoping meeting and to ensure the inclusion of stakeholder interests from the beginning, the dialogue forum can take on-board proposals for the formulation of the scope of the impact assessment. In this way, contentious issues can be dealt with early on and a shared vision of the task can be established.

In order to support the decision on the scope of the impact assessment, it is possible that an initial site-visit, a clarification of facts, or an expert hearing can be implemented as part of the dialogue forum.

(3) Create a solid foundation: Preparing the application materials and clarification of facts

Whilst the application materials are being prepared, meetings of the dialogue forum can serve to identify existing consensus and dissent and to clarify open questions arising from the interim results of the planning process. This can be done, for example, through a joint clarification of the facts (including, among others, through the common selection of experts), hearings, or through site visits. Reports and expert opinions commissioned by the forum can accompany by the dialogue forum and the (interim) results can be communicated to the stakeholders. A citizen's office can address questions from citizens and can (where beneficial) proactively report on interim results.

Such measures result in improved application materials and a modified plan or a valid comparison of variations (including non-alternatives) at the regional planning level that, ideally, take into account most issues of conflict.

(4) Inform and discuss: Public announcements and information events

The public must be comprehensively involved both before and after the public announcement and the publication of the application materials for review. The dialogue forum initiates (if applicable, with the help of a citizen's office) a series of measures (information events etc.), pays attention to the application of the measures, and ensures the flow of information.

Open questions regarding the application materials can, for example, be discussed in (mobile) citizen's offices or via the dialogue forum's website.

(5) Keeping your eye on the ball: Participation at the review of objections and the public hearing

In order to accompany the review of objections, further meetings for fact clarification are implemented before and during the hearing. This can also include further information events on the published application materials.

(6) Doing the job properly: Communication of the results and participation in the implementation

The dialogue forum can continue its work even after the formal procedure has come to an end. This can include working to communicate the final results. The project developer can also take on-board existing structures for a continuation of the dialogue (for example the dialogue forum can be changed into a neighbourhood forum).

Accompanying Public Relations

Throughout whole process the dialogue forum takes on a large portion of the public relations work. This task can be implemented by the back-office supporting the dialogue forum and, if applicable, by the (mobile) citizen's office, helping intensify the exchange with citizens. A (mobile) citizen's office serves as the contact point for transparent and trustworthy information. The information available there is legitimised by the dialogue forum.

Public relations tools accompanying the process include:

- Newsletter
- Press releases

- Dedicated website (publication of meeting minutes, live streaming of meetings if applicable, reports, discussion forum, etc.)
- Use of a (mobile) citizen's office

5. Conclusion

A contemporary and effective citizen participation infrastructure project establishes possibilities for informal participation – in addition to formal participation processes – and ensures a close interlinking between them. In this way, politics, administration, and business can meet the strengthened wishes of many citizens to be more actively involved in the design of their living environment and community, and to constructively work together on developing solutions. Participation methods in large-scale infrastructure projects are prototypical for the challenges faced in a networked society: They illustrate how participation, as a core element of modern governance, can lead to flexible solutions while, at the same time, retaining legal certainty.

For the implementation of infrastructure projects with the potential for conflict, this paper recommends beginning an informal dialogue process at the latest when the project idea is drawn up, and to continue it throughout the development process. For the implementation of the dialogue process – and therefore also the infrastructure project – the following key factors are central for ensuring success.

1. Even before the beginning of participation processes, clarify the form through which the *results* will flow in the formal development procedure. One possibility is to confer upon certain elements (such as committees) of the dialogue process the status of TöB.
2. Close *interlinking* and the forward-looking design of interfaces are necessary in order to couple the reliability of the formal structures with flexibility and informal participation instruments.
3. Good informal participation creates a *participation culture*, ensuring that the dialogue takes place at eye level. New spaces are created for exchange and conflict resolution, and a wide spectrum of actors is brought into the process.
4. There is no patented recipe for a dialogue process: *well-founded process knowledge* is necessary for aligning the informal participation process with a specific context, and to design and implement a target-orientated process.

Gaentzsch, G. (2010). Der Erörterungstermin im Planfeststellungsverfahren – Instrument zur Sachverhaltsaufklärung oder Einladung zur Verfahrensverzögerung? In K.-P. Dolde, K. Hansmann, S. Paetow & E. Schmidt-Aßmann (Eds.), *Verfassung - Umwelt - Wirtschaft: Festschrift für Dieter Sellner zum 75. Geburtstag* (pp. 219), Munich: Beck.

Riese, C., & Dieckmann, N. (2010). Der Erörterungstermin - Bestandsaufnahme und Reformvorschlag. *DVBl 2010*, pp. 1343.

Versteyl, A. (2006). Genehmigungsmanagement für thermische Abfallentsorgungsanlagen aus der Sicht des Vorhabenträgers. In K. J. Thomé-Kozmiensky & A. Versteyl (Eds.), *Texte zur Abfallwirtschaft I* (pp. 249). Nietwerder: TK Verlag.

Versteyl, A. (2008). Erweiterung der Öffentlichkeitsbeteiligung und des Rechtsschutzes im Anlagenzulassungsrecht. *AbfallR 1/2008*, pp. 8.

Versteyl, A. (2011). Partizipation durch Verfahren – Verbesserung der Öffentlichkeitsbeteiligung auf Grundlage der gesetzlichen Regelungen. *I+E 2/2011*, pp. 89.

Declining Cities as Large-scale Projects: Why it Matters how City Government Sees its Citizens

Johannes Staemmler

This chapter conceptualizes declining cities as large-scale projects for local government. It argues that the vicious cycle of economic and social decline requires a rethinking of how local administration approaches society and citizens. If the aim of local government is to trigger favorable development in the city it needs to think about which potentials there are and how to activate them. Decline is a multi-dimensional phenomenon, which requires a multitude of means and measures to deal with it. Here, the prime concern lies with the potentials of civil society that can help renovate a city in conjunction with other sectors of society. In the context of declining cities, this becomes a problem of either managing decline or actively engaging with citizens in a debate on which goals are to be pursued and who will share in achieving them.

1 Introduction

What a large-scale project is, is a matter of definition. Often we picture big infrastructure endeavors as such, especially when a multitude of stakeholders from various sectors are involved, an extended period of time is needed for planning, or when decision making and implementation as well as a number of critical issues are debated. At its core, a large-scale project is a process of change that needs governance.

All of the above applies to cities in general and to declining cities in particular. Declining cities are the most prevalent cases where the negative effects of economic and social changes amount. Often, local governments face a threefold process of deconsolidation. First, industries collapse or relocate to other places in the world due to changes in the economy. The workforce is laid-off and former employees move from being taxpayers to being in need of government support. Second, a substantial fraction of the citizens will leave in search for work and education, especially the ones that are younger or in the midst of their careers. Third, local government's capacity to respond is limited because neither its authority nor its shrinking financial resources suffice to alter the first two processes (Friedrichs, 1993). The decline is multi-dimensional. Data for Germany shows that areas with low or declining economic power also show a higher share of exiting individuals as well as a lower rate of people engaging voluntarily (Krönert et al., 2011). Popular cases of declining cities have been Manchester, Liverpool, Pittsburgh, or Detroit, but many industrialized countries know cities that show similar forms of decline (Glaeser, 2010).

This chapter conceptualizes declining cities as large-scale projects for local administrators. It argues that the vicious cycle of economic and social decline requires a rethinking of how local administration approaches society and citizens. If the aim of local administration is to put the city back on track, it needs to think about which potentials there are and how to activate them. Decline is a multi-dimensional phenomenon, which requires a multitude of means and measures to deal with it. Here, the prime concern lies with the potentials of civil society that can help renovate a city in conjunction with other sectors of society. In the context of declining cities, this becomes a problem of either managing decline or actively engaging with citizens in a debate on which goals are to be pursued and who will join in achieving them.

There are a variety of means, such as participatory budgeting, mini publics and public-private partnerships that have been tried to engage citizens in public affairs more than they used to. In a functionalist reading, one could argue that this – the sharing of governance powers – is the only choice for governments in order to sustain any governing capacity. By trading authority for participation, governments accept shared governance arrangements in order to collectively produce common goods (Geißel, 2009). In a normative reading, there is not just a need but also the chance of reconfiguring state–citizen relationships in order to foster the virtues of a stronger citizen participation in their communities. This means that a thoughtful development of government-citizen interaction increases the reflective and participatory quality of the citizen as well as the quality of government (Offe & Preuß, 1991). In short, the pressure that is produced by changing modes and location of economic production forces a new reading of means to handle the classic legitimacy-effectiveness dilemma that ideal-type democracies handle through power-sharing, electoral systems, and a strong media.

This chapter is structured in three parts. First, I will conceptualize declining cities as large-scale projects that need to be studied more closely. Declining cities are the most challenging arenas for both government and civil society to work out alternative strategies for local innovation. Second, I will analyze the potentials of civil society in declining cities, in the light of the conceptions of civil society that city administrators have. I argue that a too narrow conception of society will lead to the application of means that can be harmful to civil society and the city. The third section critically assesses means of government to engage citizens.

2 Declining cities as large scale projects

Declining cities seem to be residual places in developed democracies where only the negative impacts of macro-changes such as globalization and post-industrialism as well as local conditions amount to unfavorable conditions for citizens, business, and bureaucrats alike. Declining cities can be defined as urban areas where the weaknesses of economy and state cumulate, i.e. where the weakness of the economy cannot be compensated for by the public sector (Seibel, 1994, p. 275). They are characterized by a high degree of unemployment, worsening demographic data, high public deficits, and often appear after the breakdown of major industries around which the structure of a city has been designed (Friedrichs, 1993).

We observe urban decline as a consequence of two interlocking and global changes that put pressure on the local level. The first is commonly framed as globalization, which means that social, economic, and political arenas are no longer congruent (Zürn, 1998). Hence, no spatially bounded government authority can sufficiently govern social and economic forces that are operating within their territory. Business can and does credibly threaten to remove factories to other countries, for example. The interdependencies between the inside and the outside of the governing spaces have increased. The second change is one from predominantly industrial forms of production to post-industrial modes of value generation (Bell, 1999 [1973]). This is especially a change of the modes of production from goods to services that require different work environments and skills from the individual worker. These two changes form the background for a re-conceptualization of government-citizen interaction.

Declining cities is a growing phenomenon in Western countries. Not only do we observe that the majority of citizens in general live and work in cities, but also that the benefits of urbanization are unequally distributed (Glaeser, 2010). When mobility, demography, and modes of production change, citizens basically always threaten to exit. But cities are the life-worlds of people. It is the locus where they grow up, go to school, marry, and die. Throughout history, cities have been the hubs of ideas and creativity as well as the places for inventions and innovations (Keane, 2006). And we know of few cities that have ceased to exist. Many people seem to be staying in declining cities after all.

With Albert Hirschman (1970), we can conceptualize a citizen's situation in a declining city with a question between *exit* and *voice*. As the quality of living decreases due to lack of jobs and public funds, the citizen can choose to withdraw him/herself from this community physically or mentally. Or s/he chooses to voice discontent towards fellow citizens or the government.[1] For governments, this question is a vital one. We can assume that the exodus of citizens from a city manifests the vicious circle of decline (Friedrichs, 1993). Hence, government has a strong incentive to keep citizens from exiting. They need them as voters, taxpayers, volunteers in civil society, advisors, and addressees of its services. In order to prevent citizens from choosing the exit option, governments have in principle four means they can employ. These are based on power, incentives, nudges, and thinking which will be discussed in part IV.

1 As Amitai Etzioni puts it: "To be active is to be in charge; to be passive is to be under control, be it of natural processes, of social waves and streams, or of active others." (Etzioni, 1968, p. 4.).

Local government faces a dilemma: By law it has to provide a set of core services, which are addressed towards a shrinking and aging constituency.[2] The output-legitimacy of government (Holtkamp, Bogumil, & Kißler, 2005; Scharpf, 1999) is endangered because it has insufficient means to compensate everyone who loses due to the decline. Hence, the exit of citizens accelerates. The remaining citizens are, empirically, the least likely ones to engage themselves voluntarily. The question then is: Is decline an incentive or a barrier for city government to engage with its citizens? This paper will argue that government has the legitimacy, the need, and the tools to address these citizens because it needs their ideas and creativity to revive the city.

For social science concepts, declining cities offer at least two opportunities. First, cities are societies, in a nutshell, which allow for the testing of differing theories, especially in comparative terms. Although there is a set of urban theories, such as urban regime theory, they all are heavily linked to macro concepts from the social sciences (Mossberger & Stoker, 2001). Knowledge and concepts from cities have a high chance of being transferred to other areas (John et al., 2011). Second, the observation of declining 'mini'-societies (including their infrastructures and its effects on structures as well as processes) is a rare phenomenon. Western societies are accustomed to growth and most conceptions – sociological as well as economic – are based on the idea of increases. Government and citizens have not yet developed views or means to cope with or even to conceptualize decline.[3]

3 *Civil society conceptions*

Why should city administrators be concerned with civil society in the first place? The literature on the benefits of civil society (e.g. Priller, 2009) differentiates between benefits for the individual and for society as a whole as well as between direct and indirect benefits. In general, theory and empirical data have found a multitude of beneficial effects of civil organizations and individual engagement. First, civil society is strengthening democracy as citizens learn how to argue and associate as well as respect and trust fellow citizens (Putnam, Leonardi, & Nanetti, 1993). Second, it fosters social integration, which the state and the market have a hard time achieving. It supports individual expressions but also brings people together that would otherwise not meet. This is especially important in areas where people exit physically or mentally. Third, civil society is based on the notion of civility, which it requires and reproduces as

2 Which services the local level is responsible for varies from country to country. However, local government is always part of the multi-level governance arrangement with a given state.

3 One example for this would be the difficulties of politics and the social sciences in dealing with the economic and demographic changes that have been observed in East Germany since 1990 (Anheier, Priller, Seibel, & Zimmer, 1997; Gensicke, Olk, Reim, Schmithals, & Dienel, 2009; Kollmorgen, 2005; Staud, 2003; Steiner, 2006).

people interact in a civil manner (Evers, 2009). Fourth, civil society takes part in the production of welfare, which can take on different forms in different context and levels (Salamon & Anheier, 1997). Lastly, civil society is offering paid work to citizens, mostly in relation to the provision of welfare.

Kocka (2006, p. 40) defines civil society in three related ways: "First, as a type of social action; secondly, as an area or sphere connected to but separate from economy, state, and the private sphere, and, thirdly, as the core of a draft or project that still has some utopian features." Edwards (2009) agrees on the latter two definitions whereas offering a third one which is broader than civil society as mode of action. He perceives civil society also as the public sphere and relates it to Habermas' conception of communicative action. I will integrate both conceptions, as they share a variety of features. The argument is that the government of declining cities is in need of the beneficial effects of all forms of civil society as it helps to stabilize the social disintegration of the declining city. Government needs to carefully define civil society and be aware of its assumptions about it. A narrow conception of civil society leads to the use of means that are insufficient or even harmful to it.

Not only but especially under the condition of declining cities, all of the effects of civil society are desirable both from the perspective of the state as well as from the perspective of the citizen. However, city government has to come up with a conception of its society in order to decide how to address it. In addition, some of the benefits of civil society, such as trust or creativity, are byproducts, which cannot be produced by government or civil society directly. A vivid civil society is also an expression of citizens choosing voice over exit, which means that citizens not only support but also question the government with their civic engagement. In the following, I present three differing conceptions of civil societies and their values for city government.

3.1 Civil society as sector

The most common conception of civil society has at its core the organizations of civil society that form an own sphere or sector within society. It is separate from state and market and is known as the civil society sector, third sector, or non-profit sector (Anheier, 2004). Anheier, for example, defines civil society in a functional-operational way: "Civil society is the sphere of institutions, organizations and individuals located between the family, the state and the market in which people associate voluntarily to advance common interests" (p. 22). It is characterized by private, non-profit distributing, and self-governing organizations with voluntary membership.

The sector approach is linked to the analysis of Alexis de Tocqueville (1985 [1835/40]) who argued that the strength of American democracy is a function of its citizens' participation in clubs and associations. Within these organizations, citizens develop civic skills that are beneficial to society as a whole. This argument was taken up by Putnam et al. (1993), who argued that civic associations not only produce social capital, which is based on trust, but they also effectively put pressure on government, which in turn improves government's performance. This approach is strong because it gives civil society a shape, a function, and measurements. It has created more sensibility for the potential civic, economic, social, and democratic (by-)effects of those forms of social action that have no such explicit purposes, like many forms of volunteering, community building, and so forth (Evers, 2009). It has highlighted the multiplicity of organizational forms on the national and international level. And it has started to develop measurements for the sector showing also its economic function (Anheier, 2004).

For different reasons, the attention of policy-makers has shifted towards civil society as sector and its organizational elements. Most obviously, third sector organizations seem attractive for outsourcing government activities to, especially when it comes to welfare provision. At the same time, these organizations employ a large amount of people, which is in the interests of public administration. Besides that, organizations are easier to address than individualized citizens or public debates or spheres. Civil society as sector is also a powerful conception because it has been incorporated into neighboring social science disciplines such as the research on governance (amongst many: Benecke, Branovic, & Draude, 2008; Benz, 2004; Holtkamp & Bogumil, 2007; Kohler-Koch, 2008; Schuppert, 2005).

The focus on organizations, however, brings about a variety of problems (Evers, 2011, pp. 138-139). Not all organizations that fit the definitions of non-profit organizations are civil and civic-minded. Lobby-groups as well as hybrid organizations often have particular interests, receive money from state or business, and their voluntary memberships can be questioned. Secondly, it is not just civil society organizations that produce civility and civicness. It is also the educational system, the workplace, and others that support the development of these skills. A core problem is one of causality: The literature suggests two relationships, which researchers have a hard time disentangling. One is that civil society and its organizations improve the quality and the performance of democratic institutions (Putnam et al., 1993). The other claims that it is the state in the first place that enables the emergence of a civil society and the production of social capital ("It takes democracy to make social capital work").[4] As both arguments are plausible and have been proven empirically, one can perceive the state-society relationship as interacting systems that affect one another.

4 Anheier & Seibel, 2001; Hall, 1999; Levy, 1999; Padgett, 2000; Skocpol, 1999.

3.2 Civil society as good society

Civil society is also used with a more normative connotation. Especially since the collapse of the communist systems in Eastern Europe, which had been under pressure from their own citizens, civil society is a term related to anti-authoritarian, free, and outspoken citizens. Civil stands for the opposite of uncivil, violent, disinterested, or selfish. This conception of civil society contains a stronger historical awareness of how citizens and societies have emerged from less free conditions. It underlines not only the freedoms citizens enjoy but equally the duties to preserve and expand these freedoms against all forms of obstruction. It contains the continuous questioning of existing rules as to whether they are supportive to the civicness of society. A good society can also be – especially in the light of its historical emergence – a rebellious one (Evers, 2009).

When used as such, civil society contains one or many visions of how a society ought to be (Edwards, 2009). A 'good society' is one that has struggled for the supremacy of civil values and norms which it agrees on and on which the citizens base their behavior. Münkler argues that "The citizen is (...) someone aware of the value and preconditions of coexistence based on political participation and social solidarity, someone who knows the burdens of self-government and accepts them, fully aware of the long-term negative consequences of refusing to accept them" (Münkler, 2006, p. 94). It is a rather communitarian reading of society, based on virtues and a collective strive for civility. However, the 'good society' is conceptually and procedurally difficult to integrate into liberal democracies that allow citizens to choose freely what to do and which notion of good to follow.

The virtue of this conception is its openess towards a variety of organizational forms that also include social movements and loose forms of interaction. It is also more sensitive towards the historical preconditions under which particular civil societies emerge and in what debates and discourse they are rooted. Every city has its own narrative and points of reference. Its focus on civility and civicness helps to evaluate strategies and institutions as to whether they are conducive to the project of a good society. The state and the market are not excluded from the idea of a good society but have to become part of it as elements of a civilized society.

The problem, however, is the vagueness of this conception because civicness and civility have different meanings in different contexts. Especially in relation to the political realm, the visions of a good society differ between citizens and parties. These visions are subject to ongoing debate, reframing, and contentious struggle. Civil society can barely be used without some normative connotation. But the more normatively charged it is, the more contested the term becomes.

3.3 As mode of action in the public sphere

The third take on civil society is more focused on the characteristics of citizens' voice and action outside their private realms. Kocka starts defining civil society as mode of action which is "characterized by the fact that it (1) is oriented towards conflict, discourse, compromise, and understanding in public: civil society is realized in the public sphere; (2) stresses individual independence and collective self-organization; (3) recognized plurality, difference and tension as legitimate; (4) operates non-violently; and (5) is related to general issues [...]." (Kocka, 2006, p. 40) Hence, civil society is how citizens interact in the public.

Habermas (1992) has conceptualized the public sphere as the locus of civil society. Civil society in this concept materializes in an intermediating public sphere rather than in a separate sector. Its constitutive characteristics are political guarantees and discursive actions, i.e. deliberation, that make this sphere real and meaningful. In the public sphere, the rationalizing potentials of community, associations, and debate transform particular positions and interests into shared concepts of the common good which are then taken up by politics (Evers, 2009, 2011). It is the public sphere and the process of deliberation that help refine individual preferences not as a function of authoritative means but as a result of collective and collaborative thinking and understanding, which is enabled by means of government. However, "[i]nclusive and objective public deliberation is feasible only through channels that are not completely captured by states or markets, so the condition of associational life and the regulatory frameworks imposed by government are always important factors" (Edwards, 2009, p. 76). Not all associations within the third sector are equally important for the public sphere, because their modes of action are less dependent on discussion and individual expression.

Habermas has offered a demanding conception of the public sphere in which civil society is fundamentally contributing. This conception highlights the necessity of a democratic state for the building of a civil society because free spaces for deliberation are crucial for the overall quality of social action. The participation in debates and public conflicts is the source of democratic preferences and not a byproduct of engagement in one particular sector. "[...] [C]ivil society also plays a role in both legitimizing government intervention and imposing its own informal settlements through voluntary codes of conduct and other self-organizing principles" (Edwards, 2009, p. 71). A protected and lively public sphere allows government to interact with its citizens in between elections and to redefine its goals as they are debated in public. A public sphere that does not function because of power distribution or exiting citizens endangers both citizens and the city. The former do not take part in the process of preference refinement and are prone to radicalization. The latter only has the voting signal of the citizen and little chance to interact, activate, or receive criticism. It is a mutually reinforcing circle. Or to use Offe's and Preuss' formulation: "What is needed for effective implementation of policies, in addition to legal regulation, are enlightened, principled and refined preferences of the part of citizens" (1991, p. 202). In declining cities, the repertoire of thoughtful citizens shrinks due to the exiting of larger parts of society. Hence, the need for engaging those that would normally not be interested increases.

Participation in this conception has a rather political connotation as it emphasizes voice and dialogue more than helping or caring. It is predominantly concerned with who is able to speak under what conditions and less with the organizational preconditions. The possible loci for the public sphere remain vague, especially when it comes to instructing government on how to foster dialogue and deliberation under the conditions of exiting citizens.

All three conceptions of civil society – associations, visions, and action in the public sphere – offer valuable perspectives on civil society and hints on how to deduct governmental strategies from them. Associations are the organizational core of civil society even though not all forms contribute equally to the production of civility and trust. The 'good society' is a vision and a need for continuous contestation between citizens and between citizen and city government. Lastly, the modus of civil society is the acknowledgement of a separate way of organizing intra-citizen relationships. It will not meet the criteria of efficiency (market) and effectiveness (state) which makes it a unique force of social integration and able to produce trust and to overcome organizational boundaries.

It becomes also clear that declining cities seem in need of all three core elements to gain some ground for the future. However, the concentration on just one conception from a government point of view would come at the expense of the others (Edwards, 2009). In the following chapter, this argument will be extended to the micro level. There, I argue that the choice of government means also depends on how government conceptualizes its citizens.

4 The government's choice: from force to frame

From a city's perspective, larger economic shifts pose a problem. Local government has very few direct means to prevent layoffs and relocation of business. At the same time, they have to deal with the consequences and are deprived of its tax incomes. Especially in areas with mono-industrial structures, where industries and their suppliers employ larger portions of the local work force, the shutting of facilities has repercussions on all spheres of society. For a city, the economic and social decline is the large-scale project with the aim to trigger alternative forms of innovation and new strategies for social integration.

Local government operates under the conditions of incongruent governance spaces, scarce resources, and by and large shrinking and aging populations (Kjaer, 2009).[5] The Greek *polis*, the ideal-type democratic arena in which citizens are directly involved in debates and policymaking, has little in common with present-day cities. The number of eligible voters has increased beyond the spatial capacity of public spaces to meet physically, and the time-consuming processes of law making and implementation have led to systemic differentiations (Beck, 1996). Some do politics and others produce goods and services. However, local government has means at its disposal to approach citizens beyond elections, which will be analyzed in the following.

Every choice of government intervention – be it by means of power, incentive, nudge, or thinking - into citizens' lives has at its base an explicit or implicit conception of the citizen. These conceptions differ and lead to different policies and eventually institutional designs. In the following, I will typify governments' repertoire of means ranging from the use of power to making people think. In parallel, I will highlight three differing assumptions concerning the citizen as the micro-level of analysis – the rational citizen, the bounded-rational citizen, and the deliberative citizen. This section closes with the argument that a change in assumption about the citizen will lead to the application of alternative government strategies.

4.1 Power

Power is the classic means of government to make citizens do what they are supposed to do. This is based on the Hobbesian idea that individuals could not live together unless they agree to transfer part of their individual freedoms to the Leviathan who secures security and individual autonomy for each of them. In democratic societies, the use of power is limited because every citizen is equipped with individual positive and negative freedoms (Berlin, 2002 (1969)), which include, among others, the freedom to choose the place to live. Stating the obvious, power is a necessary condition for a (city) government to act at all, but is not sufficient to keep citizens from moving or even to engage them. Citizens in democracies can *per definitionem* not be forced to engage nor can they be forced not to exit – physically or mentally – from the city.[6]

5 This applies mostly to cities in Western democracies and former socialist countries.

6 There is much more to say about the use of power and power relations in cities, which does not directly help to understand the argument made here. The literature on urban regimes is based to a large part on power relations between different actors within the city context (e.g. DiGaetano & Klemanski, 1999; Mossberger & Stoker, 2001; Short, 2006). In non-democratic regimes, the use of force by state actors is a totally different story.

4.2 Incentives

Incentives used by government are based on the assumption that citizens want to maximize their profits. In the libertarian conception of society (e.g. Nozick, 1974), the citizen is a free and rational profit-maximizer, knowing best what he or she wants and where to get it. The state must not intervene into market and citizen affairs because it cannot know better what is good and desirable. The preferences of citizens are exogenous in this conception and cannot be changed by government. Citizens would consume government offers and change their behavior when it meets their preferences and they are given incentives to do so. The communication between government and citizens is based on votes and money. These incentives can be monetary or appreciative. The former can come as tax cuts, expense allowances, structural funds, or others. The latter often materializes in awards of different kinds.

However, this conception produces theoretical and institutional problems for declining cities. Following Offe, preferences can be flawed in three ways: First, they might follow "false assumptions about the world" (fact-regarding), second they could "immorally disregard the well-being of others" (other-regarding) and, third, they might be "short-sighted" (future-regarding) (Offe, 2003, p. 300). Without illustrating the difficulties with each of these dimensions, it becomes clear that not all preferences of citizens can be adhered to. Another difficulty with incentives posed by government is that they endanger the intrinsic tendency of citizens to engage and crowd out their motivation (Gualini, 2010). After all, the funds available for incentivizing citizens are limited in declining cities. Although city governments can draw on programs that they are offered by the regional or state level, they themselves have limited capacity to do so.

The institutional problem in declining cities is that government has to provide a minimum set of services by law such as policing and schooling. However, if larger parts of citizens start to leave the city – hence signaling their preferences for something that they cannot get within the city – government has to cut down on these services. This conception offers little help to advise government on how to react to these preferences because it would try to incentivize citizens to stay with means it lacks. However, there is no recent historical precedence of all citizens leaving a city, which then closed. Unfortunately, it is not clear whether those that stay have to or want to.[7]

7 Glaeser (2010, p. 67) pessimistically concludes: "The path back for declining industrial towns is long and hard. Over decades they must undo the cursed legacy of big factories and heavy industry. They must return to their roots as places of small-scale entrepreneurship and commerce. Apart from investing in education and maintaining core public services with moderate taxes and regulations, governments can do little to speed this process."

4.3 Nudge

Nudge seems at first sight a strange continuation when assessing government means. Stoker et al. (2011) have introduced this phrase labeling and assessing a new set of government approaches. "Nudges are about framing choices. Citizens now live in a complex world with many signals about what is the best thing to do. [...] Governments, working in cooperation with citizens, can help shape the multiple daily choices people make in ways that could be better for society and its citizens if these social cues are right" (ibid., p. 2). It is based on the assumption that citizens are boundedly rational, meaning that citizens base their decision on information they have readily available and short-sighted preferences. Governments then need to be aware of the "choice architecture" (ibid., p. 10) within which citizens seek to decide. Nudging "is about giving information and social cues so as to help people do positive things for themselves and society" (ibid., p. 9). In declining cities, this means governments know and alter the reasons upon which people base their decisions when it comes to leaving, voicing, and engaging (Corsten, Kauppert, & Rosa, 2008). An example is the introduction of volunteering agencies that assemble information on how to and where to engage. These are often co-sponsored by city government with the aim of signaling engagement opportunities. There, citizens are treated not as recipients of services but as seekers for answers.

A large literature in sociology and a growing body of work in behavioral psychology has highlighted that preferences are subject to change because of learning and that citizens are not the omnipotent decision makers as libertarian theory suggests. They are better conceptualized as bounded-rational decision makers who try to make the best decisions for themselves with the capacity and the information they have readily available. "People are rational in the sense that behavior is generally goal-oriented and, usually, they have reasons for what they do. It is just that rationality rests on the interaction of the cognitive structure and the context in which individuals are operating, and as a result sometimes they make poor quality decisions" (John et al., 2011, p. 12). Perceiving citizens as such, governments can assume that additional information and greater knowledge can change the choice architecture of their inhabitants. This conception relates to the government strategy of "nudging," saying that citizens can be, for example, brought to engage in city affairs if they get the impression that it is a good thing for them to do. "A nudge strategy advocates working by understanding the way that rationality is bounded and then nudging citizens in the right direction" (John et al., 2011, p. 13).

4.4 Deliberation

Deliberation is here used as a synonym for *thinking*. It describes the attempt of government to see citizens as thoughtful and reasonable individuals who are willing to engage in discussion when put into the right setting (John et al., 2011). Its goals are twofold. On the one hand, citizens are expected to reflect on their own preferences and positions when they are taken seriously and when others do so as well. Collective processes of deliberation are expected to enhance understanding and by that change preferences and social behavior. On the other hand, these processes of deliberation give government greater insight than election turnouts into the needs and visions of their citizens. Especially under the condition of precarious city development, citizens that voice their concerns are more inclined to view their cities as a desirable place to live.

Deliberation rests on the question how society can be able to generate the preferences in its citizens which it needs (Offe, 2003). Other than the two aforementioned conceptions, governments can also picture their citizens as thoughtful and reasonable individuals who are capable of engaging in discussions and basing their preferences and decisions on reason. If people understand the consequences of their decisions for themselves, for others, and for the future, they are more likely to rethink what they otherwise would do. Preferences are formed and refined, as Habermas (1981) argues, through communicative action between free and equal citizens. In this way, preferences are endogenized and shapeable by citizens themselves. One difficulty remains, however, as citizens might be equal according to their citizenship rights but unequal in terms of financial and educational background.

The following table summarizes this section briefly. It offers a few additional analytical categories, which will help in operationalizing the conceptions into testable hypotheses and variables.

Table 1: Classification of means of government (Extension of John et al. 2011, p. 19)

Criteria	Means			
	Power	Incentive	Nudge	Deliberate
View of the Subject	As recipient and follower of given rules, at times as agent to fulfill tasks	Benefit-maximizer with exogenous preferences	Cognitive misers, users of shortcuts, prone to flawed, sometimes befuddled thinking	Reasonable, knowledge hungry and capable of collective reflection
Costs to the individual	High, if not complying	Low but repeated	Low but repeated	High but only intermittently
Primary unit of analysis	The individual	The individual	The individual	The group
Change process	Shadow of authority, top down	Cost-benefit led shift in choice environment	Cost-benefit led shift in choice environment	Value led outline of new shared policy platform
Civic conception	Addressing the willingness to comply	Maximizing individual benefit	Increasing the attractiveness of positive-sum action	Addressing the general interest
Role of the state	Leviathan	Design financial or merit incentives, market participant	Customize message, expert and teacher	Create new institutional spaces to support citizen-led investigation, respond to citizens
Examples	Law making	Free rent for associations, compensation for voluntary work	Volunteer agencies	Debating infrastructure

4.5 Two issues with government intervention

With these differing conceptions in mind, two questions need to be addressed when thinking about government interventions and their justifications. First, one needs to be clear whether city governments should intervene in civil society at all? This is the preconditioning question before one decides where to intervene and based on which citizen conception. Second, if the answer is positive, we need to focus on the procedural quality of the intervention.

Government intervention beyond the protection of basic rights is always a matter of debate. Political parties struggle on whether resources are to be spent on social programs or economic support packages. Based on the assumption that some preferences in society are not desirable or even harmful to living in a community, a city government that is based on an elected legislative is the only legitimate actor of intervention. This is not to say that it always knows what is best for citizens and the city.

But it is the only legitimate and controllable actor with authority to introduce processes of preference articulation and discussion about what a common good is.[8] In the context of declining cities this becomes a problem of either managing decline or actively engaging with citizens in a debate on which goals are to be pursued and who will share in achieving them.

As preferences cannot be produced by city politics or government, government has to think of how to filter and amplify those preferences that are conducive to democracy in general and community living in particular. However, while there are no criteria for evaluating what a 'good' preference is, still "no political preference deserves to be taken seriously unless there is some evidence that it has been processed and supposedly enriched through efforts such as self-examination, reflection, and deliberation" (Offe, 2003, p. 308). For Offe, a good citizen is not defined by what he desires but how he has arrived there. From a city government point of view, a good citizen is more than that, if it perceives citizens as reasonable individuals. It is one who has understood that there are consequences for a community as a whole, dependant upon what he or she does as an individual. The difficulty is that governments desire active citizens, especially under the condition of limited resources. This desire is, if not domesticated in fair procedures, understandable, but at the same time dangerous as it has the tendency to reduce the active citizen to a useful citizen from a government's point of view (Gualini, 2010).

5 *Conclusion*

City government action can be directed towards the individual citizen as well as to organizations in which citizens engage. The aim is not only to integrate citizens into the delivery of services or to make them do something they would otherwise not do. It is also to know what citizens have as visions for themselves individually and collectively. The argument is that a change from exit to action will have to include a process of voice. This process of voice can have a variety of loci, which range from civil society organizations, to local media and government organized forums, or even demonstrations. Voice can be induced by government or produced by citizens themselves in forms of protest.

Declining cities are characterized by the malfunctioning of all three macro-structures of society. This threefold conception of state, market, and community, with its respective inner logics of reason, interest, and passion, are unable to produce the outcomes that are collectively desired. Offe argues, "More promising solutions are essentially 'impure': none of the three principles of social order is to be relied upon

8 This does not mean that public pressure on government is not legitimate or even unnecessary. But government has the mandate to think about the production of common goods and their protection.

exclusively, but none of them is to be denied some role within a composite and complex 'mix' of institutional arrangements" (Offe, 2003, p. 281). Singular solutions are neither available nor desirable, as the modi will eventually "undercut" each other in coping with economic and social decline. In parallel, Seibel (1991) has argued that in areas such as social welfare provision, organizations that do not adhere to one single modus are the most successful.

In order to reach these organizational mixtures, the interaction of different spheres of society is needed. For the relationship of city government and citizen, this means that the state has to open arenas for discussion with the citizen as individual as well as the citizen as organizational member. Hence, citizens' voice is a prerequisite or necessary condition for their action. The micro-conceptions of citizens offer an additional argument: Citizens are voters, consumers, volunteers, and family members, in one. They will maximize their benefits where they can but they will also argue and think about it when they are allowed to do so. It is in the hands of the government to open up for these capacities to argue, in order to know what citizens want and to give them a chance to rethink what they want.

In this approach, the three conceptions of civil society join together because they all contain an element of voice. Third sector organizations either aggregate their members' preferences or even transform their voice into action. The good society contains the visions towards which preferences and actions are to be directed. And the deliberative mode of action within the public sphere is the modus by which the citizen has a chance to move from exit to voice and increases the likeliness to move to action.

From a government point of view, the declining city is probably the most challenging arena of all. It has the duty to deliver, its output legitimacy is endangered, its citizens leave, and it is deprived of any substantial means to react. Force as a means drops out to engage citizens. And incentives, nudges, and arguments are all means of steering a context in which citizens and the city government will engage in a discussion. Government itself will enter into these dialogues as one among others. Its authority suffices only to secure for the preconditions under which these voice arenas operate. Government has to secure equal access to it, information on all eligible to participate, and its ability and willingness to integrate the results into its work. If government manages to credibly move from authority to cooperation in the sense of integration and not instrumentalization, it has a chance to achieve three goals. First, it will function of as a driver of social integration and community building. Second, it will mobilize resources that it otherwise cannot reach. And third, it will signal to its citizens and the multi-facetted context into which the city is embedded that there is search for a vision and a future.

Bibliography

Adloff, F. (2005). *Zivilgesellschaft. Theorie und politische Praxis*. Frankfurt/New York: Campus.

Anheier, H., Priller, E., Seibel, W., & Zimmer, A. (Eds.). (1997). *Erfolgreich gescheiterter Institutionentransfer: Eine politische Analyse des Dritten Sektors in den neuen Bundesländern*. Berlin: edition sigma.

Anheier, H., & Seibel, W. (2001). *The nonprofit sector in Germany: between state, economy and society*. Manchester: Manchester University Press.

Anheier, H. K. (2004). *Nonprofit organizations: theory, management, policy*. New York, London: Routledge.

Beck, U. (1996). Das Zeitalter der Nebenfolgen und die Politisierung der Moderne. In U. Beck, A. Giddens & S. Lash (Eds.), *Reflexive Modernisierung. Eine Kontroverse* (pp. 19-112). Frankfurt/M: Suhrkamp.

Bell, D. (1999 [1973]). *The Coming of Post-Instustrial Society. A Venture in Social Forecasting*. New York: Basic Books.

Benecke, G., Branovic, Z., & Draude, A. (2008). *Governance und Raum. Theoretisch-konzeptionelle Überlegungen zur Verräumlichung von Governance*. SFB 700 Working Paper 13.

Benz, A. (2004). Multilevel Governance - Governance in Mehrebenensystemen. In A. Benz (Ed.), *Governance - Regieren in komplexen Regelsystemen* (pp. 125-146). Wiesbaden: VS Verlag.

Berlin, I. (2002 (1969)). *Liberty*. Oxford: Oxforf University Press.

Corsten, M., Kauppert, M., & Rosa, H. (2008). *Quellen Bürgerschaftlichen Engagements. Die biographische Entwicklung von Wir-Sinn und fokussierten Motiven*. Wiesbaden: VS Verlag.

DiGaetano, A., & Klemanski, J. (1999). *Power and City Governance. Comparative Perspectives on Urban Development*. Minneapolis: University of Minnesota Press.

Edwards, M. (2009). *Civil Society* (2 ed.). Cambridge: Polity Press.

Etzioni, A. (1968). *The Active Society: A Theory of Societal and Political Progress*. New York: Free Press.

Evers, A. (2009). Gefährdung der Zivilität. Zum Verhältnis von Zivilgesellschaft und Drittem Sektor. *Forschungsjournal Neue Soziale Bewegung, 22*(1), 96-101.

Evers, A. (2011). Der Bezugsrahmen "Zivilgesellschaft". Unterschiedliche Definition und ihre Konsequenzen für die Konzpete der Engagementforschung. In E. Priller, M. Alscher, D. Dathe & R. Speth (Eds.), *Zivilengagement. Herausforderung für Gesellschaft, Politik und Wissenschaft* (pp.135-152). Berlin: LIT Verlag.

Friedrichs, J. (1993). A Theory of Urban Decline: Economy, Demography and Political Elites. *Urban Studies, 30*(6), 907-917.

Geißel, B. (2009). Participatory Governance: Hope or Danger for Democracy? A Case Study of Local Agenda 21. *Local Government Studies, 35*(4), 401-414.

Gensicke, T., Olk, T., Reim, D., Schmithals, J., & Dienel, H.-L. (Eds.). (2009). *Entwicklung der Zivilgesellschaft in Osteutschland. Quantitative und qualitative Befunde*. Wiesbaden: Verlag für Sozialwissenschaften.

Glaeser, E. (2010). *Triumph of the City. How our Greatest Invention Makes Us Richer, Smarter, Greener, Healthier, and Happier*. New York: The Penguin Press.

Gualini, E. (2010). Zivilgesellschaftliches Handeln und bürgerschaftliches Engagement aus stadtentwicklungspolitischer Perspektive: kritische Überlegungen zur Thematik. In E. Becker, E. Gualini, C. Runkel & R. G. Strachwitz (Eds.), *Stadtentwicklung, Zivilgesellschaft und bürgerschaftliches Engagement* (pp. 3-23). Stuttgart: Lucius & Lucius.

Habermas, J. (1981). *Theorie des kommunikativen Handelns*. Frankfurt: Suhrkamp.

Habermas, J. (1992). *Faktizität und Geltung*. Frankfurt/Main: Suhrkamp.

Hall, P. A. (1999). Social Capital in Britain. *British Journal of Political Science, 29*(03), 417-461. doi: doi:null

Hirschman, A. O. (1970). *Exit, Voice, and Loyalty. Response to Decline in Firms, Organizations, and States*. Cambridge: Harvard University Press.

Holtkamp, L., & Bogumil, J. (2007). Bürgerkommune und Local Governance. In L. Schwalb & H. Walk (Eds.), *Local Governance - Mehr Transparenz und Bürgernähe?* (pp. 231-250). Wiesbaden: VS Verlag.

Holtkamp, L., Bogumil, J., & Kißler, L. (2005). *Kooperative Demokratie. Das politische Potential von Bürgerengagement*. Frankfurt/New York: Campus Verlag.

John, P., Cotterill, S., Moseley, A., Richardson, L., Smith, G., Stoker, G., & Wales, C. (2011). *Nudge, Nudge, Think, Think. Experimenting with Ways to Change Civic Behaviour*. London: Bloomsbury Academic.

Keane, J. (2006). Introduction: Cities and Civil Society. In J. Keane (Ed.), *Civil Society: Berlin Perspectives* (pp. 1-36). Oxford/New York: Berghahn.

Kjaer, A. (2009). Governance and Urban Bureaucracy. In J. Davies & D. Imbroscio (Eds.), *Theories of Urban Politics* (2 ed., pp. 137-152): Sage.

Klein, A. (2001). *Der Diskurs der Zivilgesellschaft. Politische Hintergründe und demokratietheoretische Folgerungen*. Opladen: Leske + Budrich.

Kocka, J. (2006). Civil Society in Historical Perspective. In J. Keane (Ed.), *Civil Society. Berlin Perspectives* (pp. 37-50). New York/Oxford: Berghahn Books.

Kohler-Koch, B. (2008). Civil Society in EU Governance - A remedy to the democratic accountability deficit? *Concepts & Methods, 4*(1), 3-6.

Kollmorgen, R. (2005). *Ostdeutschland. Beobachtungen einer Übergangs- und Teilgesellschaft*. Wiesbaden: VS Verlag.

Krönert, S., Klingholz, R., Sievers, F., Großer, T., & Friemel, K. (2011). Die demografische Lage der Nation. Was freiwilliges Engagement für die Regionen leistet: Berlin Institut für Bevölkerung und Entwicklung.

Levy, J. D. (1999). *Tocqueville's revenge: state, society, and economy in contemporary France*. Cambridge, Mass.: Harvard University Press.

Mossberger, K., & Stoker, G. (2001). The Evolution of Urban Regime Theory. *Urban Affairs Review, 36*(6), 810-835.

Münkler, H. (2006). Civil Society: Desperate Wishful Thinking? In J. Keane (Ed.), *Civil Society. Berlin Perspectives* (pp. 91-102). Oxford: Berghahn.

Nozick, R. (1974). *Anarchy, State, and Utopia*: Basic Books.

Offe, C. (2003). *Herausforderungen der Demokratie. Zur Integrations- und Leistungsfähigkeit politischer Institutionen*. Frankfurt/New York: Campus.

Offe, C., & Preuß, U. K. (1991). Democratic Institutions and Moral Resources. In D. Held (Ed.), *Political Theory Today* (pp. 143-171). Cambridge/Oxford: Polity.

Padgett, S. (2000). *Organizing democracy in Eastern Germany: interest groups in post-Communist society*. Cambridge/New York: Cambridge University Press.

Priller, E. (2009). Bericht zur Lage und zu den Perspektiven des bürgerschaftlichen Engagements in Deutschland. Berlin: Bundesministerium für Familie, Jugend, Frauen und Senioren.

Putnam, R. D., Leonardi, R., & Nanetti, R. (1993). *Making democracy work: civic traditions in modern Italy*. Princeton: Princeton University Press.

Rueschemeyer, D. (2009). *Usable Theory. Analytical Tools for Social and Political Research*. Princeton: Princeton University Press.

Salamon, L. M., & Anheier, H. K. (1997). *Defining the non profit sector: a cross-national analysis*. New York: Manchester University Press.

Scharpf, F. (1999). *Governing in Europe - Effective and Democratic?* Oxford: Oxford University Press.

Schuppert, G. F. (2005). Governance-Leistungen der Zivilgesellschaft. In D. Gosewinkel, D. Rucht, W. v. d. Daele & J. Kocka (Eds.), *Zivilgesellschaft - national und transnational* (pp. 245-264). Berlin: Edition Sigma.

Seibel, W. (1991). Erfolgreich scheiternde Organisationen. Zur politischen Ökonomie des Organisationsversagens. *Politische Vierteljahresschrift, 31*(3), 479-496.

Seibel, W. (1994). *Funktionaler Dilettantismus. Erfolgreich scheiternde Organisationen im "Dritten Sektor" zwischen Markt und Staat*. Baden-Baden: Nomos.

Short, J. (2006). *Urban Theory. A Critical Assessment*. New York: Palgrave Macmillan.

Skocpol, T. (1999). How America Became Civic. In T. Skocpol & M. P. Fiorina (Eds.), *Civic Engagment in American Democracy* (pp. 27-88). Washington: Brookings.

Staud, T. (2003). Die ostdeutschen Immiganten. In T. Busse & T. Dürr (Eds.), *Das Neue Deutschland. Zukunft als Chance* (pp. 269-281). Berlin: Aufbau Verlag.

Steiner, C. (2006). Die Abwanderungsdebatte in Ostdeutschland. Zwischen regionalem Abstiegsszenario und individueller Lebensgestaltung. In F. A. B. Partizipation (Ed.), *Von der Statussicherung zur Eigenverantwortung? Das deutsche Sozialstaatsmodell im gesellschaftlichen Umbruch* (Vol. 25/26, pp. 285-296): Jahrbuch Arbeit Bildung Kultur.

Tocqueville, A. d. (1985 [1835/40]). *Über die Demokratie in Amerika*. Stuttgart: Reclam.

Zürn, M. (1998). *Regieren jenseits des Nationalstaates*. Frankfurt/M: Suhrkamp.

III

Cases of participation in large-scale projects

Where Participation Matters: The Impact of a National Level Democratic Innovation on Policymaking in Brazil

Thamy Pogrebinschi, Fabiano Santos

The present paper claims that national public policy conferences can drive legislative activity in the Brazilian Congress, thereby strengthening representative democracies through participative and deliberative experiments. The collected data will be used to empirically substantiate this claim and to raise important theoretical issues. We question the discourse that presents representative democracy in a state of crisis as well as the notion of political representation as a second best option which is only used because participatory democracy is difficult to implement in large scale. This being said, we challenge the premise that participative and deliberative forms of democracies can substitute traditional political representation as exercised by the Legislative branch.

1 Introduction

The greater the extent participative and deliberative experiments are institutionalized, the greater the stability of political representation institutions. Brazil's national public policy conferences are a possible case that supports this proposition. Arguably the largest and most innovative democratic experiment currently being held in the world, the national conferences consist of civil society deliberation forums designed to provide the federal government with guidelines for the formulation of public policy.

The national public policy conferences are organized and supported by the executive branch, structured according to policy areas and issues, and involve the equal participation of representatives from the government and from civil society. This national deliberative experiment is usually preceded by rounds at the municipal and state levels, and the combined results of the policy deliberations are then deliberated in the national conference attended by delegates elected or nominated in the previous rounds. At the end of the final national stage, a document containing guidelines for the design of public policy is drafted, as the result of a long process of deliberation and consensus formation between government and civil society.

Official data estimates that about five million people have somehow participated in the 73 national policy conferences in Brazil since 2003. These people are distributed throughout all levels of the conference process. 'Conference process' refers to the deliberation that starts at the local (municipal) or regional (aggregation of municipalities) level, continues in each of the country's 27 states, and concludes in the so-called ''national conference'', usually held in Brasília, the country's capitol. The local (municipal) level conferences are open to participation, and over the past years, strong governmental advertising and civil society mobilization has called people to engage. At this stage, a main purpose is to elect the delegates for next levels (state, then national). Some national conferences also preview upon convocation the undertaking of 'free conferences' that may be openly organized by any groups in civil society, and of 'virtual conferences' that reunites contributions submitted over the internet. Once a formal procedure is followed, the results of the free and virtual conferences are taken into consideration in the basis-document deliberated at the national level, along with the results from the local, regional and state conferences.

Figure 1: The Structure of the National Public Policy Conferences

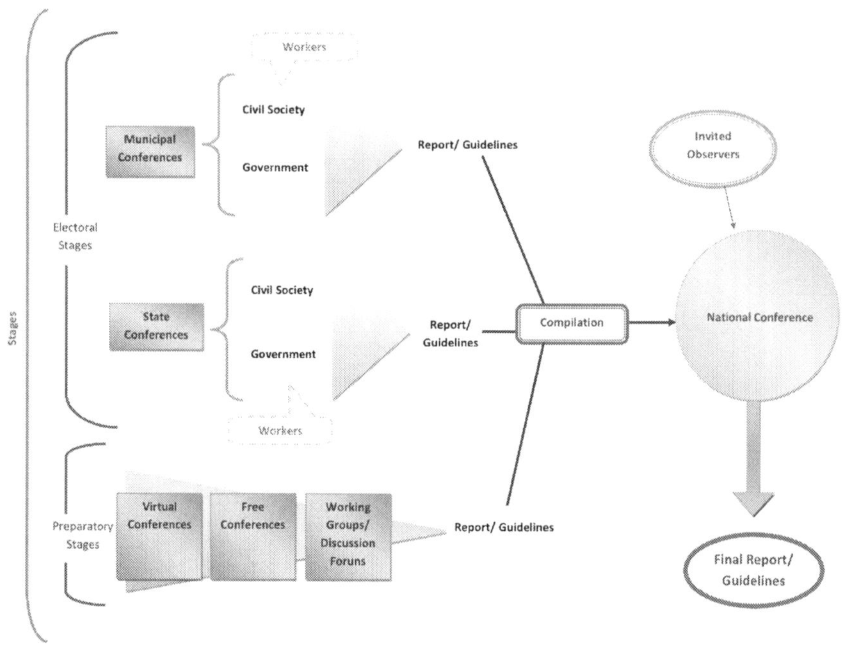

The national conferences are thus certainly an example of a ''participative institution'' (Avritzer, 2009) alongside other participative practices and deliberative experiences being institutionalized in Brazil, such as participatory budgets at the local level, to policy councils at the national level. They have a complex structure of political representation within the State and its institutions, and the participation of civil society is more direct and less mediated than traditional mechanisms of accountability, such as elections.

National public policy conferences are effective forms of political mediation and have been proving to be an appropriate means to impact the policymaking process in Brazil. This still holds true if we take into account the dynamics that might emerge in course of the eventual formation of consensus in civil society, the extent of its autonomy when acting within the State, the disputes for hegemony in different political projects, and social movements which characterize it. This notwithstanding, national public policy conferences play an important role: Brazil puts into practice what scholars of democracy around the world attempt to do by creating theoretical models and producing hypothetical simulations. They amplify the extent of participation of civil society in the political decision making process.

Though the holding of national policy conferences are not, save for a few exceptions, guaranteed by laws, and the implementation of its results are not certain nor binding, and thus dependent on the political will of federal governments, a certain degree of institutionalization has been achieved so as to ensure both its occurrence and results. Since national conferences gradually become part of the federal public policy process and therefore a part of the Executive branch structure their deliberations yield outcomes that impact the Legislative agenda. The Legislature can choose to use them for information, as a mechanism of legitimization through civil society participation, or for deliberative input for its representative activity.

The latter is the main proposition assumed and tested by this article. Our initial assumption is that the Brazilian Parliament appears to be receptive and responsive to the demands that are conjointly deliberated by civil society and government representatives in the national public policy conferences. We assume that such responsiveness can be evaluated by measuring how often the policy guidelines deliberated and approved in the national conferences are converted into legislative proposals and legal propositions deliberated and eventually approved by the Legislature. If true, then the national conferences should be considered as a component of political representation as it is exercised in the Parliament. Even more, they should then be taken as a new form of political mediation that can potentially deepen democracy, in Brazil, or wherever else such participatory experiments are successfully implemented.

2 Methodological notes: how to evaluate participatory experiments' impacts on the Congress?

We collected data on all the national policy conferences held in Brazil since 1988 (when the democratic constitution was enacted) to 2009. First, criteria were defined for classifying the national conferences that would become part of the sample. For the purposes of our investigation, not every national conference, or meeting with this name, could be considered. According to the data provided by the General Secretariat of the Presidency – the entity responsible for articulating the government's interaction with civil society and for the creation and implementation of consultation and popular participation mechanisms in the interest of the Executive,– 92 national conferences were held in Brazil from 1988 to 2009. Of this total, 80 fulfilled the criteria to be included in the sample.

As inclusion criteria we adopted indicators which would reveal the (a) deliberative, (b), normative, and (c) national scope of the policy conference. With regards to the deliberative character of the conference, we reviewed conference material, indicating the occurrence of deliberative activities (involving discussion and debate) geared towards the formulation of guidelines for public policy. With respect to the normative character of the conference, we identified in the conference material something that could be considered a final document with the voted and approved deliberations, that is the policy guidelines. As to the national character of the conference, we were concerned in verifying whether the conferences matched the criteria of serving as a space for generating inputs aimed at the formulation of nation-wide policies.

In order to classify and include policy guidelines produced by the national conferences in our database[1] we had to define a methodology. We kept our focus exclusively on guidelines prescribing and demanding any action from the Legislative branch, such as those that explicitly suggest the drafting, alteration, regulation, or rejection of bills, constitutional amendment bills, laws, decrees or any other legislative acts. We found 1,937 policy guidelines, which were then thematically grouped and classified.

Given such a large spectrum of policy guidelines we collected legislative data on Congress. The entire legislative activity of the Congress between 1988 and 2009 whose contents were pertinent to each one of the guidelines of the national conferences were classified. We researched the Congress database to identify all bill proposals being processed whose content could be related to the universe of guidelines from the national conferences.

After concluding this preliminary filter, actual classification according to the substantive pertinence between conference guidelines and Congress propositions ensued. This match was made based on the summaries of each bill proposal. At this point, the legislative production was classified into two categories: ''bill proposals and constitutional bill proposals'' and ''enacted statutes and constitutional amendments.'' After applying this content filter, the database included 2,808 bills and 321 enacted statutes or constitutional amendments.

Qualitative research – what we termed a "human filter" – followed. Each one of 3,129 legislative proposals was fully read, analyzed, and matched to the guidelines of

1 The database is online and can be accessed at www.mj.gov.br/isegoria.

each respective conference. This round of selection narrowed the bills to those specifically dealing with the demands presented by the conference produced guidelines. Bill proposals dealing with similar subjects, but pointing to directions different than those indicated by the conferences were excluded. After that, 612 bills and 52 enacted statutes or amendments remained

Finally, in order to more rigorously control the data and to establish a safety margin to confirm a particular legislative proposal resulted from the conference guidelines, a new legislative query was performed to identify and classify all bills processed in the Congress within the year immediately following each one of the 70 national conferences researched. The two filters were once again applied to the results of this collection. The following results were obtained: 2,799 bills, and 321 enacted statutes or constitutional amendments passed the thematic filter. After the qualitative filter, 612 bill proposals and 51 enacted statutes or amendments remained.

The employment of the one-year post-conference timeframe provides a distinct portrayal of the total sample researched. In reality, we ended up with 70 "snapshots", each one showing the Congress' legislative activity during the year following each one of the national conferences studied. As we apply filters and selection criteria, our total sample is simultaneously narrowed and broadened. Our snapshots overlap each other, but all reveal Brazil's Congress is significantly receptive and permeable to the policy guidelines deliberated by civil society in the national public policy conferences.

3 *The Impact of the National Conference Policy Guidelines on Legislative Production: a preliminary interpretation*

The first set of evidence, included in Tables 1 and 2 provide an idea of the relative volume of legislative production supposedly 'activated' by national conferences guidelines in the period analyzed. We first describe the figures in the table which refer to the different types of bill proposals under deliberation in the Brazilian Congress by the end of 2009. Second, we compare these results with those we produced based on a closer reading of the relationship between the conference guidelines and the decisions made in Congress in a 21 year time-spam (1988-2009), whether with regard to the initiative of bills or to the approval of new laws. We refer to this closer reading as a 'filter' because it imposes further restrictions from the guidelines. As a filter, a thematic affinity is not enough, there must also be, we believe, a clear textual alignment between guidelines, on one hand, and bills, statutes, and amendments, on the other one.

Table 1 reveals that in a total sample of 13,245 bill proposals, 2,629 (19.8%) are thematically convergent with the guidelines produced by the national conferences. In addition, of the 369 constitutional amendment proposals, 179 of them (48.5%) are included among the bill proposals that are in some way related to national conferences deliberations. Of the overall total, 2,808 bills submitted to the Legislative branch (26%) deal with contents that were also deliberated in the national conferences. If we apply one of our 'filters' these numbers are however reduced. These numbers are shown in Table 2, where we see that 566 (4.3%) of the bills and 46 constitutional amendment bills (12.5%) initiated by legislators, totaling 612 initiatives (4.5%), are directly pertinent to the guidelines contained in the conferences' final reports.

It is hard to assess the extent to which these figures are significant within the wider range of bill proposals, but it certainly requires closer attention. A first issue concerns the efficacy of such bills compared to the entire set of statutes enacted by Congress since 1988. To what extent are the bills, inspired by or directly related to the national conference guidelines, able to continue on to the floor of both houses and be enacted and then sanctioned by the president?

Table 3 suggests a first take on this issue. Of the 4,332 statutes, bill proposals which were eventually enacted in Brazil, 265 (6.1%) are in some manner thematically convergent with conference resolutions. Of the constitutional bill proposals, 8 (14%) that were enacted also belong to this subset. In Table 4 we present the figures after having had submitted the total figures through our filter. Here, 51 statutes (1.2%) and 1 constitutional amendment (1.8%) were enacted as a result of initiatives directly related to the guidelines, comprising 52 (1.2%) legal documents derived from the participatory realm of national conferences.

Table 1 – Bills and Constitutional Bills: thematic pertinence x total production in Congress [2]

	Bills	Constitutional Bills	Total
Legislative production resulting from conference guidelines	2,629 (19.8%)	179 (48.5%)	2,808 (26%)
Legislative production not resulting from conference guidelines	10,616 (70.2%)	190 (51.5%)	10,806 (74%)
Total Legislative production	13,245 (100%)	369 (100%)	13,614 (100%)

Table 2 – Bills and Constitutional Bills: qualitative filter x total legislative production by the National Congress

	Bills	Constitutional Bills	Total
Legislative production resulting from conference guidelines	566 (4.3%)	46 (12.5%)	612 (4.5%)

2 As of October 19, 2009.

Legislative production not resulting from conference guidelines	12,679 (95.7%)	323 (87.5%)	13,002 (95.5%)
Total Legislative production	13,245 (100%)	369 (100%)	13,614 (100%)

Table 3 – Enacted Statutes and Constitutional Amendments: thematic pertinence x total legislative production by the National Congress

	Enacted Ordinary and Complementary Statutes	**Enacted Constitutional Amendments**	**Total**
Legislative production resulting from conference guidelines	312 (7.2%)	9 (15.8%)	321 (7.3%)
Legislative production not resulting from conference guidelines	4,010 (92.8%)	48 (84.2%)	4,058 (92.7%)
Total Legislative Production	4,322 (100%)	57 (100%)	4,379 (100%)

Table 4 – Statutes and Constitutional amendments: qualitative filter x total legislative production by the National Congress

	Enacted Ordinary and Complementary Statutes	**Enacted Constitutional Amendments**	**Total**
Legislative production resulting from conference guidelines after classification through filter	51 (1.2%)	1 (1.8%)	52 (1.2%)
Legislative production not resulting from conference guidelines	4,271 (98.8%)	56 (98.2%)	4,327 (98.8%)
Total Legislative production	4,322 (100%)	57 (100%)	4,379 (100%)

It is difficult to gauge the political significance of the results presented thus far, nevertheless two caveats are in order. First, it is important to remember that the total sample of enacted statutes includes bill proposals initiated by the Executive branch which comprise the bulk (approximately 80%) of legislative production in Brazil. Thus, if we only take into account legislation initiated by a deputy or senator, the numbers are impressive, and include no less than 51 enacted statutes initiated with the influence of deliberative and participative processes. Second, it is worth emphasizing that a considerable number of constitutional amendment bill proposals displaying some thematic correlation were accepted in addition to the amendment which was effectively enacted. Constitutional amendment bills are, by nature, hard to submit to processing and harder still to enact. The rules that apply to the processing of this kind of bill, as well as the requirement of more robust majorities for approval, make it a rare specimen in the legislative scenario, not only in Brazil but in other countries as well. Only very high degrees of consensus or very isolated opposition explain the approval of these bills.

A second, more fundamental, issue involving the thematic areas contained by the bill proposals deserves closer scrutiny. Which issues covered in the enacted statutes and amendments were found to be pertinent to the guidelines of the national conference? The below chart and graphs present a first set of information.[3]

We start our analysis by considering the values relative to the thematic pertinence between the guidelines and legislative activity. The tables and graphs below show public policy areas initiated by legislators 'inspired' by the guidelines of the national conferences are: human rights, health, environment and minorities. The disproportional occurrence of bill proposals in the subject area of human rights is caused by several crossovers, and thus contains a wide range of issues potentially targeted by regulation proposals. The way information is presented does not allow for, in our view, any other stronger suggestions concerning the analysis. Subjects such as health, environment, and minorities, however, can provide greater insights.

The first national conferences held were on the issues of health. The participation of civil society in this domain is the most institutionalized and well established and its networks have been active in the formulation of public policies since long before the promulgation of the 1988 Constitution. Perhaps this is the main factor which explains the relative prominence of this subject area compared to the other themes dealt with in national conferences and in its capacity to produce effects in the decision making process of the Legislative branch.

The minorities and environmental thematic groups are relatively newer and yet they hold an enormous potential for interface with representative institutions. It is worth emphasizing that several studies have shown that the endogenous production of statutes in Congress is directed towards the social rights, minorities and environmental subject areas privileged and favored by Brazilian deputies and senators. The fact that these particular thematic policy areas stand out due to the participative and deliberative dynamics of civil society suggests interesting lines of investigation. It is possible to argue, for example, that the participative and deliberative manifestations are decisive cues and informational sources concerning the conflicts and issues which merit regulation by the Legislative branch, something only Congress can provide.

However, it must be acknowledged that from the perspective of bill proposal efficacy, the distribution of production according to themes is substantially different. Whereas in this regard, human rights and health continue accounting for a large portion of production, minorities and the environment lose ground to the 'state, economy and

3 Before going on to the description of the data, a technical observation is necessary. Contrary to our previous analysis, this time we were not able to avoid over-counting, as in some cases, due to the fact many bill proposals can be contained in a single thematic group, some bills were accounted for twice.

development' and 'education, culture, social assistance, and sports' policy areas. Only a finer analysis taking into consideration how bill proposals were initiated as well as their content could allow us to understand the reasons for this inversion. An examination of the figures relative to the distribution according to themes considering the filter used above sheds some light on this question.

Table 5 – Bills, Constitutional Bills, Enacted Statutes and Constitutional Amendments according to policy area (Thematic Convergence Filter)

Policy areas	Bills and Constitutional Bills	Enacted Statutes and Constitutional Amendments
Health	862	91
Minorities	412	25
The Environment	436	25
State, Economy and Development	170	28
Education, Culture, Social Assistance and Sports	286	39
Human Rights	1336	197

Graph 1 – Bills According to policy areas (thematic convergence)

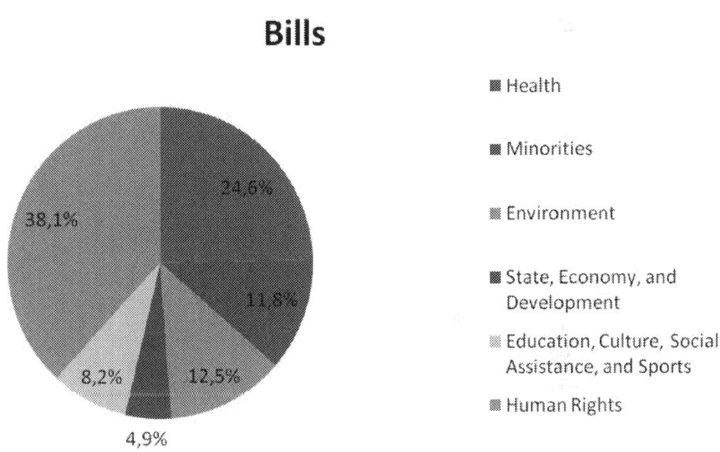

Graph 2 – Enacted Statutes and Constitutional Amendments according to policy areas

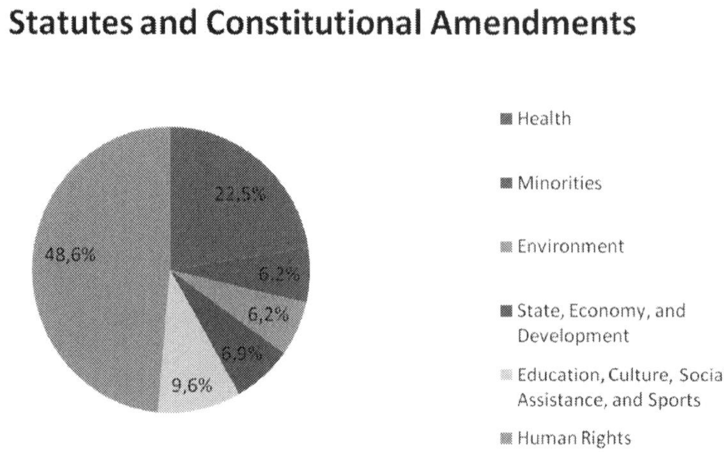

What is more, the heuristic potential of our hypotheses becomes evident when we apply the qualitative filter to the data relating to guideline themes embraced by Congress; see Table 6 and Graphs 3 and 4 below.

Human rights remains a prominent subject area, but, as seen earlier, this is significantly due to the greater extent of overlap from other areas. In other words, this is more indicative of the fact that a broader variety of issues are aggregated under this rubric, than of a clear preference on the part of legislators. With respect to bill proposals, most interesting is that health loses relative ground to minorities, on the one hand, and to education, culture, social assistance, and sports, on the other. Once again, with respect to statutes and amendments 'human rights', 'state, economy and development,' and 'education, culture, social assistance, and sports' are areas with greater concentration.

Table 6 – Bills, Constitutional Amendment Bills, Enacted Statutes and Constitutional Amendents according to policy areas (qualitative filter)

Policy Areas	Bills and Constitutional Bills	Enacted Statutes and Constitutional Amendments
Health	92	7
Minorities	117	6
The Environment	29	0
State, Economy, and Development	55	11
Education, Culture, Social Assistance and Sports	133	10
Human Rights	231	26

Graph 3 – Bills according to policy areas (qualitative filter)

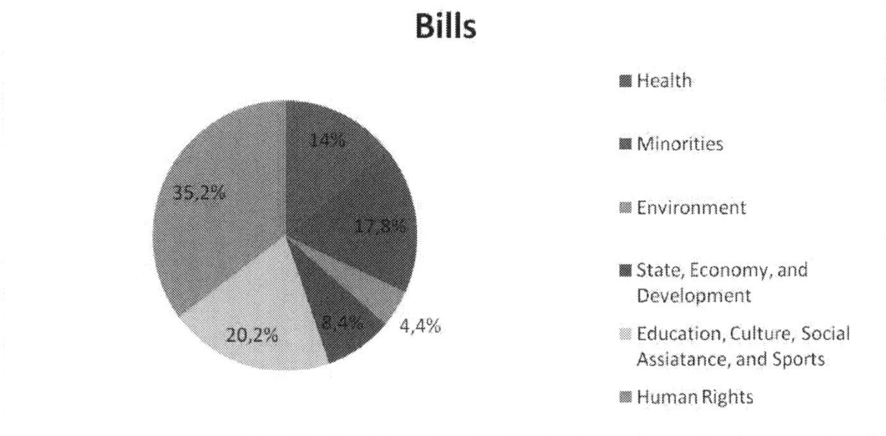

Graph 4 – Enacted Statutes and Constitutional Amendments according to policy areas (qualitative filter)

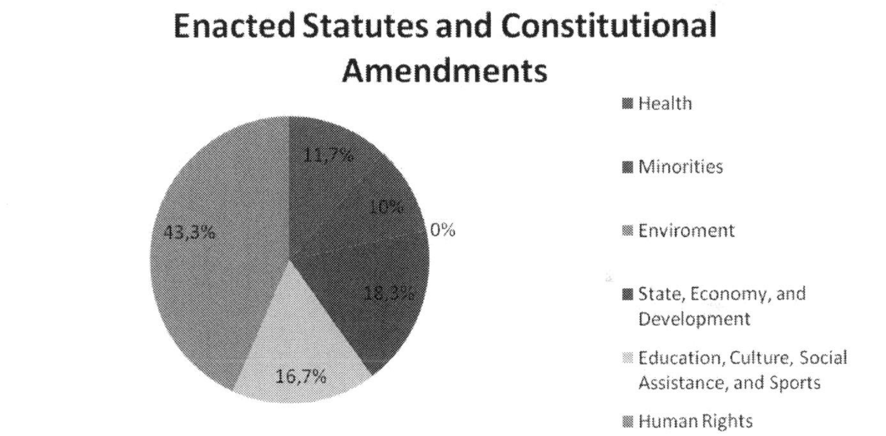

Lastly, a third and final fundamental issue concerns the temporal factor. Is the phenomenon of thematic pertinence between the guidelines of the national conferences and legislative production something new in the Brazilian political landscape? If so, to what extent? Is this something specific to a certain administration or has it been evolving continuously since the inauguration of the conferences? Let us start answering these questions by presenting the following tables.

Table 7 – Bills, Constitutional Bills, Enacted Statutes and Amendments (thematic pertinence)

Administration	Bills	Constitutional Bills	Enacted Statutes	Amendments to the Constitution
Sarney	0	0	0	0
Collor	2	0	1	0
Itamar	3	0	1	0
FHC I	68	0	39	1
FHC II	314	15	55	2
Lula I	740	73	114	5
Lula II (until 2008)	1,493	90	102	1

Table 8 – Bills, Constitutional Bills, Enacted Statutes and Amendments by Administration (qualitative filter)

Administration	Bills	Constitutional Amendment Bills	Enacted Statutes	Enacted Amendments to the Constitution
Sarney	0	0	0	0
Collor	0	0	0	0
Itamar	0	0	0	0
FHC I	22	0	7	0
FHC II	60	5	7	0
Lula I	149	17	20	0
Lula II (until 2008)	336	24	17	1

The data clearly indicates that the Legislative branch's involvement with the policy issues pertinent to the national conferences only becomes significant after President Fernando Henriques Cardoso's (1995-2002) first term in office (1995-1998). Before then, only five bills, in addition to two new statutes show some relation to the guidelines deliberated and approved in the national conferences. From 1995 to 1998, 68 bills were processed by Congress, 39 statutes and one constitutional amendment with these traits were enacted. In his second term, this sharp increase is maintained: 314 bills processed, 55 statutes and 2 amendments enacted, in addition to 15 constitutional amendments still being processed, a novel development since the inauguration of the new constitutional period in 1988.

However, during the presidency of Luís Inácio Lula da Silva (2003-2010) the numbers show an even more drastic increase in legislative production with thematic pertinence to the resolutions issued by the national conferences. From 2003 to 2008, no less than 2,233 bill proposals began being processed by the two houses of Congress (the sum of the figures on the last two lines of Table 11), in addition to the 163 constitutional amendment bill proposals presented, 216 statutes enacted and 6 constitutional amendments.

If we examine this from the perspective of the 'filter,' this evolution remains prominent. From the José Sarney (1985-1990) to the Itamar Franco administration (1992-1994), there are no bill proposals related to the resolutions of the national conferences. During the first Fernando Henrique Cardoso administration, the first bills (22 in total) and enacted statutes (7) appear. From 1999 to 2002 (his second administration), the Constitutional Amendment bills become a real feature of the political landscape. The Lula 'era' however stands out once again: 485 bills appear in the data from 2003-2009, 92 of them in the Senate, in addition to 41 constitutional amendment bills and 37 enacted statutes and 1 enacted Constitutional Amendment.

These preliminary numbers raise several issues. It seems obvious that the pre 1995 numbers (the first year of Fernando Henrique's first term) can be explained by the simple fact that national conferences were still rare and restricted to the subject area of health. It is therefore possible to conclude that thematically pertinent bill proposals only become relevant in the total calculation of legislative production when participative and deliberative activity becomes an established reality in the practices of Brazilian democracy.

This is an obvious conclusion, yet it implies a not so evident theoretical interpretation concerning the relationship between the representative and participative dimension of democracies and how they evolved in the Brazilian political context. If our assumption that increasing thematic pertinence is a true evolution rather than casual or circumstantial is correct then the claim that in Brazil representative institutions are being strengthened by participative practices must also be correct. It is nevertheless also true that the data suggests more than a temporal correlation between pertinent bills and the greater frequency of national conferences. They carry the additional suggestion that there is an affinity between the political scenario which emerged from the Workers' Party (PT) victory in the presidential elections (2003) and the surge in the legislative production 'activated' by the conferences guidelines. Graphs 5 and 6 and their data concerning solely thematic pertinence allow for a careful examination of this question, since they compare the evolution of statutes and amendments supposedly influenced by the national policy conferences and the total of bills enacted by the Congress during this period.

Graph 5 – Distribution by administrations: enacted statutes derived from national conferences (LN) x total statutes enacted by National Congress (LC)

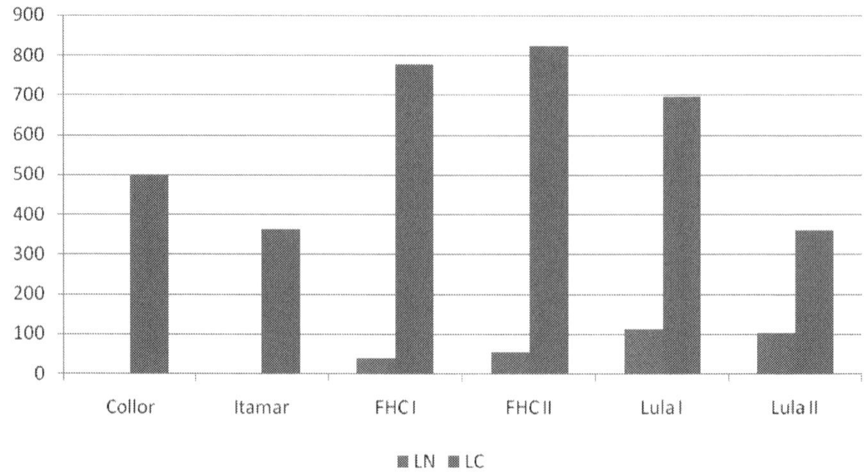

Graph 6 – Distribution by administrations: enacted constitutional amendments derived from national conferences (EC pesquisa) x total constitutional amendments enacted by Congress (EC)

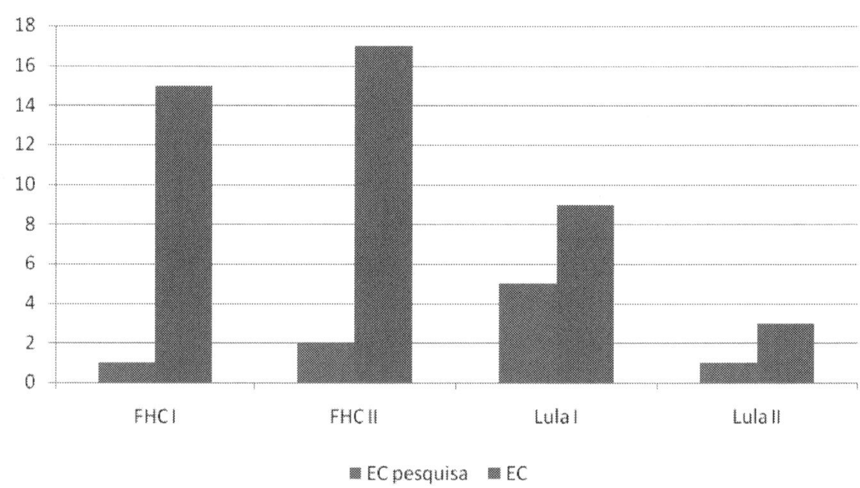

A first important observation is that the comparison between administrations in terms of initiatives is not viable because it is impossible to precisely ascertain the number of thematically convergent bills that began being processed in the Congress during each administration. Therefore, we only have access to the bills initiated after 1988 that are still being processed by Congress. We took this into consideration when describing the date and restricted ourselves to the comparison of decisions which were effectively implemented. It is noticeable that beginning with the first Fernando Henrique presidential term there is a major shift concerning the approval of legislation. Determining the extent to which this explains the increase in the number of thematically convergent bills enacted as statutes depends on a relatively simple statistical analysis which is beyond the scope of this text.

What interests us more is the fact there is a significant difference in terms of the volume of legislative activity inspired by national conference guidelines between the Fernando Henrique administration and the Lula administration. This increase is more apparent if we consider statutes and constitutional amendments enacted during Lula's first term. It therefore seems reasonable to state that starting in 2002, when Lula was elected and the dominant coalition in Congress was composed of the Workers' Party and other left-wing parties, the national conferences became more than just increasingly effective and present in the political landscape. What is more, it is also possible to state that the strengthening link between the representative and participative dimensions became more substantial.

4 *The Impact of Conference Guidelines on the Legislative Production of Congress: An Analysis with Temporal Proximity*

In the discussion above, based on the set of decisions made by Congress, whether in the sense of introducing legislation or enacting bills of statutes, we were able to detect those that are somehow thematically convergent with the guidelines of the national conferences held during the established timeframe. A reasonable objection to this selection procedure could be that the relationships found between the guidelines deliberated in the national conferences and legislative acts are in many cases random. After all, we are looking for corresponding decisions that could have eventually been made at points in time very distant from each other. If this is the case for a significant number of the cases accounted for above, we cannot know for sure whether legislative activity was prompted by participatory practices or by any other motive. Since our goal is to demonstrate that participative and deliberative practices have had an active role in strengthening representative democracy as a whole, we decided to reconsider the analysis carried out thus far by adopting the procedure of further restricting the cases of legislative decisions analyzed to those made during the period of at most one year following each national conference.

Table 9, below, provides a first glimpse of what happens after submitting the data to this new form of control. Once again, we were unable to reject the general hypothesis derived from our theoretical arguments as 12.5% of the bills submitted to Congress in the one-year period subsequent to conferences were shown to be thematically pertinent to at least one of its many guidelines. This figure is greater for constitutional amendment bills (15.7%). The aggregate figure is therefore 232 (12.6%) thematically pertinent initiatives.

Table 9 – Subsequent one-year limit: Bills and Constitutional Amendment Bills filed and still underway submitted to filter x total filed and underway

	Bills	**Constitutional Bills**	**Total**
Legislative Production (filed and underway) thematically pertinent and submitted to qualitative and one-year limit filters	214 (12.5%)	11 (15.7%)	232 (12.6%)
Legislative Production (filed and underway) thematically pertinent and submitted to one-year limit filter	1,492 (87.6%)	59 (84.3%)	1,544 (87.4%)
Legislative Production (filed and underway) submitted to one-year limit filter	1,706 (100%)	70 (100%)	1,776 (100%)

What is there to be said of the actual decisions made by Congress? In other words, which decisions effectively altered the Brazilian legal framework? Table 10, below, provides the answer we are looking for.

Table 10 – Subsequent one-year limit: Enacted statutes and constitutional amendments submitted to qualitative filter

	Enacted Ordinary and complementary Statutes	**Enacted Constitutional Amendments**	**Total**
Legislative production resulting from conference guidelines after being submitted to qualitative and one-year limit filters	15 (0.3%)	0 (0%)	15 (0.3%)
Legislative Production not resulting from guidelines of national conferences	4,271 (99.7%)	57 (100%)	4,327 (99.7%)
Total legislative production	4,322 (100%)	57 (100%)	4,379 (100%)

No less than 15 statutes related to the guidelines resulting from the national policy conferences were enacted in the one-year period after they had taken place and their deliberations were published. Although this represents a low percentage of the statutes enacted during the same 12-month period after the national conference, it should be considered that this interval is extremely short in comparison to the time it usually takes for a proposition to be submitted, processed, sent to the floor, included on the agenda and voted. Notice that no constitutional amendment was enacted within this timeframe, as this would be politically impossible without immense efforts by the Executive.

Table 11 – Bills, Constitutional Amendment Bills, Enacted Statutes and Constitutional Amendments according to policy areas (filed or underway, submitted to qualitative filter and one-year limit filter)

Policy areas	Bills and Constitutional Bills	Enacted Statutes and Amendments
Health	27	2
Minorities	36	2
The Environment	12	0
State, Economy, and Development	25	2
Education, Culture, Social Assistance and Sports	47	2
Human Rights	78	7

What is there to be said concerning the issues dealt with? Table 11, above, and graphs 7 and 8 below, show that the human right policy area still stands out, both in terms of bills and of the enactment of laws. Although this scenario is changing if we consider the relative positions of other policy areas when leaving aside the temporal restriction. The 'minorities' and 'education, culture, social assistance and sports' policy areas remain predominant in terms of initiatives, although it is possible to observe greater evenness in the distribution of final decisions. The 'health,' 'minorities,' and 'state, culture, social assistance and sports' policy areas were the subject of enacted statutes in the one-year period after the occurrence of designated national conferences.

Graph 7 – Bills and Constitutional Bills according to policy areas and considering one-year limit

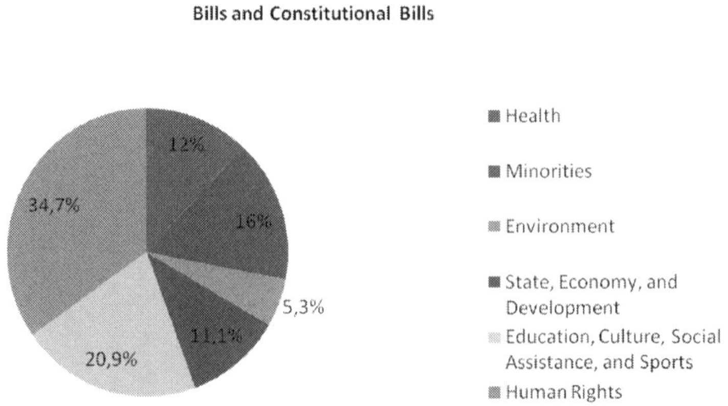

Graph 8 – Enacted Statutes and Constitutional Amendments according to policy areas and considering one-year limit

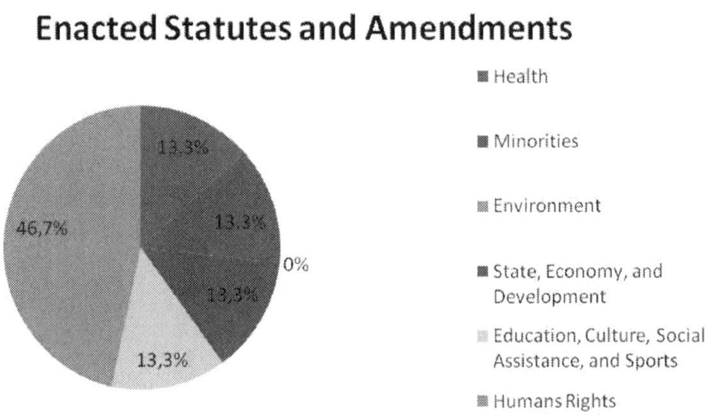

Finally, we will discuss the evolution of Congress' decisions inspired by the deliberations held in conferences throughout the different administrations which span the period following the enactment of the 1988 Constitution. Once again, from the perspective of initiatives it is clear there is a prevalent frequency of this phenomenon during the Lula administration compared to others, although it gained relevance initially during the Fernando Henrique Cardoso administration. None of this is new. However, from the point of view of the efficacy of the bills, it is possible to notice that the differences between the Lula and Fernando Henrique Cardoso administrations mentioned earlier lose their strength when we introduce the temporal restriction. This result seems natural, especially if we consider that the assessment of the Lula administration does not entirely cover his second term, since the data collection stage of our research ended in October 2009 (and Lula's second mandate ended in the end of 2010). Furthermore, it is also important to remember that we are referring to statutes enacted within the twelve months which follow the occurrence of a national public policy conference. The enactment of statutes within a year is a rare event, and it is not surprising that this only happened very few times during the two terms of Fernando Henrique Cardoso and of the current incumbent.

Table 12 – One-year limit: Bills and Constitutional Amendment Bills Government, filed and underway, submitted to qualitative filter.

Government	Bills	Constitutional Bills	Enacted Statutes	Constitutional Amendments
Sarney	0	0	0	0
Collor	0	0	0	0
Itamar	9	0	0	0
FHC I	26	0	4	0
FHC II	48	4	3	0
Lula I	73	4	7	0
Lula II (until 2008)	58	3	1	0

5 Concluding Remarks

The research results presented in this article sought to support the claim that national public policy conferences can drive legislative activity in the Congress, thereby showing that representative democracies can be strengthened through participative and deliberative practices. The data presented served not only to empirically substantiate this claim but also raised important theoretical issues. In this sense, our results seem to deconstruct the discourse that presents representative democracy in Brazil and its institutions in a state of crisis as well as the notion of political representation as a the second best option which is only chosen because of the impossibility of direct democratic procedures where citizens would be represented without the mediation of elected officials.

Furthermore, the data presented challenges the premise that participative and deliberative forms of democracies could substitute the political representation traditionally exercised by the Legislative branch. The results presented in this article therefore aspire to contribute to a more positive assessment of the Congress and to raising the level of trust in the Legislative branch by showing that it is indeed receptive and permeable to demands expressed by civil society through participatory and deliberative experiments. We thus hope to make clear that participative and deliberative experiences should be institutionalized and integrated into the power structure of the state, thereby relying less on the political good-will of more or less favorable governments.

Specifically with regards to the impacts of the national public policy conferences on legislative activity in Brazil, we can ascertain that something new is developing, something with an enormous potential in terms of deepening the exercise of democracy in the country. The national conferences have not only influenced the proposal of bills to the Congress, but have also done so in a relatively efficient manner as several bills, and statutes and constitutional amendments enacted have a content which is convergent with the guidelines extracted from the conferences.

The results presented in this article enhance our understanding that social participation should not be cast as opposing to or competing with political representation (Pogrebinschi 2012a and 2012b). Participative and deliberative practices like the Brazilian national public policy conferences internally reproduce representative dynamics similar to the logic of the Legislative branch. Yet what distinguishes these practices is not the assumed lack of electoral and party-system mediation between citizen preferences and the action of representatives, but rather the greater quality deliberations, the specialization of discussed policies and the possibility to change citizen preferences during the process, because they are exposed to information produced by sectors of civil society that are directly engaged with the issues in question.

Taking a step further, a plea can be made for the adoption of the kind of deliberation being carried out in participatory practices as valuable inputs for strengthening the deliberative dimension of the legislative process in Parliaments. Identifying the strictly deliberative dimension of participatory practices enables one to accurately map the contact zones between the so-called participative and deliberative models of democracy, and also between these models and representative democracy. The deliberative dimension is inherent to representative institutions. Social participation must be embedded into political representation and must also involve deliberative experiences. In other words, representative, participative and deliberative democracy are theoretical models that must be harmonized in practice. The national public policy conferences prove this to be possible.

Bibliography:

Avritzer, Leonardo. (2007). 'Sociedade Civil, Instituições Participativas e Representação: da Autorização à Legitimidade da Ação'. In: Dados, Rio de Janeiro), v. 50.

Avritzer, Leonardo. (2009). *Participatory Institutions in Democratic Brazil.* Johns Hopkins University Press.

Avritzer, Leonardo, & Matos, Cleber Gesteira. (2010). *Experiências Nacionais de Participação Social*. São Paulo: Editora Cortes.

Barber, Benjamin. (2004). *Strong Democracy. Participatory Politics for a New Age*. Berkeley: University of California Press.

Bendor, Jonathan, & Meirowitz, Adam. (2004), 'Spatial Models of Delegation.' *American Political Science Review*, vol. 98, no. 2, pp. 293-310.

Bohman, James. (1996). *Public Deliberation. Pluralism, Complexity, and Democracy*. Cambridge: MIT Press.

Castiglione, Dario, & Warren, Mark. (2006). 'Rethinking Democratic Representation: Eight Theoretical Issues'. Manuscript prepared for delivery at the Centre for the Study of Democratic Institutions, University of British Columbia.

Cohen, Joshua. (1997). 'Deliberation and Democratic Legitimacy'. In: Bohman, James and Rehg, William (eds). *Deliberative Democracy. Essays on Reason and Politics*. Cambridge: MIT Press.

Dagnino, Evelina, & Tatagiba, Luciana. (2007). (Eds.). *Democracia, Sociedade Civil e Participação*. Chapecó: Argos.

Dryzek, John S. (1990). *Discursive Democracy. Politics, Policy, and Political Science*. Cambridge: Cambridge University Press.

Dryzek, John S. (2000). *Deliberative democracy and beyond*. Oxford, Oxford University Press.

Fishkin, James. (1991). *Democracy and Deliberation: New Directions for Democratic Reform*. New Haven: Yale University Press.

Fung, Archon, & Wright, Erik Olin. (2003). *Deepening Democracy: Institutional Innovations in Empowered Participatory Governance*. London: Verso.

Fung, Archon, & Wright, Erik Olin. (2004). *Empowered Participation. Reinventing Urban Democracy*. Princeton: Princeton University Press.

Gurza Lavalle, Adrian et al. (2006). 'Representação Política e Organizações Civis: Novas Instâncias de Mediação e os Desafios da Legitimidade'. In: *Revista Brasileira de Ciências Sociais*, v. 21, n. 60.

Gurza Lavalle, Adrian et al. (2006b). 'Democracia, Pluralização da Representação e Sociedade Civil'. In: *Lua Nova. Revista de Cultura e Política*, v. 67, n. 67.

Gutmann, Amy. (1996). *Democracy and Disagreement*. Cambridge: Harvard University Press.

Gutmann, Amy, & Thompson D. (2004). *Why Deliberative Democracy?* Princeton: Princeton University Press.

Habermas, Jürgen. (1998). *Between Facts and Norms. Contributions for a Discourse Theory of Law and Democracy*. Cambridge: MIT Press.

Habermas, Jürgen. (1989). 'Popular Sovereignty as Procedure', in *Between Facts*

and Norms. Contributions for a Discourse Theory of Law and Democracy. Cambridge, MIT Press.

Manin, Bernard. (1996). *Principes du Gouvernement Représentatif*. Paris : Calmann-Levy.

Mansbridge, Jane. (1983). *Beyond Adversary Democracy*. Chicago: University of Chicago Press.

Mansbridge, Jane. (2003). 'Rethinking Representation'. In: *American Political Science Review*, vol. 97, n.4.

Pateman, Carole. (1970). *Participation and Democratic Theory*. Cambridge: Cambridge University Press.

Pitkin, Hanna. (1967). *The Concept of Representation*. San Francisco: University of California Press.

Pogrebinschi, Thamy. (2012a) 'Participation as Representation: Democratic Policymaking in Brazil'. In: Cameron, Max, Hershberg, Eric and Sharpe, Kenneth eds., *New Institutions for Participatory Democracy in Latin America: Voice and Consequence*. New York: Palgrave MacMillan.

Pogrebinschi, Thamy. (2012b). 'Participatory Policymaking and Political Experimentalism in Brazil'. In: Kron, Stefanie/Costa, Sérgio/Braig, Marianne (Ed): Democracia y reconfiguraciones contemporáneas del derecho en America Latina. Frankfurt & Madrid: Vervuert.

Przeworski, Adam, Stokes, Susan, & Manin, Bernard. (eds.) (1999). *Democracy, Accountability, and Representation*. Cambridge: Cambridge University Press.

Schumpeter, Joseph. (1942). *Capitalism, Socialism and Democracy*. New York: Harper.

Urbinati, Nadia. (2006). *Representative Democracy: Principles and Genealogy*. Chicago: Chicago University Press.

The Administrative State and Collaborative Governance

Carmen Sirianni

Can an agency of the federal administrative state enable productive engagement by citizens themselves to help solve public problems? In order to tackle this question it will be analyzed how a large agency, the US Environmental Protection Agency (EPA), has attempted to enable collaborative civic action. This has been done in four key ways including cognitive framing, coproducing tools, building local civic and extensive network capacity, and catalyzing change at the level of states in a federal system. Of course, a single case study only provides preliminary answers to questions as broad as the one above. There are many political, organizational, and budget obstacles that impede further learning and capacity building and no agency in the US can provide a model for other countries, which have other legal, political, and cultural traditions. However, an assessment of EPA's strategies shows that a federal agency can enable productive civic engagement to solve complex public problems.

1 Introduction

Can an agency of the federal administrative state enable productive engagement by citizens themselves to help solve public problems, and thereby take a rightful, even noble place in a democratic theory and practice of self-governance for the twenty-first century?

I propose a positive, albeit tentative, answer to this question. The obstacles, of course, are very substantial, not only taking us back to classical questions of bureaucracy posed by Max Weber, but to many emergent questions of the new governance theories: accountability, effectiveness, sustainability, and democratic anchorage of collaborative and networked forms of governance (Sørensen & Torfing 2007; Weber 2003; Behn 2001; Kettl 2002). The alignment of regulatory tools with civic and collaborative ones also presents a problem, though one that has not escaped innovators, nor those agencies and independent bodies in the US with responsibility for evaluation, oversight, and improvement, such as the Office of Inspector General, the National Academy of Public Administration, and the National Research Council.

Here I do not look directly at large projects, but at how a large agency, the US Environmental Protection Agency (EPA), has attempted to enable collaborative civic action, especially building organizational fields in which civic associations and movements play a substantial role. While EPA is active across a variety of fields, my focus here, for illustrative purposes, is watersheds. Some of what I describe is authorized legislatively, either generally (1972 Clean Water Act (CWA) norms for public participation), programmatically (National Estuary Program in CWA's 1987 revisions), or through specific other statutes that provide funding for community-based habitat restoration. But much comes from the initiative of agency staff, responding to the emerging watershed movement over several decades, to science-based justifications (especially conservation biology), and to their own understanding of the limits of command-and-control regulation in grappling with complex problems. Such staff, often networked across specific bureaucratic offices and agencies and sometimes motivated by core norms of democratic participation, such as "Jeffersonian democracy," represent significant organization culture change, a critical ingredient in sustainable change (Sirianni 2009; Fiorino 2006; Koontz et al. 2004).

EPA has enabled civic engagement and collaborative governance in four key ways: 1) cognitive framing, 2) coproducing tools, 3) building local civic and extensive network capacity, 4) catalyzing change at the level of states in a federal system.

2 *Cognitive Framing*

EPA has collaborated with the watershed movement, beginning in the 1980s, as well as with conservation biologists, legal theorists, and other policy analysts, to fashion a watershed frame that elicits collaborative action to solve complex problems. The watershed frame holds that most if not all the key problems pertaining to water – quality, supply, fisheries, habitat preservation, biodiversity, flood control – need to be understood and dealt with at the level of the watershed: hydrologically defined drainage basins that feed particular water bodies. Watersheds, including smaller watersheds nested in much larger ones, such as the Chesapeake Bay or Puget Sound, are systems defined by complex interactions among innumerable natural and social dynamics. Only holistic, problem-solving strategies tailored to specific, place-based contexts and engaging civic associations and institutional actors in active stewardship could hope to maintain and restore them. Even though fragmented federal regulations, command-and-control techniques, and massive investments in wastewater treatment have significantly reduced point-source pollution since the Clean Water Act of 1972, watersheds remain at risk owing to nonpoint source pollution, primarily from farms, transportation systems, and urban runoff, as well as innumerable everyday activities of ordinary citizens (use of lawn fertilizers). The familiar regulatory tools are inadequate for nonpoint pollution and ecosystem restoration (Sabatier, Focht, & Lubell 2005; Lavigne 2004; Goslant 1988; Adler 1995). Climate change brings still further complexity and the need for holistic and collaborative strategies for both mitigation and adaptation.

3 Coproducing Tools

The EPA has played a vital role in helping to develop useable watershed tools for public deliberation, participatory planning, citizen monitoring, collaborative management, open and usable information, and hands-on restoration. These tools are typically co-produced with an array of nongovernmental partners and are designed to be utilized effectively by ordinary citizens, community groups, watershed associations, service learning programs in schools and youth associations, and conservation partnerships that include public agencies and various other stakeholder groups (Sirianni & Sofer 2012). The co-production of tools tends to be the most effective way to tap local knowledge and meld it with professional expertise and quality assurance standards (Corburn 2005), thus ensuring greater legitimacy among various types of actors, as well as the iterative and interactive refinement of tools in response to continued feedback from practical use. Table 1 provides a schematic overview of some of these watershed tools.

Table 1: EPA Co-Produced Tools for Democratic Watershed Collaboration (Sirianni 2009)

Type of tool	**Selected examples** (overlapping, integrative uses for many tools)
Organizing	"Watersheds" as cognitive frame for civic organizing and collaboration *Community Culture and the Environment* *Community Watershed Forums: A Planner's Guide*
Network building	EPA co-sponsored conferences of watershed movement (see Table 2 below) National Estuary Program (NEP) Citizen Advisory Committees *Volunteer Monitor*
Management	NEP management conference Watershed Academy trainings, webcasts, partnership with US Office of Personnel Management
Data	Water Quality Exchange, STORET Warehouse
Planning	NEP comprehensive conservation and management plan (CCMP) *Handbook for Developing Watershed Plans to Restore and Protect Our Waters* Watershed Plan Builder
Financing	Matching grants (NEP, Chesapeake Bay; National Fish and Wildlife Foundation) Section 319 nonpoint source grants to states Targeted Watershed Grants OWOW's Watershed Financing Team University-based environmental finance centers Watershed Academy webcasts on financing watershed associations
Restoration	*Methods to Develop Restoration Plans for Small Urban Watersheds* (part of 11-volume series)
Deliberation	*Community Watershed Forums: A Planner's Guide*
Monitoring	*Volunteer Estuary Monitoring: A Methods Manual* *Volunteer Monitor*
Performance	Region 1: Charles River "measurement that matters" *The Volunteer Monitor's Guide to Quality Assurance Project Plans* *Valuing Ecosystem Services: Toward Better Environmental Decision-Making*

EPA has helped to build civic and network capacity in a variety of ways. One essential way is providing funding, often in the form of matching grants, to local watershed associations and partnerships. Such funding might be provided directly, but is often channeled through other programs and watershed movement intermediaries, such as the River Network of Restoring America's Estuaries, which are chosen on a competitive basis, based on their organizational and training capacities and democratic anchorage within broad networks of state and local groups. Thus, the River Network might be chosen, along with several other capable intermediaries, to engage dozens or even hundreds of its partners and affiliates in using tools, such as developing watershed plans. The grants are not for advocacy, but to build the problem-solving capacities of the field.

Another form of support that helps build capacity is co-sponsorship of network conferences to exchange best practices at all levels of the federal system, across various types of stakeholders, and within and across movement niches (volunteer monitoring, urban rivers, large estuaries). Collaborating with major watershed movement actors, such conferences have been critical for building the field. Table 2 provides a selective overview.

Table 2: EPA Co-Sponsored/Funded Watershed Network Building Conferences (Sirianni 2009)

Conference(s)	Date(s)	Participants
First National Conference of Estuary Groups	1987	Save The Bay (Providence, RI) convenes emerging coalitions of estuary groups as NEP is established
National Citizen Monitoring Conferences	1988-2000	Bi-annual, 100-300 participants, in conjunction with rotating civic partners (Izaak Walton League, Chesapeake Bay Alliance, etc); now part of NWQMC network (professional and volunteer monitors)
Watershed '93	1993	1,100 participants from broad range of local, state, and national watershed and conservation groups, tribes, public agencies, University Extension, business and professional associations; hundreds more via satellite broadcast on final day
Restoring Urban Waters: Friends of Trashed Rivers Conference	1993	Coalition to Restore Urban Waters (CRUW), with River Network, Izaak Walton League, National Association of Service and Conservation Corps (now Corps Network), and others; 300 participants (followed by three other trashed rivers conferences)
Watershed '96	1996	2,000 participants, plus several thousand others at 156 teleconference downlinks, from broad range of local, state, and national watershed and conservation groups, public agencies, University Extension, K-12 schools, business and professional associations
National River Rally	1995-2012	524 participants in peak year of 2006, convened by River Network, other river advocacy and watershed restoration groups, public agencies (recent falloff in EPA support, but still tools presentations)

Conference(s)	Date(s)	Participants
Regional Watershed Forums	1999-2001	13 regional, multi-stakeholder, lay/professional roundtables, 40-85 participants each; some continue as regular roundtables, with state and county offshoots; prepare agenda for National Watershed Forum
National Watershed Forum	2001	480 participants from broad range of local, state, and national watershed and conservation groups, public agencies, University Extension, and professional associations
National Conferences on Coastal and Estuarine Habitat Restoration	2003-2012	800-1500 participants, broad multi-stakeholder, convened by Restore America's Estuaries, with Save The Bay, TNC, NOAA, USFWS, local and state agencies, business partners

5 Catalyzing Change at the Level of States in a Federal System

Finally, since some powers are delegated to the fifty states, EPA has had to help catalyze change at this level, while also learning from states that have been in the forefront of such changes, such as those that participated in a nonprofit-funded initiative in the late 1990s, the Watershed Innovators Workshop. While some incentives come in the form of funding through nonpoint-source pollution grants and the like, EPA framing, tools, and network capacity building have helped innovators within state agencies. Ideally, states then also become laboratories of democracy that other states emulate.

In Colorado, for instance, some state agencies began to introduce the watershed approach in the late 1990s, in response to various actions by EPA headquarters, but especially due to the support they received from EPA's Region 8, whose main office is in Denver. A very innovative regional EPA staff network, encompassing ecosystem protection, but also with regulatory authority, as well as innovators in other programs, such as environmental justice, worked to convince state agencies to utilize the new frame and tools. The state itself then appointed regional in-state watershed coordinators to facilitate training statewide, and the number of watershed associations grew quickly over two years from 6 to 40. These associations then founded the statewide Colorado Watershed Assembly, a civic network in its governance, yet a full collaborator with state and federal agencies in its practice. The assembly, now with 75 member groups, works to build local capacity through training, funding, and network collaboration with a broad array of still other civic and professional associations, as well as schools and universities.

6 Concluding Thoughts

Strategies within EPA's watershed programs have shown us the outlines – and a good number of the basic organizational components – of how a federal agency can enable productive civic engagement to solve complex public problems. It is, however, not a model for all other agencies, or even all agencies that deal directly with place-based actors. Within EPA itself, there exist other approaches to funding, training, and network building, though also much learning across innovative programs. There are many political, organizational, and budget obstacles that impede further learning and capacity building, to be sure (Sirianni 2009). And no agency in the US can provide a model for other countries, which have other legal, political, and cultural traditions, and also have lessons from which US environmental and other agencies might very well learn. But many other countries are grappling with a similar set of problems and have to figure out how to approach the basic challenge of how national administrative agencies can enable robust civic problem solving, both for reasons of effectiveness and democratic legitimacy.

Bibliography

Adler, Robert W. 1995. "Addressing Barriers to Watershed Protection." *Environmental Law* 25: 973-1106.

Behn, Robert. 2001. *Rethinking Democratic Accountability.* Washington, DC: Brookings Press.

Corburn, Jason. 2005. *Street Science: Community Knowledge and Environmental Health Justice.* Cambridge, MA: MIT Press.

Fiorino, Daniel J. 2006. *The New Environmental Regulation.* Cambridge, MA: MIT Press.

Goslant, Kim Herman. 1988. "Citizen Participation and Administrative Discretion in the Cleanup of Narragansett Bay." *Harvard Environmental Law Review* 12: 521-568.

Kettl, Donald F. 2002. *The Transformation of Governance: Public Administration for the Twenty-First Century.* Baltimore, MD: Johns Hopkins University Press.

Koontz, Tomas, et al. 2004. *Collaborative Environmental Management: What Roles for Government?* Washington, DC: Resources for the Future.

Lavigne, Peter M. 2004. “Watershed Councils East and West: Advocacy, Consensus, and Environmental Progress.” *UCLA Journal of Environmental Law and Policy* 22:2.

Sabatier, Paul A., Focht, W., Lubell, M., et al. 2005. *Swimming Upstream: Collaborative Approaches to Watershed Management.* Cambridge, MA: MIT Press.

Sirianni, Carmen. 2009. *Investing in Democracy: Engaging Citizens in Collaborative Governance.* Washington, DC: Brookings Press.

Sirianni, Carmen, & Stephanie Sofer. 2012. “Environmental Organizations.” In Lester M. Salamon, ed., *The State of Nonprofit America,* second edition. Washington, DC: Brookings Press.

Sørensen, E. and Jacob Torfing, J. 2007. *Theories of Democratic Network Governance.* Basingstoke: Palgrave Macmillan.

Weber, Edward P. 2003. *Bringing Society Back In: Grassroots Ecosystem Management, Accountability, and Sustainable Communities.* Cambridge, MA: MIT Press.

Two Democracies Work Better Together: French and Italian Decision-Making Processes for the Turin-Lyon Railway Project

Emanuela Saporito, Daniela Ciaffi

The Pan-European Corridor V railway line connects Lisbon and Kiev and touches many European countries. The paper present focuses on the Turin-Lyon section where French and Italian authorities jointly work on this huge infrastructure project while applying different approaches. While there are provisions for a public debates on such issues in France, there is no similar institutional framework in Italy. Hence, the analysis allows to compare the dynamics of the public debate in two democratic systems with different public decision-making systems and political cultures. While the French case evidences that public institutions can activate participation by providing "invited spaces" for collective discussion, the Italian case shows that these space also can be claimed by the public. In essence, lessons learned from this comparison raise interesting questions about the use of participatory spaces to correct and improve representative democracy.

1. Introduction

The paper aims to describe how two European neighboring countries have tackled the problem of the same new, big infrastructure landing in both their own territories, starting from the 1990s until today. Its subject is the Pan-European Corridor V railway line from Lisbon to Kiev, in particular the Turin-Lyon section, and the two countries involved are France and Italy. The perspective of this analysis is focused on the dynamics of the public debate in these two democracies. On the French side of the Alps, the *Débat Public* has been low since 1983. On the Italian side, a similar institutional frame does not exist. So, the Italian public debate concerning a stretch of a highway near Genoa is a rare exception and an example of voluntarism by the promoters (Pomatto, 2011).

In Italy, during this last decade, fighting dynamics between the national top-down promoters of the Corridor V track section and the local bottom-up opposition movements to these works have been continuous. In France, on the other hand, there was no public protest and the project proceeded calmly. Recent interpretations of this gap in terms of government and governance were self-evident: France appeared to be well prepared to handle projects of public interest while Italy seemed to lack any institutional provisions for handling the opposition expressed by its citizens.

This paper, however, aims to question this image. We basically argue that the Italian bottom-up movements add some value to the French public debate system and vice versa. In the title, the key finding of this paper is mentioned already: two democracies work better than just one. The authors provide an evolutionary interpretation of the case study analyzed: from a former unidirectional dynamic, according to which "Italy should learn from France how to manage conflicts and complexity through public debate on important infrastructures project," to a bidirectional dynamic, like "and France is on her behalf learning from Italy that public debate has wide margins of improvement." Starting from the same infrastructural subject, French top-down efforts and Italian bottom-up strivings seem to work in a complementary way, towards an incremental improvement of closely related democracies. The driving belt of this mechanism, as will be argued, could be identified in the argumentative movements, which lay in contact with and listen to each other, from one side of the Alps to another.

2. The Turin-Lyon railway project: Conflicting issues

The history of the Turin-Lyon high-speed railway is a story of uncertainty and ambiguity. A story that needs a double reading tier, that implies a reference to policy analysis in order to describe the intricate system of subjects that drove or variously affected decisions, but that also needs critical reflection on planning practice in complex and conflicting conditions. In the following pages, we will try to provide a synthetic reconstruction of Italian stakeholders' positions overall, the process, and critical insight on the political and technical nature of territorial planning in the infrastructural field.

Since the beginning of the entire decision-making process, the story has been told according to two substantially different perspectives: the institutional voice of national and European governments on one hand, and the informal voice of local communities living in the territories affected by this infrastructure on the other.[1] By going throughout the chronicle of the Turin-Lyon rail layout project, from 1988 when for the first time the idea to connect the French high-speed railway *Tgv–Méditerranée* with Italy through Susa Valley came out, until today, antagonist actors have been sustaining conflicting technical and political visions about its strategic role, never coming to end with a sufficiently legitimate and effective decision. The project, strongly desired by the French government, was certainly supported from the beginning by Italian local private agencies, such as Agnelli Foundation and the *Federazione delle Unioni Industriali del Piemonte* (Federation of the Employers' Association of Piedmont), which started the

1 For a detailed chronicle of the two histories, see Ciaffi & Maroni (2006).

discussion with political players first at the local level, then at the national one (Maggiolini, 2009); Piedmont Region, the Province and the Municipality of Turin, which flew in to join the Supporting Committee, together with the most important local economic actors; the national rail agency, *Ferrovie dello Stato* (FS), that contributed in 1994 to establishing the French-Italian Alp tunnel (today's *LTF - Lyon Turin Ferroviaire*), albeit with some changes of opinion of the different chairmen in office over the years;[2] all national executives, who, since 1990, have been in favor of the project, even though each with a different position on how much local authorities had to be involved in the decision-making process. Looking at the opponents' side, it is possible to identify at least three main phases of strong contrast (Algostino, 2007; Sasso, 2006): the first lasting from the early nineties to 2000, the second, ending in 2005, culminating with the opening of the first construction site in Venaus, and the third coming up until present. Information campaigns – promoted by some environmental groups, scholars, local authorities, and ordinary citizens – are what mainly characterized the first phase (Maggiolini, 2009). However, already with the second phase, the movement crossed the borders of Susa Valley, reaching towns near Turin located alongside the planned railways, and involving not just environmental groups, but also political parties, trade unions, and social centers, thus assuming a more politicized character, questioning both legitimacy and efficacy of the project (Ciaffi & Mela, 2011). The 'No TAV'[3] movement, then, became a heterogeneous group, supported also by other radical dissent groups spread all over Italy, whose coalition and internal cohesion was facilitated by the absence of any possible contact with the counterpart. This is also the phase in which local administrators started playing a key role in opposing the infrastructure. Some of them (mostly from Low Valley) joined an Institutional Committee aimed at reinforcing the No TAV movement in further formal negotiation with national government.

2 Caruso underlines how contradiction within FS are related to different organizational levels: "on the basis of the political level of the organization (at the managers level) or of the technical level, it is possible to recognize different positions regarding the feasibility of the work" Caruso (2007), p. 5.

3 TAV is the Italian acronym for high-speed train (Treno ad Alta Velocità). The No TAV movement was born initially as a clear protest group, which doesn't leave any room for mediation.

Figure 1: The layout of Corridor V

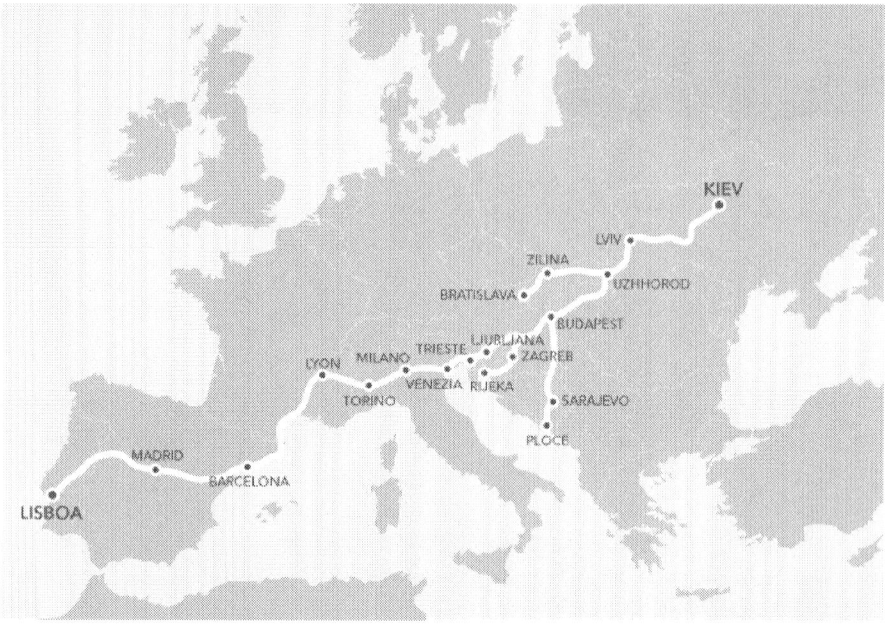

Source: http://www.tircorridoio5.com/index.php

The role of European Union Policies for Regional Planning was certainly crucial. According to Maggiolini (2009), Ciaffi & Maroni (2006), Celata (2005), and Fubini (2010) it seems that the European Community had the merit and the responsibility of including the Turin-Lyon high-speed railway project into the institutional framework of transnational policies for regional development, in particular into the Trans-European Networks (TEN), conceived according to the objectives stated in the European Spatial Development Perspective (ESDP).[4] In fact, in 1994 during the Essen Council meeting,[5] the section of Turin-Lyon became a part of the Corridor V, a multi-modal transport axis crossing southern Europe from Lisbon to Kiev, which in the EC's intentions would have ensured competitiveness to a newly enlarged EU,[6] internal market

4 The European Spatial Development Perspective (ESDP) is a document produced in 1999, which states principles for European sustainable territorial development. It is based on three general principles which were defined at Lipasi in 1994: 1- Economic and Social Cohesion 2- Sustainable development 3- A more balanced competitiveness of the European Territory. In particular among the objectives, the ESDP includes the creation of a balanced and polycentric urban system and new urban-rural relationship. For further insights see CEC (1999).

5 For further insights, see the presidency conclusions of the European Council (1994).

6 From 2004, Europe included new State Members from Est. regions and activated a new period of policies. New members were Cyprus, Czech Republic, Estonia, Hungary, Latvia, Lithuania, Malta, Poland, Slovakia, and Slovenia.

functioning and improvement, economic strengthening, and social cohesion. Although the EC position regarding the Turin-Lyon rail layout has been somehow ambiguous, becoming in different moments critical about environmental issues and citizen involvement, as being one of the main backers, EC turns out to be used either as a kind of source of the unquestionable legitimacy of this public work by those in favor or, on the other side, as one of the spheres where lobbying can take place (Maggiolini, 2009).

Figure 2: The Lyon-Turin section

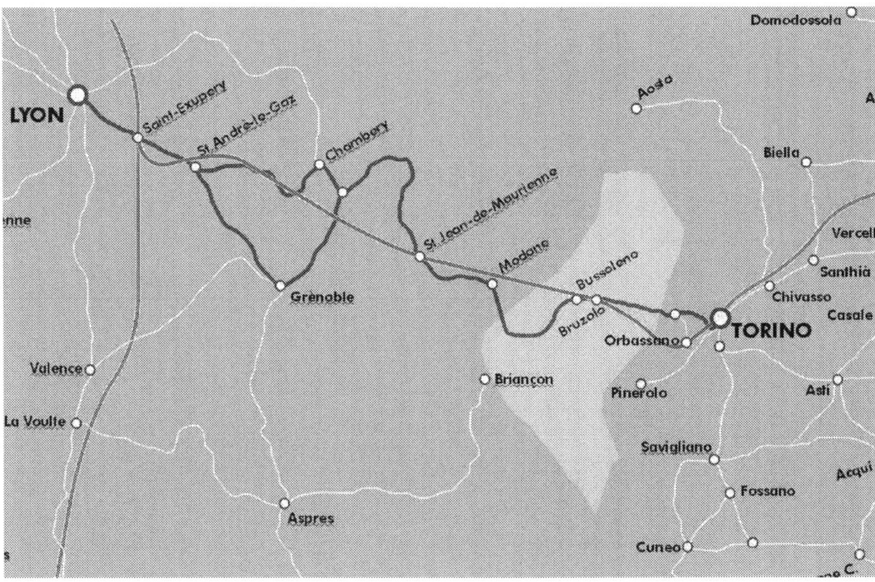

The dark gray line shows the historical railway whereas the lighter gray line indicates the new high-speed train (TAV) rail layout. Susa Valley is in the Piedmont Region which is the lighter gray area at the center-right of this map.
Source: http://www.virgolenellevirgole.it/in-evidenza/torino-lione-il-viaggio-della-discordia/

However, in terms of strategies and approaches to infrastructural planning, Corridor policies would have been conceived as a system of local interventions and investments aimed at overcoming the damage caused by a more or excessively sector-based approach, typical of infrastructural planning. In EU documents' intention, the Corridor would have promoted a more comprehensive planning approach with a special interest for local needs (Fubini, 2010), by coping with what is specifically defined as the *territorialization* process of a great work (Dematteis & Governa, 2001), which concerns localization policies within a specific territory.[7] On the other hand, national governments and local authorities would have had the duty to develop integrated spatial policies through which to lever on the new infrastructural system and to produce new territorial and economical scenarios. By looking at the Italian situation, the actual *territorialization* process does not really show a clear correspondence between local planning and Corridor policies (Fubini, 2010). If this gap is evident in correspondence with Italian big cities, intended as Corridors' strategic nodes, this is even clearer for "in-between territories," such as Susa Valley. The first and main argument used by local communities to cross the new railway project, in fact, was the infrastructural overload of the valley (especially the Low Valley), indeed, already straddled by a highway, two national roads, and a power line. Years of failing public planning policies in this area, aimed at reducing traffic congestion and at improving economic development of the region, have transformed this territory in a "service area," exploited to generate benefits for other territories (Ciaffi & Mela, 2011), and consequently it has increased local communities' skepticism and disaffection towards public policies.

It is thus evident that infrastructure planning at the above local scale raises controversial issues in practice. In fact, it has to deal with its inter-scalar nature and taking into consideration outcomes-evaluation at different levels, at different scales, and in different, even competing, territories. Although the overall project might have a rationale if taken per se, when viewed at the local scale it may appear not linked to territorial approaches and often in conflict with local policies. This kind of complexity makes decision-making processes in spatial planning uncertain and intrinsically conflicting, strictly dependent on the way in which means and goals are formulated (Christensen, 1985). Therefore, the conflicting potential of an infrastructure project may concern not just with antagonist stakeholders' values or interests, but also to what extent works' costs and benefits are intended to be distributed along different geographic areas and scales, raising issues of social and territorial justice. According to this operative framework, to enlarge decisional arenas through open and participative processes seems to be a necessary step. From a spatial planning perspective, the aim is not just to reduce conflicts and to deal with NIMBY[8] syndrome, but to collect as much knowledge as needed to design the most suitable solution for each territorial setting. The emerging necessity for planners of involving a plurality of actors in planning

7 Each "territorialization" process is determined by symbolic and material production/construction of a territory. This process necessarily implies a conflicting dimension, which concerns with representations, goals, strategies and actions of an actors' plurality, which act on different scales on the basis of different rationalities (Dematteis & Governa, 2001).

8 NIMBY (*Not In My Back Yard)* is a label used to describe reactions of local communities towards common interest projects, which are perceived as threating to local identity and territorial peculiarities or that could have negative externalities on their territory. Such projects could be, for example, incinerators, quarries, and industrial, mobility, or energy infrastructures. It is a kind of spiteful label, because it implies that opponents are moving because of selfish, and individualistic interests (Bobbio, 2004).

processes, derives both from pragmatic and political reasons: from the consciousness that making effective public policies means merging expert and experiential knowledge (Balducci, 1991), drawing on the "intelligence of democracy" (Lindblom, 1975); but also it derives from the political need of designing new and more democratic forms of public decision-making processes by introducing participatory practice as a way to solve the existent gap between public institutions and civil society (Bobbio, 2002, 2004, 2007).

In light of a persistent conflicting and uncertain situation affecting the Turin-Lyon railway decision-making process, two main questions remain: how to conceive public decision makers' action in order to produce an effective and legitimate project? And which role is there for "conflicting participation" (Ciaffi & Mela, 2011)?

3. *Coping with complexity: Two normative approaches*

In order to explore possible answers to the research questions we are proposing, we will try to understand how France and Italy, two neighboring countries sharing the same infrastructure and of course similar planning problems, have tackled and are still coping with Corridor V projects. In particular, we will critically analyze normative and institutional approaches to civic participation as a methodological way to untie a complex and conflicting planning topic.

3.1. One deliberative instrument for several projects: French Débat Public

French public management of large-scale projects in territorial development boasts a decennial experience in involving civil society in decision-making processes. During his presidency, Mitterand started a legislative path to regulate public inquiries, which led to the establishment of the 'public debate' form (***Débat Public***)[9] as a mandatory procedure to be followed in the face of big urban and territorial transformation projects.

Going back to the origins of the current French Débat Public, the first set of rules to involve civic society in spatial planning processes became law in 1976. During the following fifteen years, national legislators' perspective shifted from a generic goal of "taking into consideration environmental protection" into a growing attention towards specific large infrastructural projects regulation. In the early nineties, the

9 The Public Debate is a method of citizen participation in public decision-making processes and has been introduced by the French National Commission (Commission National du Debat Public) in 1996. The procedure of a Public Debate is includes the following steps: draft an explanatory document about the project, plan a series of public assemblies, collect and publish citizens and interest groups opinions, write a final report on the Public Debate. Further information is available at http://www.debatpublic.fr/docs/doc/brochure-in-english.pdf.

Bouchardeau's law gave a very convincing meaning to the concept of transparency: in a modern democracy all actors involved in any big spatial transformation have to participate in public presentations of projects and to debate according to specific procedures designed by the law. Public debate was definitively introduced with Barnier's law in 1995 (Hélin 1995), which defined procedures of actors' consultation and responsibilities. With the Chart de la Concertation (Consultation Chart) in 1996, the assumption of a participatory culture was clear: "consultation aimed at agreement achievement represents an enrichment for representative democracy towards a more participated democracy, and it generates minds- and behaviors- changing." Decision-making responsibility for territorial public policies was thus shared by the collectivité locale (local collectivity): in fact, members of government, third sector, and civil society are brought to work together in the public debate form. From a methodological point of view, this instrument is a deliberative device[10] aimed at facilitating a transparent and dialogical communication among participants – not just the stakeholders, but everybody who has an interest in the topic discussed. Furthermore, it has to take place at the beginning of the decision-making process and it is not compulsory to reach a final agreement: the Débat Public is merely conceived to be an argumentative time for learning more about intentions, objectives, and meanings of an intervention, rather than designing solutions (Romano, 2012).

According to contemporary procedures, the key role in a public debate is played by the national commission, which has the responsibility of managing discussion between participants. Its members are chosen at top government levels, together with three other representatives: national association for environment protection, users, and experts. As several French authors underline, the experiences of public debate are widely innovative but still characterized by a number of imperfections (Revel et al., 2007). On one hand, one of the most problematic issues concerns selecting national commission members, particularly with the choice of the president. On the other, the extremely open nature of the method, grounded on participants' self-selection (Bobbio, 2004), could be critical. In fact, it would create a sort of imbalance during the discussion, favoring one-sided argumentations.

10 In the Italian cultural framework, it has been necessary to underline the distinction between the Anglo-Saxon meaning of deliberation and Italian meaning of "*deliberazione*." While the Italian *"deliberazione"* would mean to reach a final decision, to vote a position, the English meaning is rather "to consider and examine the reasons for and against a measure." In this frame, "to deliberate" would imply a dialogical and discursive process, where participants' preferences can evolve and transform through a discursive confrontation. All Habermasian communicative theory is strictly linked to the deliberative nature of a communicative action (Habermas, 1986). Theories of Communicative and Deliberative Planning (Forester, 1989, 1999; Healey, 1997) draw on Habermasian philosophy and provide sophisticated methodological devices to facilitate collective discursive interaction in planning decision-making processes. A wide range of methods used to facilitate deliberation in planning is available on-line at www.communityplanning.net.

Nevertheless, there is no doubt about the need for public debates: the law decrees that they have to be launched if the infrastructure exceeds defined costs of the works (i.e. in 2002 the law fixed the cost of 300 million Euros for highways, railways, shipways as the threshold for public debate). The French culture of spatial planning is fully aware that any physical transformation is the result of a complex game among institutional, economic, social, and environmental actors (Melin & Choay, 1988). Any interpretation about urban and territorial changes in France pays big attention to the dynamics among the different players. This is an important cultural precondition in order to understand two core reasons of public debate on infrastructure: a successful public debate is a process that is legitimated from the different involved parties and, at the same time, it is the unique tool able to make different actors interact reflectively (Pomatto, 2011). This goal is variously achieved through "democracy matches" depending on the contexts and on the personalities involved, but what is interesting to underline is that there are just three general principles regulating the public debate: equality of participants, transparency, and arguing.

3.2. Muddling Through[11]: Italian approach to public participation

In Italy, institutionalization of participatory processes for urban and territorial planning practices takes place mainly at the regional level, because of each region's autonomy in legislating on town planning matters. As Italy has sustained a decentralized planning system since the 1970s, innovative practices in terms of civic participation in urban and territorial projects are also mostly local achievements. For this reason, regions such as Emilia Romagna or Tuscany have both reformed their main town planning instruments (Piani Strutturali Comunali) in order to include participation as a requirement for plan approval. Moreover, Tuscany has recently in 2007 enacted a Regional Law on Participation (L.R.69) for the first time in Italy (Regione Toscana, 2008). Taking into consideration that for public decision makers, participation would have broad meaning,[12] a minimum level of participation is already guaranteed in our most tradi-

11 The concept of "muddling through" is gathered from Lindblom. Drawing on Simon's "bounded rationality," Lindblom developed his theory of "disjointed incrementalism," based on "partisan mutual adjustment" (Lindblom, 1959), thanks to which the decision-making process was seen as a "plural" and "bargaining" process. Lindblom's theory is based on a pragmatic approach to planning practice, generated through the direct observation of the public sector's job.

12 In the urban and territorial planning field, "to participate" can acquire different meanings. It would mean "to engage" or "to communicate, to inform," which means on the one hand to line up, to express a personal opinion becoming an active subject of the process, or, on the other hand, to share information and opinions (Ecosfera, 2001). To define what we mean with "participation" would imply different levels of power within a public policy practice. The most famous taxonomy for participation levels is Arnstein's participation ladder (Arnstein, 1969), which has already been criticized and overcome by deliberative authors, as Forester, and in Italy by Ecosfera (2001); Mela & Ciaffi (2004); Bobbio (2004); see Saporito (2008).

tional town-planning instrument, Piano Regolatore Generale Comunale (Local Master Plan), whose revisionary process provides for consultation windows with local community. Of course, infrastructural planning, especially when conceived at an over-local and strategic scale, refers to more articulated and integrated planning instruments. This is the case of the so-called Conferenza dei Servizi[13] (Conference of Services), an institution where local authorities, together with regional and national ones, can sit at the decision table and discuss and question the advisability of an infrastructure. Moreover, thanks to Environmental Impact Assessment (EIA) and later to Strategic Environmental Assessment,[14] it became possible to strengthen and improve procedures in the perspective of increasing environmental protection and sustainable development, always empowering citizens and NGO's in the decision-making process.

In spite of all those normative instruments aimed to activate participatory spaces within infrastructure planning processes, things went differently for the Turin-Lyon railway. In 2001, Berlusconi's government introduced the Legge Obiettivo (Aim Law) as the new normative instrument to regulate and finance infrastructure planning in Italy (Mazzeo & Pinto, 2011). As soon as the new law was enacted, the Turin-Lyon project was included in the list of "strategic infrastructures" conceived by the law. In contrast with all European instructions, this new legislative measure basically centralized decision making at the national government level, excluding any form of local authority and community participation during the overall process, and basically denaturing the functioning of EIA and SEA.

Just after dramatic events of 2005, things partially changed. In December 2005, around 50,000 inhabitants of Susa Valley occupied the excavation site and set up permanent pickets, paralyzing the Venaus work site until the demonstration was repressed by police forces. When in 2006 Italian government changed,[15] the new executive body finally decided to establish two ad hoc institutional bodies to cope with this permanent conflicting situation: the Tavolo Politico di Palazzo Chigi (The Political Table) and the Osservatorio per il collegamento ferroviario Torino Lione (Observatory on the Turin-Lyon Railway). Those two bodies were interrelated. The Observatory was conceived to work as a technical consulting instrument, on which the Political Table would

13 The Conference of Services, established by the law of 7 August 1990 n. 241, *Nuove norme in materia di procedimento amministrativo e di diritto di accesso ai documenti amministrativi*, subsequently modified by the law of 11 February 2005, n. 15,dal Decreto legge 14 March 2005, n. 35 and by the law of 2 April 2007, n. 40, is created to simplify processes and speed up the decision-making process.

14 European Commission introduced SEA (in Italian VAS) in 2001. In the introduction to the European regulation 2001/42/EC it is written "In order to contribute to more transparent decision making and with them of ensuring that the information supplied for the assessment is comprehensive and reliable, it is necessary to provide that authorities with relevant environmental responsibilities and the public are to be consulted during the assessment of plans and programs, and that appropriate time frames reset, allowing sufficient time for consultations, including the expression of opinion."

15 In 2006 a new left-oriented government was elected and the Prime Minister was Romano Prodi.

have relied in order to make political choices and to facilitate negotiations among different levels of government authorities – national, regional, and local. The institutionalization of a Political Table is unique in Italy (Podestà, 2008) and it is indicative of the fragility and significance the Turin-Lyon issue reached after 2005. The Observatory's goal was to "find technical answers to political questions, by trying to tie again the threads of an interrupted dialogue and to re-establish the mutual acknowledgment between subjects variously interested in the topic" (Observatory Turin-Lyon railway, 2007, p. 9). The Observatory in fact allowed a technical debate among experts named by each of the institutional stakeholders (from Susa Valley mayors to regional and European representatives), but it didn't directly involve citizens or local NGOs.

Chaired by architect Mario Virano, named extraordinary commissioner by national government, Observatory's merit was to open up a debate that for the first time questioned the opportunity of the Turin-Lyon layout by taking into consideration other possible solutions, even those grounded on the hypothesis of enhancing existing historical lines (Ciaffi & Mela, 2011). The way in which works were managed by the president, Mario Virano, was crucial. Meetings took place every week for almost 3 years. Communication with civil society occurred through monthly reports, Quaderni, containing all meeting records, as well as questions, issues, and contrasts. At the end of this experience, two critical issues might be identified within this approach. The first concerns excluding civil society from the process, that have been able, over the years, to organize groups and associations and formulate structured and valid positions and documents (Maggiolini, 2009). Secondly, bringing the political debate just on technical issues and practical solutions would have depoliticized conflicts (Padovan, Alietti, Arrobio, 2011). Indeed, it displaces contrasts on technical arguments, as much that, at the end of all mediation processes, we have two robustly documented and fully feasible solutions, following opposite, incompatible paths: the construction of a new line and the enhancing of the historical line, the so-called Low Cost project.

4. Which results? The role of opposing groups

After a stalemate phase however, intercalated by some fight episodes, open conflicts exacerbated again in summer 2011, when police forces removed No TAV's garrison in the area assigned for construction of the exploratory tunnel. Together with the Italian government crisis in winter of the same year, further protests spread all over Susa Valley and culminated in February 2012 with a dramatic accident in which a young demonstrator was seriously injured. In spite of the latter mediation attempts, No TAV resistance to central government choices didn't really make a step backward: the amount of technical studies and economic evaluation produced by No TAV supporters is impressive and all of them are addressed to delegitimize the economical and functional Turin-Lyon project's ratio.

In an interview in March 2012, conducted by Marianella Sclavi, Italian expert of creative conflicts resolution, Mario Virano reflects upon limits of the Italian way of managing conflicting public policies (Scalvi, 2012). He raises two main points: The first is the attitude of the Italian government to act with a sort of pre-Lutheran indulgences' market approach in order to make the local population and its political representatives consent to the new big infrastructure. The traditional top-down behavior is paying the stakeholders one by one, while the bottom-up perspective reveals an ordinary acceptance of this mechanism, as much individualistic as completely complementary to the top-down attitude. The interviewed speaks ironically by defining the Italian left party as "state-controlled in a different way." As regarding the Observatory experience he states: "It is completely unreasonable to think that it can be possible to open a debate with local communities and stakeholders in general at the end of a decision-making process. First thing to do should be to modify the law [Aim Law] in order to introduce an organized debate phase, codified by determined procedures, certain duration, and a guaranteed external management system, as the preliminary phase of each infrastructure planning process. What has to be discussed should be motivations, goals, and features of a new operation." Virano is clearly referring to French Débat Public, as a virtuous model for managing conflictive planning issues by enlarging the public arena. Today, it is common opinion in Italy that "we should learn from France," as the Minister for Development, Corrado Passera, stated a few weeks ago.

But what is really happening on the other side of the Alps today? Indeed, echoes from Susa Valley's protests are crossing the regional borders to resound in France. Savoie, the French region crossed by the Turin-Lyon line, has been historically in favor of the project, which would have represented a good alternative to heavy-goods vehicles invasion, crossing the valley everyday, increasing pollution and creating safety risks. Now something seems to change. Although at first the trans-alpine rail road Lyon-Turin was conceived of to privilege just high-speed train travellers, already in 1995, with the Green party elected in the Regional Council, freight transportation issues were also taken into consideration and brought into the Lyon-Turin discussion. The Mont Blanc tunnel accident in 1999 was another turning point in the decision process for sustaining the new railway project: people were convinced that starting a process of modal shifting in the Valley was the best way of also reducing dramatic risks.

For French ecologists, in fact, it has been somehow hard to understand how Susa Valley inhabitants would prefer trucks crossing valley landscapes and be against goods-rail transports. Nevertheless, today Italian opponents' argumentations are introducing new elements for evaluating Turin-Lyon benefits so convincing that "it is necessary to revise our critical support to the project, since those are profoundly changing the game," Gérard Blanc, National Leader of EELV (Europe Ecologists the Green) Savoie, recently affirmed.[16]

In the light of a renewed consciousness, French ecologists are again opening up the debate. Michèle Rivasi, a member of European Parliament for Europe Écologies, Greenpeace France ex-manager, and vice-mayor in Valence, has recently explained very well how their positions on Lyon-Turin are evolving:

> "At first, we were more convinced that goods transportation would provide the big opportunity of crossing Alps to develop trades with Italy. Now, instead, because of the problematic situation in Susa Valley and people protests against the high speed line, we wouldn't certainly oppose the majority," and she adds "this is the reason why I asked for a new report about valley situation. After all the effort aimed at promoting rail transport against heavy-goods vehicles, we wouldn't change opinion easily. But, if Italians are still opposing, we have to face with these new problems." (Blitz quotidiano, 2012)

A public inquiry conduced by the National Agency for French Environment (AE) about the 'Turin Lyon' project, published in December 2011 in France, raised a number of evidences, according to which environmental organizations such as FRAPNA (Rhône-Alpes Federation for Nature's Protection) and FNE (France Nature and Environment) historically in support of the project are changing opinion and asking to open a public discussion on the infrastructure. According to this report, in fact, former evaluations on the Turin-Lyon line traffic system and economic returns would have been carried out from no more valid data (Sansa, 2012). Apparently the first traffic foresights were too optimistic, enough so as to weaken cost-benefit analysis results made today: by using actual traffic data and taking into consideration work site delay foresights, expected profitability would reduce dramatically. The 'Lyon-Turin' project is already costing 24 billion euros. Its completion date and use however remain unclear: the number of long-distance journeys by train is stagnating and goods traffic between Italy and France is falling. The modernization of the line, according to experts, would be sufficient to transport up to 19 million tons of goods by rail, while the current figure is less than five million. Beside that, the report tackles environmental impact issues by recommending RFF to produce more detailed studies on air pollution and flooding risks.[17]

Not surprisingly, these argumentations coincide exactly with those sustained by the Italian No TAV movement.[18]

While regional representatives from EELV are espousing this thesis (Emmanuel Coux, 2011) at the national tier, former President Sarkozy and current President Hollande, both are still strongly in favor of the project. This gap between central govern-

16 For further insights, watch interviews at the following link http://www.lavoixdesallobroges.org/environnement/396-les-ecolos-savoyards-divises-sur-le-lyon-turin

17 For more detailed information see http://www.cipra.org/en/alpmedia/news-en/4556; http://www.ilfattoquotidiano.it/2012/03/05/ricavi-traffico-dubbi-parigi-sulla/195633/

18 Full documentation at http://areeweb.polito.it/eventi/TAVSalute/ANALISI%20DOCUMENTO%20GOVERNO%2028.03.12.pdf

ment conviction and local positions is evident also within ecologist groups themselves. If at the local level representatives from EELV are criticizing the entire project's ratio, also enlarging the debate to the entire economic system this infrastructure would represent (Gérard Blanc, 2011), their delegates at the national level seem still convinced.

It is certainly hard to affirm if a new French front is going to appear in the battle against the Turin-Lyon high-speed train. For sure, French central government has made crucial work in the last 10 years, preparing public opinion to accept and welcome the infrastructure. The law of 2002, in fact, contributed to defining compensations for local communities by imposing the rate for local enterprises at 86% by favoring economic returns for hotels and residences and tax facilitations. However, the rising of new opposing movements on the French side of the infrastructure project is the demonstration that conflicting dynamics within civil society have a generative and transformative power also in an very democratic and sophisticated governance system.

5. Conclusion

The Turin-Lyon railway project is an emblematic case of when such a cross-border infrastructure becomes the occasion for two democracies to confront relative public decision-making systems and political cultures. French case evidences that public institutions can activate participatory devices aimed at improving public policies, as in the infrastructural planning field, by providing "invited spaces" for collective discussion, like public debate sessions. On the contrary, Italian government shows how such a top-down approach, imposed in an emergency regime without any margins for public debate, can produce weak public policies and exacerbate conflicts. Although many Italians are looking to France as a virtuous example, asking for the introduction of public debate forms also in its governmental system, the emerging protests in France as well as recent technocratic experiments in Italy are raising interesting questions about the use of participatory spaces to correct and improve representative democracy.

A first reflection concerns with the consensual perspective proper of those participatory practices aimed to anticipate and reduce conflicts. Even though deliberative approaches do not promote negotiation (Elster, 1991), but rather transactional learning through free speech and creative dialogue, those practices are addressed to facilitate "mutual understanding" and "preferences transformation" (Habermas, 1986). Such a culturalist perspective indeed reduces pluralistic potential of participatory practices according to which “passions and interests are incommensurable”[19] (Pasqui, 2005, p. 31). In this sense, some authors are talking about “the tyranny of participation” (Cooke & Kothari 2001; Pasqui, 2005; Miessen, 2011), whose systemic tyrannical potential do not conceive “claimed spaces” for participation and consequently systematically exclude less powerful social groups. In a recent interview given to Markus Miessen in 2011 for his work *The Nightmare of Participation*, Chantal Mouffe clearly explains the conflicting relationship between the seeking of pluralism in participatory practice and the consensus-building approach. Her point of view is certainly extreme, but it gives some interesting cues of reasoning about the deliberative model, both in its practical and political dimension. In particular, Mouffe criticizes the consensus-building perspective, by sustaining instead that interaction and collaboration, as a way for producing new knowledge, should be pursued in conflicting contexts, where relationality of powers could be broken: “Because today's networking culture is based on consensus rather than conflict, it merely produces multiplications, but rarely new knowledge.” (Mouffe quoted in Miessen, 2011) Indeed, looking at the relationship described in the last paragraph of this paper between Italian opposing movements and French ecologist groups, Mouffe's observation finds a practical relevance. If the core of public debate is deliberation, the role of those opposing movements, working outside of “invited spaces” of participation, provided by the public institutions, and producing additional reasoning, is crucial for improving deliberation by incrementing collective knowledge and public consciousness on the specific topic discussed. A conflicting conception of participation, in fact, acknowledges opposing groups as beneficial for democracy, aimed at stimulating deliberative devices and governance systems in the direction of a more pluralistic and heterogeneous social organization.

In Mouffe's words “One should therefore argue that, instead of breeding the next generation of facilitators and mediators, we should encourage the ‘uninterested outsider,’ the uncalled participator, who is unaware of prerequisites and existing protocols, but instead who has to enter the arena with nothing but creative intellect and the will to provoke change.”

The Italian experience of the Observatory, on the other side, opens an interesting reflection about the relationship between technique and politics. Virano's technocratic approach, in fact, fails when it doesn't take into consideration the communicative and discursive nature of public decision-making practices, by, on the contrary, emphasizing, in a sort of neo-Positivist manner, the power of technicalities and scientific knowledge. In doing this, he seems to be not aware of the “tricky” and “weakened”

19 An Italian policy analyst, Gabriele Pasqui, clearly explains how “on one side *planning theory* adopts the centrality of deliberative dimension as an universalized process, without being sufficiently prudent and by underestimating the fact that planning processes are mainly social constructs, produced within a plurality of multi-actor cooperative and conflictive interaction's forms, which involve interests and lives' meanings, not necessarily associate,” p, 31 in Pasqui G. (2005). *Progetto, governo, società. Ripensare le politiche territoriali*, FrancoAngeli, Milano.

nature of public issues (Rittel & Webber, 1973), by relegating problem-setting process to a technical debate. At the same time, the incrementalist approach to decision-making practices in the Observatory seems a step forward for deliberative conception of participatory planning: looking for little agreements on practical tasks seems a more pragmatic and effective approach to pluri-logical decision contexts, rather than looking for "mutual understandings." However, the choice to reduce the public arena by excluding civil society from the debate has certainly affected the legitimacy perceived by public opinion about the entire Observatory's experience.

Confrontation matters, and is useful. Decades of experimentation by French democracy on more participative forms of territorial governance are proof that "it is possible" to change the way of governing and it is time for Italian technicians and politicians to ask themselves "why not here?" At the same time, French public managers have to face the weaknesses of a rigid consulting system. Certainly, French participatory models need some revision towards more flexible, transformative structures for participation, in the light of an urgent society that is showing an increased consciousness of sharing information through ICT, and producing new knowledge itself.

Bibliography

Algostino, A. (2007). *Il movimento No Tav e le forme della democrazia.* Retrieved from: www.costituzionalismo.it, fascicolo 2, ottobre, pp. 1-36.

Balducci, A. (1991). *Disegnare il futuro. Il problema dell'efficacia nella pianificazione urbanistica.* Bologna. Il Mulino.

Balducci, A. & Tessitore, P. (1998), "Irréversibilité et processus de décisions", in Klein, O. (ed.), *Temps, Irréversibilité et Grand Projets d'Infrastructures,* Actes du colloque du 5 Mars 1998, Laboratoire d'Economie et de Transport; études & recherches n. 11, Vaulx-en -Velin (France), Lyon.

Blitz quotidiano (2012). No Tav, ecologisti francesi: "Potremo dire no anche noi" (2012, March 4). Blitz quotidiano. Retrieved from http://www.blitzquotidiano.it/cronaca-italia/no-tav-ecologisti-francesi-potremo-dire-no-anche-noi-1143285/

Bobbio, L. (2002). Le arene deliberative. *Rivista Italiana di Politiche Pubbliche,* 3, pp. 5-29.

Bobbio, L. (2004). *A più voci. Amministrazioni pubbliche, imprese, associazioni, cittadini nei processi decisionali inlcusivi.* Napoli. Edizioni Scientifiche Italiane.

Bobbio, L. (2007). *Amministrare con i cittadini.* Torino. Dps.

Caruso, L. (2007), *Nuove dinamiche dell'azione collettiva: il caso della Val di Susa in una prospettiva comparata con la Francia,*(Doctoral Dissertation), Social Science Department, Faculty of Political Science, University of Turin.

CEC (Commission of the European Communities), 1999, ESDP-European Spatial Development Perspective: Toward a Balanced and Sustainable Development of the Territory of the European Union, Office for Official Publications of the European Communities, Luxembourg.

Celata, F. (2005). Governance e partecipaizone nella progettazione della Torino-Lione. Relazioni tra attori in un contesto conflittuale. Working paper. *Dipartimento degli studi Geoeconomici Linguistici Statistici Storici per l'Analisi Regionale*. N. 28. April.

Chambru, M. (2011, July 18). *Les écolos savoyards divisés sur leLyon-Turin. Vidéos.* Retrieved from http://www.lavoixdesallobroges.org/environnement/396-les-ecolos-savoyards-divises-sur-le-lyon-turin

Christensen, K.S. (1985). Coping with Uncertainty in Planning. *Apa Journal*. Vol. (51) Issue.1. pp. 63-72.

Ciaffi, D., & Maroni, O. (2006)."Eco dalla Val di Susa: Arene Deliberative Cercasi", *CONTESTI*, pp. 54-59, Torino.

Ciaffi, D. & Mela, A. (2011). *Urbanistica Partecipata. Modelli ed esperienze*. Roma. Carocci Editore.

Comunità Val di Susa e Val Sangone. (2012). *Osservazioni al documento del Governo Italiano: "Tav Torino-Lione. Domande e Risposte"*. Comunità tecnica della Val di Susa e Val Sangone. Retrieved from http://areeweb.polito.it/eventi/TAVSalute/ANALISI%20DOCUMENTO%20GOVERNO%2028.03.12.pdf.

Cooke, B. & Kothari, U. (2001). *Participation: the new tyranny*. London. Editore Zed Books.

Dematteis, G.,& Governa, F. (2001). *Contesti locali e grandi infrastrutture. Politiche e progetti in Italia e in Europa*. Milano, Franco Angeli.

Elster, J. (1991). *Arguing and Bargaining in Two Constituents Assemblies*. Yale Law School. New Haven.

European Council (1994). *Precidency Conclusions*. Meeting held in Essen December 9 and 10, 1994. Retrieved from http://www.europarl.europa.eu/summits/ess1_en.htm#tens.

Forester J. (1989). *Planning in the face of power*. UC Press.

Forester, J. (1999). *The Deliberative Practitioner*. Cambridge. The MIT Press.

Fubini, A. (ed.). (2010). *Corridor Policies and Territorial Development. Main Infrastructure and Urban Nodes within Corridor V*. Milano. Franco Angeli.

Habermas, J. (1986). *Teoria dell'agire comunicativo*. Bologna. Vol. (1). Il Mulino.

Hélin, J.C. (1995). "La loi Barnier et la participation du public. Ajustements et innovation". *Revue juridique de l'Environnement*, 2/1995, 219-233.

Lindblom, C. (1959). The Science of Muddling Through. *Public Administration Review* 19 (2), pp. 79-88.

Lindblom, C. (1975). The Sociology of Planning: Thought and Social Interaction. *Economic Planning. East and West*. Cambridge. Balling Publishing Company.

Maggiolini, M. (2009). *L'Observatoire pour la liaison ferroviaire Turin-Lyon et les mairies. Notes sur un dispositif pour relier la démocratie représentative, la démocratie participative et la démocratie par le bas*. Lyon. Doctoral Conference. ENS-LHS. Retrieved at http://participation-et-democratie.fr/fr/system/files/46Micol%20Maggiolini.pdf

Mazzeo G. & Pinto V. (2011). Normativa 2001-2011: dieci anni di "Legge obiettivo". *TeMA* 4(3), 109-112.

Merlin, P. & Choay, F. (1988). *Dictionaire de l'urbanisme et de l'amenagément*. Paris. PUF.

Miessen, M. (2011). *The Nightmare of Participation*. London. Sternberg Press.

Mouffe, C. (2000). *Deliberative Democracy or Agonistic Pluralism.* London. Political Science Series.

Osservatorio collegamento ferroviario Torino – Lione. (2007)a ._*Linea Storica, tratta di valico.* Roma System Graphic Srl

Padovan, D., Alietti, A., Arrobbio, O. (2011). Le opportunità discorsive dell'expertise nel conflitto sulla Tav in Val di Susa. In Pellizzoni, L. (edited by). *Conflitti ambientali. Esperti, politica, istituzioni nelle controversie ecologiche*. Bologna. Il Mulino. pp. 235-258.

Pasqui, G. (2005). *Progetto, governo, società. Ripensare le politiche territoriali.* Milano. FrancoAngeli.

Podestà, N. (2008). *Nuovi strumenti di mediazione per la risoluzione di conflitti: l'esperienza dell'Osservatoriodella Valle di* Susa. Annual Congress Paper SISP 2008, section "Democrazie e democratizzazione", panel Conflitti e democrazia.

Pomatto, G. (2011). *Gioco Strategico e Deliberazione. Il Dibattito Pubblico sulla Gronda di Genova.* Torino. SPS Unibersuty Press.

Regione Toscana (2008). Legge Regionale 27 dicembre 2007, n. 69. *Bollettino Ufficiale della Regione Toscana*, 3 January 2008. Retrieved from_http://www.regione.toscana.it/regione/multimedia/RT/documents/1208532707341_1_r69_2007.pdf.

Revel, M., Blatrix, C., Blondiaux, L., Fourniau, J. M., Hériard Dubreuil, B., Lefebvre, R. (edited by). (2007). *Le débat public: une expérience française de démocratie participative.* La Découverte. Paris.

Rittel, J. & Webber, M. (1973). Dilemmas in a General Theory of Planning. *Policy Sciences.* (4) pp. 155-169.

Sansa, F. (2012). Ricavi e Traffico: I dubbi di Parigi sulla Torino-Lione. *Il Fatto Quotidiano,* 5 March 2012. Retrieved from http://www.ilfattoquotidiano.it/2012/03/05/ricavi-traffico-dubbi-parigi-sulla/195633/

Saporito, E. (2008). *Partecipazione e Progetto. La costruzione collettiva di senso nelle esperienze di progettazione partecipata.* (Master's Thesis). Faculty of Architecture (Urban and Territorial Design), Polytechnic School of Turin. Abstract at http://www.architesi.polito.it/pdf/3952_uk_abs.pdf

Sasso, C. (2006). *No Tav. Cronache dalla Val di Susa.* Roma. Carta – Intra Moenia.

Sclavi, M. (2012). Intervista a Mario Virano sul tema No-Tav. *Territorio Parma Ovest*, 6 March 2012. Retrieved from http://www.beacon.it/wordpress/territorioparmaovest/societa/polis/economia-societa/4485/marianella-sclavi-intervista-mario-virano-sul-tema-no-tav.

Schaan, FL. (2012). Lyon-Turin: Environment Ministry gave bad marks._*Cipra Living the Alps*, 22 February 2012. Retrieved from http://www.cipra.org/en/alpmedia/news-en/4556.

Schiavazzi, V. (2012). La battaglia di Luca l'anarchico No Tav. La Repubblica (27.2.2012). Retrieved at: http://torino.repubblica.it/cronaca/2012/02/27/news/la_battaglia_di_luca_l_anarchico_no_tav-30569480

Sclavi, M. (2012). Intervista a Mario Virano sul tema No-Tav. *Territorio Parma Ovest*, 6 March 2012. Retrieved from http://www.beacon.it/wordpress/territorioparmaovest/societa/polis/economia-societa/4485/marianella-sclavi-intervista-mario-virano-sul-tema-no-tav

Truzzi, S. (2012). L'esperta di mediazione: "La lezione francese? Il Dibattito Pubblico". Ma per la_TAV è tardi. *Il Fatto quotidiano*, 17 March 2012. Retrieved from http://www.ilfattoquotidiano.it/2012/03/17/lesperta-partecipazione-lezione-della-francia-dibattito-pubblico/

A Reflection on Why Large Public Projects Fail

Kjetil Holgeid, Mark Thompson[1]

> "New research shows surprisingly high numbers of out-of-control tech projects – ones that can sink entire companies and careers"
> *Flyvbjerg and Budzier (2011).*

There is overwhelming evidence that large IT projects indeed tend to fail, however the extent of failure is debated among academics and practitioners. IT projects seem to fail in both private and public sectors, however failure in public IT projects appear to be more spectacular due to size, visibility in media and political consequences. We highlight the importance of several contextual issues such as how to handle a diverse set of vendors, how to avoid vendor lock-in, strategizing towards a piecemeal approach to modernization, strategies to counter lack of skilled IT professionals in public service, the importance of organization behavior perspectives such as group dynamics and group formation and finally the importance of proper change management. By studying contextual issues related to project failure we reveal two core contextual dimensions; size and volatility, from which a new framework – The Contextual IT Project Framework – emerged. The framework is leaning towards conceptions of causal agency theory and is intended to help strategize towards successful projects, paying particular attention to projects possessing what we call "hyper emergent" characteristics. We emphasise the importance of strategizing wisely by splitting large efforts into manageable pieces according to risk profile, yet putting proper measures in place to maintain a clear view of the bigger picture.

1 Introduction

The UK government spent some £16 billion on IT in 2009, and the public sector seems to make less effective use of IT compared to the private sector, according to PASC (2011). PASC points out that continuing IT mismanagement in the public sector is leading to severe project failures and waste of taxpayers' money. Examples of large scale public projects are listed in Whitfield (2007).

The motivation for this paper is a desire to contribute in reducing the considerable waste of time and money within the public sector on spectacular IT failures. There is

1 As part of this research we reached out to a number of institutions, scholars and authorities. We appreciate their help in forming the key research questions, the identification of relevant literature and valuable feedback on our analysis. Among the contributors were Jens Nørve, Magne Jørgensen, Alexander Budzier, and Svenja Falk.

a tendency for public service IT projects to become gigantic, and consequently hard to manage.

Dunleavy et al. (2006) introduce what they call an emergent paradigm in public administration, and name it the Digital Era Government (DEG). Citizens as well as businesses expect new, transparent, public services aggregated across agencies and departments. This increased demand from society at large in combination with the pressing need to implement policy reform to reach fiscal sustainability are driving the urgent need for governments to increase efficiency in IT service delivery.

There is a pressing need for governments to avoid gigantic IT failures and rather ensure realization of public service value. Consequently, there is a need for research to better understand why some public projects fail and others succeed. We will explore to what degree projects fail, seek to understand why they fail and suggest what we can do to improve.

In spite of the various reasons cited for project failure, there appears little consensus as to any emerging pattern in the existing literature. The literature points in several directions and all claim a slice of the truth. This paper will look at some of the explanations of project failure and seek to reveal the core underlying causes. Accordingly, we attempt to pull together some of the key themes emerging from existing work on project failure. In sum, this paper will clarify underlying patterns contributing to project failure and stimulate even more debate in this important field among academics and practitioners.

Our key research questions are simple:

1. To what extent do large IT projects fail?
2. Why do IT projects fail?
3. What can be done about it?

In our quest for answers we will draw on the existing, broad literature on project failure, selecting in particular from the literature that has something relevant to say about large public service projects.

2 Main findings

When searching the literature we came across several definitions of "success" and "failure" of IT projects, for example:

- PASC (2011) defines a failure: "[..] late, over budget IT systems that are not fit for purpose".
- The Project Management Body of Knowledge PMBOK (r) Guide (PMI (2008)) does not define failure or success, but advise the definition of success to be stated in the project charter.

According to Jørgensen and Moløkken (2006) The Standish Group (www.standish-group.com) defines success and failure as follows:

- Successful project: "The project is completed on-time and on-budget, with all features and functions as initially specified"
- Challenged project: "The project is completed and operational but over-budget, over the time estimate, and offers fewer features and functions than originally specified"
- Cancelled projects

The Standish Group definition of success and failure was challenged by Jørgensen and Moløkken. They ask how to categorize a project that is on-time, and on-budget, but not with all specified functionality. The definition has also been challenged by pro-agile[2] professionals who stress the importance of delivery of value rather than delivery according to pre-determined specifications.

For the purpose of this paper we adapt a pragmatic definition for success and failure inspired by the discussion in Jørgensen and Moløkken (2006):

Project Success: The project is completed on-time and on-budget, delivering the expected value; *Project Failure:* The project is either terminated or not completed on-time, or not on budget, or not providing the value aimed for.

By value we mean the sustainable added benefit, i.e. if you need to redo major pieces of the project earlier than anticipated, it should be considered as a failure.

Before we present our literature review, it is worth mentioning that there is a very large body of literature on project failure. The aim of this paper is not to summarize all literature. Rather, we will highlight a selection that will serve as the basis for a new understanding of common denominators as these pertain to the characteristics of public service projects, such as gigantic size, massive complexity and high visibility.

The literature appears littered with 'critical success factors' to guide project success. Fortune and White (2006) highlight that the use of 'critical success factors' has many champions, but also many critics. Some of the critics argue that merely listing critical success factors does not reveal important relationships across these factors. Fortune and White suggest the Formal Systems Model as a framing device to deliver the benefits of taking account of success factors while accommodating the criticism. For further study we recommend using this framework. However, for the aim of this literature review we structure the review according to the main findings, followed by a literature review analysis.

The selected literature can be characterized along several dimensions. The matrix below illustrates how the reviewed literature can be plotted along two axes: (1) *applicability*, which means to what extent the literature is addressing a narrow segment such as one particular type of projects, a few projects, or a certain geography, and (2)

2 http://www.agilemanifesto.org/.

transparency/reliability, which indicate to what degree the literature is based on a transparent/reliable research methodology and backed by data.

Figure 1: Literature review: Applicatbility vs Transparency/Reliability (illustrative). The axes of the matrix are inspired by Flyvbjerg and Budzier (2012).

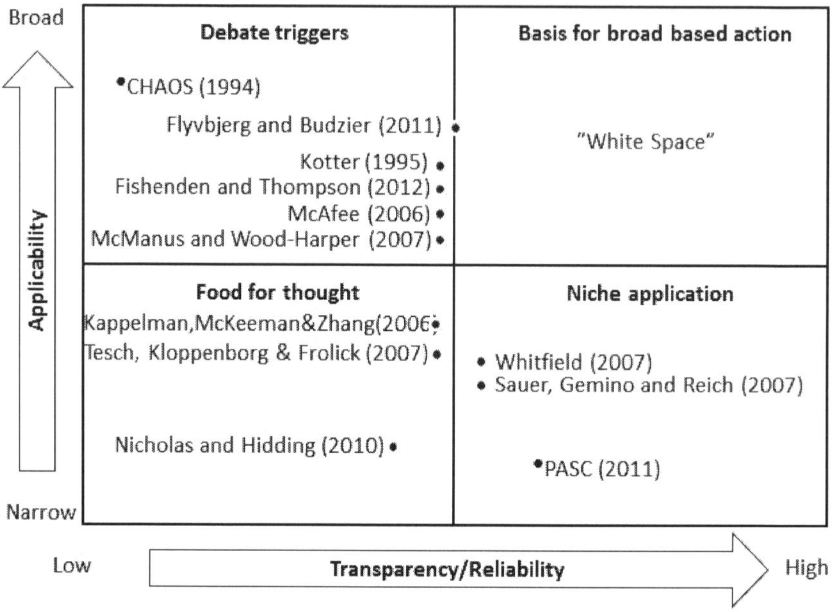

The "Food for thought" quadrant represents pieces of literature which suggest interesting ideas that might deserve further study. The "Niche application" quadrant represents pieces of literature backed by select datasets from a particular sector or region (for example "public service in UK"). The quadrant "Debate triggers" contains broadly applicable pieces of literature which might benefit from further proof and/or transparency. Finally, the quadrant "Basis for broad-based action" proposes 'universal truths' to avoid public project failure, typically backed by solid empirical evidence.

The matrix above is an illustration, and should not be viewed as a precise positioning of each piece of literature. Rather, it represents our subjective observations and illustrates why research in project success and failure indeed is interesting as there is a large "white space" for research that is both highly applicable and transparent/reliable, and upon which one can call for broad based action.

Below we will briefly present each piece of the selected literature according to main findings, and will make cross-references and analysis as we go along. This is followed by a literature review analysis where we suggest a new contextual framework to help strategize towards successful projects. In sum, the following analysis is intended as a contribution to the body of knowledge regarding project failure, as well as to stimulate discussions among academics and practitioners.

We will briefly present the selected literature, clustered around (1) contextual factors, (2) diagnosing failure, (3) understanding failure, (4) preventing failure. This is followed by a consolidated literature review analysis where we suggest a new contextual framework to help strategize towards successful projects.

2.1 Contextual factors influencing public IT project failure

The UK Public Accounts Spending Committee (PASC) review of central government ICT, PASC (2011), examined how government uses IT and what the barriers are to further improvement. PASC reports evidence of "IT mismanagement" and points out an array of high cost IT initiatives that have failed over the last 20 years.

The PASC report found that the failure of IT projects was rarely due to the technology itself (like several other reports, for example Hodgson (2002)); rather it was due to mismanagement, flaws in the underlying policy or its implementation. PASC concluded with six underlying causes of failure in government IT:

- Inadequate information, resulting in the Government being unable to manage its IT needs successfully
- An over-reliance on a small number of large suppliers and the virtual exclusion of small and medium sized (SME) IT contractors, which tend to be less risk adverse and more innovative
- A failure to integrate IT into the wider policy and business change programmes
- A tendency to commission large, complex projects which struggle to adapt to changing circumstances
- Over-specifying security requirements
- The lack of sufficient leadership and skills to manage IT within the Civil Service, and in particular the absence of an "intelligent customer" function in Departments

Source: PASC (2011, p. 9)

The lack of ICT skills in government and over-reliance on contracting out were reported as fundamental problems which have resulted in poor achievement and constitute even a "recipe for rip-offs". The PASC report stresses the pressing need for government to address the lack of skills and leadership from senior management necessary for the effective procurement and use of IT. The report states "The Government's inability to act as an intelligent customer seems to be a consequence of its decision to outsource a large amount of its IT contracts." (PASC, 2011, p. 32). Further, the PASC report quotes Mark Thompson, who argues that "there is usually really lousy management of the contract once it is in place" (Thompson quoted in PASC, 2011, p. 32).

Fishenden and Thompson (2012) take the argument further, and rather than just pointing towards lousy management, they call for a new approach to public service IT altogether. Fishenden and Thompson suggest use of open standards and architectures that allow government to become technology agnostic which over time will drive both innovation and reduce cost due to competition. This will, according to Fishenden and Thompson (2012, p. 1), "create a powerful dynamic, driving dis-integration of traditional 'black boxed' technologies and services, traditionally organized around 'system integrators' and Departmental structures, and their re-aggregation around the citizen in the form of services."

Fishenden and Thompson highlight the failure of the traditional approach to modernisation of the public sector which has been characterized as the era of New Public Management (NPM). The underlying hypothesis of NPM of private sector style, market-oriented approaches to public services often led to government disaggregating many of its functions. Further, NPM is encouraging competition between different parts of the public sector and between public and private sectors. Dunleavy et al. (2005) highlights that many of the promised benefits of disaggregation had failed to materialise, rather they provide examples of increased administrative complexity, vertical siloing of agencies, and difficulties in co-ordinating joint service delivery.

As a response, Fishenden and Thompson suggest a move towards "open architecture" if government is actually to achieve Digital Era Governance (DEG, Dunleavy et al (2006)). The core of DEG is re-aggregating of public services leveraging under direct government control around the citizen, as well leveraging new technology such as cloud computing, apps development and other recent innovations moving towards an "online civilization" (Dunleavy and Margetts, 2010).

Fishenden and Thompson suggest that Government's intention of minimizing risk in IT delivery remains unchanged within open architecture. However, the role of government will be more to create platform-based incentives for others to take risks while accepting the degree of failure that is an important part of the innovation process.

The majority of the issues discussed in both PASC (2011) and Fishenden and Thompson (2012) link back - in one way or another - to project size.

Government typically contracts for large, undifferentiated systems that have not been separated out into high- and low-risk components. Instead of bundling up standardised, low-risk components (which might be more successful), government has outsourced/developed an undifferentiated mix of high and low-risk together, resulting in a inability to identify and control key risks. Proprietary technologies are also typically deeply integrated with supporting business logic, meaning that entire departments/functions/processes need to be tackled in one go, rather than in bits.

We will link back to this discussion of contextual issues when we present a consolidated literature analysis later in the paper. Meanwhile, we suggest that these contextual issues form a useful background to our discussion of the other main findings below.

2.2 Diagnosing failure

In this section we will start building our knowledge of the extent to which IT projects fail, according to our research question #1. We will keep returning to the extent of failure in the following chapters, gradually building our understanding.

The Standish Group CHAOS reports on IT failure have been widely referenced and as mentioned earlier in this section, their definitions of success and failure have been debated. However, the CHAOS reports seem to be widely recognized in the industry. The Standish Group publishes a report on IT failures approximately every second year and claims to have been collecting case information on real-life IT environments and software development projects since 1985. Their cumulative research includes 17 years of data on why projects succeed or fail, representing more than 80,000 completed IT projects.

Examples of Standish research findings in 2009 indicate that 32% of the observed projects succeeded while 24% failed and 44% were challenged (Standish, 2009). The Standish Reports are available, but not freely in the public domain. We have therefore been careful not to reference results from CHAOS years that are not publicly available.

The Standish Group reported in 1994 that the average cost overrun of software projects was as high as 189%, while more recent cost overrun results reported by the Standish Group and others show lower results (Jørgensen and Moløkken, 2006). This could be seen as a tribute to advancement in the discipline of IT project management. However, critics such as Jørgensen and Moløkken question the validity of the 1994 CHAOS report and claim most other studies reveal cost overruns in the range of about 30%. As a general note, it is hard to compare such studies due to variations in definitions; for example, in the CHAOS report successful projects are excluded from the cost overrun % calculation.

Even though the Standish CHAOS reports are being debated, academics and practitioners seem to agree that the failure rate of IT projects is significant, as presented throughout this literature review.

2.3 Understanding failure

In this chapter we will look at several pieces of literature in order to better understand why projects fail, according to our research question #2. We cross-reference the literature and provide analysis as we go along, gradually building up to chapter 4 which is dedicated to a consolidated analysis.

2.3.1 The impact of size and volatility

In line with Jørgensen and Moløkken, Sauer, Gemino and Reich (2007) also challenge the Standish Group CHAOS reports. In a large-scale study of projects led by 412 experienced project managers in the UK, Sauer, Gemino and Reich found that 67% of projects were delivered close to budget, schedule and scope expectations, contrary to the CHAOS findings. However, even though Sauer, Gemino and Reich found the "software crisis" not to be as bad as the Standish Group, it is still alarming. The study's statistical analysis indicates that the IT projects included could be categorized into five types of performance:

- Abandoned (9%)
- Budget Challenged (5%)
- Schedule Challenged (18%)
- Good Performers (60%)
- Star Performers (7%)

Further, Sauer, Gemino and Reich reveal some very interesting connections between factors that influence project risk of failure, especially related to project size and volatility.

Size

Sauer, Gemino and Reich reveal that risk of project failure increases with project size, both in terms of effort (man-months), duration, team size and budget. This ties nicely back to our discussion above regarding PASC (2011) and Fishenden and Thompson (2012), which both raise issues linking back to project size.

While projects less than 24 man-months have 25% probability of underperforming, projects with 500-1,000 man-months have doubled the probability to 50%. Projects with 1,000-2,400 man-months have tripled the risk to 75%. No success was found above 2.400 man-months.

Volatility

Sauer, Gemino and Reich define two types of volatility which both influence project risk of failure:

- Changes in project manager or sponsor, and
- Changes in schedule, budget and scope

As the number of changes increases, the risk of project failure appears to follow. The average number of governance changes in better performing projects was 0.4, whereas the average number of governance changes in underperforming projects was 1.5. Also, regarding volatility in schedule, budget and scope, the risk of underperforming increased with the number of these changes per project.

The link between volatility and risk of underperformance is unsurprising given that we measure success based on pre-determined scope. However, pro-agile professionals (referenced earlier) would likely argue that volatility can assist in delivery of what the organization really needs, rather than what the organization thought it needed when the project was initiated.

Sauer, Gemino and Reich conclude that experienced project managers should be able to deliver close (plus or minus 7%) to the original target on two out of three projects. The authors also stress that the top management and steering committees have a significant role to play in managing project risk. Ambitious-sized projects, moving targets, and managerial turnover present challenges affecting project risk of failure.

2.3.2 The impact of over-ambitious, complex projects and lack of skills

A report from European Services Strategy Unit (Whitfield 2007) presents an analysis of 105 projects outsourced by central government, NHS, local authorities, public bodies and agencies with significant cost overruns, delays and terminations. Whitfield claims cost increases are often underestimated as the numbers reported usually only include payments to contractors, and not costs borne by the client such as additional client staff engaged. Still, he finds the average percent cost overrun at 30.5%.

- 105 outsourced public sector ICT projects with significant cost overruns, delays and terminations
- Total value of contracts is £29.5 billion
- Cost overruns totalled £9.0 billion
- 57% of contracts experienced cost overruns
- The average percentage cost overrun is 30.5%
- 33% of contracts suffered major delays
- 30% of contracts were terminated
- 12.5% of Strategic Service Delivery Partnership contracts terminated or were substantially reduced

Source: Whitfield (2007, p. 4, tables 1 and 2)

The report cites the National Audit Office's (NAO) 2003 list[3] of common causes of failure, but Whitfield states that even though these are valid, they rarely get to the root of the problems as they focus primarily on the procurement process. Whitfield's findings are very much in line with both PASC (2011) and Fishenden and Thompson (2012) in that he highlights the following additional causes:

- Some projects are over-ambitious and complex, and the long-term projects face the risk of being over-taken by new legislation, public policy and technology
- Contractors overstate their ability to deliver
- Conclusions by analysts are seldom critically assessed before accepted
- Public clients lack competence in managing large scale projects

The lack of skills in managing large scale projects have been addressed by a number of studies, including Kappelman, McKeeman and Zhang (2006)'s underscoring of the importance of communication skills, and McManus and Wood-Harper (2007)'s highlighting of (among other factors) poor stakeholder communications and poor leadership in project delivery. PASC (2011) addresses this head on by talking about "mismanagement" in public IT. The bottom line is that several studies highlight a lack of skills in managing large IT efforts as a core reason for project failure.

3 Whitfield (2007, p. 5.).

2.3.3 The impact of "black swan"-effects

Based on research of 1,471 large IT-projects, Flyvbjerg and Budzier (2011) found that the average cost overrun was 27%. This finding is in line with the figures reported by several of the papers referenced above, for example Jørgensen and Moløkken (2006) and Whitfield (2007).

However, Flyvbjerg and Budzier (2011) were more alarmed by the fact that one in six projects, or 17%, had cost overruns of 200% on average, and almost 70% experienced schedule overrun. These classic "black swan" projects, they report, can sink companies and cost the jobs of top managers. Levi Strauss, EADS, Kmart, Auto Windscreens, and Toll Collect are mentioned as examples.

Flyvbjerg and Budzier suggest taking a "black swan" stress test before engaging in a large technology project. In doing so, they advocate asking two key quesitions:

> Is the company strong enough to absorb the hit if its biggest technology project overruns budget by 400% or more, and if only 25-50% of projected benefits are realized?
>
> Can the company handle a situation where 15% of its medium-sized projects overrun by 200%?
>
> *Source: Flyvbjerg and Budzier (2011)*

Flyvbjerg and Budzier also advise managers to decompose large projects into smaller ones of limited size, complexity and duration. This is very much in line with several of the above referenced papers which stress the importance of the size factor, for example Sauer, Gemino and Reich (2007).

Flyvbjerg and Budzier recommend that organizations establish contingency plans to handle risks; and use the best possible forecasting techniques, e.g. Reference Class Forecasting – a method for predicting the future by looking at similar past situations and their outcomes (Flyvbjerg, 2006).

2.3.4 The impact of management & leadership factors versus technical factors

McManus and Wood-Harper (2007) suggest that project management is often undisciplined and chaotic. McManus and Wood-Harper reference their earlier research which found that only one in eight technology projects met the original time, cost and quality requirements criteria, and thereby could be characterized as successful.

McManus and Wood-Harper differentiate between management and technical causal factors, reporting that management causal factors account for 65% of project failures, while technical causal factors account for 35%. This resonates well with several of the above mentioned studies.

Management causal factors include:

- Poor leadership in project delivery
- Poor stakeholder communication
- Poor competencies (and skill shortages)
- Poor stakeholder management
- Poor estimation methods
- Poor risk management
- Insufficient management support

Technical causal factors include:

- Inappropriate and ill defined software requirements
- Inappropriate technical designs
- Inappropriate development tools
- Inappropriate user documentation
- Poor test planning
- Poor technical support

Source: McManus and Wood-Harper (2007, p. 39)

McManus and Wood-Harper studied 214 European public and private projects covering the period 1998-2005. They found that out of the 214 projects examined, 24% were cancelled. In 20% of the cases the cancellation was due to issues related to the business/organization. In 53% of the cases the cancellation was due to management-related issues, and in 27% cancellation was due to technology-related issues.

The average duration of the examined projects was 26 months, and the average budget was approx. €6M. It was found that more than half of the projects larger than €6 M ran over schedule more than 18 months and actual cost exceeded budget by more than €4.2M. This implication of size (both budget and duration) is also supported by Sauer, Gemino and Reich (2007) as discussed earlier.

Another major cause of failure identified by McManus and Wood-Harper was the total reliance placed on methodologies. Methods can help project managers and developers, but can also become an excuse for not engaging with people and problems. An explanation for this could be lack of leadership within the delivery process. "Processes alone are far from enough to cover the complexity and human aspect of many large projects subject to multiple stakeholders, resource and ethical constraints." (McManus & Wood-Harper, 2007, p. 43).

2.4 Preventing failure

In this section we will focus on literature addressing ways to avoid failures, according to our research question #3. Below, we focus on early detection of potential failure, IT projects as change journeys, risk management strategies and management principles.

2.4.1 Early detection of potential failure

Kappelman, McKeeman and Zhang (2006) point out that long before the failure is acknowledged there are usually significant symptoms or "early warning signs" of trouble. Their article describes the top 12 people-related and technology-related IT project risks, based on "early warning signs" data collected from a panel of 19 experts and a survey of 55 IT managers. IT project risk is grouped into three categories: people, process and product risks. The authors found that all of the highest rated early warning signs belong to the people and the process risk categories. This resonates well with the findings of McManus and Wood-Harper (2007).

The 12 dominant early warning signs according to Kappelman, McKeeman and Zhang are listed below.

Paying attention to these signs – the earlier in the life cycle of a project, the better – increases the probability of successful project outcome, either because they are being addressed or because the projects are being cancelled before they turn into disasters.

The most influential people-related risk:

- Lack of top management support
- Weak project manager
- No stakeholder involvement and/or participation
- Weak commitment of project team
- Team members lack requisite knowledge and/or skills
- Subject matter experts are overscheduled

The most influential process-related risks:

- Lack of documented requirements and/or success criteria
- No change control process (change management)
- Ineffective schedule planning and/or management
- Communication breakdown among stakeholders
- Resources assigned to higher priority project
- No business case for the project

Source: Kappelman, McKeeman and Zhang (2006)

2.4.2 IT projects as change journeys

Large IT projects can often be seen as change journeys where an organization is moving from the current state to a desired state. In his famous article "Why Transformation Efforts Fail", Kotter (1995) outlines lessons learned from watching more than 100 companies' attempts to transform themselves. He presents eight critical success factors needed in order for major change initiatives to succeed. Kotter claims that too many managers do not realize that transformation is a process, not an event, and that the change process advances through stages each with their own pitfalls.

The eight phases to successful change are, according to Kotter:

1. Establishing a sense of urgency
2. Form a powerful guiding coalition
3. Create a vision
4. Communicate the vision
5. Empower others to act on the vision
6. Plan for and create short term wins
7. Consolidate improvements and produce more change
8. Institutionalize the new approaches

Rather than focusing on success factors in isolation, Kotter prescribes a process to follow to get the organization moving in the desired direction. Several studies have pointed out the lack of ability to manage large IT projects as one key reason why they fail, for example PASC (2011) and Whitney (2007). In the light of Kotter's paper, we suggest this has not only to do with lack of traditional project management discipline but also lack of competence in leading change journeys.

McAfee (2006) states that business leaders should not underestimate resistance when they impose changes in the ways people work. The degree of change impact drives the extent to which such change needs to be facilitated by an experienced leader. Building consensus in the organisation is important, but successful implementers are also willing to push ahead without having everyone on board when needed.

The suggestions of McAfee are very much in line with the change process outlined by Kotter. McAfee further stresses that IT project success and failure seem to be attributed more towards leadership and management aspects rather than pure technology issues, also indicated by McManus and Wood-Harper (2007) and PASC (2011).

2.4.3 Risk management strategies

Tesch, Kloppenborg and Frolick (2007) identify IT project risk factors that pose threats to successful project implementation. Risks are grouped into six categories and corresponding strategies for avoiding or mitigating the risks are proposed.

Risk Category	**Top Rated Risks**
Sponsorship/Ownership	Project has inadequate top management commitment
Funding and Scheduling	Entire project must be budgeted at the outset
Personnel and Staffing	Project lacks enough staff or right skills
Scope	Requirements are ignored for the sake of technology
Requirements	Project changes are managed poorly
Relationship Management	Project fails to satisfy end-user expectations

Source: Tesch, Kloppenborg and Frolick (2007, p. 64)

Strategies for avoiding risks are often related to establishing project management processes within the organisation. However, other researchers warn that over-reliance on methodology can be a cause of failure in itself, as discussed earlier (for example McManus and Wood-Harper (2007)).

Another theme is the importance of recognizing the hidden risks that are difficult to avoid or mitigate in a planned fashion. Along these lines, Flyvbjerg and Budzier suggest taking a "black swan" stress test before engaging in a large technology project, as a systematic risk planning process - as suggested by Tesch, Kloppenborg and Frolick - might not be enough.

2.4.4 Management Principles Associated with IT Project Success

Nicholas and Hidding (2010) point out that success in IT projects remains elusive, even after decades of efforts to improve it. They argue that most of these efforts have focused on the traditional project management paradigm (for example presented in PMI (2008)) and that exploring a new paradigm called Value-Driven Change Leadership (VDCL) might be useful. The VDCL suggests tracking business value-added benefits rather than tracking conformity to plans and schedules.

The Agile Manifesto (referenced earlier) represents yet another paradigm for software development. In the Agile Manifesto Principles[4] we read, "Welcome changing requirements, even late in development. Agile processes harness change for the customer's competitive advantage."

Two schools of thought emerge here: the efficiency school and the effectiveness school. The more traditional efficiency school defines success largely by timely and on-budget delivery according to specification. In contrast, the effectiveness school promotes measurement of success according to the total project output (the value the project brings to the organization). We suggest the agile paradigm is related to the effectiveness school of thought due to its core focus on value output rather than initial scope specification.

We find no conclusive evidence as to which school of thought is the most effective in avoiding project failure (according to our definition). Rather than such an 'either-or' approach, we suggest that projects might usefully be plotted on a spectrum spanning both efficiency and effectiveness schools of thought. We will explore this contention more closely as we present the consolidated literature review analysis below.

3 *Discussion*

The literature review reveals overwhelming evidence that IT projects in general, and large public IT projects in particular, indeed tend to fail. IT projects display an alarming rate of failure in terms of both schedule and cost overruns. Perhaps even more severely, large projects have a tendency not to deliver the promised value, and some are abandoned with a huge net loss, having failed to realize any value at all. Large scale public IT projects are typically triggered by policy reform and consequently highly visible in the media as taxpayer's money is on the line.

The literature review has revealed common core themes contributing to success and failure of public IT projects. Leadership-related issues emerge as the over-arching theme. Although proper technology strategy and implementation need to be in place,

4 http://agilemanifesto.org/principles.html.

IT projects seldom fail due to technology related issues. Throughout the literature review this view seems to be a common denominator, even though each piece of literature places differing emphasis on the various leadership/management factors addressed. This is illustrated in the table below, where the main causes determining IT project failure are mapped across the literature reviewed.

Table 1: Literature review: Core causes of failure

Failure: Core causes	Dunleavy et al (2005, 2006)	Flyvjberg and Budzier (2011)	Kappelman, McKeeman and Zhang (2006)	Kotter (1995)	McAfee (2006)	McManus and Wood-Harper (2007)	Nicholas and Hidding (2010)	PASC (2011)	Sauer, Gemino and Reich (2007)	Tesch, Kloppenborg and Frolick (2007)	Fishenden and Thompson (2011)	Whitfield (2007)
Lack of proper leadership/management			x	x	x	x		x			x	x
Lack of change management skills			x	x	x	x		x			x	
Lack of large scale IT project management skills			x			x		x			x	x
Poor risk management strategies		x				x				x		x
Complexity, abmition and size		x						x	x		x	x
Naive and undifferntiated approach to contract and size								x			x	x
Fragmentation and poor co-ordination of joint service delivery	x							x			x	
Poor handling of volatility							x		x			
Over-reliance on methods and process						x						

We suggest that project size and volatility form a useful way to place the above findings in context. Sauer, Gemino and Reich (2007) suggest that risk of project failure increases with project size and volatility. The importance of the size factor is backed by numerous reports, including Whitfield (2007), Flyvbjerg and Budzier (2011), PASC (2011), Fishenden and Thompson (2012). The importance of proper handling of volatility is addressed in several papers, for example Nicholas and Hidding (2010), PASC (2011).

We propose analyzing project failure by applying project size and volatility as core contextual dimensions. We propose a new framework – the Contextual IT Project Framework – which is intended to (1) help strategize towards successful projects by leveraging contextually sound strategies, (2) facilitate discussions about project success and failure, and (3) frame our literature review analysis.

Figure 2: The Contextual IT Project Framework

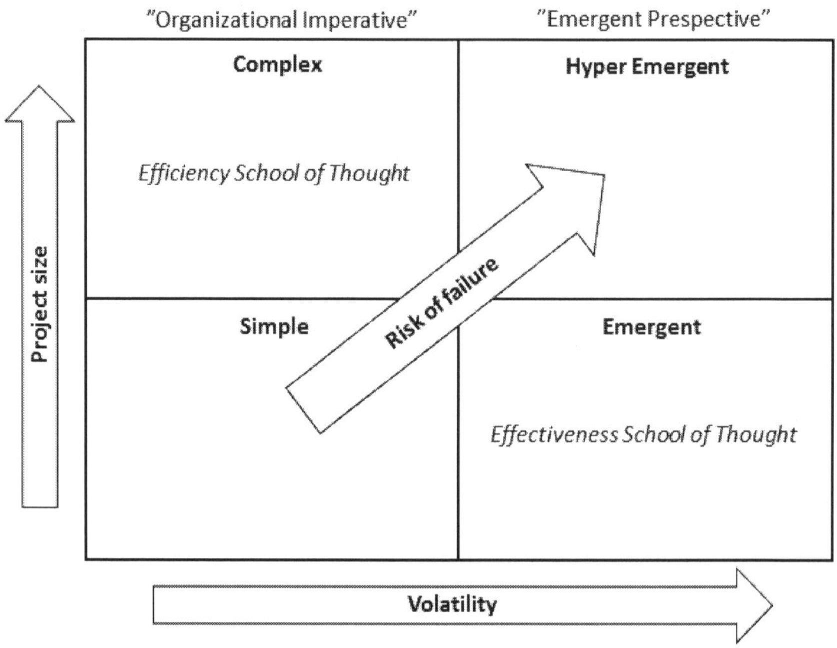

The framework fits well to the work of Markus and Robey (1988) who look at the relationship between information technology and organizational change from a causal agency point of view. They lay out three conceptions of causal agency: (1) the technological imperative where IT is viewed as a cause of organizational change, (2) the organizational imperative where designers can manage the impacts of IT systems by attending to technical and social concerns, and (3) the emergent perspective where the uses and impact of IT emerge unpredictably from complex social interactions.

The *organizational imperative,* which builds on the assumption of designer discretion, seems to fit well in analyzing situations where there is a low degree of volatility (the left quadrants in the Contextual IT Project Framework). The *emergent perspective*, which appreciates that preferences develop and change over time and behavior is hard to predict, can be applied to the right quadrants of the Contextual IT Project Framework. According to Markus and Robey, empirical research has generated contradictory findings related to the *technological imperative*, thus we do not include this perspective in the proposed framework.

As presented in the literature review, Nicholas and Hidding (2010) discuss management principles associated with IT project success, and present two schools of thought. The traditional *efficiency school* defines success by timely and on-budget delivery according to pre-determined specifications. This traditional view of IT project management, also supported by PMI (2008), seems to apply well in projects characterized by a low degree of volatility, and is well suited for "Simple" or "Complex" projects according to our suggested framework. The *effectiveness school* of thought, which defines success according to value output rather than pre-determined specifications, seems to apply well in circumstances with a higher degree of volatility.

As both project size and volatility increase, the project might end up in the "Hyper Emergent" quadrant characterized by a high risk of failure. The organizational perspective fails in explaining causality in hyper emergent projects as cause and effect in high volatile environments are by nature blurred and hard to comprehend. In such situations pre-determined specifications are likely to be subject to significant change, and even with proper change control mechanisms it is likely to be a costly experience. Among the various underlying causes of failure highlighted in PASC (2011) are over-specification of requirements and a tendency to commission large projects which struggle to adapt to changing circumstances.

Based on our experience, large public projects tend to end up being "Hyper Emergent" due to vast size and high volatility in management and/or changes in schedule, budget and scope as presented by Sauer, Gemino and Reich (2007). In the existing literature we have not found any compelling holistic strategy to cope with such hyper emergent contextual situations. Pure emergent strategies, for example instantiated by the agile movement mentioned earlier, is to our knowledge not yet applied sufficiently to huge public projects. One view might be that existing emergent strategies apply well to small and volatile projects, but are not sufficient as a measure to address the needs of the "Hyper Emergent" large and volatile public projects. This view, however, requires further study.

In the absence of a holistic approach to handle "Hyper Emergent" projects, we suggest an avoidance strategy where large public projects are divided into smaller manageable pieces scattered across the contextual IT Project Framework, yet avoiding the "Hyper Emergent" quadrant. Project slices categorized as "Simple", "Complex" or "Emergent" can be addressed by well known approaches from either the efficiency- or effectiveness camp. Avoiding large and volatile projects seems to be in the spirit of Whitfield (2007), Fishenden and Thompson (2012), PASC (2011), Flyvbjerg and Budzier (2011).

Even though the Contextual IT Project Framework presents four distinct quadrants, in reality a project will find itself on a *spectrum* along the size and volatility dimensions. The diagonal risk dimension illustrated is likewise relative. Thus, even after applying avoidance strategies, a cluster of sliced projects will differ in their relative degree of being "Hyper Emergent". Therefore we suggest Flyvbjerg and Budzier's advice of performing "black swan" stress tests still applies. Also, risk mitigation strategies are highly applicable as pointed out in numerous studies such as McManus and Wood-Harper (2007), Tesch, Kloppenborg and Frolick (2007).

Based on the literature review we believe that strategies to avoid "Hyper Emergent" situations are important, yet not sufficient, in coping with public project failure. Even though we slice projects in to manageable pieces according to their risk profile, the output from the sliced projects still need to work together in a properly orchestrated symphony. This is particularly important as we move from the era of New Public Management (James and Manning, 1996) towards Digital Era Governance (DEG) where services are re-aggregated around citizens needs (Dunleavy et.al., 2006), as discussed earlier.

Thus, in a DEG world the over-arching governance of several connected projects is still going to be a key leadership challenge, even though individual projects may, as a result of the mentioned avoidance strategy, seek to move away from the "Hyper Emergent" category. Therefore we predict that the lack of skilled leadership capacity will remain at the centre of gravity in explaining failure of large scale IT projects. Lack of skilled IT leadership/management is reported in numerous studies to be a key reason for failure (Kappelman, McKeeman and Zhang, 2006; McAfee, 2006; PASC, 2011).

We suggest that general leadership attributes should not be addressed in isolation; rather we suggest aiming for a combination of leadership attributes composed of skills and experience in leadership, change management (Kotter, 1995), project management (Whitfield, 2007) and large scale IT delivery (PASC, 2011). People possessing such skills are hard to find, since such skills typically are acquired by 'hard life experience' in large scale project delivery. Due to the very nature of large scale IT projects spanning several years, few people are privileged to experience more than one or two large scale project(s) over the course of their careers. Consequently, the supply of such professionals is scarce.

We submit that governments as well as companies will benefit from reflection on this scarcity. This implies new strategies to build and retain the necessary skills as well as an element of wise prioritization of the most skilled resources to the benefit of the most critical, large and complex projects. New strategies to build necessary skills can be married with our suggested approach towards slicing huge projects into manageable pieces paying heavy attention to risk profiles applying the Contextual IT Project Framework. In order to build the critical skills to succeed in large scale IT projects, public agencies might consider in-house delivery of low-risk components while prioritizing their (few) key IT delivery professionals towards intelligent client management of higher risk components and contracts.

As a consequence of the mentioned scarcity, public agencies typically revert to a convenient strategy of contracting out very large chunks of work, relying on contractual terms and conditions, sometimes in combination with detailed specifications. There are several flaws associated with this common strategy. First, the needs for large scale public IT delivery skills do not evaporate by outsourcing. Second, strong evidence suggests that size is a determinant of failure and work should be broken down in manageable pieces yet maintaining strong 'glue' among the pieces. Third, blending an undifferentiated mix of high and low risk components into one large contract is, according to the literature review, not best practice.

The strategy of eating the elephant one piece at a time seems logical and reasonable. However, the importance of understanding the bigger picture is still paramount. Joint IT public service delivery across agencies, and even across entities within large agencies, tends to be problematic. The importance of proper change management, common understanding of urgency, clear and shared goals, transparent status and strong focus on dependency and risk mitigation are all critical in ensuring success. Internal power struggles might undermine efficient service delivery, and the importance of a common, clear and accepted over-arching goal cannot be stressed enough. This appears to be true in both open and closed architectural strategies.

To compensate for lack of skills public agencies sometimes tend to focus heavily on methodology and processes. Industrialized and optimized delivery processes are of course important, but the literature review reveals that this cannot be a substitute for the scarce leadership skills mentioned above. Over-reliance on methodology and process can lead to a dangerous false sense of control. According to the literature review, the inconvenient truth is rather a severe lack of leadership, IT delivery skills and experience on both sides of the table (clients and contractors).

As discussed, volatility is common in large scale IT projects. As projects are assessed to be leaning towards the right quadrants "Emergent" or "Hyper Emergent" of the Contextual IT Project Framework, we submit that public agencies not only should evaluate proposals based on initial price, but putting a stronger emphasis on contractual measures to ensure long term value for money. Over-reliance on up-front detailed specifications of large projects has proven not to deliver predictable outcomes as the needs are subject to change. Long-running programs might even be subject to major policy change, making initial requirements incomplete or even irrelevant.

To sum up, we propose a new framework – the Contextual IT Project Framework – which is intended to (1) help strategize towards successful projects by leveraging contextually sound strategies, (2) facilitate discussions about project success and failure, and (3) frame our literature review analysis. We suggest an avoidance strategy for moving away from "Hyper Emergent" projects, and highlight the importance of strategizing wisely in splitting large efforts into manageable pieces according to risk profile. Still, there is clearly a need for a skilled leadership, change management and IT delivery skills to ensure large scale IT project success. The skills are acquired largely by experience from large scale projects and we suggest new strategies to address the current scarcity of such skills, putting proper measures in place to maintain a clear view of the bigger picture. Over-reliance on contractual measures, methodology and process do not lead to the evaporation of the need of proper skills, leadership and management.

4 Conclusion, limitations, and future work

The primary objective of this report has been to shed light on the research questions through a focused literature review supported by our analysis. Below we revisit the research questions and highlight the main findings. Finally, we will discuss limitations and suggest further research.

To what extent do large IT projects fail?

The literature review revealed overwhelming evidence that IT projects in general, and large public IT projects in particular, indeed tend to fail. An alarming rate of IT projects fail in terms of both schedule and cost overruns. Perhaps even more severely, large projects have a tendency not delivering the promised value and some are abandoned with a huge net loss not realizing any value at all. Large scale public IT projects are typically triggered by policy reform and consequently highly visible in media as taxpayer's money is on the line.

We found most studies reveal cost overruns in the range of about 30% (see for example Jørgensen and Moløkken, 2006). More alarming was the "black swan" effect pointed out by Flyvbjerg and Budzier (2011), reporting one in six projects had cost overruns of 200% on average, and almost 70% schedule overrun.

Why do IT projects fail?

We found that large IT projects seldom fail due to technology-related issues. Leadership-related issues emerge as the over-arching theme. A lack of skills in managing large scale IT projects was reported in several studies, which highlighted a corresponding tendency to rely instead on "hard" factors such as contracts and methodologies. Our study highlights the lack of skills in leading large scale IT efforts in general and change management skills in particular. Also, we found that contextual factors such as size and volatility are key determinants of failure or success. We suggest that ambitious, complex projects characterized by high degree of volatility in combination with lack of the mentioned skills, should be a cause for alarm within the public sector.

What can be done about it?

We suggest a new framework – the Contextual IT Project Framework – based on a conception of causal agency theory and intended to help strategize towards successful projects, paying particular attention to projects possessing what we call "hyper emergent" characteristics. Further, we propose that sustained advancement in change management and IT delivery skills is needed to ensure large scale IT project success. Such skills are acquired largely through experience of large scale projects and we suggest new strategies to address this scarcity. Over-reliance on contractual measures, methodology and process can never compensate for a lack of the aforementioned skills. We highlight the importance of strategizing wisely in splitting large efforts into manageable pieces according to risk profile and applying the Contextual IT Project Framework.

As a final remark we wonder whether the Digital Era Government (Dunleavy et al., 2006), where citizens expect aggregated services delivered across agencies, will lead to an increase in projects with emergent characteristics, where changes can no longer be handled within agency 'silos'. If so, the findings of this report in general – and the Contextual IT Project Framework in particular – will likely pay dividends for the future.

The work presented in this paper has limitations, and further work should be done to address these. The literature review is focused, yet representative. However, the literature review is not intended to be a presentation of the complete body of knowledge on IT project failure. As presented in Jørgensen and Moløkken (2004), it matters whom you ask and how you collect reasons, and in complex settings like large IT projects the respondents' role, data collection approach and approach to data analysis tend to influence the conclusions. In this paper we are referencing numerous pieces of literature, but have not done a detailed comparison with regard to the above mentioned aspects.

Further research should be aimed specifically at the "Hyper Emergent" quadrant of our suggested Contextual IT Project Framework, and we welcome empirical evidence of application of agile strategies in "Hyper Emergent" contexts.

As public projects tend to fail due to people-related issues rather than technology, we suggest further research in the lines of Orlikowski and Barley (2001) who looked at what research in technology and research on organizations can learn from each other.

We suggest further study to address the scarcity of resources possessing the proper blend of skills required to successfully manage large IT projects. Our research has provided initial evidence of what kind of skills needed, however a deep dive to add even more flesh to the bones is welcomed. An even more comprehensive and detailed literature review covering the full body of knowledge on IT project failure is highly welcomed.

Finally, we suggest further study to address issues discussed by Jørgensen and Moløkken (2004), as discussed above. We suggest a detailed comparison of the literature reviewed in this study with regard to the above mentioned aspects.

Bibliography

Dunleavy P., et al. (2005): "New Public Management is dead – long live digital-era governance", Journal of Public Administration Research and Theory 16: 467-494, 2005 (EBSCO)

Dunleavy P., et al. (2006) "Digital Era Governance", Oxford: Oxford University Press, 2006, ISBN 0-19-929619-7 978-0-19-929619-4

Dunleavy P. and Margetts, H. (2010): "The Second Wave of Digital Era Governance", American Political Science Association Conference, 4 September 2010, Washington DC, USA http://eprints.lse.ac.uk/27684/1/The_second_wave_of_digital_era_governance_(LSERO).pdf (Accessed Jaunary 2, 2012).

Fishenden, J. and Thompson, M. (2012): "Digital Government, Open Architecture, and Innovation: Why Public Sector IT Will Never Be The Same Again", accepted for publication in *Journal of Public Administration, Research and Theory*, 2012

Flyvbjerg, B. (2006): "From Nobel Prize to Project Management: Getting Risks Right", Project Management Journal, vol. 37, no. 3, August, pp. 5-15. http://flyvbjerg.plan.aau.dk/Publications2006/Nobel-PMJ2006.pdf (Accessed Jaunary 8, 2012).

Flyvbjerg, B. and Budzier, A. (2011): "Why Your IT Project Might Be Riskier Than You Think", Harvard Business Review, September 2011.

Flyvbjerg, B. and Budzier, A. (2012): "Project Success Factors and Core Beliefs", Presentation at the Value Assurance Academy, Brussels, 9-10th February, 2012.

Fortune, J. and White, D. (2006): "Framing of project critical success factors by a systems model", International Journal of Project Management 24 (2006), p 53-65.

Frese, R. and Sauter, V. (2003): "Project Success and Failure: "What is Success, What is Failure, And How Can You Improve Your Odds For Success?", December 16, 2003 http://www.umsl.edu/~sauterv/analysis/6840_f03_papers/frese/ (Accessed January 2, 2012)

Hodgson, I. (2002): "Keeping Your Head Above Water", http://www.conspectus.com/2002/november/article19.asp (Accessed January 2, 2012)

Jørgensen, M. and Moløkken-Østvold, K. (2004): "Reasons for Software Effort Estimation error: Impact of Respondent Role, Information Collection Approach, and Data Analysis Method", IEEE transactions on Software Engineering, Volume 30, Issue 12, December 2004.

Jørgensen, M. and Moløkken-Østvold, K. (2006): "How Large Are Software Cost Overruns? A Review of the 1994 CHAOS Report", Information and Software Technology, Volume 48, Issue 4, April 2006.

Kappelman, L.A., McKeeman, R. and Zhang, L. (2006): "Early Warning Sign of IT Project Failure: The Dominant Dozen", Information Systems Management, Fall 2006 (EBSCO).

Kotter, J. P. (1995): "Leading Change: Why Transformation Efforts Fail", Harvard Business Review, March-April 1995.

Markus M.L. and Robey, D. (1988): "Information Technology and Organizational Change: Causal Structure in Theory and Research", Management Science, Vol. 34, No. 5, May 1988.

McAfee, A. (2006): “Mastering the Three Worlds of Information Technology“, Harvard Business Review, November 2006 (EBSCO).

McManus, J. and Wood-Harper, T. (2007): “Understanding the Sources of Information Systems Project Failure“, Management Services, Autumn 2007 (EBSCO).

Nicholas, J. and Hidding, G. (2010): “Management Principles Associated With IT Project Success“, International Journal of Management and Information Systems, Fourth Quarter, 2010, pg 147-156. Available at http://journals.cluteonline.com/index.php/IJMIS/article/view/22/20 (Accessed February 20th, 2012)

Orlikowski, W. J.and Barley, W. R. (2001): ”Technology and Institutions: ”What Can Research on Information Technology and research on Organizations Learn From Each Other?”, MIS quarterly Vol. 25 No. 2, pp. 145-165, June 2001.

PASC (2011): “Government and IT – “a recipe for rip-offs”: time for a new approach”, Volume I, 28 July 2011. http://www.publications.parliament.uk/pa/cm201012/cmselect/cmpubadm/715/715i.pdf (Accessed December 20, 2011).

PMI (2008): “A Guide to The Project Management Body of Knowledge - PMBOK (r) Guide – Fourth edition”, Project Management Institute, pmi.org, 2008, http://marketplace.pmi.org/Pages/ProductDetail.aspx?GMProduct=00101095501

Sauer, C., Gemino, A., and Reich, B.H. (2007): “The Impact of Size and Volatility on IT Project Performance: Studying the factors influencing project risk” Communication of the ACM, November 2007, Vol. 50, No. 11 (Accessed February 20th 2012 at acm.org)

Standish (2009), “Press Release April 23, 2009”, http://www1.standishgroup.com/newsroom/chaos_2009.php (Accessed January 2, 2012)

Tesch, D., Kloppenborg, T.J and Frolick, M.N (2007): “IT Project Risk Factors: The Project Management Professional Perspective”, Journal of Computer Information Systems, Summer 2007, http://notspecial.no.funpic.de/Quellensammlung/RiskFactors.pdf (Accessed 15th January 2012)

Tress90 (2006): *Assessment of Tres90*, The Norwegian Parliament, St.prp.nr 55 (1994-1995), http://www.stortinget.no/no/Saker-og-publikasjoner/Publikasjoner/Innstillinger/Stortinget/1994-1995/inns-199495-210/7/ (Accessed 15th January 2012)

Tuckman, B.W (1965): “Developmental sequences in small groups”, Psychological Bulletin 63 (6): 384–399.

Whitfield, D. (2007): “Cost overruns, delays and terminations: 105 outsourced public sector ICT projects”, European Services Strategy Unit, ESSU Research Report No. 3, 2007 http://www.european-services-strategy.org.uk/news/2007/ict-contract-chaos/105-ict-contracts.pdf (Accessed January 8, 2012)

Sonderfall statt Prototyp: Eine prozedurale und empirische Analyse der Schlichtung zu Stuttgart 21

[Exception to the Rule: A Procedural and Empirical Analysis of the Stuttgart 21 Arbitration]

Arne Spieker, Marko Bachl

This paper analyzes public arbitration discussions as a new measure for Alternative Dispute Resolution (ADR) in local politics. In a case study of the German infrastructure project Stuttgart 21, we ask to what extent public arbitration discussions helped to resolve the conflict and pacify the city. We evaluate the arbitration in regard to fairness, inclusiveness, procedural method and influence on the local public. This evaluation will be twofold: The analysis of quality and procedural method of the process is based on a survey of the participants of the arbitration from both camps and a theoretical reflection regarding to established standards of ADR. The public influence of the arbitration is measured by an online-panel survey of the local population (n = 447), which was carried out directly before and after the arbitration. Results show that the public arbitration of Stuttgart 21 fails as a prototype for public arbitrations because of several defaults, most importantly the lack of openness for results and a jointly clarification of the facts as well as an insufficient clarity of the procedure. In regard to the local public, the arbitration led to a slight objectification of the conflict, but without altering positions. We also find signs for a selective perception of the arbitration discussions by both opponents and supporters of the project.

Summary of the most important findings:

- *The procedural analysis reveals several severe shortcomings of the Stuttgart 21 arbitration, most importantly: the proceedings' lack of clarity; lack of trust of the participants in the openness of the outcome; lack of an agreement on how both supporters and critics of the project could equally accompany the 'Stresstest' (the final fact finding procedure).*
- *According to the survey of active participants of the Stuttgart 21 arbitration sessions, the public broadcasts of the arbitration sessions increased the motivation to act up in front of the cameras and decreased the willingness to seek a compromise between the parties.*
- *The public arbitration sessions increased the satisfaction with the availability of information on Stuttgart 21 among the surveyed citizens of Stuttgart. However, they reported to have learnt mostly arguments that supported their initial opinion on the project.*

- *The arbitration did not substantially alter the citizens' beliefs on the most important arguments for and against Stuttgart 21.*
- *After the arbitration, both supporters and critics of Stuttgart 21 had a less unfavorable opinion of the communicative behavior and of several representatives of the other camp. However, in absolute terms the evaluation of the respective opposite camp still remained clearly unfavorable.*

1 Einleitung

Die aktuelle Debatte über Bürgerbeteiligung bei Großprojekten ist ohne die Auseinandersetzung um das Infrastruktur- und Städtebauprojekt Stuttgart 21 und die anschließende so genannte Sach- und Fachschlichtung nicht denkbar. Die Schlichtung zu Stuttgart 21 (im Folgenden kurz: S21-Schlichtung) hat sich in diesen Diskussionen zum Topos entwickelt, zu einem Symbol für Strategien zur Lösung großskalierter öffentlicher Konflikte. Angesichts der deutschlandweiten Beachtung, die die ursprünglich lokale Auseinandersetzung im Jahr 2010 erfuhr, erstaunt dies nicht. Die S21-Schlichtung fand in einem extrem polarisierten Umfeld statt: Nach der Eskalation der Auseinandersetzung am 30. September 2010, als es bei einer Demonstration im Stuttgarter Schlossgarten zu Zusammenstößen zwischen Polizei und Demonstranten mit über 100 Verletzten kam, wurde sowohl von den Grünen als auch der Landesregierung der Einsatz eines unabhängigen Vermittlers in einem moderierten Diskussionsprozess gefordert. Dadurch sollte ein Weg aus dem verfahrenen Konflikt gefunden und die Auseinandersetzung versachlicht werden, wie dies die Aussage, man brauche eine „Beruhigung der Leute" (Özdemir, zitiert in Kamann, 2010) durch den GRÜNEN-Politiker Cem Özdemir beispielhaft verdeutlicht. Befürworter und Kritiker des Projektes einigten sich schließlich auf den ehemaligen CDU-Generalsekretär und ATTAC-Mitglied Heiner Geißler. Am 22. Oktober 2010 begannen die Gespräche in den Räumlichkeiten des Stuttgarter Rathauses. Ihr Ziel war es laut Geißler, „über Zahlen, Daten und Fakten rund um Stuttgart 21 zu informieren, so dass man sich ein eigenes Urteil bilden könne" (Schlichtung S21, 2011). An den Sitzungen nahmen von Seiten der Befürworter und der Kritiker jeweils sieben, teils wechselnde, Repräsentanten teil. Nach acht ganztägigen Sitzungen endete die Gesprächsrunde am 30. November mit dem Schlichterspruch Heiner Geißlers. Jede Sitzung war einem umstrittenen Thema gewidmet, so beispielsweise der „Leistungsfähigkeit des Bahnknotens Stuttgart 21", „Geologie, Sicherheit und Bauablauf" oder der von den Stuttgart-21-Gegnern vertretenen Alternativlösung „Kopfbahnhof 21" (Schlichtung S21, 2011).[1] Die S21-Schlichtung wurde vollständig live im nationalen und regionalen Fernsehen und im Internet

1 Die Inhalte der Schlichtung sind ausführlich auf http://www.schlichtung-s21.de/ dokumentiert.

übertragen und stieß auf ein gewaltiges Medienecho. Heiner Geißler selbst bezeichnete das Verfahren in seiner Abschlusserklärung als „Demokratieexperiment“, dem er „eine weite Verbreitung in Deutschland“ wünsche (Geißler, 2010, S. 15). Die S21-Schlichtung wurde in der Öffentlichkeit als Prototyp bezeichnet, mit dem sich zukünftig Konflikte um Großprojekte vermeiden lassen sollen und eine bessere Bürgerbeteiligung möglich werden soll (Brettschneider, 2011).

Doch ist dem wirklich so? Kann die Sach- und Fachschlichtung tatsächlich als Prototyp für zukünftige Infrastrukturprojekte dienen? Um diese Frage zu beantworten, präsentieren wir in diesem Aufsatz Ergebnisse aus zwei Untersuchungen: Zum ersten ordnen wir die S21-Schlichtung als Prozedur zur Konfliktbewältigung ein. Die ‚Methode Geißler‘, also die Idee, auf einem informellen Weg an einem Runden Tisch einen festgefahren Konflikt lösen zu wollen, ist an sich kein neues Konzept. Verfahren der Alternativen Streitbeilegung werden schon seit mehreren Jahrzehnten auch im Rahmen von umstrittenen Großprojekten durchgeführt.[2] Wir gleichen sie deshalb mit den bereits existierenden Verfahren ab und prüfen, ob die S21-Schlichtung den in Wissenschaft und Praxis verbreiteten Qualitätskriterien gerecht wird. Neben der prozeduralen Analyse greifen wir dazu auch auf eine Befragung zurück, die mit den Teilnehmern der Schlichtungsgespräche durchgeführt wurde. Zweitens fragen wir nach den Wirkungen, die das Verfahren auf Befürworter und Kritiker innerhalb der Stuttgarter Bürgerschaft hatte. An der Schlichtung selbst nahmen zwar die Repräsentanten der Befürworter und Kritiker sowie deren Experten teil. Ein wichtiger Adressat war jedoch auch die bereitere Öffentlichkeit, die über die Fakten informiert werden sollte, um auf diese Weise, in den Worten Heiner Geißlers, zu einer „Befriedung, zu einer Versachlichung der Auseinandersetzung beizutragen“ (Protokoll 1, 2010, S. 1). Zur Beantwortung der Frage nach den Wirkungen auf die Bürger ziehen wir eine zweiwellige Panel-Studie heran, in der Einwohner aus Stuttgart und dem Umland direkt vor und nach der Schlichtung befragt wurden. Hier untersuchen wir, ob die S21-Schlichtung dazu geführt hat, dass Befürworter und Kritiker sich aneinander angenähert haben.

2 Die S21-Schlichtung als Alternatives Streitbeilegungsverfahren?

Die Schlichtung zum Konflikt um Stuttgart 21 ist ein Versuch der Konfliktlösung, der verwaltungsrechtlich nicht vorgesehen ist und auf absoluter Freiwilligkeit der teilnehmenden Akteure beruht. Als solches ähnelt es den Verfahren der Alternativen Streitbeilegung, die ihre Wurzeln in den USA unter dem Begriff „Alternative Dispute Re-

2 Für wissenschaftliche Analysen von prototypischen Verfahren in Deutschland vgl. z.B. die WZB-Begleitforschung zur Mediation um eine Müllverbrennungsanlage in Neuss (Holzinger & Weidner, 1997; Pfingsten & Fietkau, 1995) oder die Dokumentation der Mediation zum Ausbau des Frankfurter Flughafens (Geis, 2005).

solution“ (ADR) haben (Rogers & McEwen, 1994). Sie sind eine Reaktion auf die Erfahrung, dass in heutigen pluralen Gesellschaften Interessenskonflikte auf der Mikro- und Meso-Ebene immer häufiger auftreten bei einer gleichzeitig abnehmenden Legitimität der gesetzlich vorgesehenen Entscheidungsverfahren (Scharpf, 1991). Mit Methoden der ADR sollen die beteiligten Parteien gemeinsam nach Lösungen für den Konflikt suchen und so die gesetzlichen, politischen und administrativen Verfahren entlasten. Ziel ist dabei eine Ergänzung, nicht aber eine Ersetzung der formalen Verfahren. Wesentliches Element der ADR ist das kooperative Vorgehen aller Konfliktparteien, das in einem gemeinsam getragenen Konsens münden kann, aber nicht muss (Zillessen, 1998, S. 19). Als Vorteil für ADR wird üblicherweise ins Feld geführt, dass sie effektiver und effizienter als die rechtlich vorgesehenen Verfahren arbeiten. Durch die Schaffung einer gemeinsamen, informellen Plattform des Austausches sei es unter Hinzuziehung neutraler Dritter möglich, flexible und kreative Lösungen zu finden, die den Interessen der Beteiligten besser gerecht werden. Durch die Freiwilligkeit der Teilnahme hätten die vereinbarten Ergebnisse eine höhere Akzeptanz und seien damit auf Dauer belastbarer. Auch wenn die Verfahren erst einmal sehr zeit- und arbeitsintensiv sind, spare das aktive Aufarbeiten von Konflikten damit auf lange Sicht Zeit und Geld ein (Fietkau & Weidner, 1998; Hamacher, 1996; Weidner, 1996). Verbreitete Formen von ADR-Verfahren sind die Mediation, das Joint Fact Finding, Verhandlungen (mit/ohne Faszilitator) und Schlichtungsprozeduren (Bingham, 1986).

Keine der Typen ist in der Praxis in Reinform anzutreffen, vielmehr existiert eine Reihe von Mischtypen, die je nach Anforderung der konkreten Situation konzipiert werden. Die S21-Schlichtung hat mit zwei Typen besondere Ähnlichkeit: Dem *Joint Fact Finding* und der *Schlichtung*. Der Idee des Joint Fact Finding liegt die Beobachtung zu Grunde, dass die Konfliktparteien häufig mit unterschiedlichen Daten und Fakten argumentieren beziehungsweise zu völlig unterschiedlichen Interpretationen dieser Informationen gelangen. In der öffentlichen Auseinandersetzung versucht jede Seite ihre Argumente und Deutungen auf der Agenda zu platzieren, während die Argumente und Deutungen der Gegenseite dethematisiert werden. Selbst wenn diese Asynchronität der Debatte durchbrochen wird und die Diskussion sich um dieselben Argumente zentriert, steht doch nur Aussage gegen Aussage. Jede Konfliktseite besteht auf der Korrektheit ihrer Informationen und bestreitet diejenigen der Gegenseite. Diesen Problemen kann mit einem Joint Fact Finding entgegengewirkt werden, indem eine Interaktionsplattform zur gemeinsamen Feststellung der Fakten geschaffen wird. Mit bestimmten Verfahrensprozeduren - wie gemeinsamen Expertenhearings oder der Beauftragung von Gutachten - soll eine lagerübergreifend akzeptierte Faktenbasis geschaffen werden. Faktenklärungen sind häufig Bestandteil von Konfliktregelungsverfahren im öffentlichen Bereich, wie beispielsweise der politischen Mediation (Eggert & Meister, 2007).

Als *Schlichtung* wird ein Verfahrenstyp verstanden, bei dem ein neutraler Dritter starken Einfluss auf die Lösungsfindung hat. Während beispielsweise bei einer *Mediation* der sogenannte Mediator die Parteien dabei unterstützt, selbstständig eine Lösung miteinander zu vereinbaren, geht es dem Schlichter darum, eine eigene Bewertung der Sach- und Rechtslage vorzunehmen und die Streitparteien von einem Schlichtungs- und Vergleichsergebnis zu überzeugen (Breidenbach, 1995). Öffentliche Aufmerksamkeit erregen regelmäßig Schlichtungsversuche in der Tarifpolitik, aber auch im Bauwesen sind sie nicht unbekannt (Zerhusen, 2005). Die S21-Schlichtung als Verfahren der Aufarbeitung von Daten, an deren Ende ein Schlichterspruch stand, vereinigt damit sowohl Elemente einer nicht bindenden Schlichtung als auch des Joint Fact Finding – allerdings auf eine sehr untypische Weise, wie im Folgenden noch gezeigt wird.

In der akademischen Literatur zu ADR (z.B. Fietkau & Weidner, 1998; Zillessen, 1998) wie auch in Praxis-Leitfäden (z.B. Susskind, McKearnan & Thomas-Larmer, 1999) wurden zahlreiche von Voraussetzungen für den Erfolg alternativer Streitbeilegungsverfahren herausgearbeitet. Dazu gehören die Verfahrensklarheit, die Ergebnisoffenheit des Verfahrens, die Begleitung durch einen neutralen Dritten, die Freiwilligkeit der Teilnahme, die Bereitschaft zur gemeinsamen Problemlösung, die ausgewogene Repräsentation möglichst aller betroffenen Parteien sowie deren Gleichbehandlung im Prozess. Anders als bei einem rechtlich vorgesehenen formalen Verfahren, dessen Ergebnisse *de jure* bindende Gültigkeit haben, müssen ADR-Verfahren von den freiwillig teilnehmenden Konfliktparteien selbst als legitim empfunden werden. Nur wenn das Prozedere von allen Beteiligten als angemessen anerkannt wird, können sich auch die Ergebnisse des Verfahrens als langfristig bindend und stabil erweisen. Die Einhaltung der aufgeführten prozeduralen Standards ist damit nicht nur für die Beurteilung der Prozedur, sondern auch für Qualität des Verfahrensergebnisses zentral. Für eine Schlichtung kommt das Kriterium hinzu, dass der Schlichterspruch auch inhaltlich von den Parteien als ausgewogen und angemessen empfunden werden muss, sonst wird er mangels rechtlicher Bindungskraft kaum Chancen auf eine Umsetzung haben.

3 Prozedurale Beurteilung

Im folgenden Abschnitt analysieren wir die Schlichtung anhand der verschiedenen Qualitätskriterien. Bei der Einschätzung werden Ergebnisse einer Befragung der Teilnehmer an den Schlichtungsgesprächen herangezogen.[3] Die prozedurale Beurteilung ermöglicht uns, die S21-Schlichtung als Verfahrenstyp klassifizieren und bewerten zu können.

Verfahrensklarheit

Voraussetzung für Akzeptanz und Erfolg eines Streitbeilegungsverfahrens ist, dass Klarheit und Einigkeit über die Form des Verfahrens besteht. Dazu gehört, sich darüber zu verständigen, in welcher Form diskutiert bzw. verhandelt wird, welche Rolle der neutrale Dritte hat und welche Art des Ergebnisses am Ende steht. Die Klärung der Fakten kann beispielsweise durch die gemeinsame Beauftragung von Gutachten geschehen, wie es im Rahmen des Streitbeilegungsverfahrens im Konflikt um den Ausbau des Frankfurter Flughafens durchgeführt wurde: Dort einigten sich die Parteien auf gemeinsame Gutachter und gaben zudem Kontrollgutachten in Auftrag, die die Qualität der Hauptgutachten überwachen sollten (Wörner, 2010). Am Ende des Joint Fact Finding steht im Erfolgsfall ein abgestimmtes Dokument, aus dem hervorgeht, welche Fragestellungen untersucht wurden, worüber Einigkeit besteht und worüber noch Dissens. Wählt man dagegen ein Schlichtungsverfahren, ist den Teilnehmern bereits zu Beginn klar, dass am Ende ein Schlichterspruch steht (Raupach, 1964).

Die Verfahrensklarheit bei der S21-Schlichtung war nur bedingt gegeben. Heiner Geißler erklärte zu Beginn, dass ein Ergebnis wie bei einer klassischen Schlichtung nicht möglich sei. Man könne weder einen neuen Bahnhof erfinden, noch Stuttgart zu einer ebenen Stadt machen (Protokoll 1, 2010). Es gehe vielmehr darum, einen „Faktencheck“ zu machen, in dem man alle strittigen Fragen erörtere und versuche, zu einer gemeinsamen Bewertung zu gelangen. Aus diesen Ergebnissen müsse „am Ende jede Seite die Konsequenzen daraus ziehen, die sie für richtig hält“ (Protokoll 1, 2010, S. 2.). Im Gegensatz zu dieser Ankündigung, sich auf die Klärung der Fakten zu beschränken, stand am Ende jedoch ein Schlichterspruch, in dem Geißler selbst seine Schlüsse aus dem Verfahren zog, einen Kompromissvorschlag erarbeitete und diesen dann der Öffentlichkeit präsentierte. Die Zustimmung zu diesem Kompromissvorschlag (Stuttgart 21 Plus) rang Geißler den beiden Parteien zwischen Abschluss der letzten Sitzung und der Pressekonferenz unter enormen Zeitdruck ab. Dies wurde auch als „Überrumpelungsverfahren“ kritisiert (Rucht, 2010). Die S21-Schlichtung litt damit unter Verfahrensunklarheit, verursacht durch eine Vermengung von Faktenfin-

3 Die Befragung wurde durch uns von Mitte Juni bis Anfang Juli 2011 postalisch durchgeführt. Angeschrieben wurden 64 Teilnehmer der Schlichtungsrunden (ständige Teilnehmer sowie eingeladene Experten). Jeweils 17 Teilnehmer der Befürworter- und der Kritikerseite sandten den Fragebogen zurück. Die Rücklaufquote beträgt damit 53%.

dungs- und Schlichtungsverfahren, die vor Beginn des Prozesses so nicht mit den beteiligten Akteuren abgestimmt war.

Ergebnisoffenheit

Eng mit der Verfahrensklarheit verbunden ist die Ergebnisoffenheit. Eine zwingende Notwendigkeit für Methoden der Alternativen Streitbeilegung ist, dass potenziell eine Kompromisslösung existiert, die zwar beiden Seiten Opfer abverlangt, sie jedoch besser stellt als Alternativen, die ohne Verhandlungslösung wahrscheinlich zustande kommen würden (Fisher, Ury & Patton, 2011; Holzinger, 1996). Wie Geißler selbst beschrieb, war die Ergebnisoffenheit des Schlichtungsverfahrens problematisch. Es standen mit Stuttgart 21 und dem Gegenentwurf Kopfbahnhof 21 (K21) zwei sich gegenseitig ausschließende Konzepte zur Diskussion. Die Schlichtung wurde zu einem sehr späten Zeitpunkt durchgeführt, rund 16 Jahre nach der offiziellen Vorstellung des Projektes. Erste Bauarbeiten, wie der Abriss des Bahnhof-Nordflügels, waren bereits geschehen, Aufträge an Subunternehmer in großer Zahl vergeben. Daher überrascht es nicht, dass die Mehrheit der befragten Teilnehmer der Kritikerseite, ganz im Gegensatz zu den Befürwortern, eine mangelnde Ergebnisoffenheit beklagte (vgl. Abb. 1). Geißler wurde nach Ende der Schlichtungsrunden von dieser Seite auch vorgeworfen, er habe vor den geschaffenen Fakten kapituliert (Waßmuth & von Larcher, 2010).

Abbildung 1: "Das Schlichtungsverfahren war ergebnisoffen."

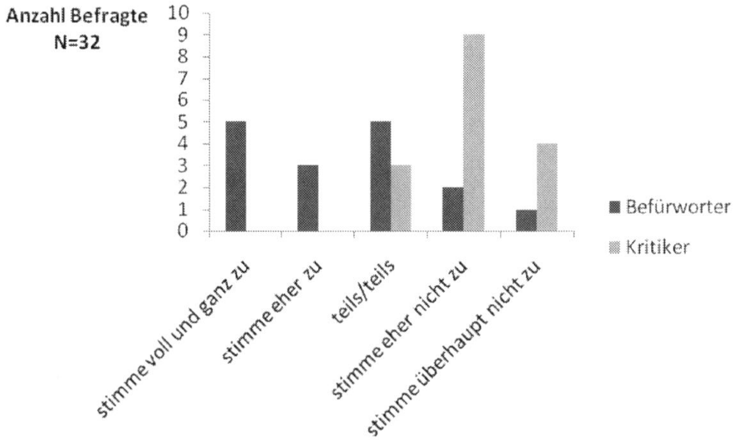

Einbindung aller Parteien

Möglichst alle Stimmen einzubinden und ihnen im Prozess Gehör zu verschaffen, ist ein wichtiges Kriterium für Alternative Streitbeilegungsverfahren. Fehlen wichtige Akteure am Tisch, fehlt auch ihre Zustimmung zu den Ergebnissen, wodurch eine Beendigung des Konfliktes unwahrscheinlicher wird (Fietkau & Weidner, 1998). An der Schlichtung waren von Seiten der Befürworter Vertreter der Landesregierung, der Stadt, der Bahn und des Aktionsbündnisses Initiative "Pro Stuttgart 21" beteiligt. Von Seiten der Kritiker nahmen diejenigen an den Sitzungen teil, die im Konflikt in der Öffentlichkeit prominent vertreten waren, wie Vertreter von Bündnis90/Die Grünen, der SÖS-Stadtratsfraktion und des BUND. Damit war die Zusammensetzung weniger durch die tatsächliche Betroffenheit von Stuttgart 21 bestimmt (so fehlten z.B. Vertreter von Hauseigentümern), sondern vielmehr durch den politischen Konflikt. Bemerkenswert war das Fehlen der "Parkschützer", einer Initiative zum Schutz des Schlossparks. Diese hatten sich vor Beginn der Gespräche gegen eine Teilnahme entschieden. Der allergrößte Teil der befragten Schlichtungsteilnehmer, sowohl von Befürworter- wie auch von Kritikerseite, schätzte die Zusammensetzung des Teilnehmerkreises jedoch als angemessen ein.

Fairness des Verfahrens

Die Gleichbehandlung der Teilnehmer ist essenziell für die Legitimität des Prozesses. Die Gewährleistung identischer Möglichkeiten zur Rede und Gegenrede, gleichverteilte Redezeiten und die gerechte Anwendung der Verfahrensregeln gehört zu den Hauptaufgaben des Gesprächsleiters. Die Gleichberechtigung der Teilnehmer als auch die Fairness des Verfahrens wurde von den Befürwortern positiv beurteilt, von den Kritikern in einem abgeschwächtem Maße ebenfalls. Dies deckt sich mit der Bewertung der Verfahrensführung durch Heiner Geißler, die von beiden Seiten überwiegend gut beurteilt wurde. Geißler erwarb sich durch einen kompromisslosen Leitungsstil Respekt, in dem er alle Beteiligten wiederholt dazu ermahnte, sachlich und verständlich vorzutragen. Ein wesentliches strukturelles Defizit war die ungleiche Ausstattung mit Ressourcen: Die Befürworter konnten sich, assistiert durch personelles Know-How und finanzielle Unterstützung der Projektträger, auf Daten, Zahlen und Argumente eines seit vielen Jahren in der Planung bestehenden Projekts stützen. Dagegen mussten die Kritiker ihre Beweisführung in ihrer Freizeit und mit vergleichsweise limitierten finanziellen Ressourcen entwickeln. Diese ungleichen Bedingungen wurden erwartungsgemäß vor allem von der Kritikerseite bemängelt.

Vorgehensweise der Faktenklärung

Erfolgsmaßstab für ein Joint Fact Finding ist, ob am Ende eine gesicherte Grundlage besteht, der beide Seiten zustimmen können. Die Fakten zu Stuttgart 21 waren in vielerlei Hinsicht umstritten: Zur Diskussion standen unter anderem die Leistungsfähigkeit des neuen Bahnknotens, die Gefährdung des Grundwassers, die geologischen Risiken der Tunnel, die zu erwartenden Kosten und die Eignung von K21 als alternatives Konzept. Die Sitzungen ähnelten einem Gerichtsprozess, in dem beide Seiten ihre Argumente vorbrachten und versuchten, diese mit Beweisen zu untermauern. Dazu konnten sie Experten in den ‚Zeugenstand' rufen. Das enge Zeitkorsett mit nur acht Sitzungen ließ es nicht zu, zu einer einheitlicheren Bewertung der Fakten zu kommen, beispielsweise indem beide Seiten gemeinsame Gutachten in Auftrag gaben. Die Auseinandersetzung beschränkte sich auf Rede und Gegenrede. Die Diskussion verhakte sich zudem zu oft in Details, was dazu führte, dass eine abschließende Betrachtung zentraler Punkte mangels Zeit nicht möglich war. Dementsprechend uneinheitlich ist die Ansicht der Befragten darüber, wie die Möglichkeit der Klärung von Sachfragen zu beurteilen ist (Abb. 2).

Abbildung 2: „Wie bewerten Sie die Möglichkeit der Klärung von Sachfragen?"

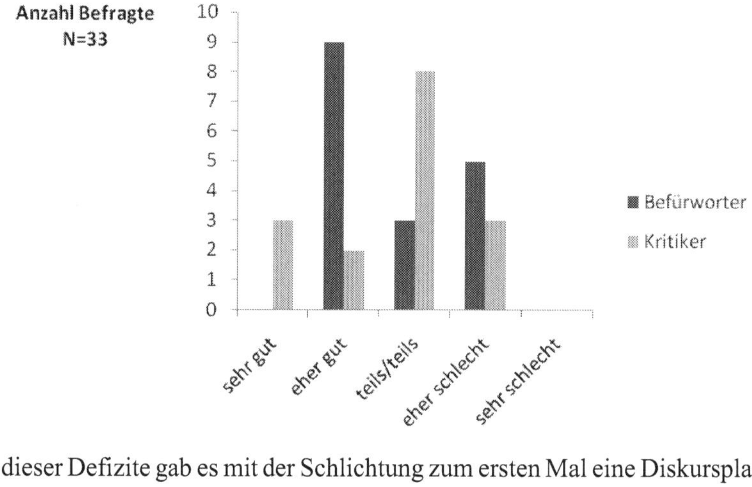

Trotz dieser Defizite gab es mit der Schlichtung zum ersten Mal eine Diskursplattform, in der es möglich war, die Fülle der Argumente und Daten beider Seiten zusammenzutragen und miteinander zu vergleichen. So bezeichnen selbst kritische Autoren das Verfahren als ein Projekt „gewaltiger Volksbildung" (Waßmuth & von Larcher, 2010), das viel für „eine demokratische Diskussionskultur, für Transparenz und Verständlichkeit" getan habe (Vonnahme & Tremml, 2010). Die befragten Teilnehmer der Befürworterseite bescheinigten der Schlichtung mehrheitlich, dass die Aufklärung über

Zahlen, Daten und Fakten gelungen sei, während bei den Kritikern darüber Uneinigkeit besteht (Abb. 3). Ähnlich sieht das Bild bei der Frage aus, ob alle wesentlichen Aspekte von Stuttgart 21 behandelt wurden (Abb. 4). Von Seiten der Kritiker wurde wiederholt die unzureichende Behandlung von K21 als Alternative bemängelt.

Abbildung 3: „Ist die Aufklärung über Zahlen, Daten und Fakten gelungen?"

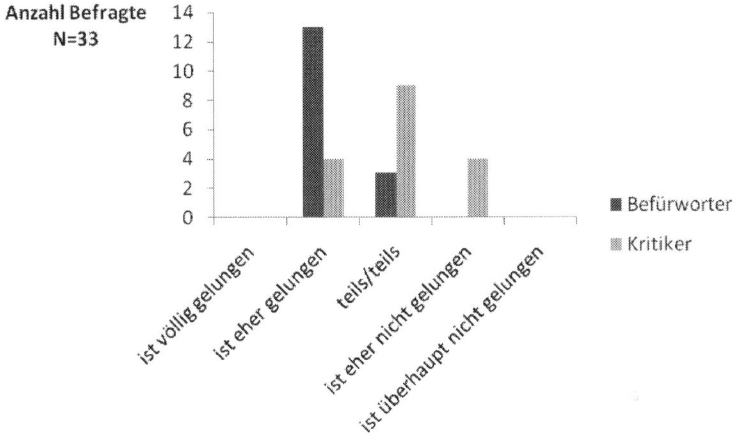

Abbildung 4: "Alle wesentlichen Aspekte von Stuttgart 21 wurden behandelt"

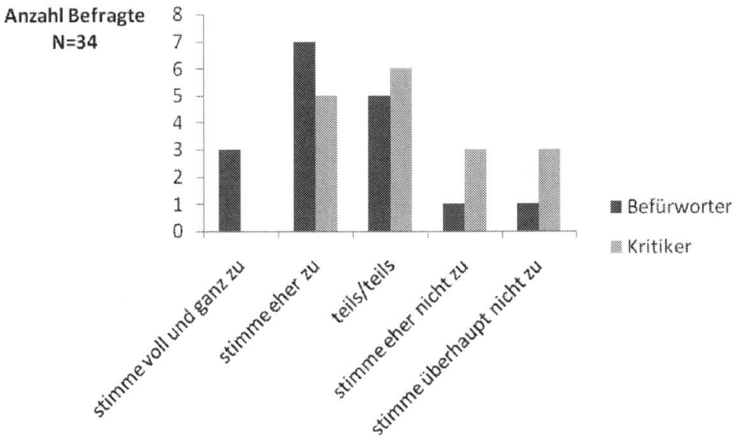

Das zentrale Element des Schlichterspruchs war der Stresstest. Die von Heiner Geißler vorgeschlagenen Modifikationen band er an die Ergebnisse einer Simulation, mit der die Bahn den Nachweis erbringen sollte, dass „ein Fahrplan mit 30% Leistungszuwachs in der Spitzenstunde mit guter Betriebsqualität möglich ist" (Protokoll 9, 2010,

S. 44). Damit lagerte Geißler den Kern der Faktenklärung aus dem Verfahren aus und gab ihn in die Hände einer der streitenden Parteien. Von Seiten der Kritiker wurde moniert, dass die Bahn den Stresstest nicht transparent durchführe und „eine kritische Begleitung durch externe Experten“ nicht zulasse (Aktionsbündnis gegen Stuttgart 21, 2010). Nach ihrer Ansicht wurden fehlerhafte Annahmen getroffen und wesentliche Unterlagen der Öffentlichkeit nicht zugänglich gemacht (Aktionsbündnis gegen Stuttgart 21, 2011). Brigitte Dahlbender, Landesvorsitzende des BUND und für die Kritikerseite Teilnehmerin der Schlichtungsgespräche, bemängelte im Rahmen der Ergebnispräsentation die unklaren Rahmenbedingungen und Interpretationsspielräume des Stresstests. Es sei „[...] unabdingbar wichtig, dass sich beide Parteien zusammensetzen, die Grundlagen gemeinsam definieren und dann geschaut wird, was bei einem Stresstest und bei einem entsprechenden Audit oder Gutachten herauskommt. Das ist erheblich versäumt worden“ (Protokoll 10, 2011, S. 20). Solche Fragestellungen hätten in einem Gremium durch beide Seiten gemeinsam transparent bearbeitet werden können. Die befragten Kritiker und auch eine knappe Mehrheit der Befürworter wünschten sich solch eine Begleitung des Stresstests und der Volksabstimmung.

Abbildung 5: „Halten Sie die Einführung eines Gremiums für besser, das den Stresstest und die Volksabstimmung transparent begleitet?"

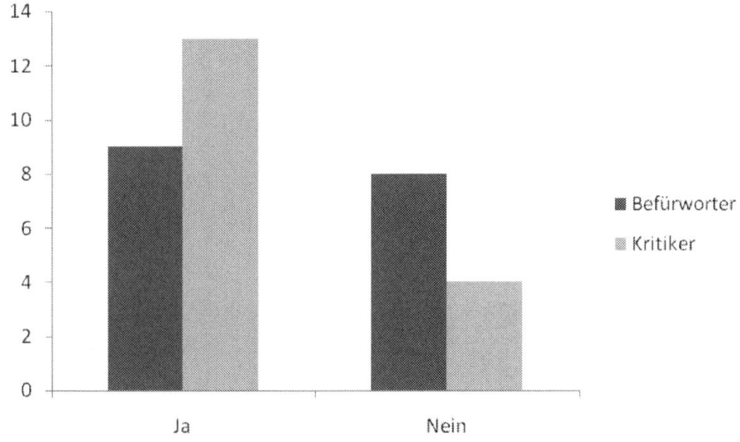

Bewertung des Schlichterspruchs durch die Schlichtungsteilnehmer

Der Schlichterspruch von Heiner Geißler mit dem Titel „Stuttgart 21 Plus“ sah mehrere Modifikationen des Projekts vor, die die von den Kritikern in der Schlichtung aufgezeigten Probleme beheben sollten (Protokoll 9, 2010). Welche Verbesserungen tatsächlich durchgeführt werden müssten, sollte sich im Stresstest erweisen. Trotz einiger zustimmender Reaktionen unmittelbar im Anschluss an die Schlichtung stieß der Schlichterspruch auf Seiten der Kritiker überwiegend auf Ablehnung, während die Befürworter ihn weitgehend positiv bewerteten (Abb. 6 und 7). Für die Kritiker wurde der Schlichterspruch als Niederlage wahrgenommen, da sie angetreten waren, Stuttgart 21 zu verhindern. Der Schlichterspruch war hingegen eine Bestätigung des Projekts, dessen ohnehin schon als zu hoch kritisierten Kosten dadurch noch weiter steigen würden. Für ein informelles Verfahren der Alternativen Konfliktlösung ist eine solche Unzufriedenheit einer Seite ein großes Problem, da sie die Legitimation und damit die Selbstbindung an das Ergebnis unterminiert. Dies zeigte sich im weiteren Verlauf des Konflikts, in dem die Positionen der Parteien unverändert hart blieben. Ein Vorwurf an die Kritiker, sich mit der Einwilligung zu einem Schlichtungsverfahren auch an das Ergebnis binden zu müssen, ginge fehl. In einem informellen, auf Freiwilligkeit basierenden Verfahren muss sich niemand an ein wie auch immer geartetes Ergebnis binden. Ein methodisch gutes Streitbeilegungsverfahren zeichnet sich vielmehr dadurch aus, dass es Ergebnisse produziert, die von den Beteiligten als fair und angemessen angesehen werden. Je legitimer die Prozedur des Zustandekommens eines Ergebnisses wahrgenommen wird, desto legitimer wird auch das Ergebnis selbst wahrgenommen. Ein autonom herbeigeführter Schlichterspruch erweist sich hierbei als weniger tragfähig als eine von beiden Parteien gemeinsam herbeigeführte Lösung oder ein Faktenklärungsprozess unter Einbeziehung gemeinsam bestellter Gutachter. Unter den gegebenen zeitlichen Rahmenbedingungen wäre dies allerdings kaum zu erreichen gewesen.

Abbildung 6: „Wie beurteilen Sie persönlich den Schlichterspruch?“

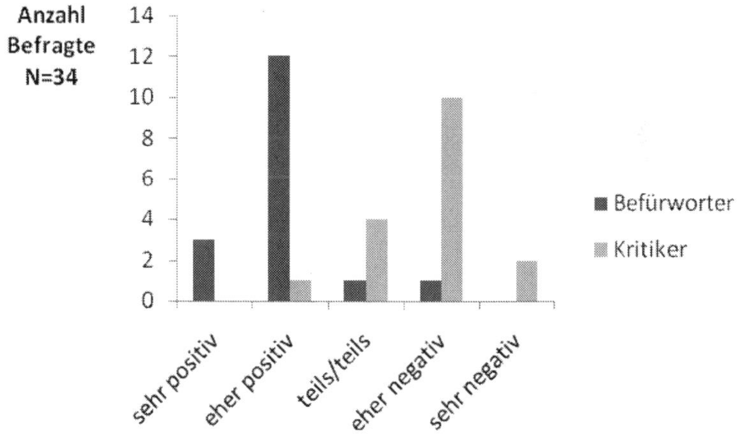

Abbildung 7: "Der Schlichterspruch war ausgewogen"

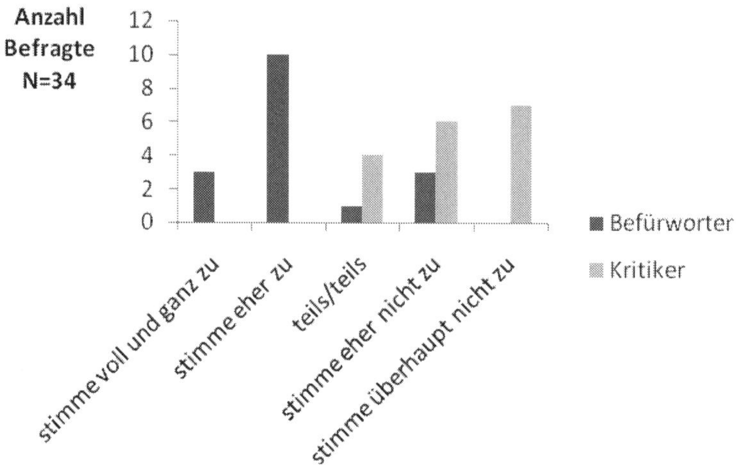

Transparenz

Die Live-Übertragung der Schlichtung löste großes öffentliches Interesse aus. Der überregionale deutsche Fernsehsender PHOENIX übertrug alle Sitzungen, der regionale SWR teilweise, und beide Sender erreichten damit über 10 Millionen Fernsehzuschauer, die zumindest Teile der Schlichtung verfolgten (PHOENIX, 2010; SWR, 2010). Zusätzlich gab es Live-Streams unter anderem auf zdf.de und fluegel.tv. Damit war eine vollständige Transparenz der Sitzungsinhalte gegeben. Heiner Geißler versuchte dem öffentlichen Interesse gerecht zu werden und legte viel Wert auf einen verständlichen und nachvollziehbaren Ablauf der Debatte. So ermahnte er Teilnehmer regelmäßig, auf Fremdworte und Abkürzungen zu verzichten. Für ein konfliktschlichtendes Verfahren war die Live-Übertragung ein Novum, denn die Sitzungsrunden solcher Verfahren sind in der Regel nicht öffentlich. Das hat einen guten Grund: Die Vertraulichkeit soll den teilnehmenden Repräsentanten gesellschaftlicher Gruppierungen einen geschützten Raum geben, in dem es ihnen möglich ist, sich von öffentlich festgezurrten Positionen loszulösen und Kompromissoptionen auszuloten (Eisele, 2011). Ist dieser geschützte Raum nicht gegeben und findet das Verfahren vollständig im Licht der Öffentlichkeit statt, dann besteht die Gefahr, dass die Teilnehmer sich weniger von sachlichen Erwägungen leiten lassen, sondern versuchen, durch einen harten Verhandlungsstil ihren Anhängern Standfestigkeit und Loyalität zu signalisieren (Stasavage, 2007). In der Tat sind mehrere Befragte der Auffassung, die Öffentlichkeit habe bei einigen Teilnehmern zum ‚Schaulaufen' geführt (Abb. 8). Dagegen ist der überwiegende Teil der befragten Teilnehmer der Auffassung, eine vertrauliche Arbeitsatmosphäre wurde dadurch nicht behindert. Das kann freilich dahingehend gelesen werden, dass eine vertrauliche Arbeitsatmosphäre gar nicht notwendig war. Schließlich hatten nicht die Teilnehmer einen Kompromiss zu erarbeiten, sondern der Schlichter.

Abbildung 8: "Die öffentliche Übertragung hat einige Teilnehmer zum Schaulaufen verleitet"

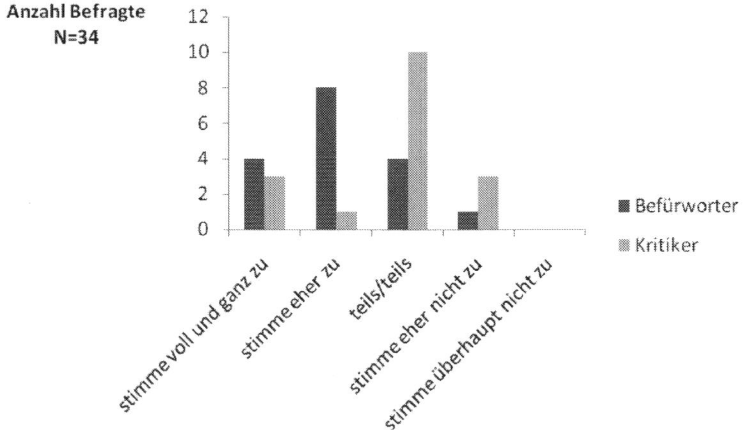

Zwischenfazit

Die prozedurale Bewertung der Schlichtung fällt zwiespältig aus. Sie wurde im gegebenen Rahmen fair durchgeführt, auch die Auswahl der Schlichtungsteilnehmer war aus Sicht der Befragten angemessen. Heiner Geißler legte zudem großen Wert auf Verständlichkeit und eine gründliche Präsentation der Fakten. Der Rahmen selbst weißt jedoch, gemessen an den Standards etablierter Verfahren, zahlreiche Mängel auf. Zu den Wesentlichsten gehören die Verfahrensunklarheit, der enge zeitliche Rahmen, die mangelnde Ergebnisoffenheit sowie das Prozedere der Faktenklärung. In Hinblick auf die Funktion der S21-Schlichtung als Joint Fact Finding ist vor allem zu bemängeln, dass eine *gemeinsame* Feststellung und Erörterung der Fakten überhaupt nicht stattfand. Stattdessen präsentierten Befürworter wie Kritiker ihre *eigenen* Ansichten mithilfe ihrer *eigenen* Experten vor dem Schlichter und der interessierten Öffentlichkeit, ohne dass ein tiefergehender Austausch über diese Fakten stattfand. Dementsprechend gespalten fiel auch das Urteil der befragten Teilnehmer zur Faktenklärung in der Schlichtung aus. Die stärksten negativen Konsequenzen hatte das nicht zwischen den Konfliktparteien abgestimmte Vorgehen bei der Faktensuche für den abschließenden

Stresstest. Vor dem Hintergrund der zeitlichen Restriktionen der Schlichtungsgespräche war es während des laufenden Verfahrens kaum möglich, gemeinsame Gutachten zu beauftragen. Hier war die Präsentation der den Parteien jeweils bereits vorliegenden Informationen ein pragmatisch sinnvoller Kompromiss. Der Stresstest als ein Gutachten, das direkt aus dem Schlichtungsverfahren abgeleitet wurde, hätte jedoch nach den Prinzipien eines guten Joint Fact Finding gemeinsam beauftragt und beaufsichtigt werden können. Diese Chance wurde verpasst, als die Deutsche Bahn als Vertreterin einer der beiden Konfliktparteien mit der Durchführung der Simulation beauftragt und auch eine Begleitung durch die anderen Verfahrensteilnehmer (inklusive des Schlichters) nicht vorgesehen wurde.[4] Indem Geißler bei seiner zentralen Maßnahme der Konfliktlösung den Ball wieder in die Arena warf und die Kontrahenten beim Streit um den Stresstest alleine ließ, raubte er seinem Schlichtungsversuch bereits zu Beginn die Erfolgschancen.

Hinsichtlich der Funktion der S21-Schlichtung als Schlichtungsverfahren muss vor allem die fehlende Verfahrensklarheit, die fehlende Ergebnisoffenheit und die – zumindest auf Seiten der befragten Kritiker – geringe Akzeptanz des Schlichterspruchs kritisiert werden. Allein die Tatsache, dass am Ende des Prozesses eine Empfehlung für das weitere Vorgehen stand, war – abgesehen von der Titulierung des Verfahrens als Schlichtung – zu Beginn nicht klar mit den Teilnehmern vereinbart. Die Entscheidung, in der letzten Sitzung einen Schlichterspruch abzugeben, überrascht. Schließlich fehlten wesentliche Voraussetzungen, die für eine dauerhafte Anerkennung des Schlichterspruchs notwendig gewesen wären. Weder gab es eine gemeinsam akzeptierte Faktengrundlage, noch war eine Kompromissformel in Sichtweite, die beiden Parteien gleichermaßen Zugeständnisse abgerungen hätte. Stuttgart 21 Plus war eine Bestätigung des Projektes, die die kritisierten Kosten noch weiter in die Höhe trieb. Die Kritik an den verschiedenen Aspekten von Stuttgart 21 war getragen von dem Interesse, K21 als Alternativkonzept zu etablieren und nicht davon, einzelne Mängel von S21 zu beseitigen. Um dieses Interesse der Kritiker zu berücksichtigen, hätte man die verschiedenen zur Debatte stehenden Alternativen (zumindest S21 und K21, Nullvariante) gleichberechtigt und transparent prüfen müssen. Da dies unterbleiben ist, fehlte es dem Schlichterspruch an Akzeptanz. Die Legitimation der ‚Lösung' war dahin, bevor sie überhaupt umgesetzt werden konnte.

In der Gesamtschau der verfahrenstechnischen Mängel ist es wenig überraschend, dass die Schlichtung nicht dazu in der Lage war, zentrale Konfliktpunkte auszuräumen und zur Faktenklarheit beizutragen. Das muss nicht bedeuten, dass die S21-Schlichtung auch bei ihrem zweiten selbsterklärten Ziel gescheitert ist: zu einer „Befriedung"

4 Der Lenkungsausschuss, in dem sich Vertreter der grün-roten Landesregierung und der Deutschen Bahn ab dem 30. Mai 2011 regelmäßig trafen, war lediglich ein allgemeines, informelles Abstimmungsgremium. Eine Einigkeit über Modalitäten des Stresstests war zu diesem Zeitpunkt ohnehin nicht mehr möglich, da dieser schon zu weit fortgeschritten war.

des Konfliktes beizutragen (Protokoll 1, 2010, S. 1). Unter Befriedung wurde verstanden, die starken Emotionen und die hohe Polarisierung innerhalb der lokalen Bevölkerung abzuschwächen und beide Seiten dazu zu bringen, sich aufeinander zuzubewegen. Wir wollen daher im nächsten Schritt untersuchen, welche Wirkungen von der Schlichtung auf die lokale Bevölkerung ausgegangen sind und ob die selbst gesteckten Ziele erreicht werden konnten.

4 Beurteilung der öffentlichen Wirksamkeit

Im Gegensatz zu klassischen Streitbeilegungsverfahren, bei denen es um konstruktive Lösungsfindungen zwischen unmittelbar von der Sache betroffenen Interessensträgern geht, richtete sich die Schlichtung von vornerein auch an die breitere Öffentlichkeit. Insofern ginge eine Bewertung der Schlichtung fehl, würde sie nicht auch ihre Wirkung auf die Bürger vor Ort mit einbeziehen. Zu diesem Zweck haben wir eine zweiwellige Panelbefragung durchgeführt, mit der wir die Einstellungen der Bürger direkt vor und nach den Schlichtungsrunden erhoben haben.[5]

Wir können positive Wirkungen des Verfahrens hinsichtlich verschiedener Dimensionen erwarten. Nach Innes (2004) können Techniken der Konsensfindung gemeinsame Lernprozesse fördern, politisches und soziales Kapital aufbauen sowie ein gemeinsames Verständnis der Fragestellungen ermöglichen. Verfahren der gemeinsamen Faktenklärung führen zu einem besseren und differenzierten Verständnis der Themen und zu legitimeren Ergebnissen und verbesserten die Beziehung zwischen den Teilnehmenden (Ehrmann & Stinson, 1999). Selbst ohne Ergebnis beendeten und somit offiziell gescheiterten Verfahren werden mitunter positive Lerneffekte zugeschrieben (Buckle & Thomas-Buckle, 1986). Prozeduren der Alternativen Konfliktlösung sind als diskursiver Aushandlungsprozess zudem durch starke deliberative Elemente geprägt (Menkel-Meadow, 2006), denen mehrere positive Effekte zugeschrieben wer-

5 Die erste Welle wurde an den beiden Tagen vor dem ersten Schlichtungsgespräch (20./21. 10. 2010), die zweite Welle im Anschluss an die Verkündung des Schlichterspruchs (1.-5. 12. 2010) erhoben. Bei der Befragung haben wir auf ein nicht-repräsentatives Online-Access-Panel zurückgegriffen, das von der Universität Hohenheim unterhalten wird. Der größte Teil der Teilnehmerinnen und Teilnehmer des Panels wohnt in der Stadt oder Region Stuttgart. Die Rekrutierung der Panelmitglieder fand unabhängig von der hier dargestellten Befragung statt. Mobilisierungseffekte durch besonders engagierte Befürworter oder Kritiker von ‚Stuttgart 21‘ können damit zumindest für die Rekrutierung ausgeschlossen werden. Von 1039 angeschriebenen Panelmitgliedern beendeten 447 Teilnehmerinnen und Teilnehmer beide Befragungswellen (43%). Eine systematische Panelmortalität in Hinblick auf Einstellung zu Stuttgart 21, Einstellungsstärke, Parteipräferenz und Themeninteresse liegt nicht vor. Die hier präsentierten Ergebnisse basieren auf einer Teilstichprobe von 355 Befragten, die vor der Schlichtung eine Meinung zu Stuttgart 21 hatten. 54% dieser Teilstichprobe konnten als Kritiker, 46% als Befürworter von Stuttgart 21 eingeordnet werden. 49% waren weiblich, 67% haben die (fachbezogene) Hochschulreife. Siehe für eine ausführlichere Analyse der Wirkungen auf die Gegner des Projekts in der Bevölkerung Bachl et al. (2011).

den: Deliberationsverfahren sollen zu einer größeren Toleranz abweichender Meinungen führen (Gutmann & Thompson, 1996) und damit Konflikte versachlichen (McCombs & Reynold, 1999); gleichfalls zu Lerneffekten führen (z.B. Gastil, 2000) sowie die Einstellungen und Meinungen der Teilnehmer verändern können (Fishkin, 1999; Fishkin & Luskin, 1999). Zusammengenommen können solche Verfahren Effekte auf *Wissen*, *Meinungen* und die *Beziehungsqualität* der streitenden Parteien haben. Der empirische Nachweis dieser positiven Effekte von ADR- beziehungsweise Deliberationsverfahren beschränkt sich allerdings auf Personen, die an den Verfahren unmittelbar und aktiv teilgenommen haben. Unklar ist, ob sich diese Effekte auch bei einer breiteren Öffentlichkeit zeigen, die – wie bei der S21-Schlichtung – das konfliktbearbeitende Verfahren lediglich als Zuschauer über die direkte und indirekte Berichterstattung der Massenmedien verfolgen konnte. In den folgenden Abschnitten werden wir überprüfen, wie sich Wissen, Meinungen und Beziehungsqualität bei den befragten Bürgern verändert haben. Alle Ergebnisse sind in den Tabellen 1 und 2 zusammengefasst.

Wissenseffekte

Die Auseinandersetzung um Stuttgart 21 war selbst für Fachleute äußert komplex. Im Einflussbereich des milliardenschweren Projektes befinden sich 360 Stationen und Bahnhöfe, 1800 Gleiskilometer und 5400 Signaleinrichtungen (DB Netz AG & Land Baden-Württemberg, 2011). Mehrere neue Bahnhöfe und 57 Kilometer Neubaustrecke sind geplant, dabei allein 30 Kilometer unterirdisch in teils schwierigem Gelände. Die Prognosen in Bezug auf Kosten, Leistungsfähigkeit und Umweltauswirkungen sind mit zahlreichen Unsicherheiten behaftet. Die Aussagen und Argumente beider Seiten widersprachen sich häufig. So war es schwierig, eindeutige und unabhängige Informationen zu bekommen. Hat sich durch die detaillierte Erörterung der fachlichen Aspekte in der Schlichtung und der Medienberichterstattung die Zufriedenheit mit den verfügbaren Informationen geändert? Die Befragungsergebnisse zeigen, dass sowohl Befürworter als auch Kritiker des Projektes nach der Schlichtung in deutlich höherem Maß mit den verfügbaren Informationen zufrieden sind. Die durchschnittliche Zufriedenheit steigerte sich substantiell. Dieser Anstieg wurde allerdings wahrscheinlich nicht durch das Lernen von Argumenten der jeweiligen Gegenseite verursacht. Vielmehr zeigt sich, dass die Anhänger beider Lager vor allem mit ihrer Voreinstellung kongruente Argumente gelernt haben. Dieser Zusammenhang zeigt sich bei den Kritikern des Projekts deutlicher als bei seinen Befürwortern. Auch wenn die Schlichtung den Bürgern nach eigener Einschätzung keine neuen Argumente der Gegenseite vermitteln konnte, so hat sie immerhin dabei geholfen, die konträre Sichtweise etwas besser zu verstehen. Die Aussage, dass auch die Gegenseite Argumente hat, die man „nachvollziehen kann“, erreichte etwas bessere Zustimmungswerte.

Tab. 1.: Wirkungen der Schlichtung auf die Stuttgarter Bevölkerung

Abhängige Variable	**Gruppe**	**Veränderung (ΔM)**	**F-Test**
Wissen			
Zufriedenheit mit verfügbaren Informationen	Gegner	+1,3	Schlichtung:p < .001
	Befürworter	+1,4	Lager: n.s.
	Gesamt	+1,3	Interaktion: n.s.
Lernen von Argumenten beider Seiten[A]	Gegner	−2,2	Richtung[A]:p < .001
	Befürworter	−0,8	Lager: n.s.
	Gesamt	−1,6	Interaktion: p < .001
Nachvollziehen der Argumente der Gegenseite	Gegner	+0,3	Schlichtung:p = .008
	Befürworter	+0,3	Lager: n.s.
	Gesamt	+0,3	Interaktion: n.s.
Meinung			
Extremität der Gesamtbewertung von Stuttgart 21	Gegner	−0,5	Schlichtung:p < .001
	Befürworter	−0,4	Lager: n.s.
	Gesamt	−0,5	Interaktion: n.s.
Bewertung der Argumente der Gegenseite	Gegner	+0,1	Schlichtung:p = .004
	Befürworter	+0,2	Lager: p < .001
	Gesamt	+0,1	Interaktion: n.s.
Beziehung			
Bewertung der Rolle der Gegenseite im Allgemeinen	Gegner	−0,1	Schlichtung:n.s.
	Befürworter	+0,3	Lager: p = .002
	Gesamt	+0,1	Interaktion: p = .03
Bewertung des Kommunikationsverhaltens der Gegenseite	Gegner	+0,3	Schlichtung:p = .003
	Befürworter	+0,1	Lager: n.s.
	Gesamt	+0,2	Interaktion: n.s.

Anmerkungen

[A] Vergleich zwischen Lernen von Argumenten für und gegen Stuttgart 21

Alle Veränderungen beziehen sich auf eine 7er-Skala

Alle Tests sind Varianzanalysen mit Messwiederholung; Innersubjektfaktor (Messung vor und nach der Schlichtung), Zwischensubjektfaktor (Lagerzugehörigkeit vor der Schlichtung, Gegner und Befürworter von Stuttgart 21) und Interaktionsterm der beiden Faktoren

Meinungseffekte

So unvereinbar die beiden Konzepte S21 und K21 nebeneinander standen, so polarisiert waren auch die Meinungen der Anhänger und Kritiker von Stuttgart 21 in der Bürgerschaft. Vor der Schlichtung standen die Kritiker dem Projekt extrem ablehnend gegenüber, während es die Befürworter äußert unkritisch betrachteten und dementsprechend einer ablehnenden Haltung nur wenig Verständnis entgegen brachten. Die Schlichtung führte dazu, dass die Extremität der Bewertung etwas nachließ. Die durchschnittliche Bewertung des Projekts durch beide Lager näherte sich um etwa einen halben Skalenpunkt der neutralen Skalenmitte an. Neben der Bewertung des Gesamtprojekts haben wir auch untersucht, wie Befürworter und Kritiker eine Reihe von Sachargumenten der jeweiligen Gegenseite einschätzen. Auf dieser Sachebene können allerdings keine substantiellen Veränderungen festgestellt werden. Der Index, der die Zustimmung zu allen Sachargumenten der jeweiligen Gegenseite zusammenfasst, ändert sich nur in sehr geringem Maße. Während die Meinung zu Stuttgart 21 als Ganzes nach der Schlichtung also etwas moderater ausfällt, verändert sich die sachliche Bewertung einzelner Projektaspekte kaum.

Tab. 2: Wirkung der Schlichtung auf die Bewertung der Rolle von Repräsentanten der Projekt-Befürworter in den Diskussionen um Stuttgart 21 durch die befragten Projekt-Kritiker

	Vor Schlichtung *M* (*SD*)	Nach Schlichtung *M* (*SD*)	Δ*M*	*p*	*N*
Repräsentanten von Stuttgart 21					
Stefan Mappus	−2,52 (0,96)	−2,12 (1,37)	+0,35	.000	188
Wolfgang Schuster	−2,42 (0,98)	−2,21 (1,20)	+0,21	.013	178
Tanja Gönner	−1,94 (1,37)	−1,81 (1,54)	+0,13	.178	155
Rüdiger Grube	−2,44 (1,09)	−2,03 (1,40)	+0,41	.000	166
Regierungsparteien					
CDU	−2,46 (0,99)	−2,05 (1,43)	+0,41	.000	185
FDP	−2,44 (1,07)	−2,08 (1,42)	+0,36	.001	155

Frage: Wie bewerten Sie die Rolle der folgenden Akteure (Parteien) in den Diskussionen um „Stuttgart 21"? Skala von −3 sehr negativ bis +3 sehr positiv
Alle Tests sind T-Tests zum Vergleich der Mittelwerte vor und nach der Schlichtung

Beziehungseffekte

Der Konflikt um Stuttgart 21 war besonders direkt vor Beginn der Schlichtung durch eine extrem scharfe Rhetorik gezeichnet. Die Projektträger wurden von Demonstranten als „Lügenpack" beschimpft, der damalige Ministerpräsident Mappus sprach von „Berufsdemonstranten" und davon, den „Fehdehandschuh" aufzunehmen (Müller, 2010). Ein erklärtes Ziel der Schlichtung war es, aus einer emotionalen Auseinandersetzung zwischen zwei sich gegenüberstehenden Lagern wieder eine Diskussion um die Sache zu machen. Gelänge dies, so sollte sich das auch in weniger extremen Ablehnungen der Gegenseite widerspiegeln. Wir betrachten die Beziehungseffekte auf drei Ebenen: die Bewertung der jeweiligen Gegenseite im Allgemeinen, die Bewertung ausgewählter prominenter Repräsentanten der Gegenseite sowie die Bewertung des kommunikativen Verhaltens der Gegenseite. Während die Befürworter das Lager der Kritiker im Allgemeinen nach der Schlichtung etwas positiver bewerteten, blieb die Bewertung der Befürworter durch die Kritiker auf unverändert gleich negativem Niveau. Allerdings verbessert sich die Bewertung von drei der vier erfassten prominenten Projekt-

Repräsentanten (Ministerpräsident Mappus, Stuttgarts Oberbürgermeister Schuster, Vorstandsvorsitzender der Deutschen Bahn Grube) sowie der hinter dem Projekt stehenden Regierungsparteien CDU und FDP (vgl. Tabelle 2) durch die befragten Stuttgart-21-Kritiker. Die Rolle dieser Akteure im Streit um Stuttgart 21 wurde vor der Schlichtung extrem schlecht bewertet. Zwei Monate und acht Schlichtungsgespräche später wird ihr Verhalten zwar noch immer sehr negativ gesehen, die Einschätzungen sind jedoch weniger extrem. Bei der Bewertung der Repräsentanten der Projektkritiker durch die befragten Befürworter konnten dagegen nur wenige bedeutsame Veränderungen gefunden werden. Schließlich finden wir eine geringe, statistisch signifikante Verbesserung der Wahrnehmung des kommunikativen Verhaltens des jeweils anderen Lagers: Der Gegenseite werden eine etwas größere Dialogbereitschaft und eine etwas ausgewogenere Argumentation zugesprochen. Wieder bleiben die absoluten Werte klar im negativen Bereich, eine leichte Verbesserung ist jedoch festzustellen.[6]

Zwischenfazit

Die Befragung der lokalen Bevölkerung zeigt, dass sich die extreme Polarisierung der beiden Seiten etwas abgeschwächt hat. Das kann man dahingehend deuten, dass der Konflikt durch die Schlichtung tatsächlich ein Stück weit versachlicht wurde. Trotzdem bleiben die Werte auf einem relativ hohen Niveau: Die Kritiker von Stuttgart 21 lehnen das Projekt stark ab und bewerten auch das Verhalten der Befürworter negativ – wenn nun auch etwas milder. Ähnliches gilt für die Befürworter. Eine deutliche Verbesserung zeigt sich bei der Zufriedenheit mit den verfügbaren Informationen. Damit geht jedoch gleichsam die Feststellung einher, dass vor allem Argumente gelernt wurden, die die bereits bestehende Meinung stützen. Dieser Effekt deckt sich mit Erkenntnissen aus der Medienwirkungsforschung zur selektiven Wahrnehmung und Dissonanzvermeidung (Iyengar, Krosnick, Hahn & Walker, 2008). Eine starke Voreinstellung erhöht demnach die Wahrscheinlichkeit, dass bei der Medienrezeption vor allem solche Argumente wahrgenommen werden, die bestehende Einstellungen stützen. Die Auseinandersetzung mit inkongruenten Argumenten wird jedoch vermieden, um kognitive Dissonanzen zu reduzieren. Diese Ergebnisse sprechen gegen die Hypothese, dass die S21-Schlichtung als ein deliberativer Moment zu einer Annäherung beider Seiten geführt hat. Sie zeigen gleichfalls die Grenzen medienvermittelter Konfliktlösungsverfahren in polarisierten Öffentlichkeiten auf. Eine aktive Einbindung der Bürger, in der diese in die Lage versetzt werden, selbst zu deliberieren und sich mit den Argumenten der Gegenseite auseinander zu setzen, wäre, nach wissenschaftlichem

6 Zusätzlich zu diesen Auswertungen haben wir auch nach moderierenden Wirkungen der Einstellungsstärke sowie der Zuwendung zu und dem Interesse an den Schlichtungsgesprächen gesucht. Hierbei konnten wir jedoch keine signifikanten Interaktionseffekte feststellen.

Erkenntnisstand, eine erfolgversprechendere Maßnahme, da die selektive Zuwendung zu Argumenten verringert würde (Bachl et al., 2011; Delli Carpini, Cook, & Jacobs, 2004).

5 Fazit: Sonderfall statt Prototyp

Sowohl unsere prozedurale Analyse der Schlichtungsgespräche zwischen Repräsentanten der Befürworter- und Kritikerseite als auch unsere Untersuchung der Wirkungen auf die Befürworter und die Kritiker in der Stuttgarter Bevölkerung zeigen einige Defizite der S21-Schlichtung auf. Die Schlichtungsgespräche konnten ihre Funktionen als ein Prozess des Joint Fact Finding und einer Schlichtung nur in begrenztem Maße erfüllen. Wichtige Erfolgsbedingungen, die in der Literatur zu ADR-Verfahren dargestellt werden – allen voran die gemeinsame Feststellung von Fakten und die ergebnisoffene Feststellung eines Schlichterspruchs –, wurden durch die S21-Schlichtung nicht erfüllt. Dies ist zu einem großen Teil externen Restriktionen wie dem späten Zeitpunkt der Durchführung und dem eng bemessenen Zeitrahmen geschuldet, teilweise aber auch auf Fehlentscheidungen in der Konzeption des Verfahrens zurückzuführen. So wäre eine gemeinsame Beauftragung und Begleitung des abschließenden Stresstests im Sinne eines vorbildlichen Joint Fact Finding wünschenswert gewesen. Auch die Entscheidung, einen formalisierten Schlichtungsspruch mit einer Bewertung zukünftiger Handlungsoptionen zu veröffentlichen, der angesichts der sich wechselseitig ausschließenden Positionen der Streitparteien von mindestens einer Seite abgelehnt werden musste, erscheint zumindest diskussionswürdig. Die Befragung der Schlichtungsteilnehmer stützt diese Einschätzung. Zwar wurde die Verfahrensführung gelobt, jedoch standen am Ende weder ein gemeinsam erarbeitetes Ergebnis noch irgendeine inhaltliche Annäherung. Ein besserer Weg wäre gewesen, dem Verfahren mehr Zeit einzuräumen, themenspezifische Arbeitsgruppen zu bilden, zumindest teilweise die Öffentlichkeit auszuschließen und gemeinsam Gutachten in Auftrag zu geben – speziell für den Stresstest als abschließende Bestandsaufnahme wäre dies zwingend notwendig gewesen. Ein Ergebnis, das auf eine solche Weise zustande gekommen wäre, hätte eine wesentlich größere Bindungskraft entfalten können. Offen bleibt, ob es selbst nach einer solchen Prozedur der Faktenklärung eine Kompromissformel oder gar einen beidseitig anerkannten Schlichterspruch hätte geben können. Denn es ist ein Irrglaube, dass jedes Alternative Streitbeilegungsverfahren seinem Namen vollkommen gerecht wird und einen Konflikt endgültig beilegen kann. Hierbei handelt es sich um den Optimalfall: Bei allen Beteiligten treten Lerneffekte ein und es werden Lösungen ermöglicht, die vorher niemand bedacht hat (Fietkau & Weidner, 1996; Hamacher, 1996; Weidner, 1998; Innes, 2004). Die Chancen auf ein größeres gegenseitiges (Fakten-) Verständnis und eine Verringerung des Konflikts wären mit einem besser gestalteten Verfahren sicher höher gewesen. Dazu hätte es allerdings die Zustimmung beider Seiten und den politischen Willen bedurft.

Synchron zu diesen Beobachtungen fallen auch die Veränderungen, die wir in der öffentlichen Wahrnehmung des Konflikts finden konnten, gemessen an den potenziellen Wirkungen von ADR- und Deliberationsverfahren nur gemäßigt aus. Die Polarisierung zwischen Befürwortern und Kritikern wurde etwas geringer, vor allem konnte das weithin wahrgenommene Informationsdefizit behoben werden. Allerdings finden wir auch deutliche Hinweise darauf, dass die Informationen aus den Schlichtungsgesprächen vor allem selektiv in Kongruenz zu den Voreinstellungen verfolgt und verarbeitet wurden – die Bürgerinnen und Bürger lernten vor allem von ‚ihrer' Seite, eine größere Akzeptanz der Argumente der Gegenseite war nicht festzustellen. Ebenso wie die Teilnehmer der Schlichtung blieben auch die Fronten zwischen Befürwortern und Gegnern auf Zuschauerseite verhärtet.

Wir möchten jedoch nicht mit einem Verriss der S21-Schlichtung enden – dies würde den Akteuren, die sich für diese Maßnahme eingesetzt und an ihr mitgewirkt haben, nicht gerecht. Daher plädieren wir dafür, die S21-Schlichtung vor allem im spezifischen Kontext ihrer Entstehung zu bewerten. Gemessen an den eigenen Ansprüchen war die Schlichtung nicht unbedingt erfolglos: Es wurde die bis zu diesem Zeitpunkt schmerzlich vermisste detaillierte Erörterung der fachlichen Aspekte von Stuttgart 21 in der Öffentlichkeit vorgenommen. Nach der Eskalation des Konfliktes auf der Straße wurde ein Forum geschaffen, in dem sich die Debatte auf die strittigen Inhalte des Projektes zentrierte. Die Polarisierung in der Bürgerschaft konnte nicht beseitigt, wohl aber vermindert werden. In den Fokus rückte statt der Konfrontation von „Lügenpack" und „Berufsdemonstranten" wieder der – immer noch erbittert ausgefochtene – Streit um das Infrastrukturprojekt. In Anbetracht ihrer faktischen Ergebnislosigkeit war die S21-Schlichtung jedoch nicht die Lösung selbst, sondern nur das Symbol einer Lösung. Ein Symbol mit friedensstiftender Wirkung, das mutmaßlich dazu beigetragen hat, die Öffentlichkeit zu beruhigen, da nun ein als legitim wahrgenommenes Verfahren gefunden wurde. Ob das als ein Erfolg gewertet werden kann, hängt vom Standpunkt des Betrachters ab. Gemessen an den Standards Alternativer Streitbeilegungsverfahren – und an diesen muss man die S21-Schlichtung messen, wenn sie als Prototyp für die Zukunft gehandelt wird – ist sie gescheitert. Sie hat keinen Weg aus dem Konflikt finden können und vermochte es nicht, beide Seiten aneinander anzunähern. Dieses Scheitern war systemisch veranlagt. Es war einerseits situationsbedingten Hindernissen wie dem späten Zeitpunkt der Durchführung und der Politisierung des Konflikts geschuldet. Andererseits offenbarten sich aber auch zahlreiche Konstruktionsfehler, wie die fehlende Verfahrensklarheit, die mangelnde Ergebnisoffenheit und die unzureichende Vorgehensweise bei der Faktenklärung. Diese Analyse lässt sich am besten nachvollziehen, wenn wir uns in Erinnerung rufen, wer die dominierende Persönlichkeit der S21-Schlichtung war: Heiner Geißler ist kein ausgebildeter Mediator, er ist ein Vollblutpolitiker. Aus dieser Perspektive müssen wir auch die S21-Schlichtung einordnen: Sie war ein Sonderfall: eine politische Prozedur, die dazu dienen sollte, in einen festgefahrenen politischen Konflikt wieder Bewegung zu bringen. Als solche ist sie geglückt, da sie zu einer Versachlichung der Debatte und so zu einer „Beruhigung der Leute" tatsächlich beigetragen hat. Inhaltlich erreichen konnte sie nichts – die später durchgeführte Volksabstimmung war so gesehen unvermeidbar. Eine weitere Verbreitung ist dem Modell der S21-Schlichtung nicht zu wünschen, dem vermehrten Einsatz von frühzeitigen und professionell durchgeführten Bürgerbeteiligungs- und Streitbeilegungsverfahren dagegen schon.

Literatur

Aktionsbündnis gegen Stuttgart 21. (2010, 16. Dezember). *Stresstest: Intransparent wie eh und je*. Verfügbar unter http://www.kopfbahnhof-21.de/index.php?id=110&tx_ttnews[pointer]=9&tx_ttnews[tt_news]=561&tx_ttnews[backPid]=108&cHash=a63dbc34e7.

Aktionsbündnis gegen Stuttgart 21. (2011, 15. Juni). *Aktionsbündnis gegen Stuttgart 21 fordert weiteren Bau- und Vergabestopp bis Mitte September*. Verfügbar unter http://www.kopfbahnhof-21.de/index.php?id=110&tx_ttnews[pS]=1306265758&tx_ttnews[tt_news]=617&tx_ttnews[backPid]=108&cHash=700bc8776c.

Bachl, M., Spieker, A., Kercher, J. & Brettschneider, F. (2011, September). *A Song for the Deaf? The Effects of Public Arbitration in a Polarized Atmosphere*. Vortrag auf der 64. Jahrestagung der World Association for Public Opinion Research (WAPOR), 21.-23. 9. 2011, Amsterdam. Verfügbar unter http://wapor.unl.edu/wp-content/uploads/2011/09/Bachl_Spieker_Kercher_Bretschneider.pdf

Bingham, G. (1986). *Resolving environmental disputes: a decade of experience*. Washington: Conservation Foundation.

Breidenbach, S. (1995). *Mediation. Struktur, Chancen und Risiken von Vermittlung im Konflikt*. Köln: Schmidt.

Brettschneider, F. (2011). Kommunikation und Meinungsbildung bei Großprojekten. *APuZ*, *61*(44-45), 40–47.

Buckle, L. G., & Thomas-Buckle, S. R. (1986). Placing environmental mediation in context: Lessons from "failed" mediations. *Environmental Impact Assessment Review*, *6*(1), 55–70. doi: doi:10.1016/0195-9255(86)90040-5

DB Netz AG & Land Baden-Württemberg. (2011). *Audit zur Betriebsqualität Stuttgart 21*. Schlussbericht. Verfügbar unter http://www.deutschebahn.com/site/shared/de/dateianhaenge/presse/stuttgart21__stresstest.pdf.

Delli Carpini, M. X., Cook, F. L., & Jacobs, L. R. (2004). Public Deliberation, Discursive Partizipation and Citizen Engagement: A Review of the Empirical Literature. *Annual Review of Political Science*, *7*, 315–344. doi:10.1146/annurev.polisci.7.121003.091630

Eggert, R., & Meister, H.-P. (2007). Transparente Public Affairs - Die Politische Mediation. In J. Rieksmeier (Hrsg.), *Praxisbuch: Politische Interessensvermittlung* (S. 95–105). Wiesbaden: VS.

Ehrmann, J. R., & Stinson, B. L. (1999). Joint Fact-Finding and the Use of Technical Experts. In L. Susskind, S. McKearnan, & J. Thomas-Larmer (Hrsg.), *The consensus building handbook. A comprehensive guide to reaching agreement* (S. 375–400). Thousand Oaks: Sage.

Eisele, J. (2011). Öffentliche Streitbeilegungsverfahren – Zwischen Mediation, Schlichtung, Moderation und Schaulaufen der Akteure. *Zeitschrift für Rechtspolitik*, *44*(4), 113–116.

Fietkau, H.-J., & Weidner, H. (1998). *Umweltverhandeln. Konzepte, Praxis und Analysen alternativer Konfliktregelungsverfahren.* Berlin: Edition Sigma.

Fisher, R., Ury, W., & Patton, B. (2011). *Getting to yes: negotiating agreement without giving in* (3., überarb. Aufl.). London: Penguin.

Fishkin, J. S. (1999). Toward a deliberative democracy: experimenting with an ideal. In S. L. Elkin & K. E. Soltan (Hrsg.), *Citizen competence and democratic institutions* (S. 279–290). University Park: Pennsylvania State University Press.

Fishkin, J. S., & Luskin, R. C. (1999). Bringing deliberation to the democratic dialogue. In M. E. McCombs & A. Reynolds (Hrsg.), *The poll with a human face the National Issues Convention experiment in political communication* (S. 3–38). Mahwah: Lawrence Erlbaum.

Protokoll 1: Schlichtungsverfahren zu Stuttgart 21: Strategische Bedeutung und verkehrliche Leistungsfähigkeit des Bahnknotens Stuttgart 21. Stenographisches Protokoll. (2010, 22. Oktober). Verfügbar unter http://www.schlichtung-s21.de/fileadmin/schlichtungs21/Redaktion/pdf/ 101022/22_10_2010_Wortprotokoll_Schlichtungsgespraech_S21.pdf.

Protokoll 9: Schlichtungsverfahren zu Stuttgart 21: Abschlussplädoyers der Projektbefürworter und der Projektkritiker, Empfehlungen des Schlichters Dr. Heiner Geißler. Stenographisches Protokoll. (2010, 30. November). Verfügbar unter http://www.schlichtung-s21.de/fileadmin/schlichtungs21/Redaktion/pdf/101130/2010-11-30%20Wortprotokoll.pdf.

Protokoll 10: Schlichtungsverfahren zu Stuttgart 21: Audit zur Betriebsqualitätsüberprüfung Stuttgart 21: Präsentation des Abschlussberichts von SMA und Partner AG. Stenographisches Protokoll. (2011, 29. Juli). Verfügbar unter http://www.schlichtung-s21.de/fileadmin/ schlichtungs21/ Redaktion/pdf/110729/Protokoll29072011.pdf.

Gastil, J. (2000). *By popular demand. Rrevitalizing representative democracy through deliberative elections.* Berkeley: University of California Press.

Geis, A. (2005). *Regieren mit Mediation: Das Beteiligungsverfahren zur zukünftigen Entwicklung des Frankfurter Flughafens.* Wiesbaden: VS.

Geißler, H. (2010, 30. November). *Schlichtung Stuttgart 21 PLUS.* Verfügbar unter http:// www.stuttgart.de/img/mdb/item/415843/60751.pdf.

Geißler, H., & SMA und Partner AG. (2011, 29. Juli). *Frieden in Stuttgart: Eine Kompromiss-Lösung zur Befriedung der Auseinandersetzung um Stuttgart 21.* Verfügbar unter http:// www.schlichtung-s21.de/fileadmin/schlichtungs21/Redaktion/pdf/110729/frieden_in_stuttgart.pdf.

Gutmann, A., & Thompson, D. F. (1996). *Democracy and disagreement.* Cambridge: Harvard University Press.

Hamacher, W. (1996). *Konfliktmanagement im Umweltbereich: Instrument der Umweltpolitik in Entwicklungsländern.* Eschborn: Deutsche Gesellschaft für Technische Zusammenarbeit.

Holzinger, K. (1996). Grenzen der Kooperation in alternativen Konfliktlösungsverfahren: Exogene Restriktionen, Verhandlungsleitlinien und Outside Options. In W. v. d. Daele, & F. Neidhardt (Hrsg.), *Kommunikation und Entscheidung* (S. 232–274). Berlin: edition sigma.

Holzinger, K. & Weidner, H. (1997). *Das Neusser Mediationsverfahren im politischen Umfeld. Befragungsergebnisse und -methodik* (Schriften zu Mediationsverfahren im Umweltschutz Nr. 17. (= WZB Discussion Paper FS II 97 - 303)). Berlin: WZB.

Innes, J. E. (2004). Consensus Building: Clarifications for the Critics. *Planning Theory, 3*(1), 5-20. doi: 10.1177/1473095204042315

Iyengar, S., Hahn, K. S., Krosnick, J. A., & Walker, J. (2008). Selective Exposure to Campaign Communication: The Role of Anticipated Agreement and Issue Public Membership. *The Journal of Politics*, *70*(01), 186–200. doi:10.1017/S0022381607080139

Kamann. (2010, 5. Oktober). Schlichter und Anheizer - Grüne im Zwiespalt. *Berliner Morgenpost* [Online]. Verfügbar unter http://www.morgenpost.de/printarchiv/politik/article1414785/ Schlichter-und-Anheizer-Gruene-im-Zwiespalt.html.

McCombs, M. E., & Reynolds, A. (Hrsg.). (1999). *The poll with a human face the National Issues Convention experiment in political communication*. Mahwah: Lawrence Erlbaum.

Menkel-Meadow, C. (2006). Deliberative Democracy and Conflict Resolution: Two theories and practices of participation in the polity. *Dispute Resolution Magazine*, *12*(2), 18–22.

Müller, A. (2010, 15. Oktober). Umstrittener Polizeieinsatz: Hilferufe aus dem Schlossgarten verhallen. *Stuttgarter Zeitung* [Online]. Verfügbar unter http://www.stuttgarter-zeitung.de/ inhalt.umstrittener-polizeieinsatz-hilferufe-aus-dem-schlossgarten-verhallen.b450e947-c2b6-47c4-984b-060ed5e7f9c5.html.

Pfingsten, K. & Fietkau. H.-J. (1995). *Das Neusser Mediationsverfahren aus Sicht der Beteiligten. Ergebnisdarstellung der schriftlichen Befragung* (Schriften zu Mediationsverfahren im Umweltschutz Nr. 9. (= WZB Discussion Paper FS II 95 - 302)). Berlin: WZB

PHOENIX (Hrsg). (2010, 1. Dezember). *Rekordquote für Abschlussrunde zu Stuttgart 21 / In der Spitze mehr als fünf Prozent Marktanteil.* Verfügbar unter http://www.presseportal.de/ pm/6511/ 1727553/phoenix-rekordquote-fuer-abschlussrunde-zu-stuttgart-21-in-der-spitze-mehr-als-fuenf-prozent.

Raupach, H. (1964). *Die Schlichtung von kollektiven Arbeitsstreitigkeiten und ihre Probleme.* Berlin: Duncker & Humblot.

Rogers, N. H., & McEwen, C. A. (1994). *Mediation: Law, policy, and practice*. Rochester & San Francisco: Bancroft-Whitney.

Rucht, D. (2010, 30. November). *Legitimation durch Verfahren oder Neutralisierung von Kritik?* Verfügbar unter http://www.kopfbahnhof-21.de/index.php?id=691.

Scharpf, F. W. (1991). *Die Handlungsfähigkeit des Staates am Ende des Zwanzigsten Jahrhunderts*. Köln: Max-Planck-Institut für Gesellschaftsforschung.

Schlichtung S21 (2011, 29. November). Verfügbar unter http://www.schlichtung-s21.de.

Stasavage, D. (2007). Polarization and Publicity: Rethinking the Benefits of Deliberative Democracy. *Journal of Politics*, *69*(1), 59–72. doi:10.1111/j.1468-2508.2007.00494.x

Susskind, L., McKearnan, S., & Thomas-Larmer, J. (Hrsg.). (1999). *The consensus building handbook: A comprehensive guide to reaching agreement*. Thousand Oaks: Sage.

SWR (Hrsg.). (2010, 1. Dezember). *Millionen sahen Schlichtungsgespräche im SWR Fernsehen: Abschluss der Gespräche am 30. November 2010 erfolgreichster Tag.* Verfügbar unter http://www.swr.de/unternehmen/presse/-/id=4224/nid=4224/did=7887060/1mu6xbd /index.html.

Vonnahme, P., & Tremml, B. (2010, 20. Dezember). Demokratie 21. *Telepolis* [Online]. Verfügbar unter http://www.heise.de/tp/artikel/33/33865/1.html.

Waßmuth, C., & van Larcher, D. (2010, 30. November). *Der schale Geschmack nach der Party*. Verfügbar unter http://www.attac.de/aktuell/stuttgart21/schlichtungs-debatte/der-schale-geschmack-nach-der-party/?L=2.

Weidner, H. (1996). Freiwillige Kooperationen und alternative Konfliktregelungsverfahren in der Umweltpolitik. In W. v. d. Daele, & F. Neidhardt (Hrsg.), *Kommunikation und Entscheidung* (S. 195–231). Berlin: edition sigma.

Wörner, J.-D. (Hrsg.) (2010). *Abschlussdokumentation RDF 2000-2008*. Verfügbar unter http://www.forum-flughafen-region.de/fileadmin/files/Archiv/Archiv_RDF-Dokumentation/RDF_Abschlussbericht_2010.pdf.

Zerhusen, J. (2005). *Alternative Streitbeilegung im Bauwesen: Streitvermeidung, Schlichtung, Mediation, Schiedsverfahren*. Hamburg: Carl Heymanns.

Zilleßen, H. (1998). Mediation: Kooperatives Konfliktmanagement in der Umweltpolitik. Opladen: Westdeutscher.

IV

What's next?

Large-Scale Projects and Democratic Legitimacy: Problems, Challenges and Some Solutions

Stefan Schaible

Many lessons are to be learned from the assessment of large-scale infrastructure projects. Based on practical experiences in the field, the present report sketches out challenges and opportunities which arise in the course of planning and implementing large-scale projects. It will be argued that there is a clear need for a transparent and open discourse that goes far beyond formal procedures and discussions about advantages and disadvantages of a project. In doing so, reasonable and transparent debates may promote solutions for the good of both, political and corporate stakeholders as well as society as a whole.

1 Introduction

There are lessons to be learned from the assessment of large-scale infrastructure projects. While most articles compiled in this book look at the challenges at hand from an academic point of view, the present paper has a different approach. It is based on practical experiences rather than scientific work in the field. One might of course wonder what a management consultant's perspective might add to a debate on democratic legitimacy. Their mandate sure does not carry a very high degree of formal democratic legitimacy which would make the profession a valuable source for the examination of large-scale projects. As a matter of fact, a consultant's mandate is temporary – borrowed if you wish. However the consultant's perspective provides evidence-based observations of the interplay of various stakeholders. Consultants work at the intersection of the public and private sector and, thus, investigate planning and permitting processes and aim at improving implementation procedures.

Against this background and with a long experience of jointly working on highly complex projects with various key players from different sectors and professions, this paper might give an impression of the challenges and opportunities which arise in the course of planning and implementing large-scale projects.

2 The problems of large-scale projects: Niklas Luhmann comes to his limits

In Germany, infrastructure projects and large-scale reform projects usually are subject to vast public criticism. We observe a defensive reaction on the part of the public towards practically any plans involving major change or transformation, and this skepticism is articulated through a variety of channels. Nevertheless, it would be wrong to call Germany a true participatory democracy: a lack of public acceptance does not necessarily cause a project to stop. Public participation other than protest is often impossible, formal ways of civic involvement in the planning and implementation processes of large scale projects are limited. On the federal level there are only very few provisions for participation and even opportunities to participate on the regional levels come with major barriers.

This notwithstanding, there are many reasons for the public's general skepticism and their defensive reaction. On the societal level, new avenues for activism in today's network democracy appeared for a public that is frustrated by the lack of transparency in the decision-making process. At the same time, communication on the part of decision makers is often poor. And the significant financial impact, complexity and lack of clarity of such projects make people feel very hesitant towards this kind of development. On the individual level, we see an unwillingness to accept reforms which is coupled with a significant increase of personal values like independence and self-determination in the last decades as opposed to the former notion of society as a community where a "common sense" is key for development. Furthermore, demographic change (an aging society is less interested in reform) and general prosperity result in an over-attachment to the status quo. Looking at the global dimension, the global crisis of confidence caused by the ongoing financial and monetary chaos is another very important, but often neglected, factor. This upheaval challenges what we have come to accept as a given, such as the superiority of the capitalist system.

3 A hungry, young and confident society?

There are many examples of German infrastructure projects facing major public opposition, among others the railway project Stuttgart 21, the question of carbon capture storage, large-scale pipeline projects, the crossing of the Fehmarnbelt, the new airport in Berlin, the investment in pumped-storage electricity, wind farms, and even bypasses in rural areas. A recent study by the Allensbach Institute found that only one-third of Germans think infrastructure projects, such as extending transportation and power networks, are important. 75% of the German population sympathize with public demonstrations against large-scale projects and 54% even react negatively to only the term "large-scale construction project" (cf. IfD-Allensbach, 2011).

One might conclude that Germany has lost its willingness for reform. This trend, if true, does not necessarily manifest itself in other countries: in Switzerland, the construction of the Gotthard basis tunnel was celebrated as a great feat of engineering. In the USA and China, skyscrapers are showcases of groundbreaking architecture. Large scale projects may even cross national borders as shown by the recent completion of the Channel Tunnel connecting France and the United Kingdom. In Germany, however, it seems that anything new or unfamiliar – the Transrapid high-speed monorail project, for instance – is doomed to fail. Even projects such as the joint Winter Olympic bid by the cities of Munich and Garmisch-Partenkirchen are able to mobilize almost half the population – to oppose it.

It seems like Germany's planning and decision-making culture has reached a dead-end – very much like the old Stuttgart railway terminus. This holds not only true for the initial step, obtaining the permit for a project, but also for the entire construction process that follows. The planning and decision-making processes of large-scale projects have been crippled by lengthy procedures. It has become clear that securing "legitimacy via the process", as coined by Niklas Luhmann (cf. 1995), does not suffice in a democratic state any more.

4 The challenges of large-scale projects: Michel Foucault has become reality

The challenge is not an easy one, but burying one's heads in the sand or even resigning because of public criticism is not the way forward. The shift in the public's stance touches the fundaments of society, and reinventing the attitude in Germany towards large-scale projects seems to be called for. Both politicians as well as private companies must learn how to argue, to convince, to fight if they want to realize such projects. It seems that the paradigm shift in the public's attitude has occurred largely unnoticed or has been observed too late.

Political commentator Franz Walter (2011) recently wrote that the typical member of a citizens' protest group is a retired engineer who is not fundamentally opposed to progress. He speaks from a high level of technical expertise and uses his "expert knowledge" to prevent power transmission projects that threaten his environment. Walter concludes that the kind of protest those citizens engage in are a social phenomenon that is here to stay. The protesters have plenty of time on their hands to represent their own clear interests. This is what makes the movement so powerful. Political commentators go even further and describe the group of people as "Wutbürger" or enraged citizens (Kurbjuweit 2010).

And indeed, the protesters in Germany differ fundamentally from the young people in Spain protesting against unemployment and their lack or prospects, or British youth protesting against discrimination and desolation in run-down industrial districts, or Greeks who feel that their country is being undermined by corruption, bureaucracy and waste. So, one might think of the German movement as quite sustainable and rooted within society compared to the protests in other European countries. This, again, backs the assumption that German society has to discuss the very essence of the protest and the skepticism of its citizens in order to overcome the innovation deadlock described above.

In his essay "the blackmail of enlightenment", Foucault (1991) describes that the individual has the right to refuse a legitimacy that has been installed by pure procedures. The right of the individual to say No and to refuse common sense is a part of society – and with the rise of effective communication via text messaging and Internet in advanced democracies – will become even more important. Foucault, with his defense of the individual, was more successful than many have hoped to be and identified in doing so what might be the most important challenge for future large-scale projects.

5 Some solutions: a pledge for an open discourse

Communicating solid convictions and clear facts is what might help to overcome current obstacles in the long run, pointing out the need to initiate a real public discourse about large-scale projects. This is relevant for the political side as well as for the (mostly private) companies that want to build large infrastructure projects. On the political side it is no coincidence that people today widely respect individuals who have strong opinions and speak their mind such as former Chancellor Helmut Schmidt and former President Roman Herzog. The unexcited, rather severe type of politician with lucid arguments is back in fashion, take for example Federal Ministers Thomas de Maizière and Wolfgang Schäuble, or opposition leaders Peer Steinbrück and Frank-Walter Steinmeier. All of them currently enjoy great popularity.

Politicians need to rediscover their ability to fight, to be passionate, and to argue. Powerful personalities are necessary, but they cannot solve the rather structural "crisis of legitimacy" in decision-making processes on their own. Procedures which became increasingly formal need to be replaced by forms of participation that really allow for an open discourse. This discourse has to be about all the different aspect of the large-scale project: its set up, the planning, the technical design. This has a number of consequences:

- Firstly, the democratic system in Germany has to be expanded. This means allowing for referendums on a national level, modifying existing regulations at federal level, and creating new tools at municipal level. While this might not be a solution for everything, it is an essential first step to win back public trust in politics. The participation initiative of the state of Rhineland-Palatine provides interesting insights (Zukunftsinitiative Rheinland-Pfalz, 2012).
- Secondly, mediation and arbitration processes will become the rule rather than the exception for large-scale projects. Dialogue must begin in the planning stage, before the decision processes start as is already done in Scandinavia. Initially this

may seem even more complex and time-consuming but in the long run it will lead to simplicity, speed and greater public acceptance.

- Thirdly, the political world must become better at strategic, holistic planning. Hasty, short-term political action for action's sake and random politicizing only fosters resentment and frustration. This approach should not be confused with the anemic bureaucracy practiced by political functionaries. Personalities and political communication skills are an essential part of strategy and planning. With Aristotle we could say, the "zoon politikon" or "political animal" is in great demand (cf. Mulgan 1974).
- Fourthly, authorities and infrastructure companies must increasingly make use of all available communication channels, like the new media, as participation in today's network democracy uses all these different channels.
- Fifthly and lastly, the infrastructure companies or maybe even the private sector has to reposition itself drastically in the field of large-scale projects. It has to become standard in future to anticipate resistance and critical points from the beginning of a project and to reflect on them already in the planning and design phase. Therefore, it is necessary to break up the classical logic of a project, which starts with the technical planning and then looks at financing. These disciplines should be considered only at a later stage and environmental, legal as well as political and communicative issues have to be considered early on in the process, for example in the feasibility assessment of a project in direct interaction and discourse with relevant stakeholders. This is commonly referred to as an integrated project approach and it has proven to be very successful.

This however also requires a change in the mindset of infrastructure companies. They cannot delegate the process to authorities and politics or define resistance against a project as purely irrational. They have to take the opposition seriously and have to convince by strong arguments and facts. This has not always happened in the past.

In conclusion, there is a clear need for a transparent and open discourse that goes far beyond formal procedures and discussions about advantages and disadvantages of a project, a discourse close to what Habermas (1999) described. Experiences with large-scale projects have shown the influential presence of the critical individual. If one puts forward valid and transparent arguments, it is possible to reflect on these in the project set up, separating them from the ones that are based on self-interest only. And while pure self-interest is unlikely to win in the end, this is not self-evident. Skeptical individuals require valid arguments in order to change their minds. However, in its very essence, arguing reasonably and transparently may promote solutions for the good of both, political and corporate stakeholders as well as society as a whole.

Foucault, Michel (1991). What is Enlightenment?, in: Rabinow, Paul (Hrsg). *The Foucault Reader*, London: Penguin.

Habermas, Jürgen 1999 [1992]. Between facts and norms: contributions to a discourse theory of law and democracy. Cambridge, MA: MIT Press

IfD-Allensbach (2011). IfD-Umfrage 10076. Allensbacher Archiv.

Kurbjuweit, D. (2011). Der Wutbürger. Der Spiegel (41), 26-27.

Luhmann, Niklas (1995) [1984]. *Social Systems*, Stanford: Stanford University Press.

Mulgan, Richard G. (1974). Aristotle's Doctrine That Man Is a Political Animal, in: *Hermes* 102. Bd., H. 3, S. 438-445

Walter, Franz (2011). Alt, stur egoistisch. Spiegel Online. Retrieved at: http://www.spiegel.de/politik/deutschland/studie-ueber-wutbuerger-alt-stur-egoistisch-a-784664-2.html (13.06.2012).

Zukunftsinitiative Rheinland-Pfalz (2012). Wir tun was. Retrieved at: http://www.wir-tun-was.de (13.06.2012).

Participation in Large-Scale Projects – From Porto Alegre to Stuttgart and Beyond…

Andreas Hoffelder

1 Introduction

In 2011, Stuttgart 21 became one of the political main topics. A wave of protest had overrun Germany. People everywhere came out against large-scale projects. Democracy seemed alive, but oftentimes self-interest and the general welfare collided. Nevertheless, the protests led to a referendum and started an intense debate about participation in political decision making.

The most prominent example of participation is the participatory budgeting in Porto Alegre. It is a regional capital of 1.3 million people, which since 1989 has been governed by the *Partido dos Trabalhadores* (PT or Workers' Party), Brazil's largest left-wing party. Its flagship policy, the Participatory Budget, involves thousands of city residents in decisions about municipal expenditures. In a country where public funds are typically spent through a mixture of corruption, patronage, and obscure technocratism, this was a revolution in political practice. In 2001, Porto Alegre hosted the first World Social Forum. At that time it had become a global beacon for participatory democracy, winning 'best practice' recognition from mainstream international development agencies such as the World Bank, the United Nations Development Program, and UN-Habitat. In Latin America it is practiced in, depending on how one defines it, between 250 and 2,500 municipalities. The smaller figure refers to those cities where the process was implemented as a local government initiative, while the larger number would include all the municipal governments recently required by national laws to consult civil society on budget priorities, as is now prescribed in Bolivia, Nicaragua, and Peru. Hence, political participation is practiced and happening yet.

Coming back to Germany there seems to be protests everywhere and against everything. Whether it's a new train station in Stuttgart, school reforms in Hamburg, a smoking ban in Bavaria, a permanent disposal site for nuclear waste, or a new runway at every possible airport in the nation, it's bound to bring demonstrations. The power of the people is swelling.

The message of the people on the street is the same everywhere: "we are trying to improve our living conditions." They defy governors, mayors, and parliamentarians, challenging their decisions and opposing their projects and laws. The main battle line in the country these days is being drawn between the citizens and the state.

In dealing with the fear of the people, mediations could be a possible solution. For example, while the expansion of the airport in Frankfurt was being prepared, mediation took place. The aim was to keep those people living around the airport informed and updated on what was going to happen. Indeed, it must be noted that the mediation result was 15 years ago and the determined and contracted points are in part no longer contemporary.

A possibility to fasten the whole process and to deal with the powerlessness of the people towards the political decisions their representatives make in their name, is participation. With a referendum, politicians are able to present their pro and contra-arguments towards a project and receive (or don't receive) the legitimation directly from the voters to go ahead with the construction or whatever the referendum is about.

At first glance that seems a salutary development. Democracy is alive, people are taking part. But that won't necessarily make a better society. Many of the protests are against infrastructure and energy projects and this could prevent the modernization of the country. So the question is how to deal with the problem. Is participation, like that mentioned above in the example of Porto Alegre, the answer?

2 Modes of participation in large-scale projects: ten examples

The next pages will now give an overview of the recent large-scale projects worldwide and highlight the different ways of dealing with the problems. Especially in the emerging countries it is very interesting if they are able to find a balance between the modernization of the country and the interests of the people. And of course there are also a lot of large-scale projects all over the world causing similar protest by the population to that of Stuttgart 21.

At the same time, however, the cases presented below show that infrastructure/ transportation is just one out of many issues which are subject to public protest. In Germany, the most current demonstrations are assignable to airports and the noise they cause. Whether it's Frankfurt, Munich, Berlin, Cologne, or Hamburg, there are people demonstrating against the extension of runways, night flight permissions, and air routes. In Frankfurt, the travellers must jam their way through the terminal every Monday across the demonstrating masses. And on April 05, 2012, the demonstrations seemed to show an effect. A judicial decision prohibited night flights at Germany's largest airport hub. Other large-scale transportation projects causing resistance in the population are the crossing of the Fehmarn Belt by a bridge, the extension of the city highway A100 in Berlin, the deepening of the Elbe River in Hamburg, and a train high-speed connection in northern Germany between Hannover, Bremen, and Hamburg. When it comes to energy supply, the situation is especially critical. All the different types of energy plants cause some kind of public protest, ranging from skepticism against power plants exploiting fossil resources, to the fear of nuclear fallout, to the anticipated damage wind energy parks on and offshore can do to the environment.

Moreover, energy infrastructure can also be perceived as a threat to those who live nearby, as shown in the case of the construction of new high voltage power lines which are supposed to connect the shore and the agglomeration areas in the western and southern part of Germany.

2.1 The Belo Monte Dam

In Brazil, the construction of the Belo Monte Dam caused strong criticism by indigenous people and numerous environmental organizations. The dam is a hydroelectric dam complex on the Xingu River in the state of Pará. The planned capacity would be 11,233 megawatts (MW), which would make it the world's third-largest dam in installed capacity, behind the Three Gorges Dam in China and the Brazilian-Paraguayan Itaipu Dam. However, there is opposition among the international community to the project's potential construction regarding its economic viability, generation inefficiency, and impact to the region's people and environment. Belo Monte's 668 square kilometers of reservoir will flood 400 square kilometers of forest, which is in total about 0.01% of the Amazon forest. Furthermore, the loss of vegetation and natural spaces, changes in the quality and path of the water supply and fish migration routes, and the temporary disruption of the water supply in the Xingu riverbed for 7 months are feared most by the project opponents. The hydroelectric energy project is meant to be a solution to Brazil's periodic blackouts and a 'clean development' approach to global climate change. However, the National Amazon Research Institute (INPA) has calculated that the forests flooded by Belo Monte's reservoirs will generate enormous quantities of methane, a greenhouse gas that is 25 times more potent than CO_2 which queries the climate change impact in a huge amount.

The idea to build a dam on the Xingu River is not new. It was first proposed in the 1970s during the time of the military dictatorship in Brazil, but it never went forward and the plans were just put on hold. During the 1990s, energy-problems came back in the focus and plans for Belo Monte were again renewed. Former President Lula da Silva agreed to the Belo Monte Dam project. In April 2010, Norte Energia was formed. Norte Energia is a consortium made up of more than ten mining, engineering, and construction companies that finally won the rights to build the dam. Ibama, the environmental regulatory agency, signed off on the $14 billion project.

More than one million Brazilians signed a petition against the dam in less than a week and in 2010 the American filmmaker James Cameron came to Brazil to take up the cause of fighting against the dam.

Further Reading:
http://www.aljazeera.com/indepth/features/2012/01/201212015366764400.html
http://www.bbc.co.uk/news/world-latin-america-16228680
http://www.internationalrivers.org/campaigns/belo-monte-dam
http://amazonwatch.org/work/belo-monte-dam

2.2 Tipnis National Park

A conflict in Bolivia for a road through the Tipnis National Park forced the President of Bolivia, Evo Morales, in October 2011 to sign off a law known as Ley Corta declaring the Indigenous Territory National Park Isiboro Sécure as "untouchable." The bill came up after an indigenous march led by the Confederation of Indigenous Peoples of Bolivia (CIDOB in Spanish) covered more than 600 kilometers to the seat of government in La Paz demanding to stop a road project attempting to cross through the middle of the national park.

Nevertheless, the Bolivian government has always maintained the road will lead to development for the indigenous communities living in TIPNIS and for the country as a whole. The government maintains that agricultural producers in that area will have an easier access to the markets for their goods. And in early January 2012, the government received surprising support. A pro-road march organized by the newly-gathered Indigenous Council from the South (CONISUR) began its 500-kilometer march from the southern borders of the national park to La Paz, calling for the road to be built. This action was strongly criticized by other indigenous organizations claiming that it was fully backed by the government as a political chess move. CONISUR is an organization that groups together 21 indigenous communities with 12 living in the south of the TIPNIS territory. In the middle of January 2012, Gumercindo Pradel, President of CONISUR, said that the law banning the road was approved without consulting all the communities within the TIPNIS and therefore it should be repealed. Meanwhile, a second march of the project-enemies was organized. But while the agenda of the first march was limited to the proposed highway, the new march is planned as a national mobilization for indigenous, environmental, and human rights. However, the highway project has divided the inhabitants of the TIPNIS and of the Beni and Cochabamba departments, which would be linked by the planned road, and a solution that can be useful for both sides is not yet in sight.

Further Reading:

http://nacla.org/blog/2012/4/27/bolivia-tipnis-protesters-launch-national-march-seek-indigenous-urban-alliance

http://climate-connections.org/tag/tipnis-national-park/

http://www.lab.org.uk/index.php?option=com_content&view=article&id=1094:bolivia-the-tipnis-conflict-key-issues-underpinning-the-conflict-part-3&catid=66:analysis&Itemid=39

http://globalvoicesonline.org/2012/02/17/bolivia-conflict-over-road-through-tipnis-national-park-continues/

2.3 La Rioja Mining

In Argentina, more precisely in the north-western province of La Rioja, thousands of people mobilized to stop an open-cast gold mining project in the Nevados de Famatina, a snowy peak that is the semi-arid area's sole source of drinking water. And they did it with success.

Local residents, supported by environmental groups such as Greenpeace, had been holding a series of protests against the project that made the Canadian mining firm Osiska stop the project. After that, the authorities of Argentina respected the ongoing grassroots protests and started to consider a possible referendum on the whole project. Also the company itself said that it would put its operation in northwestern La Rioja province on hold if it did not get the backing of the local population. A main point of the demonstrating masses was water. It will take about 1 million liters of water per day in that very dry region to extract gold, silver, copper, and other minerals. Another fear of the people living there was the polluting of the environment because of the necessary tons of cyanide needed for the whole process. Governor Beder Herrera mentioned that he has instructed his staff to inform people about the real impact of the mining operations in La Rioja. The local residents shall learn what will be done and what results will be obtained through metal and mineral exploration in the province. But they also will be informed about La Rioja's mineral wealth, the benefits the province will obtain, and how the mining work will be conducted.

Further Reading:

http://www.osisko.com/en/

http://www.bbc.co.uk/news/world-latin-america-16827158

http://www.pcasc.net/2012/01/25/thousands-protest-canadian-mining-project-in-argentina/

http://en.mercopress.com/2012/01/31/argentine-province-suspends-open-pit-gold-mining-project-following-protests

2.4 Citizen Participation in the New Orleans Plan

After New Orleans was devastated by Hurricane Katrina, the city government was unable to organize the evacuation of the city, supplies for the refugees, and the planning of the reconstruction process. It was rather dysfunctional. State agencies, nonprofit resources, and thousands of volunteers came into the city after the flood, but there was almost no coordination in planning the help for the people and operating the clearing operations. Furthermore, the city has always been deeply divided by race and class, and any rebuilding plan would unequally affect the various groups of citizens. To make the whole situation even worse, poor people and African Americans were much more likely to have been forced into exile by the flooding and therefore unable to express their views about their own city's reconstruction. Given that, a transparent and public deliberation was indispensable.

Initiated by the Mayor of New Orleans, the City Council, and the City Planning Commission, and after five months of intensive citizen engagement with expert planning teams – made possible through funding from the Rockefeller Foundation – the Greater New Orleans Foundation, and the Bush-Clinton Katrina Fund, a team of planners submitted the Unified New Orleans Plan (UNOP) to the City Planning Commission. From its inception, UNOP's designers and implementers insisted on wide public participation in the plan to develop a concept to recover and rebuild the City of New Orleans. Current residents and displaced former residents were recruited via recorded phone calls from the mayor and celebrities. They were offered transportation, meals, and childcare to enable them to participate. Neutral briefing materials in English, Spanish, and Vietnamese were provided. Almost two thirds of the participants were African American and they worked at small tables convened together in large public spaces. Each table was equipped with a laptop and some voting keypads. Comments, ideas, and votes from the tables were shared simultaneously with participants on big screens or via webcasts. Including a citizen and leader-liaison board with biweekly opened sessions, four rounds of interactive meetings in 13 planning districts, and three citywide Community Congresses that brought together the residents of New Orleans, a plan to reconstruct the city and to consider the needs of the inhabitants was developed.

Further Reading:
http://www.unifiedneworleansplan.com/home3/
http://www.rockefellerfoundation.org/news/publications/citizen-participation-unified-new

2.5 Recife Participatory Budget

Recife Participatory Budget is the winner of the Rheinhard-Mohn Prize 2011 of the Bertelsmann Foundation, assigned for vitalizing democracy, and it marks a new generation of municipal budget experiences where participation extends from decision making through to the practical side of budget implementation. The Recife Participatory Budget was made to run with program-costs for the municipality of about €385,000 a year. Much of that amount is still spent on communication, electronic voting systems, and support for meetings. Although the budget team in the mayor's office is small and supported by a number of public-service workers in different policy areas, about 70 additional staff members were involved and there were also 80 volunteers to assist in the organization of forums, plenary sessions, and other meetings. Specific territorial based actions and improvements are complemented by thematic discussions on municipal-wide issues and investments in information technology are used for the involvement of as many people as possible. Furthermore, public works contractors are required to hire local community members and train their staff in community relations. City employees and volunteers in each of the city's neighborhoods encourage people to get involved and even children in over 200 municipal schools are also included with proposals for their schools and the city. Mobile voting tools and the internet are used to extend access to those unable to attend meetings. In a special child-participatory budget, the children discuss the needs of their schools as well as their city and communities. Some 89,000 children from five to 15 years are involved in the process.

More than 100,000 adults and young people joined local forums or made themselves heard via the internet, which stands for nearly 20% of the adult population of the city. The impact has been significant in influencing the direction of public expenditure (some €220 million over 10 years) and in broadening and expanding the everyday democratic processes. So the whole budget process works very well to strengthen capacities and develop new structures. The first step to a more open and horizontal style of government and governance is done in Recife.

Further Reading:

http://www.recife.pe.gov.br/op/index.php (Portuguese)

http://www.youtube.com/watch?v=JXln0EqW9gc

http://www.newdemocracy.com.au/index.php?option=com_content&view=article&id=73&Itemid=94

http://participedia.net/cases/recife-participatory-budgeting

2.6 Abuja Town Hall Meetings

In Abuja, the Federal Capital Territory of Nigeria, the former administration had enormous difficulty in getting their messages to the inhabitants and receiving informative feedback. A method of engaging positively with local citizens was established, namely, the use of town hall meetings. So in Nigeria, a new democratic space was created to facilitate dialogue between political leaders in local government and citizens. Through the use of public meetings and a range of media, decision-making processes became more transparent. The town hall meetings in Abuja were regular quarterly forums where all residents of the city could meet with the Minister of Abuja and his team and raise matters of interest. Each town hall meeting was broadcast live on radio and later via a 30-minute television documentary. Many people in the community were formally invited to the events; some heard through word of mouth and others through advertisements on the radio. The participation of all six suburbs of Abuja was coordinated through the Area Council Chairpersons, who helped organize the events and encouraged different categories of people to participate. A team from the Minister of Abuja's office specially dedicated to the project also drew on people from the community who were already involved in formulating the Federal Capital Territory Economic and Empowerment Strategy. The outcome of every town hall meeting was documented and adopted by the Federal Capital Territory's Executive Committee as action points. The Executive Committee was made up of ministers and secretaries who met weekly to look at the outcome of the meeting. By following some initial skepticism within the administration of Abuja, the town hall meetings are now viewed as a positive activity for the citizens as well as for the government. Since this first meeting took place, further town hall meetings have been held covering issues affecting Abuja, including the banning of lorries used to transport workers into the city center and the introduction of a new bus system. At one of the Town Hall Meetings, the decision was taken to ban commercial motorcycles from the city center. Before this decision was made, around 50 accidents involving these motorcycles were reported in the city every day. So the use of town hall meetings has demonstrated the important role this approach can have for Nigeria.

Further Reading:
http://www.modernghana.com/news/233027/1/transcipt-hillary-clinton-town-hall-meeting-in-abu.html
http://www.slgpnigeria.org/uploads/File/5318%20-%20FCT%20THM.pdf

2.7 Participatory Chinatown

The project Participatory Chinatown took place in one of Boston's densest immigrant communities to help open up urban planning and bring new aspects into the process. It is a 3-D game designed to be part of the master planning process for Boston's Chinatown. The player was able to assume the role of one of 15 virtual residents and complete their assigned quest like finding a job, a house, or a place to socialize. Sometimes language skills, income level, or other circumstances can make the game more challenging.

It could be played either as a multi-player experience with other players gathering in a physical meeting hall provided with networked computers, or as a single-player experience on the web. The game was available in English as well as in Chinese. Whatever the experience of the player was, s/he was tasked with considering the future of the neighborhood by walking through and commenting on proposed development sites. The player's comments and decisions were transmitted to the real life decision makers. Participatory Chinatown combined elements of digital worlds such as Second Life with the engaging mechanics of digital games to transform the way people think and deliberate about community issues. It turned game design into a community process by recruiting the youth from Chinatown. To help make planning concepts and scenarios more intuitive, proposed scenarios for Chinatown were built into fully 3D environments that participants could walk through and discuss, both in person and with in-game comments. The ultimate goal of the project was to engage more Chinatown stakeholders in the 2010 Chinatown Master Planning Process. The game gave people the possibility to take the perspective of others in the community, and to think about how the planning decisions affect Chinatown's diverse population. In 10 months, about 450 active participants took part in the game and gave their input to improve Boston's Chinatown. Their dialogues and comments were provided to the 2010 Chinatown Master Planning Committee, and included in the community's final master plan.

Further Reading:
http://participatorychinatown.org/
http://www.youtube.com/watch?v=CxOC1MPAHd4

2.8 The G1000 in Belgium

An independent group of Belgian citizens from various walks of life and different parts of the country launched the idea of organizing a large citizens' summit called G1000, after Belgium had been without a government for more than 500 days. G1000 was conceived in early 2011 by a small group of Belgian citizens consisting of academics, journalists, and civil society activists who were concerned about the failure of their political system. Exercised by the inability of Belgium's politicians to create a new government and the resulting political warfare, the group's manifesto was published. The statement was "if the politicians can't find a solution, let the citizens do it." G1000 seeks to show the country's political leaders that they should engage with them in finding a way out of the trouble. Their principal objectives are to show that deliberative democracy can work, and to produce concrete proposals for the government to consider.

The G1000 is designed as a three-stage rocket. The first part, which was launched during the summer of 2011, was an online survey built in order to find out which issues citizens really care about. More than 5,000 suggestions were put forward and ranked by thousands of citizens. After clustering similar themes and the final counting, 25 themes were put forward for a second round of voting from which 4 were tackled. Next, a full day of deliberation bringing one thousand people together took place on November 11, 2011 at Tour & Taxis in Brussels. Spread across 100 tables of 10 people each, and after having been briefed by experts, the participants made a number of proposals around the themes from the online process. Finally, a smaller group of citizens continued to gather regularly over the next months in order to refine these proposals and transform them into concrete recommendations.

Running alongside the G1000, there evolved groups of citizens around the country that met in their communities and replicated the same discussions, sending their recommendations to the main hall electronically.

Further Reading:

www.g1000.org

http://www.euronews.com/2011/11/12/europe-weekly-the-g1000-gives-a-voice-to-the-people/

http://participedia.net/cases/g1000

http://www.deliberative-democracy.net/index.php?option=com_content&view=article&id=178:g1000&catid=1:general&Itemid=68

2.9 Geraldton 2029 and beyond: Developing civic deliberation and collaborative governance to co-create a sustainable future

The project is integral to the '2029 and Beyond' vision, strategy, and actions to develop a future that is sustainable culturally, environmentally, economically, and socially. The city has committed to achieve this by revitalizing their democratic practice, developing a deliberative community, and collaborative governance. The whole population of the Greater Geraldton City Region, which is approximately 40,000 people and from which 17% are indigenous, were requested to participate in the joint project. The project is governed by the Greater Geraldton City Region Alliance Governance Group, which includes government, industry leaders, and a random sample of community members also consisting of indigenous people who oversee the project and help to fast-track community recommendations. The aim is to enhance the community's interest in and understanding of complex issues. Furthermore, the effectiveness of a public discourse should be improved.

The Greater Geraldton City Region in Australia is facing serious challenges to its future resilience and sustainability. Traditional industries of fishing and agriculture are in decline. Climate change experts have highlighted this region as being of high ecological and infrastructure vulnerability. Now, the project is moved by the theory and practice of deliberative democracy, defined as an inclusive form of democratic public discourse, characterized by dialogue and deliberation which influences political action. The project utilizes a range of innovative deliberative techniques and social media tools to get people involved in creating the future they envision. One of the first actions of the Alliance was to create a team of around 40 community 'champions,' ordinary community people who have volunteered to be trained and then run a variety of public deliberations. These deliberative processes are being integrated with other planning processes implemented by the City of Geraldton-Greenough.

Further Reading:
http://2029andbeyond.com.au/
http://www.youtube.com/watch?v=QOOKpnv 43Kk
http://www.linkedin.com/groups/Greater-Geraldton-City-Region-2029-2718371?mostPopular=&gid=2718371

2.10 The Gotthard Base Tunnel

The Gotthard Base Tunnel is a railway tunnel beneath the Swiss Alps with a surveyed opening in 2016. With a route length of 57 km, it is the world's longest rail tunnel. Its main purpose is to increase total transport capacity across the Alps. The Alps make shipping freight especially expensive, so notably between Germany and Italy the travelling time of cargo will be reduced by a noteworthy amount. Particularly to shift freight volumes from road to rail to reduce environmental damage caused by the increasing number of trucks on the streets is another desired effect.

Passenger trains will be able to travel up to 250 km/h. So also the cut of the journey-time for passenger trains from Zürich to Milan by about an hour and from Zürich to Lugano to 1 hour 40 minutes makes the tunnel, with an estimated amount of 200 to 250 trains a day, a very useful project. The tunnel consists of two single-track tunnels and is part of the AlpTransit project, including the Lötschberg Base Tunnel between the cantons of Bern and Valais and the still-under construction Ceneri Base Tunnel (scheduled to open at the end of 2019). The 'Gotthardbahn' and the old Gotthard-Tunnel, a winding mountain route opened in 1882 across the Saint-Gotthard Massif and now operating at capacity, will be bypassed and the direct route usable by high-speed rail and heavy freight trains established. Nevertheless, the current 15 km tunnel will be retained as part of the Swiss network. To provide this faster and furthermore, flatter passage through the Swiss Alps, the tunnel is established about 600 meters below the older tunnel. On the current track, the heavy cargo trains need to use two locomotives in front of the train with an additional pushing engine at the end of it. Otherwise they won't be able to pass through the narrow mountain valleys and through the spiral tunnels climbing up to the entrance of the old tunnel at a height of 1,100 meters above sea level.

The $10 billion project started in 1996, after, typical for the 'motherland' of referendums, 64% of Swiss voters accepted the Alp-Transit project in a referendum in

1992. In Switzerland, referendums have a long tradition. Swiss voters can demand a binding referendum at federal, cantonal, and municipal level. They are a central feature of Swiss political life.

Further Reading:
http://www.swissinfo.ch/eng/specials/gotthard_base_tunnel/index.html?cid=28292860
http://www.railway-technology.com/projects/gotthard-base-tunnel/
http://www.spiegel.de/international/europe/0,1518,723202,00.html

3 Deliberative governance: where to find it and how to participate?

Participation seems to be desired by a large amount of the population and seems to be able to solve a lot of conflicts and to shorten the planning and implementation of large-scale projects. There are a lot of platforms inviting people to participate in the political process.

The list below will give you a short overview.

Name	**Website**	**Description**
Week in e-democracy	http://www.edemocracy-forum.com/2009/12/database-eparticipation.html	European database to promote e-participation.
Citizenside	http://www.citizenside.com	Citizenside is the world's biggest open-source news service.
National Coalition for Dialogue & Deliberation (NCDD)	http://ncdd.org	The NCDD promotes the use of dialogue, deliberation, and other innovative group processes to help people come together across differences.
America speaks: Engaging citizens in governance	http://americaspeaks.org	Platform to develop online activities and to support online participation and transparency.
Participedia	http://participedia.net	Participedia is an open global knowledge community for researchers and practitioners in the field of democratic innovation and public engagement.
Deliberative Democracy Consortium	http://www.deliberative-democracy.net	Global network of researchers and practitioners working to advance *deliberative democracy.*
CIVICUS: World Alliance for Citizen Participation	https://www.civicus.org	CIVICUS is an international alliance of members and partners, which constitutes an influential network of organizations at the local, national, regional, and international levels, and spans the spectrum of civil society.
Global Voices	http://globalvoicesonline.org	Global Voices is an international community of bloggers who report on blogs and citizen media from around the world.

About the Contributors

Marko Bachl is a Research Associate at the Institute of Communication Science at the Universität Hohenheim.

Henning Banthien is a communication and strategy expert and managing partner of IFOK.

Sarah Bastgen is a Research Associate at the International Institute for Politics and Society, Berlin.

Daniela Ciaffi is architect and Professor of Urban Sociology at the University of Palermo.

Dr. Christopher Gohl is an Associate at the Weltethos-Institut, Tübingen.

Andreas Hoffelder is a Research Associate at the Hertie School of Governance, Berlin.

Kjetil Holgeid is a management consultant and EMBA alumni of Cambridge Judge Business School, University of Cambridge, UK.

Mathias König is a Research Associate at the Institute of Social Sciences at the Universität Koblenz-Landau.

Wolfgang König, is a Research Associate at the Institute of Social Sciences at the Universität Koblenz-Landau.

Thamy Pogrebinschi is Professor at the Institute of Social and Political Studies at the State University of Rio de Janeiro, and Visiting Researcher at the Social Science Research Center Berlin.

Martina Richwien is a communication and strategy expert in field of sustainability strategies and renewable energy development at IFOK.

Claudia Ritzi is a Research Associate at the Chair of Political Theory at the Helmut Schmidt University, Hamburg.

Andrea Römmele is Professor for Communication in Politics and Civil Society at the Hertie School of Governance, Berlin.

Fabiano Santos is Professor at the Institute of Social and Political Studies at the State University of Rio de Janeiro, and President of the Brazilian Political Science Association (ABCP).

Emanuela Saporito is an architect and PhD Candidate in Spatial Planning and Urban Development at the Architecture and Planning Department of the Polytechnic School of Milan.

Stefan Schaible is Head of the international Civil Economics, Energy & Infrastructure Competence Center at Roland Berger Strategy Consultants, and a member of the company's board of supervisors.

Henrik Schober is the head editor of the Journal for Political Consulting and Policy Advice and a Research Associate at the Hertie School of Governance, Berlin.

Gunnar Folke Schuppert is Professor of state and administrative law at the Humboldt University, Berlin, and the managing director of the Rule of Law Center at the Social Science Research Center Berlin.

Carmen Sirianni is the Morris Hillquit Professor of Labor and Social Thought and professor of Sociology and Public Policy at Brandeis University.

Arne Spieker is a consultant for public dialogue in the fields of energy and infrastructure.

Johannes Staemmler is a Research Fellow at the Hertie School of Governance, Berlin.

Mark Thompson is Senior Lecturer in Information Systems at Cambridge's Judge Business School and Strategy Director at ICT London-based Methods Innovation & Delivery.

Andrea Versteyl is a lawyer and honorary professor at the Leibniz Universität, Hannover.

Paul Webb is Professor of Politics at the School of Law, Politics and Sociology, University of Sussex.

Katrin Winkler is a project manager at the Bundesnetzwerk Bürgerschaftliches Engagement.